WATER UTILITY ACCOUNTING

Prepared for the

MUNICIPAL FINANCE OFFICERS ASSOCIATION

of the United States and Canada

and the

AMERICAN WATER WORKS ASSOCIATION

by

Leon E. Hay
Indiana University
Graduate School of Business

and

D. J. Grinnell
University of Connecticut

10094

Published jointly by the

MUNICIPAL FINANCE OFFICERS ASSOCIATION

of the United States and Canada

Chicago

and the

AMERICAN WATER WORKS ASSOCIATION

New York

1970

Printed in the United States of America
by Edwards Brothers Inc., Ann Arbor, Mich.

FOREWORD

WATER UTILITY ACCOUNTING, published jointly by the Municipal Finance Officers Association and the American Water Works Association, answers the need for a single book integrating all pertinent existing data on the subject. So did its predecessor, WATER WORKS ACCOUNTING, when published in 1938 by these same organizations.

However, this new manual represents much more than just a revision of the earlier work. For one thing, whereas WATER WORKS ACCOUNTING was a basic textbook written on a level that would permit the layman to utilize accounting procedures, WATER UTILITY ACCOUNTING reflects recognition of the tremendous increases in accounting complexity and sophistication that have taken place during the past 32 years. It is written on the level of the formally trained accountant operating in the water works field. For another, this new manual suggests implementation of accounting procedures that reflect the utility status of today's water works.

Thus the principles discussed in this new work conform to recommendations by the National Committee on Governmental Accounting, upon which most state public service commissions base their accounting requirements both for municipally-owned (in this book, referring to water works owned by governments generally) and investor-owned utilities in all four classes specified by The National Association of Regulatory Utility Commissioners (see Chapter 1: Introduction).

WATER UTILITY ACCOUNTING was prepared for the American Water Works Association and the Municipal Finance Officers Association by Leon E. Hay and D. J. Grennell of the Indiana University Graduate School of Business under the supervision of an American Water Works Association committee chaired by Ralph L. Swingley, President, Indianapolis Water Co. Indianapolis, Indiana, and a Municipal Finance Officers Association committee chaired by John R. Shields, Controller, City Water Board, San Antonio, Texas. The names of other members of these Water Utility Accounting Committees are listed on the next page.

The sponsoring associations intend to revise this manual periodically as called for by changes in practical water works accounting procedure.

The undersigned wish to acknowledge with thanks the assistance of many other members of both associations, and many non-members who contributed their knowledge, talents and time to the task of preparing and reviewing the material contained in this manual. Without their assistance, its realization would not have been possible.

Joseph F. Clark, Executive Director
Municipal Finance Officers Association
of the United States and Canada

Eric F. Johnson, Executive Director
American Water Works Association

April 15, 1970

iii

MEMBERS OF THE COMMITTEES FOR PRODUCTION
OF WATER UTILITY ACCOUNTING

MUNICIPAL FINANCE OFFICERS ASSOCIATION
of the United States and Canada

John R. Shields, Comptroller, City Water Board, City of San Antonio, Texas 78206, *Chairman*

William J. Boal, Fiscal Control Officer, Board of Water Commissioners, City and County of Denver, Colorado 80202

Leigh B. Hebb, Chief Fiscal Officer, Water Department, City of Philadelphia, Pennsylvania 19107

James R. McInnes, C.A., Executive Director and Treasurer, The Metropolitan Corporation of Greater Winnipeg, Winnipeg 1, Manitoba, Canada

Ex-Officio Members

Joseph F. Clark, Executive Director, Municipal Finance Officers Association of the United States and Canada, Chicago, Illinois 60637

Representing Association's General Committee on Accounting:

Nathan J. Sindelar, Treasurer, East Bay Municipal Utility District, Oakland, California 94623

THE AMERICAN WATER WORKS ASSOCIATION

Ralph L. Swingley, President, Indianapolis Water Company, 1220 Waterway Boulevard, Indianapolis, Indiana 46202, *Chairman*

William B. Gamble, Jr., Vice President, American Water Works Service Company, Inc., 3 Penn Center Plaza, Philadelphia 2662, Pa.

Harvey D. Goff, Vice President, Elizabethtown Water Company, Elizabethtown Plaza, Elizabeth, New Jersey

John A. Gubanich, Vice President, Finance, General Waterworks Corp., 1500 Walnut Street, Philadelphia 2, Pa.

Joseph J. Kenney, Controller, Jamaica Water Supply Company, 16120 89th Avenue, Jamaica 32, New Jersey

Herbert L. Plowman, Secretary and Assistant Treasurer, Gary-Hobart Water Corporation, 650 Madison Street, Gary, Indiana

Stanford I. Roth, Water & Sewers Department, Water Accounting Division, 251 W. Washington, Room 611, Phoenix, Arizona 85003

Richard G. Small, Controller, Portland Water District, 255 Douglas Street, Portland, Me. 04104

William C. Welmon, Sr. Vice President and Treasurer, Southern California Water Company, 11911 S. Vermont Avenue, Los Angeles, 44 California

Charles E. Woods, Treasurer and Controller, New Haven Water Company, 100 Crown Street, New Haven, Conn.

Ex-Officio Member

Eric F. Johnson, Executive Director, American Water Works Association, New York, New York 10016

CONTENTS

PART ONE—WATER UTILITY ACCOUNTING SYSTEM

PART FOUR—PLANNING AND CONTROLLING ASSETS, LIABILITIES, AND EQUITIES

APPENDIX—A SUGGESTED SYSTEM OF ACCOUNTS FOR CLASS A AND B WATER UTILITIES

ILLUSTRATIONS

Part One
WATER UTILITY
ACCOUNTING SYSTEM

CHAPTER 1. INTRODUCTION

This book is intended to serve a twofold purpose: (1) to give water utility managers an understanding of how accounting information can aid them in performing the management function more efficiently and effectively, and (2) to give the accountant an insight into the types of information needed by management, regulatory authorities, taxing authorities, creditors, customers, stockholders, and other interested groups. It is assumed that the reader has some knowledge of basic accounting; for that reason an explanation of the detailed mechanics of accounting has been omitted.[1]

The primary purpose of an accounting system is to meet the information needs of interested parties. In meeting this objective, an acceptable water utility accounting system is one that (1) fulfills regulatory and other legal requirements regarding record keeping and reporting, (2) provides for the recording and accumulation of financial data in such a form that it can be utilized effectively as a guide to managing the water utility, and (3) provides interested parties with information sufficient to evaluate the performance of the water utility management group.

Water utilities are subject to many regulatory and other legal requirements which often result in considerable demands on the accounting system. Such requirements may, for example, prescribe the chart of accounts to be used, the nature and content of records, and the frequency and form of reports. The extent of these legal requirements will differ, of course, depending on the state within which the utility is located and depending on whether the utility is municipally-owned or investor-owned.

The management of many phases of water utility operations would be impossible without the aid of financial information. For example, managers must be kept informed of costs of carrying out particular phases of the utility's activities under their supervision, in order that the performance of subordinates can be evaluated and corrective action taken when and where necessary. In addition, a water utility's budget, to be workable, must be based on past experience modified by information regarding the future; this past experience is reported in financial reports and accounting and statistical records. Financial information is also a necessary part of a good system of internal control. The success of management planning and control of operations depends to a large extent on the adequacy of financial information derived from the accounting system.

Finally, the accounting system must provide information to many groups external to the everyday operations of the water utility. Public service commissions, municipal governments, creditors, stockholders of investor-owned water utilities, customers, and other groups have a valid need for information to evaluate the performance of the water utility management group and the financial condition and operating results of the utility.

It can be seen that the demands on a water utility accounting system are extensive. Accordingly, it is hoped that this book may prove to be valuable to both municipally-owned and investor-owned water utilities in designing or improving their accounting and reporting systems. Further, a major objective of the book is to reflect current thinking in the area of accounting for water utilities. Sound principles of water utility accounting and financial reporting are advocated with the intent of providing planning and control guidelines for management in their efforts to utilize water utility resources efficiently.

---

[1] Readers who do not have a knowledge of basic accounting may refer to any one of a number of introductory accounting textbooks for an explanation of fundamentals of accounting. For example, see: Harold Bierman Jr., Financial and Managerial Accounting: An Introduction (New York: The Macmillan Company, 1963); C. Rollin Niswonger and Philip E. Fess, Accounting Principles (9th ed.; Cincinnati: South-Western Publishing Company, 1965); Robert R. Milroy and Robert E. Walden, Accounting Theory and Practice: Introductory (Cambridge: Houghton Mifflin Company, 1960); and Lawrence L. Vance and Russell Taussig, Accounting Principles and Control (rev. ed.; New York: Holt, Rinehart, and Winston, 1966).

The Water Utility Industry

Every business enterprise is concerned with a public interest to some extent and, consequently, is subject to a measure of public regulation. Certain types of enterprises, however, are so greatly concerned with public interest that they have been subjected to far-reaching regulation by government. Among these enterprises are public utilities.

Within the extensive area of public utilities, one of the most important sectors is the water utility industry. The importance of this industry is great, particularly when the role it plays in everyday industrial and economic life is considered. With its many ramifications, the water utility industry touches every phase of national economic life.

In the case of American business in general, the economic law of supply and demand will act, at least in theory, as an invisible hand to regulate the economy. The demand for a commodity should bring forth the capacity to produce the commodity in such quantities as are necessary to fulfill the demand. At the same time, the consumer is able to exercise his influence over the price by choosing among alternative sources of supply. Thus, it is said, competition will act as a regulator.

With a public utility type of enterprise, the duplication of productive facilities is usually considered to be unsound. In the water utility industry, large capital expenditures are required to build source-of-supply facilities, transmission lines, pumping stations, treatment plants, and water distribution systems. If duplicate facilities were constructed by competing water utilities, the consumer, in effect, would have to pay for such economic waste through higher prices for water. In addition, while the aggregate value of water is enormous, the marginal value of such water is usually low, making the consumer unwilling to pay a price sufficient to cover the high costs incurred by competing water utilities.

Such conditions have resulted in the granting of monopolistic privileges by governmental units to water utilities as well as to other public utilities. When the economic law of supply and demand cannot perform its function, and, as a result, monopolistic privilege is granted, there arises the need for another form of regulation. Such regulation

has been established by governmental bodies basically in one of two ways: (1) the water utility is operated directly by an agency of government, such as a water department of the municipal government, a water district, or a water authority; or (2) governmental units have established public utility commissions or other agencies to regulate the operations of investor-owned water utilities.

The fundamental purposes of this regulation have been to establish and control reasonable rates of earnings of public utilities, to establish and maintain satisfactory levels of services rendered by utilities, and to insure the financial stability of these utilities.

Classifying Water Utilities by Size

The National Association of Regulatory Utility Commissioners (NARUC),[2] divides water utilities into four classes for the purpose of applying its systems of accounts, as follows:

Class A. Utilities having annual water operating revenues of $500,000 or more

Class B. Utilities having annual water operating revenues of $250,000 or more, but less than $500,000

Class C. Utilities having annual water operating revenues of $50,000 or more, but less than $250,000

Class D. Utilities having annual water operating revenues of less than $50,000.[3]

"The class to which any utility belongs shall originally be determined by the average of its annual water operating revenues for the last three consecutive years. Subsequent changes in classification shall be made when the annual water operating revenues for each of the three immediately preceding years shall exceed the upper limit, or be less than the lower limit, of the annual water operating revenues of the classification previously applicable to the utility."[4]

The principles discussed in this book are applicable to all sizes of utilities, although the examples presented in the following chapters generally illustrate applications to Class A and B utilities.

[2] Formerly the National Association of Railroad and Utilities Commissioners.
[3] Committee on Accounts and Statistics, National Association of Regulatory Utility Commissioners, Uniform System of Accounts for Class A and B Water Utilities 1957 (Washington, D.C.; National Association of Regulatory Utility Commissioners, 1958), p. 4.
[4] Ibid.

Classifying Water Utilities by Type of Ownership

The legal organization of a water utility may take many different forms, all of which can be categorized either as investor-owned or as governmentally-owned. The term "municipally-owned" is used in this book to refer to governmentally-owned utilities in general, in keeping with the common usage of the term "municipality" to refer to any governmental unit subordinate to a state.

The legal form of organization has little or no effect upon most facets of water utility operation; therefore, unless otherwise indicated, the discussion in this book applies to both investor-owned and municipally-owned utilities. The legal form of organization does result in significant differences in the instances described briefly in Fig. 1-1. The effects of these differences are discussed in subsequent chapters.

Accounting Requirements

Most investor-owned water utilities are subject to regulation by state public service commissions.

Figure 1-1
IMPORTANT DIFFERENCES IN WATER UTILITIES RESULTING FROM TYPE OF OWNERSHIP

Subject	Municipally-Owned Water Utility	Investor-Owned Water Utility
Chart of Accounts	Often no requirement to adopt the state public service commission's uniform system of accounts.	Usually required to adopt a uniform system of accounts prescribed by the state public service commission.
Water rates	Rate schedules are usually not subject to control by state public service commissions. (However, in some states, municipally-owned utilities are subject to regulation by state public service commissions on the same basis as investor-owned utilities.)[a]	Rate schedules are usually subject to the approval of the state public service commission.
Financing	Acquisition, replacement, or expansion of facilities may be financed by existing cash balances, the issuance of bonds to be retired from the income of the utility, contributions from the municipality with the repayment of any resulting bond issue accomplished through taxation or other sources, long-term advances from the municipality, contributions and advances from customers for construction, and contributions from state and federal governments.	Acquisition, replacement, or expansion of facilities may be financed from existing cash balances, the issuance of various types of securities (including preferred stock, common stock, and bonds), contributions and advances from customers for construction, and contributions from state and federal governments.
Taxes	Do not pay income taxes and usually do not have to pay property taxes. In some instances, municipally-owned water utilities are required to pay taxes on property (such as source of supply facilities) which is located outside their service area boundaries and within the taxing jurisdiction of other municipalities. Municipally-owned water utilities may also be required to render free services to other municipal departments or to make payments to the general fund in lieu of taxes.	Required to pay all forms of taxes. (In a few states, investor-owned water utilities are exempt from payment of certain taxes, such as those on property.)
Organization[b]	May be a legal entity in itself as in the case of a water district or authority; or the utility may be a subdivision of a municipality as in the case of a water department.	Usually incorporated, although smaller utilities may be either partnerships or individual proprietorships.

[a] See: American Water Works Association, Water Utility Management, Manual AWWA M5 (New York: American Water Works Association, 1959), p. 4.; and National Committee on Governmental Accounting, Governmental Accounting, Auditing, and Financial Reporting (Chicago: Municipal Finance Officers Association, 1968), Chapter 6.
[b] For an expanded discussion of the organization of water utilities, see: American Water Works Association, Water Utility Management, Manual AWWA M5 (New York: American Water Works Association, 1959), Chapter 1.

In some cases, municipally-owned utilities also are subject to regulation by state public service commissions on the same basis as investor-owned utilities. In addition, the National Committee on Governmental Accounting (NCGA) recommends that uniform classifications of accounts, prescribed by state public service commissions for investor-owned utilities, be utilized by municipally-owned utilities as well.[5] The accounting requirements of the state commissions are based, for the most part, on the recommendations of the NARUC. Therefore, the account classification and other recommendations of the NARUC have been followed in the preparation of this book; however, accounting terminology generally adopted since the publication of the NARUC classification has been incorporated in this book. Principles of accounting and accounting terminology as used in this book are also in agreement with pronouncements of the NCGA.

Organization of the Book

The book is arranged in four parts: Part One is devoted to a discussion of the objectives of accounting for water utilities. Part One also includes a brief discussion of the system of accounts used by water utilities and the relationship of the accounts to fund accounting and management accounting.

Part Two is concerned with accounting reports for water utilities. This discussion includes the purposes of reports, the need for them, applica-

tion of principles of report preparation to water utilities, internal management reports, reports to governmental authorities, and reports to other interested groups such as stockholders, creditors, customers, and employees.

Part Three is devoted to planning and controlling operations. This part includes a discussion of management functions in general, planning and control in general, and the general principles of management accounting. Separate chapters are devoted to planning for and controlling revenues, operating and maintenance expenses, depreciation and amortization, taxes, and the cost of money.

Part Four deals with planning for and controlling assets, liabilities, and equity interests. Particular attention is paid to various aspects of planning for and controlling utility plants, current assets, restricted assets, current liabilities, long-term liabilities, capital paid in by stockholders (applicable to investor-owned water utilities), retained earnings, operating reserves, customer advances for construction, and contributions. The recommendations of the NCGA have been augmented, where necessary, to incorporate terms peculiar to water utilities as these have been developed by organizations such as the NARUC and other bodies concerned with water utilities.

Examples, such as illustrative reports, are presented throughout the book. The purpose of these examples is to illustrate accounting principles and procedures generally applicable to water utilities and to emphasize sound accounting and reporting practices for water utilities.

---

[5]National Committee on Governmental Accounting, Governmental Accounting, Auditing, and Financial Reporting (Chicago: Municipal Finance Officers Association, 1968), p. 54.

CHAPTER 2. OBJECTIVE OF ACCOUNTING FOR WATER UTILITIES

The primary objective of any entity's accounting system is to meet the information requirements of all interested groups having a valid need for information concerning that entity. In the case of a water utility, the accounting system should furnish information to the following major groups:

1. Regulatory Authorities
2. Management
3. Taxing Authorities
4. Creditors
5. Stockholders (for investor-owned water utilities)
6. Customers and the General Public
7. Employees.

In this chapter, the information needs of the above-listed groups are discussed. The subject of internal control is reviewed separately since it is of such vital interest and importance to all groups interested in the affairs of the water utility.

Meeting the Information Needs of Regulatory Authorities

As described in Chapter 1, due to the essential character of the service rendered, water utilities are said to be "affected with a public interest." As a result, water utilities are subject to government regulation. The governmental agency exercising regulatory control over water utilities varies with the state in which the utility is located and the form of ownership of the utility.

Regulating Investor-Owned Water Utilities. In the case of investor-owned water utilities, general regulatory control is usually exercised by an appropriate state body. In addition, there are other governmental agencies which exercise control in more specific areas of interest. State health departments establish requirements relating to the potability of the water supply. On the federal level, the Securities and Exchange Commission has regulatory power over many important phases of the marketing of securities, as well as supervision of various aspects of the affairs of water utilities. There are, of course, many other federal,

state, and local governmental bodies which, under varying circumstances, have other regulatory responsibilities. For example, final approval of a franchise granted to a water utility by a municipality must, in some states, be obtained from the conservation department or some other agency concerned with water resources.

Regulating Municipally-Owned Water Utilities. While the control of state public service commissions and similar bodies covers a wide range, it does not, except in a few states, extend to municipally-owned water utilities. Regulatory control of a municipal water department usually rests with the local government. Such control may be the direct responsibility of the mayor alone, or with the city council, but here again the particular organization dictates which subdivision of local government exercises control. In the cases of water districts and authorities, regulatory control is usually specified by the statute enabling the creation of the entity. Further, as is true of investor-owned water utilities, state health agencies frequently establish requirements for municipally-owned water utilities with respect to the potability of the water supply.

Information Requirements. Whatever the form of ownership, or the regulatory authority having control, the information required for particular purposes is generally the same. Regulation of water utilities, while varying considerably, usually demands information about such aspects of a water utility's affairs as general accounting practices, financial position and operating results, rates, cost of utility property, metering and billing practices, construction methods, financing requirements and purposes, quality of service, and other matters of concern to the general public. Therefore, a water utility's accounting system must be designed to meet all requirements of regulatory authorities. Regulatory authorities generally prescribe the system of accounts to be used, stipulate the accounting records to be kept, and require routine accounting and statistical reports. Special reports are also required by regulatory agencies in the event of proposed mergers, consolidations, reorganizations, abandonment of facilities, transfer of property, financing, and rate changes. Reports for regulatory authorities are discussed in detail in Chapter 5.

Meeting the Information Needs of Management

In addition to serving regulatory authorities, a water utility's accounting and reporting system must furnish information to help management plan and control the operation of the utility. Planning involves the selection of the utility's objectives and the means for achieving them. Controlling is defined as obtaining conformity to plans.[1]

When utility management is faced with a particular problem, such as establishing a rate schedule or obtaining funds for expansion, the accounting system must be capable of supplying information which will aid management in selecting the most appropriate course of action from the available alternatives. Once the course is chosen, plans can be expressed in terms of budgets. Again, the accounting system must generate much of the information needed to develop the budgets. Through the use of budgets, plans can be coordinated and communicated to water utility personnel. These budgets reflect performance standards and serve as a basis for judging performance.

Management control is dependent upon performance reports. The information required to develop performance reports must be generated by the accounting system. Such reports allow management to measure performance, compare actual performance with standards, and make a fair appraisal of performance. The results shown by performance reports may indicate that corrective action is in order to obtain conformity with plans.

Chapter 6 is concerned with internal management reports; Chapters 8 through 18 cover, in detail, planning and control of operations and balance sheet items.

Meeting the Information Needs of Taxing Authorities

As the functions of government have expanded, taxes levied on water utilities have increased in number. In the case of investor-owned water utilities, the result has been a contribution to the support of federal, state, and local governments through property taxes, federal income taxes, state income taxes, city income taxes, sales and use taxes, payroll taxes, taxes on gross receipts,

and franchise taxes. With the exception of payroll taxes, municipally-owned water utilities do not pay federal taxes and are generally exempt from state and local taxes. In lieu of taxes, a municipally-owned water utility may be required to make contributions of cash to the municipal general fund, or to render free water services to other municipal departments.

It can be seen that federal, state, and local taxing authorities have a valid need for information pertaining to the water utility. Hence, the requirements of these taxing authorities will influence the accounting and reporting system. The record-keeping function must be well planned to meet the widely diverse pattern of federal, state, and local tax laws. The nature of records is, of course, related to the complexity of the taxes involved. The accounting system must be capable of producing records which will support the tax returns.

Reports to taxing authorities are discussed in detail in Chapter 5. Planning for specific types of taxes is the subject of Chapter 13.

Meeting the Information Needs of Creditors

Although the types of debt instruments issued by investor-owned and municipally-owned water utilities differ, the information needs of present and prospective creditors of these utilities are basically the same. However, the information needs of the short-term creditor will differ somewhat from those of the long-term creditor.

While financial information is extremely important to creditors, it is not the only type of information needed. For example, information pertaining to the quality of the water utility management and future prospects for the water utility industry are also of considerable importance.

From the standpoint of financial information, short-term creditors are largely interested in the short-term debt-paying ability of the organization. Long-term creditors, on the other hand, are interested in the earning power of the organization and its ability to repay the debt over an extended period of time. Both short- and long-term lenders are concerned with the utility's ability to repay the debt at maturity; therefore the future is of primary importance.

Information needed by creditors concerning the future may be expressed in terms of budgets, forecasts, and pro forma statements of financial

---

[1]See: Harold Koontz and Cyril O'Donnell, Principles of Management (New York: McGraw-Hill Book Company, Inc., 1959), pp. 35-38.

position and operating results.[2] Creditors also should be given data concerning past and present financial position and operating results, expressed in terms of comparative financial statements. In addition, creditors are interested in such matters as the disposition of funds obtained from the credit source, other fixed payment obligations, insurance coverage, contingent liabilities, capitalization ratios, detailed descriptions of existing short- and long-term debt, age of utility plant assets, and information concerning behavior of revenues and expenses, and interest and debt service coverage.

Reporting to creditors is discussed in Chapter 7. Planning and controlling the cost of borrowing is discussed in Chapter 14. Chapter 18 is concerned with planning and controlling liabilities.

Meeting the Information Needs of Shareholders

Present and potential shareholders are interested in the operations, financial condition, and abilities and philosophies of the management of an investor-owned water utility in order to arrive at a decision regarding the purchase, sale, or holding of stock in the utility. It is management's responsibility to furnish investors with information on the water utility's operations and financial condition sufficient to help form an opinion as to the worth or potential worth of securities.

The information needs of any one group are not mutually exclusive of the needs of others. Such is the case of shareholders and creditors. Much of the information previously suggested as being useful to creditors is the same as that required by shareholders, present and potential.

While a shareholder is interested in much of the information desired by creditors, his primary interest is in dividends and earnings of the water utility. As a result, the shareholder requires a great deal of information about these matters, and the accounting and reporting system must be capable of supplying it. In addition, the shareholder has a great need for information concerning future prospects and plans of the water utility and their effect on earnings.

The published annual report is the primary document for transmitting this information from management to the security holders. The annual report and its contents, as well as other reports to shareholders, are discussed in Chapter 7.

Planning and controlling the cost of stockholder equity is discussed in Chapter 14.

Meeting the Information Needs of Customers and the General Public

There is some disagreement as to the extent of the responsibility a water utility has for the dissemination of financial information to customers and the general public. It might be argued that information furnished to regulatory authorities is sufficient to protect the interests of customers and the general public and that additional information need not be furnished directly to the latter. Although it is true that much of the information furnished to regulatory authorities is legally available to interested groups, customers and the general public are interested in particular aspects of the water utility operation, and the direct dissemination of certain information to these groups seems advisable, if only from the standpoint of promoting good customer and public relations.

Water customers are interested in obtaining quality water service at a reasonable cost; hence, the customer is interested in information related to service and water rates. In order to meet these customer information needs, the utility may find it feasible to furnish information pertaining to such matters as future plans for replacement and expansion of facilities, research activities, main extension policies, reasons for changes in water rate schedules, and new legislation affecting water utilities. In some municipalities the customers of the municipal utility, as taxpayers, vote on proposed bond issues. In such instances, information concerning the utility's financial position and future capital expenditure plans should be publicized to show the need for this type of additional financing.

The information needs of the general public parallel, to a great extent, those of water customers, since the general public is the source of existing and potential customers. In addition, the general public has an interest in other aspects of the water utility. For example, various taxes may serve as direct or indirect sources of financing a considerable portion of the activities of a municipally-owned water utility. Further, in the case of municipally-owned water utilities, the is-

---

[2] Pro forma statements of financial position depict forecast or projected levels of balance sheet items at a selected date or dates in the future. These statements are based on a proposed financing plan or alternative financing plans. A pro forma statement of operating results depicts forecast or projected revenues and expenses for a given future period or periods of time.

suance of bonds to finance utility activities may be subject to the approval of the general public. Therefore, the general public, as taxpayers, may desire reports of the utility's operating results, financial position, and future plans. Reports to customers and the general public are considered in Chapter 7.

Meeting the Information Needs of Employees

It is generally recognized that employees are entitled to information about the water utility's operations. However, as in the case of customers and the general public, there is the problem of determining the interests of employees and deciding what information should be shared with them. Edward R. Healy[3] states that "Responsibilities to employees may be fulfilled by managing the business so that the employee is provided with stable employment at fair compensation. The employee also makes an investment in the business. He invests his time, knowledge, and abilities. As a part of his compensation he wants stability of employment, in addition to the security for himself and his family that is derived from salary compensation and fringe benefits. Also important are other conditions of employment, such as the general atmosphere in which he works, the tools provided, the identification with a successful business rendering an essential service, and the acceptance of his importance in the life of the community."

The employee is interested in information such as that involving wages, hours, working conditions, pension plans and other fringe benefits, labor policies, expansion plans and educational opportunities. He is also interested in how the water utility is doing financially and how the utility's operation relates to his own job. He may be interested in how much income the utility receives and what happens to it. In addition, the employee is concerned with comparisons between his wage rate and wage rates for similar jobs in other water utilities, and the benefits received by employees of other utilities. Reports to employees are presented in Chapter 7.

Internal Control

One of the most important considerations in the design of a water utility accounting system is provision for internal control. Internal control is a management responsibility and therefore a discussion of internal control could logically be included in the section of this chapter concerned with the information needs of management. However, since internal control is of importance to all interested groups, the subject deserves separate emphasis.

The American Institute of Certified Public Accountants defines internal control as comprising "the plan of organization and all of the coordinate methods and measures adopted within a business to safeguard its assets, check the accuracy and reliability of its accounting data, promote operational efficiency, and encourage adherence to prescribed managerial policies."[4]

This definition implies the use of all appropriate management control techniques for the purpose of attaining adherence to plans. In this section, however, emphasis is placed on those aspects of internal control designed to minimize errors and fraud and to discourage waste. There are certain principles involved in the establishment and maintenance of an adequate system of internal control.[5]

1. High quality of personnel. The water utility accounting system will be ineffective unless reliable personnel are employed. The utility must follow sound employment practices, utilize employee training programs, and adopt procedures for measuring employee performance in order to attract and retain highly qualified personnel. Over the long run, the use of inferior personnel may prove costly from the standpoint of productivity as well as fraud.

2. Separation of duties. Personnel having record-keeping responsibilities should not have access to the physical handling of assets. Ideally, there should be a complete separation of the accounting, operating, and custodial functions. For example, the person receiving payments from customers should not have access to the accounts receivable subsidiary ledger. Such procedures will help to eliminate errors in accounting records and prevent fraud by requiring the collusion of at least two persons in any dishonest activities.

3. Adequate supervision. The organization structure of the water utility should be such that every employee has a superior who supervises and evaluates performance.

[3] Edward R. Healy "Management Responsibilities and Objectives in Investor-Owned and Municipal Utilities," Journal American Water Works Association, Vol. 58, No. 5 (May 1966), p. 514.

[4] Committee on Auditing Procedure, Internal Control (New York: American Institute of Certified Public Accountants, 1949), p. 6.

[5] The discussion of these principles relies in part on Charles T. Horngren's Cost Accounting: A Managerial Emphasis (2nd ed.; Englewood Cliffs, N.J.: Prentice-Hall, Inc., 1967), pp. 704-706.

4. Assignment of responsibility. The organization structure of the utility should provide for proper allocation of responsibilities. The effect of assigning responsibilities is that individuals tend to be more diligent in carrying out their assigned tasks, and perform their jobs more efficiently. Another important consideration is that the qualifications of personnel should be commensurate with responsibilities.

5. Establishing routine procedures. Written instructions should be issued to specify procedures to be followed in carrying out routine functions. Such instructions should include procedures for authorization, review, and record-keeping as a means of providing control over assets, liabilities, revenues and expenses. The requirement that checks be signed by authorized personnel only after presentation of a voucher, prepared from supporting source documents, is an example of a routine established to control disbursements.

6. Job rotation. The rotating of routes among meter readers and the rotating of accounts among receivables clerks is a useful device for preventing dishonesty. In addition, the requirements that all employees take vacations and that key personnel be bonded are additional measures for pro-viding against fraud.

7. Investigations. Water utility activities should be reviewed periodically to insure that established procedures actually are being followed. This may be accomplished through investigations conducted by outsiders, such as certified public accountants, or by internal auditors.

8. Physical control over property. Protective facilities and other safeguards should be installed to prevent removing of property by unauthorized persons.

The extent to which these principles of internal control can be applied will vary with the size of the water utility. For example, a small utility having a limited number of employees may not be able to attain complete separation of duties. However, sufficient separation is always possible to achieve adequate control over such key assets as cash, securities, and receivables.

This section has dealt only with the general nature and principles of internal control. The subject of internal control, as applied to specific areas of a water utility's operation, is discussed within each of the appropriate chapters of this book.

CHAPTER 3. THE SYSTEM OF ACCOUNTS

The Use of the Double-Entry System

The assets of a water utility equal its liabilities and equities. Liabilities and equities represent the rights or interests of various groups in the property held by the utility; the equality of the assets to the liabilities and equities is the foundation upon which the double-entry system is constructed. Transactions carried out by the utility bring about changes in the assets and equities, and accounts based on the double-entry system record these changes.

The double-entry system provides a continuous and complete record of the utility's transactions. Further, double-entry accounting assists one in understanding the significance of the relationship between balance sheet and income accounts, as well as between asset and equity accounts.

The discussion in this book is based on the assumption that the double-entry system is employed.

The Use of Accrual Accounting

There are two bases which can be followed in accounting: cash and accrual. Under the cash basis, revenues are recognized as earned when cash is received, and expenses are charged when cash is disbursed. Under the accrual basis, revenues are recorded in the period in which service is given, although payments may be received in a prior or subsequent period; expenses are recorded in the period in which the benefits are received, although payments may be made in a prior or subsequent period. Systems may also exist which are partly accrual and partly cash; such systems are described as modified accrual or modified cash systems.

To obtain a statement of revenues and expenses for an accounting period it is essential that all revenues and expenses for the period be recorded. The use of the accrual basis allows a water utility to match costs against the revenues generated by these costs, thereby producing a statement of revenues and expense which is more accurate than one based on cash accounting.

In general, use of the accrual basis of accounting is recommended for water utilities, both municipally-owned and investor-owned. The illustrations and discussion in this book are based on the assumption that the accrual basis of accounting is employed.

A Recommended System of Accounts

Before the accounting staff of a water utility can record the transactions of the utility meaningfully, assets, liabilities, equities, revenues, and expenses must be classified. A system of accounts should be designed that facilitates record-keeping and report preparation, and provides for control and accountability. The system of accounts must provide for accumulation of data in sufficient detail, and in such a manner, as to facilitate the preparation of reports to meet the needs of all interested groups.

The accounts to be kept by an investor-owned water utility are usually prescribed by an appropriate agency of the state in which the utility operates. Some states also require municipally-owned water utilities to follow a prescribed uniform system of accounts. The system of accounts set forth in this chapter is representative of systems required by regulatory agencies. It is based on the recommendations of the Committee on Accounts and Statistics of the National Association of Regulatory Utility Commissioners (NARUC), and on the recommendations of the National Committee on Governmental Accounting (NCGA).

The NARUC's published system of accounts for each class of water utilities consists of: (1) general instructions and definitions, (2) instructions concerning utility plant and operating expense, (3) a prescribed list of accounts, (4) a definition of each account and instructions concerning the types of transactions to be recorded in each account, and (5) the general sequence for balance sheet and income statements item.[1] The NARUC also

---

[1] For example, see: Committee on Accounts and Statistics, National Association of Regulatory Utility Commissioners, Uniform System of Accounts for Class A and B Water Utilities 1957 (Washington, D.C.: National Association of Regulatory Utility Commissioners, 1958).

issues, periodically, interpretations of the Uniform System of Accounts.[2]

Basic Framework of Recommended System. The detailed listing of accounts recommended for use by municipally-owned and investor-owned water utilities is presented in the Appendix. In this section the logic of the system is explained.

Figure 3-1 is a graphic presentation of the interrelationships of the groups of accounts provided in the recommended system. This figure, as well as the detailed listing of accounts given in the Appendix, reflects the coding scheme employed by the NARUC. Accounts are assigned code numbers to facilitate identification and to allow for proper consolidation or combination of accounts when preparing and presenting reports to regulatory agencies.

The accounts are divided into two main sections, the first consisting of summary balance sheet accounts, the second of summary income accounts. Summary balance sheet accounts are grouped within two categories: Assets and Other Debits, and Liabilities and Other Credits. The summary balance sheet categories are further divided into groups of summary balance sheet accounts as shown in Fig. 3-1. One particular group of summary accounts, Utility Plant, is supported by detailed plant accounts. The detailed structure is desirable because of the importance of information concerning plant facilities to regulatory bodies for determining the appropriate rate base. Detailed utility plant information also promotes effective management control of plant assets.

The summary income categories consist of Utility Operating Income, Other Income, Miscellaneous Income Deductions, Interest Charges, and Retained Earnings.[3] The categories of summary income accounts have no account or code numbers; the title given to each category serves only as an income statement caption.

Utility Operating Income is the net income derived from the normal operations of the water utility during a stated period. Utility Operating Income is computed by subtracting Operating Expenses (which include all expenses applicable to the furnishing of water utility services) from

Operating Revenues (which summarize the revenues derived from normal operations of the water utility).[4] In cases where income is derived from the leasing of utility plant facilities, the difference between Operating Revenues and Operating Expenses is entitled Net Operating Revenues. Adding income from leasing utility plant results in Utility Operating Income.

Utility Operating Income is closely associated with the concept of "above and below the line," which reflects the regulatory point of view of the public service commissions. A regulated water utility is entitled to operating revenues sufficient to cover operating expenses and to provide for a fair or reasonable return. From the viewpoint of a public service commission, the return to a water utility is the amount in dollars which remains after operating expenses have been subtracted from operating revenues; it is named Utility Operating Income. Revenue and expenses recognized in the determination of Utility Operating Income are considered to be "above the line" items and enter into the determination of a fair or reasonable return for rate-making purposes. "Below the line" items, although included as adjustments of Utility Operating Income in arriving at the net income of the water utility, are not included in calculations of rates and the determination of a fair or reasonable return.

Expenses are "above the line" if such expenses are reasonable in amount and of such a nature as to be considered chargeable against customers for services rendered. Interest charges and other items (Miscellaneous Income Deductions) considered by regulatory bodies to be of doubtful propriety as operating expenses are classified as "below the line" items. Further, income resulting from activities of a nonutility nature (nonoperating revenue less the nonoperating expense incurred in obtaining that revenue) also is considered to be "below the line."

As shown in Fig. 3-1, the summary account entitled Operating Revenues and two summary accounts for Operating Expenses, namely Operation Expense and Maintenance Expense, are supported by detailed revenue and expense accounts.[5] The detailed structure is desirable because of the

[2] See: Committee on Accounts and Statistics, National Association of Regulatory Utility Commissioners, Interpretations of Uniform System of Accounts for Electric, Gas and Water Utilities (Washington, D.C.: National Association of Regulatory Utility Commissioners, 1965).

[3] In accord with current usage the term "Retained Earnings" has been substituted for the older term "Earned Surplus," used in the NARUC publication.

[4] The accounts for Operating Expenses are also called Operating Revenue Deduction accounts. The term Operating Expenses is more nearly in accord with generally accepted terminology.

[5] Note the difference in the terms "Operating Expenses" and "Operation Expense." The term "Operating Expenses" has a broader meaning in that it includes depreciation, amortization, and taxes as well as the charges to the operation and maintenance accounts.

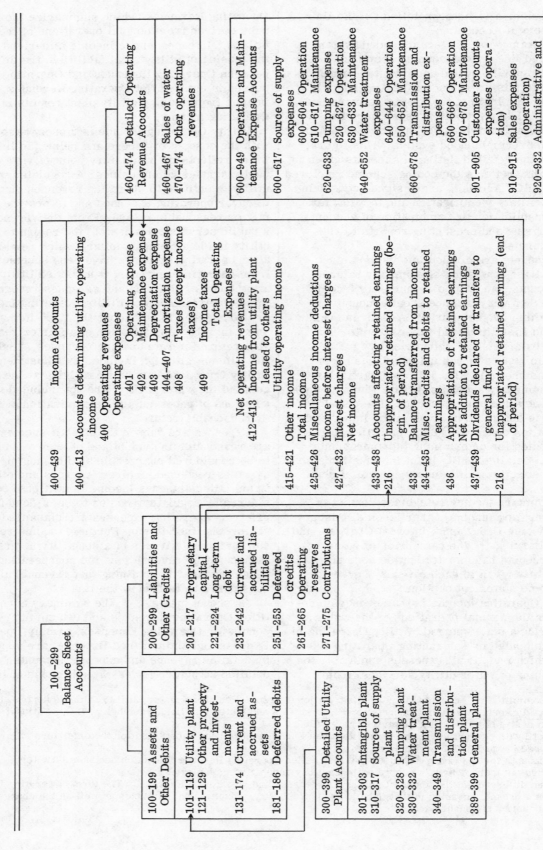

Figure 3-1

A SYSTEM OF ACCOUNTS FOR WATER UTILITIES
(Based on NARUC and NCGA Recommendations)

importance of operating revenue and expense information for rate determination by regulatory authorities. It is also an aid to effective control of revenues and expenses by management.

The Other Income category includes income of the utility which does not result from its normal business of supplying potable water. The Miscellaneous Income Deductions category includes expenses, other than interest, which are not includable elsewhere. Interest Charges includes interest on both long-term and short-term debt; the amortization of debt discount, debt premium, and debt issue expense; and interest charged to construction (a credit balance account which reduces the amount of interest charged to operations).

The net income of the water utility, determined from the accounts described above, is transferred to an account entitled Balance Transferred from Income in the Retained Earnings category. The Retained Earnings category is composed of a group of accounts that form the connecting link between the income accounts used to determine net income of the water utility, and the balance sheet accounts. The purpose of the Retained Earnings category is to explain changes in a water utility's retained earnings balance over a fiscal or calendar year, due to net income, accounting adjustments not properly attributable to a particular period, appropriations of retained earnings during the period, and transfers to the municipal general fund (or in the case of investor-owned water utilities, dividend declarations).

Limitations of the Recommended System of Accounts. Any system of accounts such as that suggested in this chapter is based upon a set of assumptions as to the organizational structure and operating activities of a water utility. If a given utility varies in organizational plan or in operating activities from the assumptions underlying the suggested system, the details of the system should be adapted to fit the actual conditions. The essential features of the suggested system should be retained by all water utilities, however, because the system is based on accounting principles advocated by the NARUC and NCGA. Use of the essential features of the suggested system of accounts will promote uniform reporting by water utilities, which is a prerequisite to effective regulatory control. In addition, uniform reporting enhances understanding of financial reports of water utilities and permits comparison of individ-

ual utility enterprises with each other and with the industry in general.

Fund Accounting and the Recommended System of Accounts

The NCGA defines a fund as "an independent fiscal and accounting entity with a self-balancing set of accounts recording cash and/or other resources together with all related liabilities, obligations, reserves, and equities which are segregated for the purpose of carrying on specific activities or attaining certain objectives in accordance with special regulations, restrictions, or limitations."[6] A fund represents a particular aspect of the activities of a governmental unit and the classification of accounts must be designed to record all the financial transactions and yield reports pertaining to the fund as a separate and complete accounting entity. Funds are established in order to demonstrate compliance with laws, or for reasons of policy and administration.

A municipally-owned water utility should be accounted for as a separate enterprise fund. Within the framework of the enterprise fund, it is generally recommended that a municipally-owned water utility use essentially the same system of accounts as an investor-owned water utility. The fund concept, however, necessitates certain minor variations in the system of accounts for municipally-owned and investor-owned water utilities. These variations are indicated in the detailed listing of accounts in the appendix to this chapter. In general, the variations are a result of two aspects of fund accounting: interfund transactions and restricted assets.

Interfund Transactions. In most municipalities a municipally-owned water utility, as a separate accounting entity, has important and continuing relationships with other funds for centralized services such as purchasing and transportation. Centralized services are usually rendered by a working capital fund. Conversely, various activities of the municipality use the services provided by the water utility. Further, there may be other important transactions between the water utility and other funds of the municipality, such as the transfer of a portion of the utility's retained earnings to the general fund, or the transfer of resources from the general fund to the utility for financing purposes; and payments by the water

---

[6] National Committee on Governmental Accounting, Governmental Accounting, Auditing, and Financial Reporting (Chicago: Municipal Finance Officers Association, 1968), p. 6.

utility to the general fund or special revenue funds in lieu of property taxes. The NCGA states: "In all of these inter-fund relationships it is most important to recognize a strict adherence to individual fund entities. . . ."[7] The system of accounts must be designed to record the interfund transactions resulting from the relationships between municipal funds.

Restricted Assets. A water utility may have cash and investments, the use of which is restricted by statute, contractual agreement, a special trust relationship, or utility management policy. While the restrictions can pertain to both investor-owned and municipally-owned water utilities, the latter group is more frequently subject to such restrictions.

To meet the requirements imposed by the restrictions, the appropriate liquid assets are segregated within the utility enterprise fund. The segregated assets may include assets restricted for debt service (for both general obligation bonds and revenue bonds), assets restricted for construction purposes, assets restricted for replacement of utility plant, and assets derived from customers' deposits. While the restricted assets bear some resemblance to funds, being offset by corresponding liabilities or restrictions of retained earnings, they are not funds as that term is defined in governmental accounting, since they are not completely independent self-balancing entities. The segregated assets are commonly referred to as funds (for example, sinking funds and construction funds); however the NCGA recommends that the portions of a water utility's assets restricted for a particular purpose be referred to as restricted asset accounts.[8]

The restricted assets of a municipally-owned water utility are offset by corresponding liabilities or restrictions of retained earnings. The recommended system of accounts differentiates between operating reserves and the restriction of retained earnings (called Appropriated Retained Earnings). Accretions to operating reserve accounts are made by charges to operating expenses; the reserve accounts represent provisions for estimated liabilities or contingent losses. Appropriations of retained earnings arise directly from charges to the Unappropriated Retained Earnings account.

The Operating Reserves category includes accounts entitled Property Insurance Reserve, Injuries and Damages Reserve, Pensions and Benefits Reserve, and Miscellaneous Operating Reserves. The Appropriated Retained Earnings category includes restrictions of retained earnings for bond debt service, construction, replacement, and similar purposes. Restricted assets are discussed in detail in Chapter 17. Operating reserves and appropriations of retained earnings are discussed in Chapter 18.

Management Accounting and the Recommended System of Accounts

The central idea of management accounting is that managers should be provided with sufficient timely information so that the entity may be managed efficiently and effectively. Management accounting for water utilities is concerned with providing accounting and statistical information to facilitate the performance of utility management functions, particularly those of planning and controlling.

The NARUC Uniform System of Accounts emphasizes the grouping of cost data on a functional basis, such as source of supply, pumping, water treatment, and transmission and distribution. For planning and control purposes, however, management is interested in cost information based on a natural classification such as labor, fuel, and rent. Therefore, within each functional group, costs are identified according to their natural classification.

Effective cost control requires that definite responsibility for costs be established. Further, a manager should be held responsible only for those costs which he can control. Therefore, the system of accounts must allow for the identification and presentation of costs incurred by each responsibility segment of the water utility organization. Cost data and related operating statistics enable utility management to set standards of performance and to prepare realistic operating plans (budgets). Comparison of actual costs and operating statistics with the planned costs and performance standards, by responsibility segment, enables management to control cost and performance and to improve future planning.

In addition to providing information to facilitate planning and controlling current activities of the water utility, a good system of accounts should be designed to facilitate evaluation of proposed alternatives to current technology and current activities. Proposed alternatives often involve capital expenditures. Information needed for capital expenditure decisions is discussed in Chapter 16.

7 Ibid., p. 52.
8 Ibid., p. 52.

Part Two
WATER UTILITY
ACCOUNTING REPORTS

CHAPTER 4. WATER UTILITY REPORTING—GENERAL

The purpose of accounting and statistical reports is to communicate information about the water utility. The information presented in accounting and statistical reports serves as an important foundation upon which decisions by regulatory authorities, taxing bodies, management, creditors, stockholders, and other groups interested in the affairs of a water utility are based. The information needs of each group are discussed in Chapter 2.

The end products of the accounting system employed by the water utility are the financial reports presented to interested groups in an effort to satisfy the information requirements of each. While the data accumulated by the accounting system are not the only sources of information available to those interested in the affairs of the water utility, they represent a significant portion. Therefore, it is important that the financial reports generated by the accounting system present information relevant to the specific needs and problems of the interested groups in a form readily understood by the intended readers.

Application of Principles of Report Preparation

The format and content of certain reports to public service commissions, the Securities and Exchange Commission, and taxing authorities are usually designed by these particular groups. When this is the case, the water utility merely furnishes the information in the manner prescribed. In preparing reports for which the format and content are not specified by law, the accountant is free to apply the general principles of report preparation. Briefly, these principles may be stated as:

1. The requirements of the readers for whom the report is intended should dictate the nature of the data presented and the manner of presentation.

2. The data reported should be arranged in a logical and readily understandable manner.

3. The wording of the report should convey to the reader the precise meaning intended.

4. The information should be reported at the time that it is needed.

5. No more time or effort should be expended in obtaining the information reported than the information is expected to be worth.

The first of these principles is the most important. Reports are made in order to convey a message. In order to succeed in having the message read and understood, the preparers of the report must understand the uses that the intended readers may be expected to make of the report. The second and third principles amplify the first. The ideas embodied in the second are: like items should be grouped; as much or as little detail should be shown as the intended readers are expected to need; and the significance and relative importance of the various groups of data should be brought out through the use of subtotals, totals, various typographic styles, and other devices. The third principle suggests that language familiar to the intended readers should be employed; i.e., technical terminology should be used in a report only if intended readers have a technical background.

The fourth of the general principles of report preparation is obvious, but it is often violated in practice. To report information by the time it is needed, the needs of the intended readers must be foreseen and a system designed to provide the needed information routinely. The design of the information system should also facilitate the presentation of data needed occasionally but not routinely. Accuracy is often of less importance than timeliness; estimates are adequate for many purposes.

The fifth principle is a corollary of the fourth: some of the information desired by water utility managers, or by individuals or groups outside the management team, would cost more to obtain than the information would be worth. The fifth principle also places a lid of reasonableness upon the other four; however, it should not be used as an excuse for failure to be diligent and creative in attempting to meet the needs of those who have a valid claim for information about the water utility and its activities.

The preparation of reports involves the accumulation, sorting, and summarization of detailed financial and statistical data generated by the accounting system. Report preparation is costly, and procedures must be employed which minimize its expense. The procedures instituted are, to a certain extent, dictated by the size of the water utility organization. In some instances, manual preparation may be the most economical. For larger systems, the use of accounting machines and punched cards, or electronic data processing equipment, will be feasible. In other cases, a combination of these data processing systems may be the most efficient and economical. The application of various combinations should be studied before a decision is reached concerning the most appropriate procedures for report preparation. How to apply the general principles for reporting to regulatory and tax authorities, management, creditors, and other interested groups, is the purpose of Part Two of this book.

Reports to Regulatory and Tax Authorities. Chapter 5 is concerned with reports to regulatory and tax authorities; in this context the general reporting principles may be stated as:

1. Each report to a regulatory or tax agency must contain the information specified by the agency.

2. Each report to a regulatory or tax agency must be in a format acceptable to the agency.

3. The terminology used in reports to regulatory or tax agencies must be in conformity with the requirements of the agency.

4. The timing of reports to regulatory or tax agencies must be in conformity with the requirements of the agency (legal penalties may be incurred for noncompliance with reporting requirements of regulatory and tax agencies).

Reports to Management. Chapter 6 discusses reports to water utility management. In that chapter the following reporting principles are brought out:

1. A report to a member of a water utility management team should present information concerning the particular area over which the manager has responsibility.

2. A report to a member of a water utility management team should emphasize the information needed by the manager to discharge his planning and control responsibilities efficiently and effectively.

3. The amount of detail presented in a management report should be inversely related to the breadth of responsibilities exercised by the manager for whom the report is intended.

4. All important information relevant to a decision should be provided at the time needed.

5. The terminology used in a report and the manner of presentation of the information should be understandable by the individual for whom the report is intended.

6. The expenditure of time and effort to provide information must be no greater than the expected value of the information.

Reports to Creditors and Other Interested Groups. Chapter 7 illustrates the application of the general principles of reporting to creditors and other groups outside the water utility management. Briefly, the principles of reporting to such groups may be stated as:

1. Reports intended for creditors, customers, stockholders, and other external groups should present information designed to show the extent to which water utility management has fulfilled its stewardship function.

2. The form, content, and frequency of reports to creditors and other groups interested in the activities of a water utility are generally dictated by custom.

3. Reports intended for readers without accounting knowledge should employ descriptive rather than technical language insofar as possible.

4. Reports in narrative or graphic form should be used to direct attention to significant amounts and relationships shown in accompanying financial statements, and to present important information in addition to that shown in the statements.

CHAPTER 5. REPORTS TO REGULATORY AND TAX AUTHORITIES

Regulatory and Tax Reports—General

Water utilities are required to submit numerous routine and special reports to state public service commissions, the Securities and Exchange Commission, and federal, state, and municipal tax authorities. Generally, the form and content of reports for regulatory and tax purposes are prescribed by the governmental agency having jurisdiction and are not within the discretion of the water utility. In many jurisdictions, municipally-owned water utilities are not subject to as extensive reporting requirements as are investor-owned water utilities. Figure 5-1 presents a concise comparison of the differences in relationship of investor-owned and municipally-owned utilities to regulatory and tax agencies.

The remainder of this chapter is devoted to a description of the form and content of reports to three major groups: state public service commissions, the SEC, and tax authorities.

Reporting to State Public Service Commissions

The purpose of reports to a state public service commission is to provide in useful and convenient form the information required by the commission to facilitate the fulfillment of the commission's regulatory responsibilities. Accounting and statistical reports to a state public service commission provide useful factual information concerning revenue, expenses, property cost, and other aspects of the utility's activities which are used to regulate the earnings and price structure, service, and financial structure of a water utility subject to the commission's jurisdiction.

The Annual Report. The principal medium through which information for control over the affairs of a water utility is received by a state public service commission is the annual commission report. (In some instances reports are required semi-annually or quarterly.)

A major portion of the data for the annual report is produced by the system of accounts employed by the water utility. The prescribed form of the annual report reflects the prescribed uniform system of accounts. To the extent that uniform systems of accounts prescribed by various state public service commissions differ, the form of annual reports to these commissions will also differ. Accounting terminology used in annual reports rendered by water utilities subject to different commissions also may vary and must be

Figure 5-1
DIFFERENCES IN THE RELATIONSHIP OF REGULATORY AND TAX AGENCIES TO
INVESTOR-OWNED AND MUNICIPALLY-OWNED WATER UTILITIES

Governmental Agency	Investor-Owned Water Utilities	Municipally-Owned Water Utilities
State Public Service Commission	Generally subject to regulation.	Generally not subject to regulation. May, however, be required to submit reports to commission solely for information purposes.
Securities and Exchange Commission	Frequently subject, to some extent, to regulation.	Not subject to regulation.
Tax authorities	Generally subject to taxes levied by federal, state, and municipal governments.	Do not pay federal income taxes and generally do not pay other federal taxes (with the exception of some payroll taxes). Frequently exempted from payment of state and municipal taxes; in some instances municipally-owned water utilities are required to pay taxes on property (such as source of supply facilities) which is located outside their service area boundaries.

21

Figure 5-2
CONTENT OF A TYPICAL ANNUAL REPORT FOR A STATE PUBLIC SERVICE COMMISSION

Category of Information	Nature of Information Typically Included Within Applicable Information Category
Identity of the water utility and general information.	Name of the utility, type of organization, legal history, character of service, location of main business office, location of office where accounts and records are kept, and territory served (franchises and permits).
Identity of officers and management	Names of officers and key management personnel, addresses, and yearly compensation.
Description of ownership	Number of stockholders, names and addresses of principal stockholders, number of shares held by principal stockholders, and voting powers of each class and series of stock.
Description of affiliations with other companies	Names and addresses of affiliates, and extent of control.
Financial statements	A comparative balance sheet at the end of the accounting period with supporting notes and schedules showing details of significant accounts, and a comparative statement of income and retained earnings with supporting notes and schedules showing details of significant accounts.
Description of major units of property	Location, year of construction, and other information concerning major items such as reservoirs, standpipes, boiler equipment, and pumping equipment.
Significant operating statistics	Data concerning water production, water consumption, treatment, pumping, fire service, number and classification of customers, number and classification of employees, and accidents.
Description of important changes during the year	Acquisition of other companies, reorganization, merger or consolidation with other companies, important replacements and extensions of water system, changes in leasehold agreements, effect of important rate changes, new security issues, and other important changes affecting the water utility and not included elsewhere in the report.

interpreted by reference to the applicable uniform system of accounts.

The annual report is very comprehensive and is designed to furnish information about many aspects of the water utility's activities over which the commission considers it necessary to exercise effective control. The annual report to the public service commission contains information concerning the nature and extent of the water utility's operations, financial position, efficiency of operation, nature and extent of construction activities, and other information which will keep the commission informed as to the condition of the entire water utility.[1]

Annual reports to public service commissions by water utilities typically include the kind of information outlined in Fig. 5-2.

In general, the annual report to a public service commission is complete in itself; there is no need to refer to annual reports of prior years except to analyze long-term trends. On receipt of the annual report, the commission's accounting staff checks the report for completeness and accuracy. If major irregularities in accounting, operating, or financial practices are found, a field audit by the commission's auditing staff may be required. Further, information furnished in the annual report serves as a basis for making interutility comparisons and statistical studies of the industry.[2]

A typical balance sheet found in the annual report to a state public service commission is depicted in Fig. 5-3. A typical statement of income and retained earnings included in the annual report

---

[1] Herman H. Trachsel, Public Utility Regulation (Chicago: Richard D. Irwin, Inc., 1947), p. 370.
[2] See: Eli W. Clemens, Economic and Public Utilities (New York: Appleton-Century-Crofts, Inc., 1950), p. 455.

Figure 5-3
THE WILLING WATER UTILITY
BALANCE SHEET
As of December 31, 19XX

ASSETS AND OTHER DEBITS		LIABILITIES AND OTHER CREDITS	
Utility Plant		**Proprietary Capital**	
Utility Plant in Service Classified	$33,150,000	Common Stock Issued	$ 5,495,400
Property Held for Future Use	203,000	Preferred Stock Issued	2,250,400
Construction Work in Progress	1,250,000	Premium on Capital Stock	25,000
Total Utility Plant	$34,603,000	Other Paid-in Capital	52,500
Accumulated Provision for Depreciation and Amortization of Utility Plant	(4,635,000)	Capital Stock Expense	(37,600)
Net Utility Plant	$29,968,000	Appropriated Retained Earnings	320,200
		Unappropriated Retained Earnings	3,112,200
Other Property and Investments		Reacquired Capital Stock	(73,400)
Nonutility Property	$ 34,300	Total	$11,144,700
Accumulated Provision for Depreciation and Amortization of Nonutility Property	(7,400)	**Long-Term Debt**	
Other Investments	337,500	Bonds Payable	$16,545,000
Special Funds	626,200	Reacquired Bonds	(220,000)
Total	$ 990,600	Total	$16,325,000
Current and Accrued Assets		**Current and Accrued Liabilities**	
Cash	$ 267,300	Notes Payable	$ 37,300
Special Deposits	80,600	Accounts Payable	332,600
Temporary Cash Investments	23,500	Customer Deposits	237,400
Notes Receivable	41,800	Taxes Accrued	757,700
Accounts Receivable	674,400	Interest Accrued	93,400
Accumulated Provision for Uncollectible Accounts	(29,300)	Dividends Declared	37,400
Materials and Supplies	287,700	Matured Long-Term Debt	150,000
Prepayments	16,200	Miscellaneous Current and Accrued Liabilities	87,500
Accrued Utility Revenues	148,200	Total	$ 1,733,300
Total	$ 1,510,400	**Deferred Credits**	
Deferred Debits		Unamortized Premium on Debt	$ 8,200
Unamortized Debt Discount and Expense	$ 53,700	Customers Advances for Construction	2,120,400
Extraordinary Property Losses	18,700	Other Deferred Credits	9,300
Preliminary Survey and Investigation Charges	8,000	Total	$ 2,137,900
Temporary Facilities	9,200	**Operating Reserves**	
Miscellaneous Deferred Debits	38,600	Pensions and Benefits Reserve	$ 256,800
Total	$ 128,200	Miscellaneous Operating Reserves	32,600
		Total	$ 289,400
Total Assets and Other Debits	$32,597,200	**Contribution in Aid of Construction**	
		Contributions in Aid of Construction	$ 966,900
		Total Liabilities and Other Credits	$32,597,200

is shown in Fig. 5-4. These financial statements are based on the NARUC classification of accounts for an investor-owned water utility which is outlined in the Appendix.

Special Reports. In addition to filing the annual report, water utilities may be required to render special reports to public service commissions. Among the more important special reports are those concerned with establishing rates and those concerned with proposed security issues.

Rate studies have as their objective the determination of the prices various classes of cus-

tomers will be required to pay for water service. The rate study is very detailed; it is a result of the efforts of accountants, engineers, statisticians, and other experts. For example, from the standpoint of the accountant, the rate study requires an exhaustive analysis of income and expense accounts for several years as a basis for the preparation of statements of pro forma operating revenue and expenses at present and proposed rates. Further, the rate base value of utility plant devoted to the production, distribution, and sale of water must be determined. Rate studies are dis-

Figure 5-4
THE WILLING WATER UTILITY
STATEMENT OF INCOME
AND UNAPPROPRIATED
RETAINED EARNINGS
For the Year Ended December 31, 19XX

UTILITY OPERATING REVENUE
Operating Revenues		$6,764,100
Operating Expenses:		
Operation Expense	$1,632,700	
Maintenance Expense	328,100	
Depreciation Expense	455,600	
Amortization of Limited-Term and		
Other Utility Plant	3,700	
Amortization of Property Losses	3,200	
Taxes Other than Income Taxes	1,093,900	
Income Taxes	1,406,800	
Total Operating Expenses		$4,924,000
Utility Operating Income		$1,840,100

OTHER INCOME
Income from Nonutility Operations	$ 7,400	
Interest and Dividend Income	9,600	
Miscellaneous Nonoperating Income	2,100	
Total Other Income		$ 19,100
Total Income		$1,859,200

MISCELLANEOUS INCOME DEDUCTIONS
Miscellaneous Amortization	$ 1,800	
Other Income Deductions	3,300	
Total Miscellaneous Income		
Deductions		$ 5,100
Income Before Interest Charges		$1,854,100

INTEREST CHARGES
Interest on Long-Term Debt	$ 513,700	
Amortization of Debt Discount		
and Expense	15,400	
Amortization of Premium on Debt-Cr.	(3,100)	
Other Interest Expense	8,700	
Interest Charged to Construction-Cr.	(12,100)	
Total Interest Charges		$ 522,600
Net Income		$1,331,500

UNAPPROPRIATED RETAINED EARNINGS
Unappropriated Retained Earnings (at		
beginning of period)		$2,638,700
Credits:		
Balance Transferred from Income	$1,331,500	
Miscellaneous Credits to		
Retained Earnings	1,800	
Total Credits		$1,333,300
Debits:		
Miscellaneous Debits to		
Retained Earnings	$ 3,100	
Appropriations of Retained Earnings	32,700	
Dividends Declared-Preferred Stock	101,300	
Dividends Declared-Common Stock	722,700	
Total Debits		$ 859,800
Unappropriated Retained Earnings (at		
end of period)		$3,112,200

cussed in Chapter 6 and Chapter 9.

Public service commissions may require reports concerning proposed security issues. Typically, permission by the commission is needed prior to the issuance of securities by the water utility. For example, the issuance of capital stock or long-term indebtedness would normally require approval by the commission. In addition, informational reports on short-term financing may also be required even though commission approval may not be needed. A securities report might include information pertaining to expected proceeds, use to be made of the proceeds, pro forma financial statements, interest rate and repayment schedule (in case of debt), and any other information relating to the particular proposal.

Certainly, the preceding discussion concerning reports to public service commissions is not exhaustive. However, the reports discussed are among the more important and common documents submitted to public service commissions. Other reports also may be required by particular commissions. Other examples are reports rendered in connection with a merger or consolidation (which would normally involve the preparation of consolidated financial statements); reports rendered in connection with a reorganization (which normally involve pro forma financial statements and a critical study of the reorganization plan); reports concerning abandonment of facilities; and reports concerning construction plans or programs.

Reporting to the Securities and Exchange Commission

The information included in the various routine and special reports submitted to the Securities and Exchange Commission (SEC) results from the purposes of the statutes under which the reports are required. The general purpose of the statutes administered by the SEC "is to protect the interests of the public and investors against malpractices in the securities and financial market."[3] The SEC derives its authority and powers from a number of acts of Congress including the Securities Act of 1933 and the Securities Exchange Act of 1934. Investor-owned water utilities which issue securities falling within the provisions of these acts must comply with the reporting requirements of the SEC. The management of an investor-owned water utility should be aware of the impact of the

---

[3] J. Brooks Heckert and James D. Willson, Controllership (2nd ed.; New York: The Ronald Press Company, 1963), p. 622.

SEC and of the possibility that the utility may be subject to SEC reporting requirements. In anticipation of meeting SEC requirements, management should seek the expert counsel of outside consultants or its own staff in order to insure that all requirements are adequately met.

Financial Statements Included in Reports to the SEC. The financial statements required in reports to the SEC include the balance sheet, income statement, statement of retained earnings, and certain supporting schedules. Under the Securities Act of 1933 and the Securities Exchange Act of 1934, the SEC has the authority to prescribe the form of reports submitted and the accounting methods used in the preparation of the reports. Pursuant to such authority, the SEC developed Regulation S-X, together with related Accounting Series Releases, which govern the form and content of most of the financial statements and supporting schedules filed with the SEC under the 1933 and 1934 Acts as well as other acts administered by the commission. Additional specific requirements are contained in the instructions accompanying the individual forms which are to be used in particular circumstances for reporting to the SEC.

Although Regulation S-X governs content and form of reports to a large degree, the SEC does not want the regulation to serve as a barrier to the evolution of more useful and informative statements. Regulation S-X states that "Financial statements may be filed in such form and order, and may use such generally accepted terminology, as will best indicate their significance and character in light of the provisions applicable thereto."[4] However, a large degree of statement standardization has developed, and water utility management should refer to Regulation S-X, Accounting Series Releases, and instructions accompanying individual forms prior to preparation of particular reports.

Reporting to Tax Authorities

Municipally-owned water utilities are exempt from federal income taxation. Further, municipally-owned water utilities are exempt from most state and municipal taxation. As a result, the tax reporting requirements faced by municipally-owned water utilities generally are small in comparison with the requirements faced by investor-owned water utilities which are subject to federal, state, and local taxes. Municipally-owned water utilities may be required to provide free water service to other departments of the municipal government as an alternative to the payment of local taxes, or they may be required to transfer cash to the municipal general fund as a "payment in lieu of taxes." Planning and controlling the tax burden is discussed in Chapter 13. The present chapter is concerned only with tax reports to governmental agencies.

Reports to Federal Tax Authorities. The federal tax law, as set forth in the Internal Revenue Code and Regulations, is administered by the Internal Revenue Service. At the federal level, investor-owned water utilities are subject to income taxation. Every investor-owned water utility must file an income tax return, even if it has no taxable income. Income tax returns must be prepared and filed in accordance with the regulations and the instructions accompanying the return. The format of the return is designed to aid in determining the water utility's tax liability. The return contains spaces for (1) computing taxable income, (2) applying the appropriate normal tax and surtax rates against the computed taxable income to determine the income tax, and (3) subtracting any tax prepayments from the income tax liability to determine the balance due the IRS.

The preparation and filing of returns involves more than merely reporting taxable income and the tax liability thereon. It is necessary that the return be accompanined by any supporting information or statements required by regulations or instructions. The net income as shown in the financial statements of an investor-owned water utility may differ from the taxable income shown on the federal income tax return because the accounting treatment of certain income and expense items differs from the tax treatment. The income tax laws are written with feasibility of collection and enforcement in mind and are not necessarily in agreement with sound accounting principles. As a result of the differences, the corporation return contains a schedule which reconciles book income with taxable income. In addition, a schedule is included with the return which analyzes changes in retained earnings from the beginning to the end of the taxable year. Other detailed information must also be submitted in support of the deductions claimed on the return.

In addition, water utilities may be required to file information returns which report payments of taxable income made to others. For example, in-

---

[4] U.S. Securities and Exchange Commission, Regulation S-X, Form and Content of Financial Statements, as amended to October 15, 1964 (Washington D.C.: U.S. Government Printing Office, 1964), Rule 3-01, p. 3.

formation reports must be filed for interest paid on debt obligations and, in the case of investor-owned water utilities, dividends paid to shareholders.

Other reports to the federal government disclose information related to payroll taxes and employee income tax withholding. Federal payroll taxes encompass Federal Insurance Contribution Act (FICA) taxes and Federal Unemployment Tax Act (FUTA) taxes. FICA taxes are taxes on employees' salaries to finance the federal social security program, which provides for old age, survivor, disability, and medical benefits. The employees of an investor-owned water utility are covered by the federal social security program. Municipally-owned water utilities also are subject to payment of FICA taxes if the employees of the utility have been brought into social security coverage through agreements with the Secretary of Health, Education, and Welfare.

The purpose of the FUTA tax on wages and salaries is to build a fund to help finance the joint federal-state unemployment insurance program; the federal tax is levied on the employer but not on the employee. However, in a few cases, state unemployment contributions taxes are levied on both employers and employees.

Investor-owned water utilities generally are subject to FUTA taxes. However, the federal act establishing unemployment compensation insurance excludes employees of municipally-owned water utilities from coverage on a mandatory basis since, under the United States Constitution, the federal government cannot tax state and local governments, or their instrumentalities. Nevertheless, a majority of the states participate in the unemployment compensation program through legislation which affords some form of unemployment insurance coverage, either on a compulsory or voluntary basis, for employees of municipally-owned water utilities.

Employee income tax withholding applies to both investor-owned and municipally-owned water utilities. Federal law requires employers to withhold certain amounts from an employee's wages to be applied to the latter's federal income tax liability. The amount to be withheld from wages and salaries depends on the amount of the payment, the time period for which the payment is made, and the amount of the employee's deduction for personal exemptions.

Federal tax reporting requirements are extremely complex and change frequently in response to new or amended federal tax legislation and regulations. In order to insure that all reporting requirements are adequately met and that tax payments are minimized within the context of existing tax legislation and regulations, water utility management should have a utility tax department, employing qualified specialists in tax law and accounting, either on a full-time basis or as consultants. A utility tax department should be responsible for meeting tax reporting and tax payment deadlines in order to avoid the incurrence of legal penalties associated with noncompliance. The tax department also should maintain appropriate tax records and worksheets in support of tax reports.

Reports to State and Municipal Tax Authorities. At the state and municipal government levels, water utilities are subject to a wide variety of taxes. Further, the types of taxes levied on water utilities by state and municipal governments also differ among the various tax jurisdictions. State and municipal taxes may be classified as: income taxes, property taxes, gross receipt taxes, sales taxes, and other miscellaneous taxes.

Income taxes are becoming increasingly important as a source of revenue for state governments and municipalities. In some cases, state and municipal income tax returns correspond to the federal income tax return. Under such conditions the state and municipal income tax returns usually can be prepared from the federal return and supporting schedules. In other cases, even though the state and municipal income tax is patterned after the federal tax, the income subject to taxation and the deductions allowed may differ somewhat from that reported on the federal return. In such a situation, the income tax return for the state or municipal government may still utilize the taxable income figure derived from the federal return, allowing adjustments to be made at the bottom of the return or on a separate schedule for the differences between federal and state or municipal taxable income.

Taxes based on the value of property are a major source of revenue for state and municipal governments. Property taxes are not levied by the federal government. A water utility may be liable for payment of several different types of property taxes and may pay property taxes to many different tax authorities, including states, counties, school districts, cities, or any other tax district. The expression "property tax" generally means an ad valorem (i.e., in proportion to the value) levy on tangible or intangible property. In general, a property tax in its true form is a tax on all property not specifically exempt. All property is valued uniformly and taxed at a uniform rate. In many instances, property is classified as real property or tangible or intangible personal property; each class of property is individually valued and a tax rate (which may be the same or may be different for each class of property) is applied to each class. The basis for valuing real property and tangible or intangible personal property varies widely among the various taxing jurisdictions; the basis for valuation may be established by law or regulation as original cost-less depreciation, reproduction cost-less depreciation, cash value, or some other value.

Frequently the tangible and intangible property of a water utility is valued on a going-concern basis, as opposed to a piecemeal assessment of specific items of property. In some instances, the assessed value may be determined by the total market value of securities outstanding or by capitalizing utility net income. Once the value of all property subject to tax is assessed, the tax rate per unit value of property, such as $100 or $1000, is fixed. Property tax returns typically include information concerning the class of property subject to the tax, a listing of such property, the assessed value of the taxable property, and the tax liability on the assessed valuation.

Gross receipts taxes are levied on the revenue of the water utility. They may be based on all operating revenue, revenue from sales to particular classes of customers such as residential and commercial, or all revenues, both operating and nonoperating. Taxes actually levied on revenue or receipts may carry different descriptive titles among different tax jurisdictions; for example, they may carry the title of franchise taxes, privilege taxes, occupational taxes, or license taxes. A gross receipts tax return may include data on total receipts, sales originating in the taxing jurisdiction, and sales by class of customer.

Sales taxes are taxes based on sales of utility services to customers. Sales taxes usually are levied on retail sales (sales to final water customers). A tax may also be levied on sales for resale in some instances. Whereas gross receipts taxes are levied on the water utility, sales taxes are levied on the water utility customers, with the utility serving as a collecting agency. Sales taxes are normally stated as separate items on the bills for service, and are neither expenses to the utility nor are they revenues. The water utility must collect the tax, maintain appropriate records, and make periodic reports and payments to the tax authorities. The sales tax return typically includes data concerning gross receipts from taxable sales to customers as well as data regarding sales for resale and to governmental authorities which are exempt from taxation.

There are, of course, many other types of taxes levied on water utilities by state governments and municipalities. These other taxes include state unemployment insurance taxes, workmen's compensation insurance taxes, franchise taxes based on flat annual fees, and capital stock taxes. Periodic returns also must be rendered by the water utility in connection with these taxes.

Summary

The discussion in this chapter illustrates that a number of principles exist which may be used as guidelines in the preparation of reports to regulatory and tax authorities. These principles may be stated as:

1. Each report to a regulatory or tax agency must contain the information specified by the agency.
2. Each report to a regulatory or tax agency must be in a format acceptable to the agency.
3. The terminology used in reports to regulatory or tax agencies must be in conformity with the requirements of the agency.
4. The timing of reports to regulatory or tax agencies must be in conformity with the requirements of the agency. (Legal penalties may be incurred for noncompliance with reporting requirements of regulatory and tax agencies.)

CHAPTER 6. MANAGEMENT REPORTS

Effective decisions by water utility management are critical to the successful operation of the utility. In order to make effective decisions managers must be provided with appropriate timely information. The general principles of report preparation presented in Chapter 4 are particularly relevant to management reports:

1. The requirements of the readers for whom the report is intended should dictate the nature of the data presented and the manner of presentation.

2. The data reported should be arranged in a logical and readily understandable manner.

3. The wording of the report should convey to the reader the precise meaning intended.

4. The information should be reported at the time it is needed.

5. No more time or effort should be expended in obtaining the information reported than the information is expected to be worth.

The purpose of this chapter is to illustrate the application of these general principles to reports for water utility management.

The Nature of Accounting Reports for Management

Accounting reports provide water utility management with information required for the fulfillment of its basic tasks: the formulation of plans to achieve the objectives of the enterprise, and the control of operations to accomplish planned results. Management, as well as groups external to the operations of the water utility, is interested in the income statement and balance sheet. These conventional financial statements report revenue earned and expenses incurred during a given accounting period and report asset, liability, and equity balances as of the end of an accounting period. The income statement and balance sheet furnish a means of evaluating prior decisions and serve as a basis for planning the future operations and future financial conditions of the enterprise.

The General Structure of the Management Reporting System

The degree of detail presented in a report to management depends on the level of management for which the report is intended. The generally accepted reporting rule is that the higher the echelon of management to which a report is directed, the more summarized and broadened in scope the report should be.

Each manager should receive action reports concerning those activities for which he is responsible. Typically, managers at the level in the organization indicated by Meter Reading in Figs. 6-1 or 6-2 have direct responsibility for detailed operation of their segment of the organization, and at succeeding higher levels the responsibility becomes more general in nature. Consequently, action reports to managers with direct operating responsibility for a relatively small segment of the utility should furnish quite detailed information as to that segment. However, reports to managers at successively higher levels should furnish less and less detail about larger and larger segments. If managers at higher echelons desire, their summarized reports may be accompanied by supporting schedules of detailed information.

The concept of reporting discussed above is sometimes called "responsibility reporting." In applying the responsibility concept to report preparation, and to the underlying information collection system, historical costs must be accumulated and reported by responsibility unit to provide managers with a basis for budgeting future operations. Thus, the management information flow is designed to coincide with lines of responsibility and authority within the water utility's organization structure. Individual managers and supervisors receive reports that emphasize the costs which they can control and for which they are held responsible.

For control purposes, exception reporting may be employed. In applying the exception concept within the framework of the responsibility reporting system, material or significant deviations from plans are emphasized. Water utility managers, particularly those managers holding high level

Figure 6-1
AN ASSUMED ORGANIZATION STRUCTURE FOR A
MUNICIPALLY-OWNED WATER UTILITY

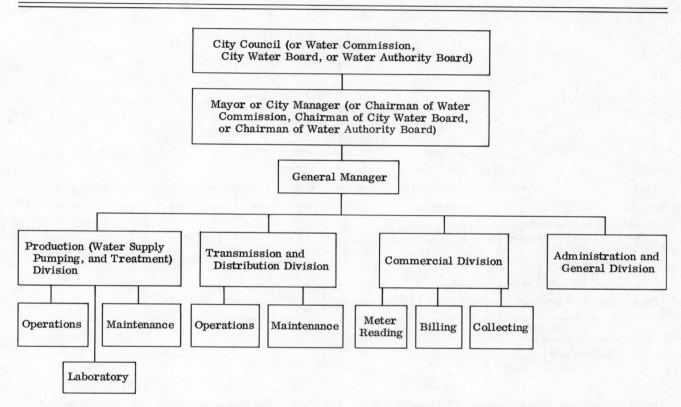

positions within the water utility's organization structure, do not have time to oversee continually every aspect of the operations for which they are responsible. Therefore, reports to managers should highlight the trouble spots that require the attention of management, rather than emphasizing those aspects of the water utility's activities that are proceeding satisfactorily and are conforming to plans.

Each water utility's management reporting system should, of course, be tailored to the existing organization structure. In order to discuss adequately a management reporting system that encompasses the concept of different reports for different levels of management, and the concept of responsibility reporting, hypothetical organization structures have been assumed for municipally-owned and investor-owned water utilities. Fig. 6-1 represents the assumed organization structure of a municipally-owned water utility. Figure 6-2 represents the assumed organization structure of an investor-owned water utility.

In Figs. 6-1 and 6-2, it is assumed that a city council (or water commission, city water board,

or water authority board) maintains a position in relation to a municipally-owned water utility comparable to that of the board of directors of an investor-owned water utility. Further, it is assumed that a mayor or city manager (or chairman of the water commission, chairman of the city water board, or chairman of the water authority board) occupies a position in the hierarchy of a municipally-owned water utility comparable to the position occupied by the chairman of the board of directors of an investor-owned water utility. A third assumption is that the position held by the general manager of a municipally-owned water utility and the position held by the president and and general manager of an investor-owned water utility are comparable. A fourth assumption is that the operating divisions within the water utility are organized in essentially the same manner in municipally-owned and investor-owned water utilities. Finally, it should be noted that the organization structures shown in Figs. 6-1 and 6-2 are somewhat simplified in that only lines of direct authority and responsibility are depicted; specialized staff or advisory personnel who have func-

Figure 6-2
AN ASSUMED ORGANIZATION STRUCTURE FOR AN
INVESTOR-OWNED WATER UTILITY

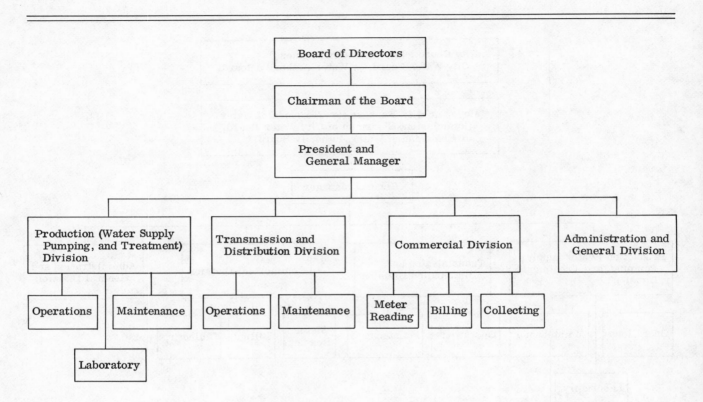

tional but not operating responsibility have been omitted from the figures. Organization structures differ markedly among water utilities; consequently, Figs. 6-1 and 6-2 are intended to serve only as a basis for discussion of a water utility management reporting system and are not presented as models which should be followed in practice.

Types of Management Reports

Although reports to water utility management can be classified in several different ways, a convenient grouping consists of planning reports, control reports, and informational reports. Each of these categories of reports has a different purpose and requires different report design, content, and timing.

Planning reports are concerned with proposed programs for the water utility's operating activities, capital investment, and financial condition. The purpose of control reports is to assist in controlling operations, capital investment, and financial condition, by emphasizing areas in need of corrective action. Information reports are in-tended to furnish water utility management with pertinent information for use in future planning, in coordinating activities of the various segments of the organization, and for determining policy.

Many planning, control, and information reports are prepared routinely for management. However, routine reports are not always suited to meeting particular problems faced by water utility management—special reports may be needed to furnish information relevant to particular decisions. The accounting and reporting system must be capable of producing information appropriate to these special needs. Examples of non-routine situations requiring special reports or studies are proposed rate changes and the issuance of new securities. While each special study is unique, certain steps are common to all. These steps may be visualized as (1) defining the problem; (2) estimating the costs and revenues affected by alternative proposals; (3) comparing costs and revenues associated with the alternatives; and (4) choosing among the alternatives.

The scope and content of planning, control, and informational reports will vary depending on the particular level of management to which the reports are directed. In the remainder of Chapter 6 the application of specific planning, control, and informational reports to each level of management will be considered. The discussion in this chapter is limited to a description of the data included in reports to water utility management. The development of the reports themselves is discussed in Parts Three and Four.

Planning Reports

Planning reports may be very broad in scope, encompassing a major portion of the activities of a business. Planning reports may also be specialized, focusing on a specific aspect of the activities of the water utility. Planning reports are a formal expression of the utility's objectives and the means to be used in achieving those objectives. Budgets, forecasts, proposals, or estimates are names given to reports in this category.

Routine Planning Reports for Policy Making Groups. The policy making group for a water utility establishes the objectives of the utility. This group is responsible for authorizing plans and overseeing the activities of the water utility. It is generally not involved with the day-to-day operations of the utility. In the case of the municipally-owned water utility depicted in Fig. 6-1, it is assumed that the policy making group includes the city council (or water commission, city water board, or water authority board) and the mayor or city manager. In the case of the investor-owned water utility depicted in Fig. 6-2, the board of directors serves as the policy making group.

Planning reports for the policy making group include both utility-wide planning reports and specialized planning reports. Major utility-wide routine planning reports may include:

1. An operating budget
2. A capital expenditures budget (or plant investments program)
3. A financing plan
4. Estimated financial statements.

Each of these reports should be presented in summarized form accompanied by detailed supporting statements. A summary statement of estimated revenue and expense (or operating budget summary statement), for example, should be submitted to the policy making group to aid it in its review of the detailed budget. Approval by that group is a necessary legal step for a municipal utility, and a customary step for an investor-owned utility. Figure 6-3 shows a statement of estimated revenue and expense based on the operating budget. The proposed budget figures for the budget year (19BY) in Fig. 6-3 are compared with the adopted budget figures and the actual figures for the current year (19CY). The comparison permits the reader of the statement to observe significant changes in revenues and expenses occuring from one year to the next.

The operating budget should be developed along the lines of authority and reponsibility. Budgets should be developed for each operating department of the utility, for each section of each department, and for any further subdivisions within the utility organization. Referring to Figs. 6-1 and 6-2, the operating budget would be composed of budgets for the Production (Water Supply, Pumping, and Treatment) Division, the Transmission and Distribution Division, the Commercial Division, and the Administrative and General Division. In turn, each of the four divisional budgets would be made up of budgets for each of its sections.

It should be emphasized that budgets should be prepared on a responsibility basis for municipality-owned as well as investor-owned utilities. The NCGA stresses that: "In some jurisdictions, utilities and other enterprises are required to adopt and operate under budgets in the same manner as non-enterprise operations of governmental units, whereas in others a formal budget is optional or not required at all. Regardless of legal requirements in this respect, however, it is widely recognized that sound financial administration requires the preparation and adoption of a comprehensive annual budget for each enterprise activity. . . .

"While the preparation and adoption of a comprehensive budget is essential for good management, this does not mean that the same degree of budgetary control must be exercised in executing an enterprise budget, or that there be a formal system of budgetary accounting such as that required for the General and Special Revenue Funds. On the contrary, since a utility or other enterprise is a self-supporting operation of a commercial nature, its expenditures should not be controlled by means of detailed and rigid appropriations. These expenditures will vary with the timing and level of demand for service, and if rigidly controlled may delay necessary expansion of activities or impede satisfactory performance. In the interests of managerial flexibility and practicality, therefore, it is recommended that no formal system of budgetary accounting and control be employed for enterprise funds, but that, instead, the budgetary estimates upon which the legally adopted budget is based be retained in memorandum form

Figure 6-3
THE WILLING WATER UTILITY
STATEMENT OF ESTIMATED REVENUE AND EXPENSE
For the Year Ending December 31, 19BY
(With Comparative Figures for the Current Year)

	Original Budget 19CY	Actual(a) 19CY	Proposed Budget 19BY
Operating Revenues:			
Metered Water Sales	$5,869,000	$6,188,900	$6,337,000
Sales for Resale	126,200	137,300	145,300
Public Fire Protection	397,800	405,200	412,700
Other	27,000	32,700	35,000
Total Operating Revenues	$6,420,000	$6,764,100	$6,930,000
Operating Expenses:			
Operation Expense	$1,651,200	$1,632,700	$1,663,200
Maintenance Expense	316,800	328,100	346,500
Depreciation and Amortization Expense	462,500	462,500	485,100
Taxes	2,467,200	2,500,700	2,564,100
Total Operating Expense	$4,897,700	$4,924,000	$5,058,900
Utility Operating Income	$1,522,300	$1,840,100	$1,871,100
Net Non-Operating Income	27,000	14,000	10,500
Total Income Before Interest Charges	$1,549,300	$1,854,100	$1,881,600
Interest Charges:			
Interest on Long-Term Debt	$ 517,300	$ 513,700	$ 556,350
Other Interest Expense	8,900	8,900	9,200
Total Interest Charges	$ 526,200	$ 522,600	$ 565,550
Net Income	$1,023,100	$1,331,500	$1,316,050

(a) The figures in this column represent actual expenses for the first ten months of the current year plus estimated expenses for the remaining two months.

and utilized in the preparation of comparative operating statements."[1]

Figure 6-4 depicts an operating budget program developed along the lines of responsibility and authority shown in Figs. 6-1 and 6-2. Only a portion of the operating budget is shown in the illustration, and it is extremely simplified. Nevertheless, the budgeted operating expense structure depicted in Fig. 6-4 indicates the manner in which the budget is developed to fit the organization structure of a water utility. Although the entire budget (including the budget details for every level of operations within the water utility organization) may be furnished to them, the city council or board of directors is primarily interested in the broadest aspects of the budget, such as budget level 1 in Fig. 6-4. The city council or board of directors may wish to investigate the details underlying a particular budget figure by referring to the appropriate portion of the operating budget.

In addition to a report concerning the operating budget, the policy making group generally receives reports concerning the capital expenditures budget. These reports frequently are prepared for a five-year period. (Some water utilities prepare capital expenditures budgets to cover more extended periods of time, such as ten, fifteen, or twenty years.) Usually the five-year budget is revised annually, the current year being dropped and the plan extended for an additional year, so that it remains a five-year plan. As in the case of reports concerning the operating budget, reports to the policy making group concerning proposed capital expenditures are typically composed of a summary statement supported by detailed information concerning individual capital expenditure projects. Figure 6-5 presents an example of a five-year capital expenditures budget summary. The budget shows the estimated cost of additions and the credits to the utility plant accounts which reflect retirements. The budget depicted in Fig.

[1] National Committee on Governmental Accounting, Governmental Accounting, Auditing and Financial Reporting (Chicago: Municipal Finance Officers Association, 1968), p. 51.

Figure 6-4
THE WILLING WATER UTILITY
STRUCTURE OF AN ANNUAL OPERATING BUDGET

Statement of Estimated Revenue and Expense
(see Fig. 6-3)

	Budget 19BY
Operating Revenues	$6,930,000
Operating Expenses:	
Operation Expense	$1,663,200
Maintenance Expense	346,500
Depreciation and Amortization Expense	485,100
Taxes	2,564,100
Total Operating Expenses	$5,058,900
Utility Operating Income	$1,871,100

Budgeted Utility Operation and Maintenance Expenses

Cost Center	Budgeted Amount-19BY	
Office of the General Manager	$ 36,400	
Production Division	748,370	
Transmission and Distribution Division	324,850	(Budget or Responsibility Level 1)
Commercial Division	268,960	
General and Administrative Division	631,120	
Total Budgeted Operation and Maintenance Expenses	$2,009,700	

Transmission and Distribution Division
Budgeted Operating Expenses

Cost Center	Budgeted Amount-19BY	
Office of the Division Manager	$ 23,200	
Operations Section	116,485	
Maintenance Section	185,165	(Budget or Responsibility Level 2)
Total	$324,850	

Maintenance Section
Budgeted Operating Expenses

Cost Center	Budgeted Amount-19BY	
Maintenance Supervision	$ 12,480	
Maintenance of Mains and Storage Facilities	61,120	
Maintenance of Customer Services	70,365	(Budget or Responsibility Level 3)
Maintenance of Meters	41,200	
Total	$185,165	

Meter Maintenance Shop

Budgeted Operating Expenses	Budgeted Amount-19BY	
Salaries and Wages:		
Foreman	$ 5,150	
Meter Repairmen	13,435	
Laborers	10,105	
Total Salaries and Wages	$28,690	
Materials and Supplies:		
Small Tools	$ 200	
Maintenance Materials and Supplies	10,900	
Other	710	
Total Materials and Supplies	$11,810	(Budget or Responsibility Level 4)
Other Expenses:		
Maintenance of Meter Testing Equipment	$ 210	
Utility Services	360	
Incidental Expenses	130	
Total Other Expenses	700	
Total Budgeted Operating Expenses	$41,200	

Figure 6-12
THE WILLING WATER UTILITY
STRUCTURE OF MONTHLY CONTROL REPORTS FOR OPERATING EXPENSES
For The Month of June, 19CY

STATEMENT OF REVENUE AND EXPENSE
(See Illustration 6-11)

	Month of June			Year to Date		
	Actual	Budget	Over (Under)	Actual	Budget	Over (Under)
Operating Revenues	$733,500	$693,000	$40,500	$3,632,750	$3,465,000	$167,750
Operating Expenses:						
Operation Expense	$170,200	$158,150	$12,050	$ 850,700	$ 831,600	$ 19,100
Maintenance Expense	32,700	28,890	3,810	167,500	173,250	(5,750)
Depreciation and Amortization Expense	40,425	40,425	0	242,550	242,550	0
Taxes	277,830	256,410	21,420	1,401,200	1,282,050	119,150
Total Operating Expenses	$521,155	$483,875	$37,280	$2,661,950	$2,529,450	$132,500
Utility Operating Income	$212,345	$209,125	$ 3,220	$ 970,800	$ 935,550	$ 35,250

UTILITY OPERATION AND MAINTENANCE EXPENSES

	Month of June			Year to Date		
Cost Center	Actual	Budget	Over (Under)	Actual	Budget	Over (Under)
Office of the General Manager	$ 2,990	$ 3,030	$ (40)	$ 11,850	$ 12,200	$ (350)
Production Division	82,830	74,830	8,000	371,900	374,190	(2,290)
Transmission and Distribution Division	36,890	29,780	7,110	172,900	162,430	10,470
Commercial Division	25,510	26,890	(1,380)	127,800	134,480	(6,680)
Administration and General Division	54,680	52,510	2,170	333,750	321,550	12,200
Total Operating and Maintenance Expenses	$202,900	$187,040	$15,860	$1,018,200	$1,004,850	$13,350

(Responsibility Level 1)

TRANSMISSION AND DISTRIBUTION DIVISION
Operating Expenses

	Month of June			Year to Date		
	Actual	Budget	Over (Under)	Actual	Budget	Over (Under)
Office of the Division Manager	$ 1,915	$ 1,935	$ (20)	$ 12,470	$ 12,600	$ (130)
Operations Section	14,425	10,650	3,775	55,170	58,290	(3,120)
Maintenance Section	20,550	17,195	3,355	105,260	91,540	13,720
Total	$36,890	$29,780	$7,110	$172,900	$162,430	$10,470

(Responsibility Level 2)

MAINTENANCE SECTION
Operating Expenses

	Month of June			Year to Date		
Cost Center	Actual	Budget	Over (Under)	Actual	Budget	Over (Under)
Maintenance Supervision	$ 1,010	$ 1,040	$ (30)	$ 6,170	$ 6,240	$ (70)
Maintenance of Mains and Storage Facilities	8,150	6,095	2,055	39,010	30,560	8,450
Maintenance of Customer Services	7,620	6,340	1,280	39,170	34,140	5,030
Maintenance of Meters	3,770	3,720	50	20,910	20,600	310
Total	$20,550	$17,195	$3,355	$105,260	$91,540	$13,720

(Responsibility Level 3)

METER MAINTENANCE SHOP
Operating Expenses

	Month of June			Year to Date		
	Actual	Budget	Over (Under)	Actual	Budget	Over (Under)
Salaries and Wages:						
Foreman	$ 430	$ 410	$ 20	$ 2,695	$ 2,575	$ 120
Meter Repairman	1,155	1,090	65	7,185	6,720	465
Laborers	740	740	0	5,090	5,055	35
Total Salaries and Wages	$2,325	$2,240	$ 85	$14,970	$14,350	$ 620
Materials and Suppies:						
Small Tools	$ 10	$ 20	$(10)	$ 105	$ 100	$ 5
Maintenance Materials and Supplies	910	890	20	5,325	5,450	(125)
Other	480	510	(30)	175	355	(180)
Total Materials and Supplies	$1,400	$1,420	$(20)	$ 5,605	$ 5,905	$(300)
Other Expenses:						
Maintenance of Meter Testing Equipment	$ 5	$ 20	$(15)	$ 115	$ 105	$ 10
Utility Services	25	30	(5)	180	180	0
Incidental Expenses	15	10	5	40	60	(20)
Total Other Expenses	$ 45	$ 60	$(15)	$ 335	$ 345	$ (10)
Total Operating Expenses	$3,770	$3,720	$ 50	$20,910	$20,600	$ 310

(Responsibility Level 4)

capital expenditure projects; minor projects may be grouped. Figure 6-13 presents a monthly statement of actual and budgeted capital expenditures for projects completed during the month. Figure 6-14 presents a monthly statement of actual and budgeted capital expenditures for projects not yet completed. This report indicates for each project the amount authorized for expenditure, the amount of actual expenditures to date, the amount committed or encumbered (purchase orders, contracts, or salary commitments not yet paid or recorded as a liability), the balance of authorized funds available to complete the project, and the percentage of completion.

For projects which show an insufficient balance of authorized funds to complete the projects, status reports should include an explanation of the reason for the deficiencies. If total costs to complete a given project are expected to exceed budget authorization by a substantial amount, authorization to make additional expenditures should be required. In the case of municipally-owned water utilities subject to a legally binding capital expenditures budget, it may be necessary for utility management to obtain a supplemental appropriation in order to issue commitment documents and make expenditures beyond original authorizations.

Control reports concerning financial condition also would be submitted to individuals at the policy making level. Balance sheets ordinarily are rendered on a monthly or quarterly basis, and should present comparative data for at least two comparable periods. Data for as many periods as are relevant to the decisions of the policy making group may be presented. Particular balance sheet accounts such as cash, receivables, materials and supplies, utility plant, and retained earnings may be supported by detailed schedules if the policy making group desires the information. Supporting schedules may indicate the detailed composition of accounts, or may analyze changes in particular balance sheet accounts from the end of a preceding period to the end of the current period.

Control Reports at the General Manager Level. As in the case of control reports at the policy making level, the major control reports at the general manager level also include reports concerning operating results, capital expenditures, and financial position. Whereas the reports at the policy making level are stated in summary form, reports for the general manager include as much detailed information as is necessary for effective control of operations of the utility and its operating divisions.

The primary report for controlling operations is the report that compares actual operating results with budget estimates or other standards of performance. For control purposes, reports of operating results should classify expenses by responsibility areas. Referring to Fig. 6-12, the general manager is interested primarily in reports of operating results generated for responsibility level 1. He also is interested in responsibility level 2, because control reports at this level are used by him to guide and evaluate the performance of division managers. Responsibility reports should be prepared and submitted to the general manager on a monthly basis, or more frequently if needed for adequate control of operations.

The general manager also is concerned with the status of capital expenditure projects. Periodic project status reports for him, preferably rendered on a monthly basis, should include information similar to that included in the capital expenditure control reports submitted at the policy making level (see Figs. 6-13 and 6-14). For each project, information concerning actual labor costs, material costs, and overhead costs should be included in the status report and compared with original estimates. If actual labor costs, material costs, or other costs vary (or will vary) from original estimates, the reasons for each variance should be explained in the status report.

The financial condition of the water utility is also of concern to the general manager. Therefore, reports concerning the financial position, and particularly the working capital position, are required by him. To keep abreast of the working capital position, frequent reports may be developed for him concerning current assets and current liabilities. For example, daily or weekly reports of cash receipts, disbursements, and balances reflect the cash position of the water utility. Other monthly status reports concerning current assets and current liabilities include aged listings of accounts receivable, listings of investment in and usage of materials and supplies, and statements of bank borrowings and loan repayments.

Control Reports for Division Managers and Supervisors. The primary control reports at the division manager and supervisor levels concern operating results. Responsibility reports concerning operating expenses should be prepared on a monthly basis. Division managers are primarily interested in reports that reflect their performance (responsibility level 2 in Fig. 6-12) and which reflect the performance of supervisors directly accountable to the division managers (responsibility level 3 in Fig. 6-12). Supervisors

Figure 6-13
THE WILLING WATER UTILITY
CAPITAL EXPENDITURE PROJECTS COMPLETED DURING OCTOBER, 19CY

Project Number	Description of Projects	Budgeted Expenditures	Actual Expenditures	Amount Over (Under) Budget
	Source of Supply Plant			
309	Replacement of Bridges & Culverts	$ 37,000	$ 34,300	($2,700)
310	Construction of Well	60,000	63,700	3,700
	Transmission & Distribution Plant			
323	Landscaping Around Standpipes	10,000	11,000	1,000
332	24" Main Extension—Cayuta Avenue	58,000	61,200	3,200
333	12" Main Replacement—Orchard Street	69,600	65,400	(4,200)
337	6" Main Extension—Elm Street	47,000	43,300	(3,700)
358	Meter Installations(a)	2,000	2,300	300
359	Hydrants(a)	7,000	7,400	400
	General Plant			
362	New Accounting Machine	2,000	2,000	- 0 -
364	Replacement of Service Trucks	18,000	17,900	(100)
	TOTALS	$387,000	$394,200	$7,200

(a) These projects constitute a number of minor projects included under blanket project numbers 358 and 359.

Figure 6-14
THE WILLING WATER UTILITY
STATUS OF UNCOMPLETED CAPITAL EXPENDITURE PROJECTS(a) AS OF OCTOBER 31, 19CY

Project Number	Brief Description of Project	Originally Authorized	Amount			Status of Progress
			Committed	Expended	Not Expended or Committed	
	Source of Supply Plant					
307	Purchase of Reservoir Land	$ 41,000			$ 41,000	Not started
	Pumping Plant					
314	New Booster Pumping Station	275,000	$ 50,200	$ 12,000	213,800	70% completed
	Transmission and Distribution Plant					
327	20" Main Replacement—Clark Street	67,000	18,400	32,600	16,000	80% completed
328	12" Main Extension—Park Avenue	172,000	13,000	165,500	(6,500)	95% completed
334	24" Main Replacement—Waverly Street	104,000		21,400	82,600	20% completed
339	6" Main Replacement—Penna. Avenue	23,000	1,500	11,500	10,000	50% completed
340	8" Main Extension—Route 17	312,500	18,900		293,600	Not started
	General Plant					
366	Replacement of Special Service Equipment	22,000	12,500	4,200	5,300	75% completed
368	New Office Furniture	9,500		10,200	(700)	95% completed
369	Replacement of Office Equipment	4,500			4,500	Not started
	TOTALS	$1,165,500	$125,800	$316,300	$723,400	

(a) This list includes all capital expenditure projects scheduled to begin on or before December 31, 19CY which are not yet completed.

are interested in control reports which relate to their particular duties (responsibility levels 3 and 4 in Fig. 6-12).

Division managers and supervisors are also concerned with progress reports concerning capital expenditure projects which relate to their particular areas of responsibility. Since division managers and supervisors may be directly involved in the construction activity and may be directly responsible for control of labor and material costs incurred in particular capital expenditure projects, they should be furnished with periodic status reports.

There are, of course, control reports other than those dealing with operating expenses and capital expenditure projects, which may be required by division managers and supervisors. For example, in the case of the commercial division manager, and the supervisors within his division, monthly reports which compare actual and budgeted (or estimated) revenue by customer classification, monthly aged listings of accounts receivable, and monthly tabulations of customer complaints, may prove helpful devices for pointing out deficiencies and improving future operations. In the case of all division managers and supervisors, weekly labor cost reports which indicate labor costs for regular operations, and overtime costs incurred due to special work conditions or emergencies, are helpful control devices.

Informational Reports

There are other reports to various levels of water utility management which cannot be classified as planning reports or control reports—they may be called informational reports. The purpose of informational reports is to supply information to water utility management for use in future planning, coordinating activities of the various segments of the organization, and policy determination. Informational reports may be broad in scope or may focus on specific aspects of the activities of the water utility.

Informational reports should not be confused with planning reports. Planning reports involve proposed programs concerning the water utility's operating activities, capital investment, and financial condition; they relate to the means for achieving predetermined objectives. Informational reports, on the other hand, provide data to be used by management to evaluate alternatives to proposed programs and to establish future plans and objectives.

Informational reports may also be utilized to familiarize divisional management and supervisors with all aspects of the utility's activities. It is desirable to furnish divisional managers and supervisors with information about segments of the organization other than their own in order to promote coordination among all segments of the utility. Information indicating to the manager the contribution made by his responsibility area to the overall effort of the water utility can aid in keeping morale at a high level.

A major informational report is the long-range study concerned with various aspects of the water utility's future, including estimates of the future demand for water and future sources available for water supply. Long-range studies, frequently conducted by outside research organizations, may serve as the basis for developing future capital expenditure programs.

Another type of informational report is the trend report. It is concerned with changes over a period of time in various aspects of the utility's activities or in conditions affecting the utility's activities. Types of information pertaining to various aspects of the utility's activities found in trend reports are:

1. Relationships between various balance sheet accounts, expressed in terms of ratios or percentages.

2. Relationships between revenues and various expense accounts, expressed in terms of ratios or percentages. Examples include maintenance expense as a percentage of operating revenue, taxes as a percentage of revenues, and taxes as a percentage of net income.

3. Relationships between particular balance sheet accounts and particular expense or revenue accounts expressed in terms of ratios. Examples are accounts receivable turnover and materials and supplies turnover.

4. Sources of revenue, such as the number of customers within various classifications, and the number of fire hydrants.

5. Operating revenues and operating costs on a per unit basis. Average revenue per customer per unit of time, revenue per million gallons metered, operating cost per million gallons metered, are examples.

6. Water pumpage and usage. For instance, millions of gallons pumped per unit of time, average daily pumpage, maximum daily pumpage, and average metered water usage per day.

Information pertaining to external conditions affecting the water utility's activities should also be presented in trend reports. Important categories are:

1. Rainfall. Examples include actual inches of rainfall per unit of time, normal rainfall in inches for a particular period of time, and the number of days of rain during a period of time.

2. Temperature. Examples include actual temperature over a period of time and normal temperature for a particular period of time.

3. Population in franchised areas. Examples include industrial firms, residential homes, and people.

Another type of informational report may be called the "analytical" report. Analytical reports are concerned with many facets of the activities of a water utility. Examples of analytical reports include analyses of operating revenues by customer or territory, changes in net operating revenues, and changes in retained earnings. Analytical statements concerning revenues and expenses are discussed in Part Three of this book. Analytical statements concerning balance sheet items are presented in Part Four.

Summary

Chapter 6 outlines a basic structure for a water utility management reporting system and presents some basic guidelines for the development of management reports. The management reporting principles outlined in Chapter 4 serve as useful guidelines for preparing management reports. To restate the management reporting principles:

1. A report to a member of a water utility management team should present information concerning the particular area over which the manager has responsibility.

2. A report to a member of a water utility management team should emphasize the information needed by the manager to discharge his planning and control responsibilities efficiently and effectively.

3. The amount of detail presented in a management report should be inversely related to the breadth of responsibilities exercised by the manager for whom the report is intended.

4. All important information relevant to a decision should be provided at the time needed.

5. The terminology used in a report and the manner of presentation of the information should be understandable by the individual for whom the report is intended.

6. The expenditure of time and effort to provide information must be no greater than the expected value of the information.

The first and third principles are applied primarily through a system of responsibility reporting, the structure of which, as discussed in the chapter, should coincide with organizational lines of authority and responsibility. The second management reporting principle is applied primarily through the use of exception reporting. Interpretative remarks should be included in management reports to explain significant deviations from plans and to indicate the action taken to correct the deficiencies.

The fourth principle concerns the timeliness of reports. The purpose of reports determines their required frequency and promptness. To be useful, reports, particularly control reports, must be prompt; forfeiture of a certain amount of accuracy may be called for to insure against tardy reports. Further, care in report preparation should be commensurate with use. While all water utility reports should be accurate to the degree consistent with timeliness, the more important a report, the greater should be the care exercised in its preparation.

The fifth principle concerns the format of management reports and the terminology used in management reports. The format of a report should be suited to the individual using the report. Formal accounting statements, statistical tabulations, pictorial presentations (graphs, charts, and diagrams), or a combination of these may be used to present information. The forms used depend on the desires and sophistication of the reader. Where possible, the format of reports should be consistent from one period to another—people become accustomed to certain formats, and frequent changes may cause confusion. However, where desirable changes can be made, a standard format should not serve as a barrier to improvement. Reports also should be concise, simple, and clear in order that the reader may secure essential facts with a minimum of time and effort. In addition, the language and terms employed in the report should be familiar to management. The use of accounting terms and language should be commensurate with the sophistication of the reader.

Finally, the sixth principle concerns the cost of report preparation. The cost of any report (in terms of time, effort, and money), should be no greater than the benefits derived from having the report (or the loss incurred from not having the report). The cost of report preparation is substantial, and water utility management should make sure that the information it requests can be supplied at a reasonable cost.

CHAPTER 7. REPORTS TO CREDITORS AND OTHER INTERESTED GROUPS

Creditors, stockholders (in the case of investor-owned water utilities), and the general public seek information about the water utility relevant to their special interests. Such information is furnished through reports to these interested groups.

The form and content of reports to creditors, stockholders, employees, customers, and the general public are not dictated by law or regulation to the same extent as are the reports to governmental authorities discussed in Chapter 5. Generally, in the case of reports to employees, customers, and the general public there are no legal requirements. The information to be included in reports, the form of reports, and the frequency of reports are largely dictated by conventional corporate reporting practice.

In the case of reports to investors (creditors and stockholders), there generally are some reporting constraints, either legal or conventional, within which water utility management must operate. For example, bond indentures typically require that reports containing information of special interest to creditors be rendered periodically by the utility. The form and content of a report to potential investors (prospectus) concerning a new securities issue may be dictated by the SEC if the investor-owned water utility issuing the securities falls within the jurisdiction of the SEC. The SEC also influences the form and content of other reports, such as the annual report to stockholders and proxy statements, rendered by investor-owned water utilities falling within the SEC's jurisdiction. Even when there are no legal requirements, a reporting requirement is imposed upon the utility by the fact that reports, such as the the annual report to stockholders, are normally expected by various groups external to the operations of the water utility. Within the dictates of regulations and conventions, the form, frequency, and content of reports to creditors and stockholders as well as employees, customers, and the general public are within the discretion of water utility management.

Some financial reports may be multi-purpose in design, serving the needs of different users of financial information. For example, the annual re-port to stockholders may prove of interest not only to stockholders but to creditors, employees, customers, and the general public. Other reports may be designed as single-purpose, serving the needs of a specific group external to the water utility. Reports to each of the major classes of external users of financial data concerning a water utility are discussed in the remainder of this chapter.

Reporting to Creditors

Present and prospective creditors are interested in a water utility's financial condition, the results of its operations, and other information that can be used to evaluate the risk involved in lending funds to the utility. Loans obtained from commercial banks, although varying significantly in length of maturity, are in the broad category of short-term credit. Bonds generally are in the category of long-term credit. Therefore, information included in reports for commercial bankers is relevant to other short-term credit grantors, while information included in reports for bondholders or their representatives is relevant to other long-term creditors.

Reports to Commercial Banks. Reports to bankers must answer questions such as: Why does the utility need money? How much is required? How and when will the loan be repaid? The particular reporting requirements (the specific financial statements and the extent of detail) accompanying the extension of credit to a water utility by a bank typically depend on the size and term of the loan. There are, of course, other factors, such as the size of the water utility and the quality of management, both of which affect reporting requirements. The request for a small loan does not require as much information as does a request for a large loan, since bankers are assuming less risk in accepting the small loan. In granting short-term loans, bankers are primarily interested in reports that emphasize the manner in which the proposed loan is to be repaid. If the loan is to be repaid from cash generated from operations, bankers frequently require a cash flow forecast showing estimated sources and uses of cash and the estimated future cash balance available for repaying the loan. If the loan is to be repaid by issuing long-term debt, bankers are interested in the effect of the added burden of noncurrent indebtness on the capital structure of the utility and of the ability of the utility to market proposed long-term issues successfully. Bankers also are interested in the income statement as an indication of the earning power or potential of the utility.

Therefore, in seeking credit extensions from commercial banks, water utility management may be required to furnish a cash flow forecast, an interim income statement and balance sheet, and possibly forecasts relating to future income (pro forma statement of income) and future financial position (pro forma balance sheet). In some cases, bankers may require the utility's financial statements to be accompanied by the opinion of an independent certified public accountant. In other cases, financial information may be supplied on a form supplied by the bank without audit.

In addition to financial statements, the report accompanying a request for short-term loan or a line of credit typically includes supplementary information related to other aspects of the water utility including:

1. Contingent liabilities
2. Assets pledged as collateral
3. Insurance carried
4. Names and addresses of officers and directors
5. A statement by Board of Directors or other policy making group indicating that the proposed loan is authorized or approved by them.

As the size or term of the requested loan increases, commercial bankers desire additional, more detailed financial statements. In such instances, audited financial statements and supporting schedules similar to those found in the annual report to a state public service commission ordinarily serve the needs of commercial banks. The financial statements and supporting schedules that accompany a request for an intermediate-term or long-term loan customarily include:

1. The accountant's opinion
2. Balance sheet
3. Statement of income
4. Statement of retained earnings
5. Notes to financial statements.

The preceding discussion has been limited primarily to historical financial statements. However, it should be emphasized that since commercial bankers are concerned with whether or not the water utility will be able to repay the loan at maturity, the future is of great interest. Therefore, requests by water utilities for bank loans should be supported by future projections expressed in terms of forecasts and budgets. It is suggested that requests for loans be accompanied by:

1. A statement of estimated revenue and expense for the forecast period
2. A statement of estimated cash flow for the forecast period indicating source and application of cash
3. A statement of financial position at the end of the forecast period.[1]

Once the loan is obtained or a line of credit is established, the utility should render to the bank periodic financial reports, reports regarding the fulfillment of protective covenants, and reports concerning any material changes affecting the water utility. The desired frequency of reports, the size of the loan, and the term of the loan are included among factors which may influence a bank's request for additional audited statements during the period when loans are outstanding.

It should be mentioned that protective covenants contained in loan agreements impose restrictions on the financial activities of the water utility. The purpose of protective covenant clauses is, of course, to provide increased security for creditors. Protective covenant clauses in loan agreements may include provisions which limit the issuance of additional debt instruments until the loan is repaid, and provisions which limit the payment of dividends (in the case of investor-owned water utilities) or payments to the general fund (in the case of municipally-owned water utilities). Water utility management must understand the provisions contained in the loan agreement in order that the restrictions and obligations imposed on the utility be respected.

Reports to Bondholders. Another major class of creditors to whom reports should be rendered are present and prospective bondholders, or their representatives. The prospectus is the major report to prospective bondholders rendered by water utilities. In the case of bonds already issued, periodic reports by water utilities to bond-

---

[1] Adapted from J. Brooks Heckert and James D. Willson, Controllership (2nd ed.; New York: The Ronald Press Company, 1963), p. 658.

holders, or trustees acting as agents for the bondholders, may be required.

In the case of an investor-owned water utility under the jurisdiction of the SEC, a prospectus relating to the sale of bonds must comply with the requirements of that regulatory agency. Bonds of an investor-owned water utility generally are issued under an indenture which defines the rights and privileges of the bondholders and the duties and obligations of the water utility. Among other provisions, the indenture typically includes a requirement that the water utility render annual and periodic reports to bondholders or their trustees.

While a bond issue of an investor-owned water utility generally is covered by a trust indenture, some municipally-owned water utility bonds, such as general obligation bonds, usually are not issued under the terms of a trust indenture. In instances where bonds issued by a municipally-owned water utility are not covered by an indenture, the rights and privileges of the bondholder and the duties and obligations of the municipally-owned water utility typically are defined by statutes and ordinances

Figure 7-1
SAN ANTONIO WATER REVENUE BONDS
PROJECTED DEBT SERVICE REQUIREMENTS

Calendar Year	$20,135,000 Revenue Bonds Outstanding		$6,000,000 Revenue Bonds—Series 1966		Total Annual Principal	Total Annual Interest	Total Annual Requirement
	Principal	Interest	Principal	Interest(a)			
1966	$	$369,807	$	$	$	$369,807	$ 369,807
1967	750,000	725,077		240,000	750,000	965,077	1,715,077
1968	785,000	695,308		240,000	785,000	935,308	1,720,308
1969	895,000	662,406		240,000	895,000	902,406	1,797,406
1970	910,000	627,500		240,000	910,000	867,500	1,777,500
1971	950,000	592,277		240,000	950,000	832,277	1,782,277
1972	965,000	556,427	100,000	238,000	1,065,000	794,427	1,859,427
1973	990,000	520,265	100,000	234,000	1,090,000	754,265	1,844,265
1974	1,015,000	483,268	100,000	230,000	1,115,000	713,268	1,828,268
1975	1,030,000	445,868	100,000	226,000	1,130,000	671,868	1,801,868
1976	1,060,000	407,965	100,000	222,000	1,160,000	629,965	1,789,965
1977	1,085,000	369,153	100,000	218,000	1,185,000	587,153	1,772,153
1978	1,105,000	329,617	100,000	214,000	1,205,000	543,617	1,748,617
1979	1,145,000	289,066	100,000	210,000	1,245,000	499,066	1,744,066
1980	1,185,000	247,112	100,000	206,000	1,285,000	453,112	1,738,112
1981	1,220,000	203,827	100,000	202,000	1,320,000	405,827	1,725,827
1982	1,265,000	159,030	200,000	196,000	1,465,000	355,030	1,820,030
1983	1,305,000	112,426	200,000	188,000	1,505,000	300,426	1,805,426
1984	1,395,000	62,568	200,000	180,000	1,595,000	242,568	1,837,568
1985	205,000	33,012	600,000	164,000	805,000	197,012	1,002,012
1986	205,000	26,087	700,000	138,000	905,000	164,087	1,069,087
1987	215,000	18,993	700,000	110,000	915,000	128,993	1,043,993
1988	215,000	11,731	700,000	82,000	915,000	93,731	1,008,731
1989	240,000	4,050	800,000	52,000	1,040,000	56,050	1,096,050
1990			900,000	18,000	900,000	18,000	918,000

(a) Series 1966 interest rate assumed as 4.00% per annum.

Ratio of Net Revenues Available for Debt Service for Fiscal Year Ending December 31, 1965 ($4,096,335.40) to Estimated Average Annual Requirements 1966-1990 ($1,639,133) (Coverage) . . . . 2.50 to 1

Ratio of Net Revenues Available for Debt Service for Fiscal Year Ending December 31, 1965 ($4,096,335.40) to Estimated Maximum Requirement in any Year (1972) ($1,861,427.50) (Coverage) . . . . 2.20 to 1

Note: The above ratios are based on actual Net Revenues as of December 31, 1965 and so do not include either the effect of the 17% rate increase effective October 1, 1966 or of the revenues to be derived from the operation of the central heating and cooling plant.

The Engineer's estimates of future net revenues and future coverages are set forth in Fig. 7-2.

Source: Prospectus relating to the sale of $6,000,000 Water Revenue Bonds, Series 1966, City of San Antonio, Texas.

which may require, among other provisions, that periodic reports be rendered to bondholders. On the other hand, revenue bonds, particularly those issued by water authorities and water districts, may be covered only by the bond indenture requirements. (General obligation bonds and revenue bonds are described in Chapter 14.)

The content of a prospectus relating to the sale of water utility bonds typically includes the following information:

1. The history and nature of the water utility's operations

2. The purpose of the bond issue

3. Description of the bond issue to include details concerning interest rates, interest payment dates, maturity schedule, redemption provisions, security, and priority

4. Authority for the issuance of the bonds (in the case of municipally-owned water utilities) and provisions of the bond indenture

5. Description of the management and operating personnel of the utility including names, addresses, background, and experience of members of the board of trustees or board of directors of the utility, executive officers, and key operating personnel

6. Important terms of franchises under which the utility operates

7. Details of bonded debt, other long-term debt, short-term debt, and capital stock (in the case of investor-owned water utilities)

8. Details of utility plant and other property including cost, accumulated depreciation, age, and location of major units of property

9. Financial statements including comparative balance sheets, and condensed operating statements for a number of prior years

10. Forecasts, including projected debt service requirements (see Fig. 7-1), and projected revenues, expenses, and net operating income available for principal and interest requirements (see Fig. 7-2)

11. Other financial and statistical data of a historical nature reflecting the operations of the water utility (see Fig. 7-3).

Figure 7-2
PROJECTION OF WATER WORKS SYSTEM REVENUE, EXPENSES
AND NET REVENUE AVAILABLE FOR PRINCIPAL AND INTEREST
REQUIREMENTS, WITH ESTIMATED REQUIREMENTS AND COVERAGE

Year	Estimated Revenue	Estimated Operating Expense	Net Revenue	Present Debt Requirements	Requirements This Issue	Combined Requirements	Times Coverage
1966	$ 7,703,500	$3,163,200	$4,540,300	$ 369,807		$ 369,807	
1967	8,770,200	3,284,600	5,485,600	1,475,077	240,000	1,715,077	3.20
1968	9,799,400	3,795,200	6,004,200	1,480,308	240,000	1,720,308	3.49
1969	9,387,700	3,726,000	5,661,700	1,557,406	240,000	1,797,406	3.15
1970	9,512,200	3,860,700	5,651,500	1,537,500	240,000	1,777,500	3.18
1971	9,636,700	4,000,000	5,636,700	1,542,277	240,000	1,782,777	3.16
1972	9,761,100	4,144,400	5,616,700	1,521,427	338,000	1,859,427	3.02
1973	9,885,600	4,294,000	5,591,600	1,510,265	334,000	1,844,265	3.03
1974	10,010,100	4,448,800	5,561,300	1,498,268	330,000	1,828,268	3.04
1975	10,134,600	4,609,200	5,525,400	1,475,868	326,000	1,801,868	3.07
1976	10,259,100	4,775,400	5,483,700	1,467,965	322,000	1,789,965	3.06
1977	10,383,600	4,947,100	5,436,500	1,454,153	318,000	1,772,153	3.07
1978	10,508,100	5,125,200	5,382,900	1,434,617	314,000	1,748,617	3.08
1979	10,632,600	5,309,900	5,322,700	1,434,066	310,000	1,744,066	3.05
1980	10,757,000	5,500,900	5,256,100	1,432,112	306,000	1,738,112	3.02
1981	10,757,000	5,500,900	5,256,100	1,423,827	302,000	1,725,827	3.05
1982	10,757,000	5,500,900	5,256,100	1,424,030	396,000	1,820,030	2.89
1983	10,757,000	5,500,900	5,256,100	1,417,426	388,000	1,805,426	2.91
1984	10,757,000	5,500,900	5,256,100	1,457,568	380,000	1,837,568	2.86
1985	10,757,000	5,500,900	5,256,100	238,012	764,000	1,002,012	5.25
1986	10,757,000	5,500,900	5,256,100	231,087	838,000	1,069,087	4.92
1987	10,757,000	5,500,900	5,256,100	233,993	810,000	1,043,993	5.03
1988	10,757,000	5,500,900	5,256,100	226,731	782,000	1,008,731	5.21
1989	10,757,000	5,500,900	5,256,100	244,050	852,000	1,096,050	4.80
1990	10,757,000	5,500,900	5,256,100		918,000	918,000	5.73

Note: Estimates by Black and Veatch, Consulting Engineers. Assumed rate of 4.00% used for these bonds.
Source: Prospectus relating to the sale of $6,000,000 Water Revenue Bonds, Series 1966, City of San Antonio, Texas.

Figure 7-3
CITY WATER BOARD
FINANCIAL AND STATISTICAL INFORMATION

	1965	1964	1963	1962	1961	1960	1959	1958	1957	1956	1955
OPERATING RESULTS											
Total Revenue and Other Income*	$ 6,934,184	$ 7,022,656	$ 7,782,993	$ 7,287,770	$ 5,992,920	$ 5,051,126	$ 5,030,271	$ 4,687,671	$ 4,723,104	$ 5,426,438	$ 3,957,233
Operating Expense	2,837,848	2,851,611	2,916,476	2,777,069	2,720,234	2,783,691	2,744,949	2,716,236	2,512,575	2,461,200	2,033,552
Depreciation and Amortization	1,495,754	1,393,805	1,309,439	1,240,997	1,163,177	1,090,588	940,363	743,402	707,505	649,990	580,540
Interest on Bonded Debt	774,788	792,487	808,803	808,129	733,165	716,949	699,473	638,188	378,317	171,490	184,277
Redemption of Bonds and Bond Reserve Additions	619,551	521,831	513,094	489,697	469,044	420,855	446,115	415,238	386,989	255,000	242,000
Revenue Available For Plant Additions	$ 1,206,243	$ 1,462,922	$ 2,235,181	$ 1,971,878	$ 907,300	$ 39,043	$ 199,371	$ 174,607	$ 737,718	$ 1,888,758	$ 915,864
Revenue Per 1,000 Gallons Pumped—Cents	24.1	23.7	23.9	23.6	22.1	18.8	18.9	18.5	18.9	18.4	15.2
Operating Expense Per 1,000 Gallons Pumped—Cents	9.9	9.6	9.0	9.0	10.0	10.4	10.3	10.7	10.0	8.3	7.8
FINANCIAL DATA											
Gross Plant Additions	$ 5,083,408	$ 4,996,017	$ 4,554,048	$ 4,350,703	$ 2,485,809	$ 4,093,047	$ 5,037,676	$ 8,762,707	$ 3,924,303	$ 1,676,573	$ 2,720,661
Total Utility Plant	67,614,106	63,534,640	59,230,517	55,140,023	51,436,982	50,218,695	46,622,299	41,999,127	33,496,606	29,572,303	27,895,729
Accumulated Depreciation	14,755,150	14,143,130	13,279,767	12,278,250	11,503,260	11,411,740	10,719,859	10,069,667	9,524,410	8,861,511	8,234,622
Inventory	402,525	311,353	382,953	355,970	452,484	458,504	636,257	748,625	1,009,243	725,253	648,341
Bonded Debt	20,885,000	21,218,000	21,517,000	21,809,000	20,115,000	18,380,000	18,607,000	15,860,000	16,098,000	3,033,000	3,288,000
Municipal Equity (Including Reserves)	37,756,828	34,815,490	32,013,349	28,495,101	25,395,667	23,245,511	21,852,841	20,547,283	19,141,237	17,579,770	15,681,211
Total Revenue Less Operating Expenses	4,096,336	4,171,045	4,866,517	4,510,701	3,272,686	2,267,435	2,285,322	1,971,435	2,210,529	2,965,238	1,923,681
Average Annual Debt Requirements	$ 1,213,322	$ 1,208,741	$ 1,204,843	$ 1,200,074	$ 1,088,311	$ 1,178,182	$ 1,168,896	$ 1,160,572	$ 966,953	$ 436,299	$ 436,254
Times Debt Coverage	3.38	3.45	4.04	3.76	3.01	1.92	1.96	1.70	2.29	6.80	4.41
OTHER STATISTICS											
Water Pumped—Million Gallons	28,721	29,631	32,549	30,930	27,098	26,861	26,558	25,332	25,010	29,472	25,983
Metered Usage—Million Gallons	25,430	25,577	28,861	26,690	22,555	22,262	22,525	20,873	21,491	25,183	21,122
Annual Rainfall—Inches	36.65	31.88	18.65	23.90	26.46	29.76	24.50	39.69	48.83	14.31	18.18
Customers at End of Year	136,902	134,724	132,181	129,301	127,190	124,962	123,816	119,800	113,421	112,042	109,224
Average Use Per Customer—Thousands of Gallons	185.8	189.8	220.7	206.4	177.3	178.2	181.9	174.3	189.4	224.7	193.3
Average Revenue Per Customer	$ 50.65	$ 52.13	$ 58.88	$ 56.36	$ 47.12	$ 40.21	$ 40.63	$ 39.13	$ 41.64	$ 48.43	$ 36.23
Miles of Main Installed	86.90	95.76	66.91	60.69	63.02	48.86	87.45	140.45	29.70	40.99	66.37
Miles of Main Replaced and Abandoned	51.80	52.88	18.83	27.46	26.26	9.20	21.64	29.62	10.13	5.65	3.53
Miles of Main In Place	1,796.05	1,760.95	1,718.07	1,669.99	1,636.76	1,600.00	1,560.34	1,494.53	1,383.70	1,364.13	1,328.79
New Services Installed	3,534	3,192	3,237	3,189	2,815	3,131	4,783	6,703	2,886	3,322	5,810
Fire Hydrants Installed	574	508	307	316	316	189	347	341	96	112	215
Fire Hydrants In Place	6,879	6,563	6,279	6,046	5,888	5,720	5,540	5,227	4,886	4,781	4,672
Number of Employees	527	532	536	542	553	604	628	662	657	585	511
Total Salaries and Wages Paid	$ 2,330,274	$ 2,220,369	$ 2,124,314	$ 2,024,613	$ 2,045,006	$ 2,101,298	$ 2,133,209	$ 2,198,921	$ 1,950,830	$ 1,744,847	$ 1,396,258
*Excludes Metered Sales to City of San Antonio Which Amount To	$ 200,619	$ 197,129	$ 189,119	$ 190,472	$ 155,619	$ 130,009	$ 127,891	$ 127,956	$ 84,387		

Source: Prospectus relating to the sale of $6,000,000 Water Revenue Bonds, Series 1966, City of San Antonio, Texas.

The financial and statistical information discussed in items 10 and 11 of the preceding list, and which is exemplified in Figs. 7-1 through 7-3, has been taken from a prospectus relating to the sale of water revenue bonds by the City of San Antonio, Texas.

As indicated earlier in this section, once the bonds are issued, periodic reports to bondholders or their representatives may be required under the terms of the purchase agreement. The reports rendered by a water utility to bondholders include annual financial statements, audited by an independent certified public accountant, and interim financial statements.

An annual report to bondholders typically includes a comparative balance sheet, a statement of income, and a statement of changes in retained earnings. Illustrations from the NCGA's *Governmental Accounting, Auditing and Financial Reporting* are included on the following pages as an indication of recommended financial statement presentation for municipally-owned water utilities. Among the illustrations are a balance sheet (Fig. 7-4), a comparative statement of revenue and expense (Fig. 7-5), and an analysis of changes in retained earnings (Fig. 7-6). It should be noted that current assets and current liabilities are positioned first within the respective portions of the balance sheet shown in Fig. 7-4, in contrast with the customary order of a balance sheet of a utility subject to public service commission jurisdiction, in which fixed assets and fixed liabilities

Figure 7-4
Name of Governmental Unit
WATER AND SEWER FUND
BALANCE SHEET
December 31, 19×2

ASSETS

Current Assets:			
Cash	$	$ 257,036	$
Accounts Receivable	23,900		
Less: Estimated Uncollectible Accounts Receivable	1,920	21,980	
Notes Receivable		2,350	
Due from General Fund		2,000	
Unbilled Accounts Receivable		7,150	
Inventory of Materials and Supplies		18,120	
Inventory of Stores for Resale		4,910	
Prepaid Expenses		1,200	
Total Current Assets			314,746
Restricted Assets:			
Cash with Fiscal Agent		80,444	
Revenue Bond Debt Service:			
Cash		5,000	
Revenue Bond Reserve:			
Cash	8,822		
Investments (Certificates of Deposit)	101,000	109,822	
Revenue Bond Contingency:			
Cash	1,533		
Investments (Certificates of Deposit)	12,800	14,333	
Revenue Bond Construction:			
Cash		17,760	
Customers' Deposits:			
Investments (Certificates of Deposit)	63,000		
Interest Receivable on Investments	650	63,650	
Total Restricted Assets			291,009
Utility Plant in Service:			
Land		211,100	
Buildings	447,700		
Less: Allowance for Depreciation	90,718	356,982	
Improvements Other than Buildings	3,887,901		
Less: Allowance for Depreciation	348,944	3,538,957	
Machinery and Equipment	1,841,145		
Less: Allowance for Depreciation	201,138	1,640,007	
Total Utility Plant in Service			5,747,046
Construction Work in Progress			22,713
TOTAL ASSETS			$6,375,514

LIABILITIES, RESERVES, CONTRIBUTIONS,
AND RETAINED EARNINGS

Current Liabilities (Payable from Current Assets):
Vouchers Payable... $ 131,071
Accrued Wages Payable...................................   850
Accrued Taxes Payable...................................   2,020
Construction Contracts Payable   8,347
Accrued General Obligation Bond Interest Payable   14,000
Advance from Municipality—General Obligation Bonds   50,000
                                                                          $ 206,288

Current Liabilities (Payable from Restricted Assets):
Construction Contracts Payable   17,760
Due to Fiscal Agent   139
Accrued Revenue Bond Interest Payable   32,305
Revenue Bonds Payable   48,000
Customer Deposits   63,000   161,204
    Total Current Liabilities   367,492
Other Liabilities:
Revenue Bonds Payable   1,798,000
Advance from Municipality—General Obligation Bonds   650,000
    Total Other Liabilities   2,448,000
    TOTAL LIABILITIES   2,815,492
Reserves:
Reserve for Revenue Bond Debt Service   5,000
Reserve for Revenue Bond Retirement   109,822
Reserve for Revenue Bond Contingency   14,333
    TOTAL RESERVES......................................   129,155
Contributions:
Contribution from Municipality   450,000
Contribution from Customers   72,000
Contribution from Subdividers   870,666
    TOTAL CONTRIBUTIONS   1,392,666
Retained Earnings   2,038,201
    TOTAL LIABILITIES, RESERVES, CONTRIBUTIONS, AND RETAINED
    EARNINGS $6,375,514

Source: National Committee on Governmental Accounting, Governmental Accounting, Auditing, and Financial Reporting (Chicago: Municipal Finance Officers Association, 1968), p. 62–63.

are shown first (see Fig. 5-3). For municipally-owned water utilities, both of the balance sheet formats are considered acceptable.

In the case of an investor-owned water utility, the form and the degree of detail of the financial statements included in annual bondholder reports are analogous to those found in annual reports to stockholders. The financial statements included in annual reports to stockholders are discussed and illustrated at a later point in this chapter.

Quarterly financial statements generally include:

1. A comparative balance sheet as of the end of the quarter and the quarter ending a year earlier

2. A comparative statement of income for the quarter and the quarter ending a year earlier; in addition, a statement of income for the year to date, or the 12 months ending with the quarter, together with corresponding results for the year prior, may also be included

3. A statement or analysis of changes in retained earnings for the quarter and the quarter ending a year earlier; in addition, a statement or analysis of changes in retained earnings to date, or the 12 months ending with the quarter, together with corresponding statements a year earlier, may also be included.

There is, of course, information other than financial statements included in reports to holders of debt instruments issued by water utilities. In each particular case, the trust indenture or other agreement between the water utility and the security holder must be considered in determining what information, as a minimum, must be included in creditor reports. Such information may include detailed financial and statistical information concerning utility plant and other property, operating

Figure 7-5
Name of Governmental Unit
WATER AND SEWER FUND
COMPARATIVE STATEMENT OF REVENUE AND EXPENSE
For the Months of September, 19×1 and 19×2 and
Nine Months Ending September 30, 19×1 and 19×2

| | | | Nine Months Ending | |
	September 19×2	September 19×1	Sept. 30, 19×2	Sept. 30, 19×1
Operating Revenues:				
Metered Water Sales	$60,250	$59,700	$448,330	$437,700
Bulk Water Sales	450	475	4,120	4,240
Sewer Service Charges	10,240	9,950	92,450	90,480
Sales of Stores	650	580	5,680	5,420
Customers' Forfeited Discount	450	420	4,020	3,900
Total Operating Revenues	72,040	71,125	554,600	541,740
Less: Operating Revenue Deductions Before Depreciation:				
Operating Expenses	39,600	37,960	300,250	296,400
Cost of Stores Sold	580	600	6,000	5,850
Taxes	6,500	6,000	13,900	13,000
Total Operating Revenue Deductions Before Depreciation	46,680	44,560	320,150	315,250
Net Operating Income Before Depreciation	25,360	26,565	234,450	226,490
Less: Depreciation	12,000	11,000	108,100	107,000
Net Operating Income	13,360	15,565	126,350	119,490
Add: Non-operating Income:				
Rent—Non-operating Property	—	—	5,000	5,000
Interest Earnings	300	300	2,700	2,600
Total Net Income	13,660	15,865	134,050	127,090
Less: Non-operating Expenses:				
Interest Expense—Revenue Bonds	5,384	5,512	48,457	49,612
Interest Expense—General Obligation Bonds	2,333	2,500	21,000	22,500
Fiscal Agents' Fees	—	—	189	200
Total Non-operating Expenses	7,717	8,012	69,646	72,312
Net Income	$ 5,943	$ 7,853	$ 64,404	$ 54,778

Source: National Committee on Governmental Accounting, Governmental Accounting, Auditing, and Financial Reporting (Chicago: Municipal Finance Officers Association, 1968), p. 66.

Figure 7-6
Name of Governmental Unit
WATER AND SEWER FUND
ANALYSIS OF CHANGES IN RETAINED EARNINGS
For the Fiscal Year Ended December 31, 19 × 2

Balance of Retained Earnings, January 1, 19 × 2		$1,991,569
Add:		
Net Income for the Fiscal Year 19 × 2		78,812
Total Balance and Additions		2,070,381
Deduct:		
Increase in Reserve for Revenue Bond Debt Service	$ 2,000	
Increase in Reserve for Revenue Bond Debt Retirement	26,832	
Increase in Reserve for Revenue Bond Contingency	3,348	
Total Deductions		32,180
Balance of Retained Earnings, December 31, 19 × 2		$2,038,201

Source: National Committee on Governmental Accounting, Governmental Accounting, Auditing, and Financial Reporting (Chicago: Municipal Finance Officers Association, 1968), p. 64.

revenues and expenses, and other aspects of the water utility's activities. In addition, information relating to the fulfillment of protective covenants may also be reported.

As in the case of protective covenants contained in loan agreements, protective covenants included in a trust indenture are quite detailed and complex, and impose restrictions on the financial activities of the water utility as well as providing increased security to the creditors. Protective covenants contained in a trust indenture or other agreements between the water utility and the security holders may include provisions which: (1) limit the issuance of additional debt instruments; (2) limit the payment of dividends (in the case of investor-owned water utilities) or payments to the general fund (in the case of municipally-owned water utilities); (3) limit the sale of mortgaged plant assets and stipulate that the money received from the sale of such property be substituted as security; (4) require that specified amounts be expended annually for the maintenance, replacement, and improvement of mortgaged property (this requirement frequently may be met, in part, by certifying that plant additions shall not serve as the basis for issuing additional bonds); and (5) require the segregation of assets for the purpose of retiring bonds. It is important that water utility management understand the provisions contained in trust indentures or other agreements between the water utility and security holders to insure that the restrictions and obligations imposed on the utility are respected and to enable management to certify in reports to bondholders or their representatives that the provisions of indentures or other agreements are being fulfilled.

Reporting to Stockholders

A stockholder, or a prospective stockholder, of an investor-owned water utility, may be assumed to lack complete knowledge of a water utility's activities if he is not involved in the day-to-day operations of the enterprise. Therefore, to a considerable extent, the stockholder depends upon reports rendered by the water utility as his principal source of information. In examining the reports of an investor-owned water utility, a stockholder is particularly interested in the utility's earnings and dividend record, financial position, and growth (in revenues, profits, and assets) during recent years. Information concerning these aspects and other information of interest permits the stockholder to estimate future financial success of the water util-

ity and the risk and return associated with ownership of its stock.

The Prospectus. The major report to prospective stockholders rendered by water utilities is the prospectus relating to the sale of capital stock. In cases where the proposed issue of stock falls within its jurisdiction, the SEC regulates the form and content of the prospectus prepared by the investor-owned water utility. Although some of the information contained in a prospectus relating to the sale of water utility bonds differs from that included in a prospectus relating to the sale of capital stock, much of the information is the same, particularly with respect to financial statements and other financial and statistical data of a historical nature, which reflect the operations and financial condition of the water utility. The financial statements included in the annual report to a state public service commission (see Figs. 5-3 and 5-4), exemplify the sort of financial statements found in a prospectus relating to the sale of capital stock. In addition, financial and statistical data similar to that shown in Fig. 7-13 may be included.

Annual Reports. The annual report is the principal source of information to stockholders. The annual report is primarily an account of management's stewardship. Prospective security holders, customers, employees, and the general public also are interested in the stewardship of managers of municipally-owned utilities as well as investor-owned utilities. Thus, the discussion in this section relates to published annual reports for both investor-owned and municipally-owned water utilities.

The annual report explains the results of operations and the financial position of the water utility. In addition, a portion of the report is frequently devoted to plans and prospects for the utility. The bases of the annual report are the financial statements and their interpretation; the basic problem is to present the financial statements and their interpretation in a manner that the reader can understand.

The structure and content of annual reports to shareholders vary among water utilities, but typically they include:

1. A presentation of the results of the year, in brief. This summarization of financial results may be compared with that of the previous year and is presented in non-technical accounting terms understandable to all users of the annual report (see Fig. 7-7).

2. A letter to stockholders by the president or board chairman, or both. The letter generally includes a brief statement concerning the year's

Figure 7-7
Indianapolis Water Company
COMPARATIVE HIGHLIGHTS

	1967	1966	Increase or (Decrease)
We received from our customers in Revenues	$14,972,802	$14,745,715	1.5%
We paid out for all Operating Expenses and Taxes, and set aside for Depreciation	10,364,184	10,186,931	1.7%
Leaving a balance as Net Income from Operations	4,608,618	4,558,784	1.1%
We had Other Income after Expenses	238,806	54,867	335.2%
Operating and Other Income was	4,847,424	4,613,651	5.1%
We paid out for Interest and related charges	1,410,545	1,275,463	10.6%
That left Net Profit for our Shareholders	3,436,879	3,338,188	3.0%
Then came Dividends paid to our Preferred Shareholders	203,249	203,249	—
Leaving a balance applicable to Common Stock	3,233,630	3,134,939	3.1%
Dividends paid to our Common Shareholders	2,139,074	2,032,120	5.3%
We then put back into the business	1,094,556	1,102,819	(.7%)
Number of Common Shares outstanding end of year	2,139,074	2,139,074	—
Common dividends paid per share	1.00	.95	5.3%
Earnings per Common Share	1.51	1.47	2.7%
Taxes per Common Share	2.40	2.38	.8%
Net Utility Plant at Cost at end of year	73,954,687	68,731,712	7.6%
Number of customers served at end of year	155,394	153,988	.9%
Miles of mains at end of year	1,614.43	1,553.17	3.9%
Number of fire hydrants at end of year	13,628	13,172	3.5%
Water pumpage (million gallons)	31,292.42	31,181.07	.4%
Population in Service Area	657,000	647,000	1.5%

Source: Indianapolis Water Company Annual Report—1967.

activities and the plans and prospects of the utility.

3. A detailed narrative review of the activities of the water utility. This review may include brief discussions concerning revenues, operating expenses, pumpage and production, new construction, new franchise areas, subsidiary operations, water rates and service, stockholder relations, employee relations, customer and public relations, marketing programs, new financing, and plans for the following year and beyond. The discussions may be supplemented by graphs, charts, maps, and pictorial representations where applicable. Fig. 7-8 presents six examples of graphs or charts which have been used by various water utilities to supplement the narrative reviews included in annual reports to stockholders.

4. Financial statements. Financial statements, in comparative form, supplemented by footnotes or supporting schedules, and accompanied by the opinion of an independent certified public accountant, provide the basic data concerning the results of operations and financial position of the water utility. The financial statements include a balance sheet (see Fig. 7-9), an income statement (see Fig. 7-10), and a statement of changes in retained earnings (see Fig. 7-10). The income statement and statement of retained earnings may be presented separately or combined in a statement of income and retained earnings. A statement of sources and uses of funds (Fig. 7-11) and a statement of cash flow (Fig. 7-12) may also be included.

5. Summary of comparative operating statistics. This summarization of pertinent financial and operating statistics typically covers a period of at least ten years (see Fig. 7-13).

A primary requirement is that the annual report be made useful and informative to the reader. Report preparation is not simple; care must be exercised when preparing financial statements and other information for inclusion in the annual report to insure that the report is understandable to the average reader. Financial statements are often supported by footnotes that present information not customarily included in the body of the statement. In addition, charts and graphs are often presented in the report to explain significant relationships or to emphasize trends. Also, the use of lucid and descriptive wording in financial statements and other portions of the annual report, in place of specialized accounting terminology and

(Text continues on page 64)

Figure 7-8
ILLUSTRATIVE CHARTS AND TABLES

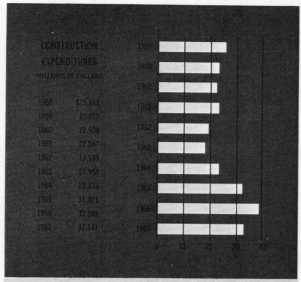

	1967	1966
New services, meters, and fire hydrants	$ 5,627,700	$ 5,987,700
Transmission and distribution facilities	16,621,000	23,338,600
Sources of supply	1,796,200	1,007,900
Treatment and pumping facilities	6,139,200	7,116,800
General structures and equipment	1,957,000	2,134,200
	$32,141,100	$39,585,200

	1967	1966
New services, meters, and fire hydrants	$ 5,627,700	$ 5,987,700
Transmission and distribution facilities	16,621,000	23,338,600
Sources of supply	1,796,200	1,007,900
Treatment and pumping facilities	6,139,200	7,116,800
General structures and equipment	1,957,000	2,134,200
	$32,141,100	$39,585,200

Source: 1967 Annual Report, American Water Works Company, Inc.

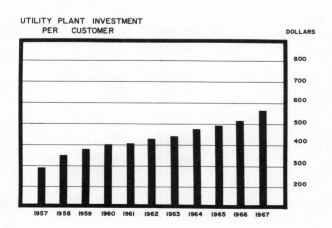

HOW 1967 REVENUE DOLLAR WAS USED

Retained in Business	$ .07
Dividends—Pref. Stock	.01
Dividends—Common Stock	.14
Interest Charges	.09
Depreciation	.07
Maintenance	.04
Operation	.24
Taxes	.34
TOTAL	$1.00

Source: 1967 Annual Report, Indianapolis Water Company.

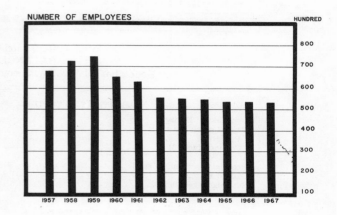

A CLASSIFICATION OF ACCOUNTS AND THEIR CONTRIBUTIONS TO REVENUE

Type of Service	Number of Active Accounts	% of Active Accounts	Water Sold (thous. gals.)	% of Gals. Consumed	Metered Revenue	% of Revenue
Domestic	190,357	96.2	15,181,010	70.8	$12,994,573	80.1
Commercial	5,879	3.0	3,174,563	14.8	1,785,910	11.0
Industrial	692	0.3	2,714,594	12.7	1,075,892	6.6
Public	564	0.3	351,701	1.6	249,370	1.5
Metered Fire	457	0.2	11,865	0.1	119,758	.8
Metered Building	7	—	10,411	—	6,646	—
	197,956	100.0	21,444,144	100.0	$16,232,149	100.0

Source: 1967 Annual Report, Philadelphia Suburban Water Company.

Figure 7-9
Philadelphia Suburban Water Company
BALANCE SHEET
December 31, 1967 with comparative figures for 1966

ASSETS	1967	1966
Property, Plant and Equipment (including $1,763,293 construction work in progress; 1966—$1,174,933), at original cost (note 1)	$117,470,646	$112,219,038
Less accumulated depreciation (note 1)	7,599,409	7,141,152
Net property, plant and equipment	109,871,237	105,077,886
Investments:		
Real estate held for investment, at cost less accumulated depreciation, $11,559 (1966—$8,919)	102,140	81,861
Other, at cost	51,750	62,750
Total investments	153,890	144,611
Current Assets:		
Cash:		
Demand deposits and on hand	566,635	1,068,410
Special deposits, bond interest and other	673,644	667,694
Marketable securities, at cost which approximates market	—	300,000
Customers' accounts receivable, less allowance for doubtful accounts, $57,531 (1966—$59,272)	1,086,166	1,054,502
Unbilled water revenues, estimated	1,777,011	1,560,998
Materials and supplies, at average cost	551,367	524,763
Prepayments and other current assets	64,401	73,878
Total current assets	4,719,224	5,250,245
Deferred Charges:		
Unamortized debt expense	244,365	235,466
Preliminary survey and investigation charges	138,110	127,470
Other deferred charges (note 1)	263,393	231,141
Total deferred charges	645,868	594,077
	$115,390,219	$111,066,819

See accompanying notes to financial statements.

Source: 1967 Annual Report, Philadelphia Suburban Water Company.

Philadelphia Suburban Water Company
BALANCE SHEET
December 31, 1967 with comparative figures for 1966

LIABILITIES AND CAPITAL	1967	1966
Stockholders' Equity:		
Capital stock (note 2):		
Preferred	$ 7,750,000	$ 7,750,000
Common (note 3)	9,701,790	9,419,216
	17,451,790	17,169,216
Premium on common stock	2,253,914	2,253,914
Capital surplus	14,332,343	12,896,952
Retained earnings	6,394,692	6,981,869
	22,980,949	22,132,735
	40,432,739	39,301,951
Less 16,081 shares of common stock in treasury, at cost (1966—14,641 shares)	356,957	332,063
Total stockholders' equity	40,075,782	38,969,888
Long-Term Debt (note 4)	59,375,000	58,375,000
Current Liabilities:		
Note payable to bank	2,500,000	—
Accounts payable	821,417	766,443
Accrued interest	909,398	899,730
Federal and State income taxes	892,954	1,590,237
Other accrued taxes	193,256	121,264
Customers' deposits	189,602	205,829
Other current and accrued liabilities	189,604	139,688
Total current liabilities	5,696,231	3,723,191
Deferred Credits:		
Unamortized premium on funded debt	21,223	23,049
Investment credit (note 1)	470,969	398,294
Customers' advances for construction	7,273,375	7,450,758
Total deferred credits	7,765,567	7,872,101
Contributions in Aid of Construction	2,477,639	2,126,639
	$115,390,219	$111,066,819

See accompanying notes to financial statements.

Source: 1967 Annual Report, Philadelphia Suburban Water Company.

Figure 7-9 Continued
Philadelphia Suburban Water Company
NOTES TO FINANCIAL STATEMENTS
December 31, 1967

(1) PROVISION FOR DEPRECIATION, INCOME TAXES AND OTHER MATTERS:

The 4% compound interest method is used to compute depreciation on utility plant and the straight-line method is used with respect to transportation and mechanical equipment and non-utility property. Depreciation of utility plant charged to income in 1967, $711,669, and in 1966, $682,937, are less than the amounts deducted or to be deducted in the comany's income tax returns by approximately $1,224,000 in 1967 and $1,181,000 in 1966.

Such excess of tax depreciation over book depreciation had the effect of reducing the provision for Federal and State income taxes for 1967 and 1966 by approximately $629,000 and $602,000, respectively. These current tax reductions have been reflected in income in accordance with policy followed by the Pennsylvania Public Utility Commission.

Federal income taxes provided for 1967 have been reduced by $100,534 under the investment credit provisions of the Revenue Act of 1962 and an amount equal to such reduction (less amortization over a 20-year period of current and prior years deferrals) has been charged as provision for investment credit as directed by the Pennsylvania Public Utility Commission. The unamortized amount so provided has been reflected in the accompanying balance sheet as a deferred credit.

At the direction of the Pennsylvania Public Utility Commission certain costs previously classified as property, plant and equipment have been reclassified as other deferred charges; comparative figures for 1966 have been restated to reflect this change.

(2) CAPITAL STOCK:

Details of the authorized and outstanding capital stock as of December 31, 1967 are as follows:

Preferred stock of $100 par value.
Authorized—125,000 shares

Outstanding:	Shares	Amount
3.65% cumulative	27,500	$2,750,000
3.95% cumulative	10,000	1,000,000
4.95% cumulative	20,000	2,000,000
5.00% cumulative	20,000	2,000,000
	77,500	$7,750,000

Common stock of $3.75 per value.
Authorized 5,000,000 shares; issued 2,587,144 shares, of which 16,081 shares are in treasury (1966— 2,511,791 shares, of which 14,641 shares were in treasury) $9,701,790

(3) STOCK OPTIONS:

At December 31, 1967 there remained outstanding restricted stock options granted to officers and key employees to purchase 9,769 shares of common stock at prices ranging from $19.18 to $21.55 a share, such prices being not less than 95% of the fair market value at the dates of granting. In addition there were outstanding qualified stock options granted to officers and key employees to purchase 15,897 shares of common stock at prices ranging from $23.07 to $25.24 a share, such prices being the fair market value at date of grant. Options under both plans are fully exercisable one year from date of grant and no option period exceeds ten years (five years with respect to the qualified plan). During 1967, no options were granted, exercised or cancelled.

(4) LONG-TERM DEBT:

The following issues of First Mortgage Bonds (secured by utility plant) were outstanding at December 31, 1967:

Issue	Amount
3-1/4% due January 1, 1971	$16,375,000
3% due July 1, 1978............	2,000,000
3-3/8% due July 1, 1982.........	4,000,000
3.90% due July 1, 1983..........	5,000,000
3-1/2% due January 1, 1986	6,000,000
4-1/2% due January 1, 1987	4,000,000
4-1/8% due May 1, 1988	4,000,000
5% due September 1, 1989	4,000,000
4-5/8% due May 1, 1991.........	3,000,000
4.70% due April 1, 1992	3,000,000
4.55% due March 1, 1994	4,000,000
5-1/2% due November 1, 1996	4,000,000
	$59,375,000

In December, 1967 negotiations were finalized for the issuance in 1968 of $4,500,000 principal amount of 6-7/8% First Mortgage Bonds due in 1993.

Provisions of the trust indenture and supplements thereto relating to the First Mortgage Bonds require, among other things, annual sinking fund payments amounting to 1/2 of 1% of the maximum aggregate principal amount of bonds outstanding. The sinking fund requirement may be satisfied by certification to the Trustee of net available permanent additions to utility plant. All prior sinking fund requirements have been satisfied by the certification of utility plant and the requirement for 1968 will be satisfied in this manner.

(5) EMPLOYEE RETIREMENT PLAN:

The company has a retirement plan covering substantially all of its employees. The total retirement expense for the year was $102,000, applicable to current cost. The company's usual policy is to fund retirement cost accrued; however, $27,000 of the current year's accrual had not been funded at December 31, 1967. Vesting under the plan commences at age 56 to the extent of 20% and increases at that rate until full vesting occurs after five years. The assets of the plan at the date of the last valuation, December 31, 1966, not only exceeded the vested benefits under the plan but exceeded the actuarial value of all benefits accrued thereunder.

(6) CONSTRUCTION COMMITMENTS:

At December 31, 1967, the company had construction commitments for property, plant and equipment of approximately $3,350,000. The estimated cost of the company's tentative construction program for 1968 is $5,650,000.

Source: 1967 Annual Report, Philadelphia Suburban Water Company.

Figure 7-10
Indianapolis Water Company
STATEMENT OF INCOME
Year ended December 31, 1967 with comparative figures for 1966

	1967	1966
Operating revenues..	$14,972,802	$14,745,715
Operating expenses and taxes:		
Operations and administration	3,625,798	3,558,190
Maintenance	621,066	601,615
Depreciation and amortization, excluding $65,402 and $55,642 charged to other accounts	989,614	942,474
Taxes (other than Federal income taxes)	2,497,706	2,209,652
Federal income taxes (note 4)...........................	2,630,000	2,875,000
Total operating expenses and taxes	10,364,184	10,186,931
Operating income	4,608,618	4,558,784
Other income (notes 1 and 6)	238,806	54,867
	4,847,424	4,613,651
Interest and other deductions:		
Interest on long-term debt.............................	1,286,881	1,194,937
Other interest	129,756	65,414
Interest allocated to construction (credit)	(66,677)	(39,512)
Amortization of debt discount, premium and expense—net ...	12,970	23,409
Other charges	47,615	31,215
Total interest and other deductions	1,410,545	1,275,463
Net income (per share of common stock: 1967—$1.51; 1966—$1.47)	$ 3,436,879	$ 3,338,188

See accompanying notes to financial statements.

Source: 1967 Annual Report, Indianapolis Water Company.

Indianapolis Water Company
STATEMENT OF RETAINED EARNINGS
Year ended December 31, 1967 with comparative figures for 1966

	1967	1966
Balance at beginning of year...........................	$4,212,291	$3,101,224
Less excess of cost over equity in The Shorewood Corporation at January 1, 1967 (note 1)...	104,560	—
	4,107,731	3,101,224
Net income for the year...............................	3,436,879	3,338,188
Net gain on sales of land, less Federal income tax (note 6)	—	8,248
	7,544,610	6,447,660
Less cash dividends declared (note 2):		
On preferred stock..................................	203,249	203,249
On common stock	2,139,074	2,032,120
	2,342,323	2,235,369
Balance at end of year................................	$5,202,287	$4,212,291

See accompanying notes to financial statements.

Source: 1967 Annual Report, Indianapolis Water Company.

Indianapolis Water Company
NOTES TO FINANCIAL STATEMENTS
December 31, 1967

(1) Investment in The Shorewood Corporation
On September 19, 1960, the Company's Board of Directors authorized the formation of The Shorewood Corporation as a wholly-owned subsidiary, for the purpose of acquiring, operating, developing and selling certain real estate around Geist and Morse Reservoirs which was not considered necessary for the Company's utility operations.

Figure 7-10 Continued

Prior to 1967 this investment was carried at cost ($2,288,760). As of January 1, 1967, in keeping with Opinion Number 9 of the Accounting Principles Board of the American Institute of Certified Public Accountants, the basis for carrying the investment was changed to the equity method by reducing the investment by the accumulated loss of The Shorewood Corporation from its inception to December 31, 1966 ($104,560) with a concurrent charge to retained earnings. Shorewood's 1967 net income ($60,286) has been added to the investment account and included in "other income" in the statement of income. Figures for 1966 have not been restated to give retroactive treatment to this change, as the effect would not be significant.

(2) Capital stock

Details of the authorized and outstanding capital stock as of December 31, 1967, are as follows (unchanged during the year):

	Shares outstanding	Amount
Cumulative preferred stock of $100 par value per share. Authorized 94,194 shares:		
Series A—5%	10,549	$ 1,054,900
Series B—4-1/4%	10,000	1,000,000
Series C—4%	4,500	450,000
Series D—4-1/2%	20,000	2,000,000
	45,049	4,504,900
Common stock of $7.50 par value per share. Authorized 2,500,000 shares	2,139,074	$16,043,055

Cash dividends declared comprised:	1967	1966
Preferred stock:		
Series A—$5.00 per share	$ 52,745	$ 52,745
Series B—$4.25 per share	42,504	42,504
Series C—$4.00 per share	18,000	18,000
Series D—$4.50 per share	90,000	90,000
	203,249	203,249
Common stock—$1.00 per share in 1967, and $.95 per share in 1966	2,139,074	2,032,120
	$ 2,342,323	$ 2,235,369

The cumulative preferred stock, which has a liquidation value of $100 per share, is redeemable at the option of the Company at $100 per share for Series B and Series C and $105 per share for Series A and Series D, an aggregate redemption value of $4,657,645.

(3) Long-term debt

The following issues of First Mortgage Bonds (secured by Company property) were outstanding at December 31, 1967, and December 31, 1966:

	1967	1966
First Mortgage Bonds, 3% Series due 1975	$ 2,000,000	$ 2,000,000
First Mortgage Bonds, 2-3/4% Series due 1976	16,725,000	16,725,000
First Mortgage Bonds, 3-1/4% Series due 1985	3,000,000	3,000,000
First Mortgage Bonds, 4-7/8% Series due 1989	6,000,000	6,000,000
First Mortgage Bonds, 4-3/4% Series due 1992	6,000,000	6,000,000
First Mortgage Bonds, 5-7/8% Series due 1997	6,800,000	—
	$40,525,000	$33,725,000

During 1967, the Company arranged to place with institutional purchasers, without public offer, $8,000,000 principal amount of First Mortgage Bonds, 5-7/8% Series due 1997, at face amount plus accrued interest. On August 17, 1967 and October 31, 1967, $2,100,000 and $4,700,000 principal amounts, respectively, were issued; and on January 15, 1968, the remaining $1,200,000 principal amount was issued. Proceeds of these bond issues were used to discharge short-term note obligations and to reinstate working capital reductions arising from expenditures for utility plant.

Provisions of trust indentures relating to the First Mortgage Bonds require annual sinking or improvement fund payments amounting to 1/2 of 1% of the maximum aggregate amount outstanding. As permitted, this requirement has been met by certification to the Trustee of permanent additions to utility plant.

(4) Federal income taxes

Federal income tax liabilities of the Company for all years prior to 1965 have been settled with the United States Treasury Department. Settlement of the liability for the years 1962 through 1964 resulted in refunds of approximately $35,000, which have been reflected as a reduction of the provision for 1967 taxes.

Source: 1967 Annual Report, Indianapolis Water Company.

(Figure 7-10 continues on next page)

Figure 7-10 Continued

Under provisions of the Revenue Act of 1962, and in accordance with a directive of the Public Service Commission of Indiana, the Company records its Investment Credit as a reduction of the liability for current Federal income taxes and as an increase in Unamortized Investment Tax Credit. The credit (which amounted to $118,900 for 1967 and $118,500 for 1966) aggregated $575,514 at December 31, 1967, after deducting amortization which is being recorded ratably over the depreciable lives of the applicable assets.

Depreciation deductions since 1954 for eligible plant and equipment have been computed for Federal income tax purposes by an accelerated method and, beginning in 1962, on the basis of "guideline lives" permitted by the Internal Revenue Service. These deductions exceed those recorded on the books, which are computed on the straight-line method at rates prescribed by the Public Service Commission of Indiana. The Company recognizes the estimated future tax effect of these accelerated depreciation deductions by increasing the provision for Federal income taxes, with corresponding additions to the reserve for deferred Federal income taxes. Net additions to the reserve amounted to $280,491 in 1967, and $249,643 in 1966. Appropriate portions of this reserve will be restored to income in years when depreciation deductions for tax purposes will be less than amounts computed at the normal rates.

(5) Pension costs
The Company has a noncontributory pension plan covering substantially all of its employees. The total pension plan expense for the year was $225,000 ($204,000 in 1966), which includes amortization of prior service cost over a period of ten years. The Company's policy is to fund pension cost accrued. The market value of the pension fund assets was substantially equivalent to the actuarially computed value of vested benefits at December 31, 1967.

The pension plan provides that, in the event it is terminated, the Company is obligated to contribute the amount which would be required to increase the pension fund to the full value of all accrued benefits. This obligation is recognized in the Company's accounts by reflecting the amount which would be required, in event of termination, as both a deferred charge and a liability ($431,285 at December 31, 1967, and $477,857 at December 31, 1966).

(6) Accounting for sales of land
Prior to 1967 net gains or losses on sales of land were reflected by direct credits or charges to retained earnings. Such transactions resulted in net gains of $73,421 in 1967, and $8,248 (after income taxes) in 1966. Beginning in 1967, in keeping with Opinion Number 9 of the Accounting Principles Board of the American Institute of Certified Public Accountants, such gains or losses are reflected as "other income" or "other charges" in the statement of income. Figures for 1966 have not been restated to give retroactive treatment to this change, as the effect would not be significant.

Source: 1967 Annual Report, Indianpolis Water Company.

other technical language, serves to make the report more understandable to the reader who does not have a technical background.

Other Reports to Stockholders. In addition to the annual report, interim financial reports issued semi-annually or quarterly may be useful to stockholders. Interim reports keep stockholders informed concerning the operations of the water utility. Interim reports need not be as elaborate as the annual report and may include only the basic financial statements and other information of material importance or immediate interest. Interim financial reports are often distributed with quarterly or semi-annual dividend checks of investor-owned utilities; information may also be communicated to stockholders through the notice of the annual meeting of stockholders, minutes of the annual meeting, and special letters.

Reporting to Customers, the General Public, and Employees

The extent of reporting to customers, the general public, and employees is largely at the dis-

cretion of the water utility. Distribution of detailed and comprehensive reports to customers, the general public, and employees is not deemed necessary or advisable by some water utilities. Others believe that the communication of selected information is useful for maintaining or promoting the goodwill of customers and the general public, and for maintaining or increasing the loyalty and efficiency of employees.

Investor-owned and municipally-owned water utilities may wish to design a single published annual report to stockholders (in the case of investor-owned water utilities), customers, the general public, and employees. A single comprehensive report to all interested groups may be adequate in situations where stockholders, customers, the general public, and employees form a homogeneous group whose information needs and interests are similar. More likely, however, the needs and interests are widely divergent; therefore, specialized reports directed to particular groups may be the most effective. As an alternative, the published annual report may be issued to all interested groups, supplemented by specialized

Figure 7-11
American Water Works Company, Inc. and Subsidiary Companies
CONSOLIDATED STATEMENT OF SOURCES AND USES OF FUNDS

	Year ended December 31	
	1967	1966
SOURCES OF FUNDS		
Funds provided from operations:		
Income before gain on dispositions of properties	$10,200,865	$ 11,535,233
Depreciation and amortization	7,688,604	7,017,757
Deferred federal income taxes and investment credits	718,931	836,102
Other	1,044,739	935,092
	19,653,139	20,324,184
Net proceeds from dispositions of properties	43,594,125	
Sales of securities		
Preferred stocks	850,000	4,550,000
Long-term debt	9,435,000	70,575,000
Short-term bank debt	11,509,300	1,994,800
Customer advances and contributions in aid of construction	2,219,422	2,179,299
Other, net	645,363	715,736
	87,906,349	100,339,019
USES OF FUNDS		
Additions to utility plant	32,141,100	39,585,200
Participation in loans by banks to subsidiaries	19,000,000	
Purchase of water utilities	2,508,327	42,796,164
Redemptions of securities		
Preferred stocks	882,425	3,454,325
Long-term debt	20,457,000	10,307,000
Dividends paid	6,074,831	6,086,316
	81,063,683	102,229,005
INCREASE (DECREASE) IN WORKING CAPITAL	$ 6,842,666	$ (1,889,986)

Source: 1967 Annual Report, American Water Works Company, Inc.

reports intended to meet the particular needs of customers, the general public, and employees.

Reports to Customers and the General Public. To create good relations with customers and the general public, many water utilities publish pamphlets or booklets to acquaint customers and the general public with facts concerning the water utility's operations. These publications often stress the history of the utility, the relationship of the water utility to the community, research activities, the quality and cost of water service, and future plans and outlook for the water utility.

Information for customers (such as operating income as a percentage of operating revenue, comparison of current income with that of other periods, the cost of water service, reasons for rate increases, and facts relating to the quality of water) may be included in reports accompanying customer water bills. Additionally, some utilities supply each customer with a rate schedule and a set of rules and regulations governing the relationship between the customer and the water utility.

The general public, the source of present and potential customers, is interested in much of the same information as are customers. In addition to the information supplied customers, reports to the general public may include other financial data, such as taxes and contributions paid by the water utility to finance publicly supported activities (for example, municipal government operations). In the case of municipally-owned water utilities, the general public may require reports concerning the efficiency of the utility's operations (in terms of meeting budgeted costs), the degree to which the utility is self-supporting, and the extent, if any, to which the taxpayer is supporting the operations and capital construction activities of the water utility. Media for distributing information to the general public include direct mail and notices or advertisements in the financial or other sections of the public press.

Reports to customers and the general public must be presented in an understandable manner. Generally, detailed financial information should be omitted and pertinent information expressed in terms of basic relationships and trends, using graphs and charts as aids. Such reports should utilize wording which is familiar and understandable to customers and the general public.

Figure 7-12
STATEMENT OF CASH FLOW
For The Year Ended December 31, 1965

Cash at January 1, 1965		$ 403,116
Cash provided from:		
Operating revenues	$10,778,985	
Increase in notes payable . .	4,005,000	
Increase in accounts payable and accrued expenses	578,660	
Federal income tax refund and related interest	394,680	
Investment credit—net	182,113	
Decrease in mortgages receivable	170,710	
Increase in main extension advances	137,440	
Others—net.	217,540	16,465,128
Total		16,868,244
Cash used for:		
Additions to property:		
Mains	4,538,680	
Other	1,695,161	
	6,233,841	
Operating expenses:		
Wages	1,656,767	
Supplies and services	2,517,537	
Taxes	2,872,709	
Interest	1,125,915	
Dividends	914,793	
Increase in accounts receivable	248,812	15,570,374
Cash at December 31, 1965 . .		$ 1,297,870

Source: 1965 Annual Report, Elizabethtown Water Company, Elizabeth, N.J.

Reports to Employees. Employee earnings reports, such as federal wage and tax statements (Form W-2), must be furnished to employees in accord with applicable regulations. With the exception of earnings statements, the nature of reports submitted to employees is determined largely by water utility management. As in the case of reports to customers and the general public, reports to employees should present the message in a clear and understandable manner. Financial statements generally should be expressed in simple, non-technical language. For example, a summary of information relating to the utility's activities might be expressed in a manner similar to that shown in Figs. 7-7 and 7-8.

In addition to general information (such as that shown in Fig. 7-7), employee reports often emphasize information pertaining to wages, pension plans, fringe benefits, and any other data of particular concern to employees; for example, labor costs (wages, pension plan costs, and other fringe benefits) may be expressed as a percentage of revenues or operating expenses. Labor costs and other employee benefits also may be compared with similar elements in other water utilities or in other industries. Employee reports also may emphasize employee productivity and efficiency. For example, operating costs per unit of processed water and the extent of customer complaints may be compared for a number of years. In addition, information expressed in terms of investment, profit, taxes, and labor cost, per employee, may be included in employee reports.

Where possible, information expressed in terms of pie charts, bar graphs, and other pictorial representations should be used to emphasize various relationships and trends to employees. The financial and statistical data furnished to employees should be supplemented with a narrative report which further explains the data, indicates future plans and outlook for the utility, outlines future job opportunities, and explains any changes in wage, pension, welfare, and other employee benefits and policies. Media for communicating information to employees include annual or other periodic reports, letters, and payroll inserts.

Summary

This chapter discusses the application of the general principles of reporting presented in Chapter 4 to reports to creditors and other groups interested in the operations and financial condition of a water utility. In the context of such reports, the general principles may be restated as:

1. Reports intended for creditors, customers, stockholders, and other external groups should present information designed to show the extent to which water utility management has fulfilled its stewardship function.

2. The form, content, and frequency of reports to creditors and other groups interested in the activities of a water utility are generally dictated by custom.

3. Reports intended for readers without accounting knowledge should employ descriptive rather than technical language insofar as possible.

4. Reports in narrative or graphic form should be used to direct attention to significant amounts and relationships shown in accompanying financial statements, and to present important information in addition to that shown in the statements.

Figure 7-13
Elizabethtown Water Company
(Including Subsidiary Companies)
COMPARATIVE REVIEW OF STATISTICS

	1967	1966	1965	1964	1963	1962
OPERATING REVENUE						
General customers	$ 8,486,418	$ 8,456,305	$ 7,945,924	$ 7,532,469	$ 7,153,214	$ 6,378,968
Other water systems	1,978,961	2,276,604	1,762,122	1,004,277	916,279	703,797
Fire protection service	1,137,292	1,089,452	1,037,784	976,726	950,726	921,078
Other	24,202	32,649	33,155	27,752	43,465	65,706
TOTAL OPERATING REVENUE	11,626,873	11,855,010	10,778,985	9,541,224	9,063,684	8,069,549
OPERATING EXPENSES:						
Purchased water	936,376	710,270	456,222	241,437	199,799	136,787
Payrolls	1,972,504	1,891,145	1,806,962	1,733,807	1,682,425	1,451,839
Other operating expenses	2,147,369	2,222,574	1,911,120	1,528,003	1,522,304	1,249,966
Depreciation	1,191,837	1,102,423	1,007,404	859,836	764,267	694,601
Taxes	2,500,912	2,891,677	2,874,476	2,782,205	2,602,196	2,444,171
TOTAL OPERATING EXPENSES	8,748,998	8,818,089	8,056,184	7,145,288	6,770,991	5,977,364
UTILITY OPERATING INCOME	2,877,875	3,036,921	2,722,801	2,395,936	2,292,693	2,092,185
INTEREST CHARGES	1,766,947	1,458,912	1,125,915	979,346	869,031	813,513
INCOME BEFORE EXTRAORDINARY ITEM	1,104,549	1,577,491	1,630,371	1,470,939	1,473,986	1,344,626
Profit on sale of land (net of taxes)	122,279	47,060	57,422			
NET INCOME (1)	$ 1,226,828	$ 1,624,551	$ 1,687,793	$ 1,470,939	$ 1,473,986	$ 1,344,626
Dividends	$ 914,793	$ 914,793	$ 914,793	$ 762,328	$ 762,328	$ 762,328
Reinvested in business	$ 312,035	$ 709,758	$ 773,000	$ 708,611	$ 711,658	$ 582,298
RATIO OF OPERATING EXPENSES TO OPERATING REVENUES	75%	74%	75%	75%	75%	74%
PER SHARE OF COMMON STOCK (2)						
Earnings:						
Before extraordinary item	$ 1.45	$ 2.07	$ 2.14	$ 1.93	$ 1.93	$ 1.76
After extraordinary item	$ 1.61	$ 2.13	$ 2.21	$ 1.93	$ 1.93	$ 1.76
Dividends	$ 1.20	$ 1.20	$ 1.20	$ 1.00	$ 1.00	$ 1.00
Book value	$ 27.99	$ 27.58	$ 26.65	$ 25.60	$ 24.69	$ 23.77
NUMBER OF STOCK HOLDERS	2,174	2,187	2,182	2,031	1,843	1,744
CAPITALIZATION (3)						
Common stock and surplus	$21,315,217	$21,027,057	$20,317,299	$19,516,415	$18,818,972	$18,124,030
Funded debt	18,815,000	18,820,000	18,825,000	19,020,000	19,027,500	18,450,000
Term loan		4,500,000	4,500,000	4,500,000		
TOTAL CAPITALIZATION	$40,130,217	$44,347,057	$43,642,299	$43,036,415	$37,846,472	$36,574,030
RATIOS (3)						
Common stock equity	53%	47%	47%	45%	50%	50%
Long-term debt	47%	53%	53%	55%	50%	50%
UTILITY PLANT						
Gross utility plant	$75,313,720	$69,787,883	$64,276,724	$58,238,392	$53,005,831	$48,496,216
Reserves for depreciation	$14,247,226	$13,189,386	$12,453,480	$11,532,463	$10,769,535	$ 9,615,678
Net utility plant	$61,066,494	$56,598,497	$51,823,244	$46,705,929	$42,236,296	$38,880,538
Percent of long-term debt to utility plant	24%	33%	36%	40%	36%	38%
Percent of reserve for depreciation to utility plant	19%	19%	19%	20%	20%	20%
OTHER PERTINENT STATISTICS						
Pumpage (millions of gallons)						
Total for year	38,033	40,515	33,872	28,182	26,608	22,655
Average day	104	111	93	77	73	62
Maximum day	152	152	137	124	111	85
Rainfall (Normal 48.3 inches)	47.1	45.7	32.6	41.3	35.4	45.3
Meters in service	117,426	116,348	114,793	111,265	108,951	103,437
Miles of mains	1,513	1,419	1,358	1,330	1,290	1,181
Fire hydrants served	7,493	7,149	7,260	7,151	6,916	6,291
Total employees	234	238	237	234	235	204

(1) Net income has been increased $47,060 ($.06 per share) in 1966, $59,337 ($.078 per share) in 1965, $11,168 ($.015 per share) in 1964 and $29,623 ($.039 per share) in 1963, due to the restatement, in accordance with a recent pronouncement of the American Institute of Certified Public Accountants, of certain previously reported special items.

(2) Computed for each of the years 1962 through 1967 on the basis of the average number of shares outstanding during each period.

(3) Short-term debt not included.

Source: 1967 Annual Report, Elizabethtown Water Company.

Part Three
PLANNING AND
CONTROLLING OPERATIONS

CHAPTER 8. PLANNING AND CONTROLLING THROUGH MANAGEMENT ACCOUNTING

It is the responsibility of management to conduct the affairs of the water utility to reach the enterprise goals as set by the utility's policy making group. To reach these goals, management must determine the needs of customers for quality water service, provide and organize water production and distribution facilities to satisfy customers' desires, and plan and control the activities of the water utility.

Planning and controlling are the responsibilities of every manager at every level within the water utility organization. The character and scope of planning and control vary with the responsibility and authority of a manager. Thus it is necessary that the organization structure of the utility be clearly defined.

Effective planning and control by water utility management requires the use of relevant information for making decisions. One of the chief aids to management in making its planning and control efforts productive is accounting. The role of accounting as an aid to management is the subject of this chapter.

Management Accounting—General

Traditional water utility accounting is concerned with measuring the net income of the utility for each time period of its life and determining the asset, liability, and equity balances at the end of a given time period. The measurement of what has happened to the stream of revenue and related expense, and the asset, liability, and equity balances is complex. The traditional accountant feels that he has done his job when he has obtained the data, arranged it according to best practice, and reported it. The traditional accountant is satisfied to leave it up to others to use the accounting reports as they see fit.

On the other hand, management accounting for water utilities is concerned with providing accounting and statistical information to facilitate the performance of utility management functions, particularly those of planning and controlling.

The Central Idea and Its Corollaries. The central idea of management accounting is that managers should be provided with sufficient timely information so that the water utility may be managed efficiently and effectively. If this central idea is accepted, certain corollary ideas follow:

1. The focus of management accounting is on the future. The past is of importance only as a guide to the future.
2. All important information relevant to a decision should be provided at the time it is needed. Implicit in this statement are the thoughts that:
   a. Information as to legal, political, and social conditions, as well as economic and business conditions, (and expected changes in these conditions) is often more important than internal information. Much of the external information must be derived from judgement and instinct. Therefore, although the expected effects of external forces must often be expressed numerically, the reliability of the numbers is open to question.
   b. Internal information as to employee attitudes and behavior must be considered, as well as accounting and statistical information relating to the production of water, distribution of water, and other activities of the water utility.
   c. No more time or money should be spent in obtaining an item of information than the item is expected to be worth. Thus, it is true that:
      (1) Accuracy is often less important than timeliness; estimates may be adequate for many purposes.
      (2) Integration of all information systems must be accomplished. It is inconsistent with the objective of efficient and effective operation of the water utility to allow accountants, statisticians, economists and operating executives to maintain overlapping systems for deriving information. The

71

system involves foreseeing what data will be needed, by whom, in what form, and when, in order to determine whether data should be collected routinely or only on occasion.

Basic Concepts of Management Accounting

To fulfill the role that accounting can and should play in assisting management planning and control, there are a number of basic concepts of management accounting which should be employed in the design of the water utility accounting system.

Figure 8-1 presents a concise statement of the basic concepts of management accounting. These concepts are discussed in the remainder of this section.

Collecting Cost and Revenue Data by Responsibility Center. It is the responsibility of the owners of a water utility to state the major objectives of the utility and to communicate these objectives to the managers so that they will know what goals they are expected to attain. The owners must also set the major policies under which water utility management will operate the enterprise. If the ownership is far removed from the operation of the water utility, the setting of major

objectives and policies becomes the duty of the representatives of the owners. In the case of a municipally-owned water utility, the representatives of the owners (the general public) are the members of the city council (or water commission, city water board, or water authority board). In the case of an investor-owned water utility, the representatives of the owners (the stockholders) are the members of the board of directors.

The setting of objectives and policies for a water utility does not in itself require any management accounting or information system. Rather, the system must be designed so that the owners, or their representatives, are informed as to the degree to which water utility management is attaining the goals that have been set for the utility, and the extent of water utility management's adherence to major policies.

Within the framework of the major objectives and policies established by the owners, or their representatives, and considering forecasts of social, economic, and political conditions, the general manager of the water utility must establish objectives and policies for each major segment of the utility, since the overall objectives must be attained through the operations of the segments of the water utility.

Figure 8-1
THE BASIC CONCEPTS OF MANAGEMENT ACCOUNTING FOR WATER UTILITIES

Basic Concepts	Example of Techniques Used to Apply the Basic Concepts
1. Historical costs and revenues should be collected routinely for each responsibility center.	Responsibility Accounting.
2. Historical cost and revenue data for each responsibility center must be related to the factors which caused the behavior of past data, so that the manager of each center may prepare realistic future plans.	Budgets or Profit Plans, for most important items of cost and revenue, at least.
3. Standards of performance are established for each activity and communicated to the manager so he knows how he is being judged. Formal cost standards are established if their expected benefit exceeds the cost of establishing them.	Standard or Estimated Costs. Return on Investment, or other measure of output attained for input of money or time.
4. Alternatives to present operations are evaluated before management makes a decision or takes action.	Return on Investment.
5. Actual performance is compared with budgeted or standard performance, and variances are investigated to determine necessary management control action.	Periodic reports flowing from responsibility accounting, and work measurement programs; and special reports.
6. Adequate internal control is established over resources—including physical control, insurance coverage, accounting and statistical controls.	Control accounts and subsidiary ledgers. Perpetual inventories. Locked storerooms. Night watchman.
7. Internal audit and external audit are utilized to make sure management plans and policies are being followed, and that the internal control system and information system are functioning as they are supposed to.	

Responsibility for the operations of each segment of the water utility, and commensurate authority to perform the operations, must be assigned to specific individuals in order for the general manager to be able to control the segmental operations, since control can be achieved only through human actions. Thus, one of the principal management accounting concepts is that costs and revenues must be measured routinely for each responsibility segment of the water utility.

The Use of Historical Cost and Revenue Data for Planning Purposes. Each manager who is responsible for the operations of a major segment of the water utility implicitly is responsible for the preparation of realistic plans, or budgets, to attain the objectives that the general manager has set for the segment. Ordinarily, each major segment must be further divided, and responsibility for these subdivisions, and commensurate authority, must be delegated to specific individuals who are assigned goals and prepare realistic plans to meet the goals.

A second principal management accounting concept, therefore, is: In order to aid water utility managers in preparing realistic plans, the management accounting or management information system must provide information which relates past cost and revenue data to all conditions which caused the past data to behave as it did—conditions external to the water utility and each responsibility segment, as well as conditions within each responsibility segment.

Effective planning by water utility management, however, does not simply involve the forecasting of causative conditions and the subsequent computation of cost and revenue figures on the same basis as in past periods. Effective planning by water utility management involves a determination of whether the relationships which existed in the past should continue to exist in the period for which plans are being prepared. Thus, the first question to be asked by each water utility manager in charge of a responsibility segment is: "Should a particular activity be performed at all?", not "How much will it cost to perform a particular activity next year?"

Standards of Performance. If it is determined that a particular activity needs to be performed in order to help the water utility reach the goals which have been set for it by the owners, or their representatives, it is then time to determine the standards by which the results of the activity are to be judged—standards which are consistent with the objectives and policies of the water utility. Thus, a third principal concept of management ac-

counting for water utilities is that standards should be established for the performance of each activity. It is fundamental that standards be established for quality of output of each activity and communicated to the person responsible for the activity, so that he knows how he is to be judged. Standards as to procedures, quantity of output related to input, and costs, are desirable refinements in all instances in which the expense of establishing such refinements can be justified by the expected benefits.

Evaluation of Alternatives. After standards have been established and translated into requirements for manpower, equipment, and money, the decision must be made by water utility management as to whether a particular activity (extension of mains, for example) should be performed by the water utility itself, or by an outside contractor. If it is to be performed by the water utility, the decision must be made as to the most logical and efficient manner in which to fit the activity into the organization structure of the utility.

The process of planning the future operations of each activity, or responsibility segment, of the water utility may disclose a number of alternatives to present operations. A system needs to be established so that the alternatives are objectively and impartially evaluated before management commits the resources of the water utility. The information for this evaluation logically comes from the management accounting system; therefore, the evaluation of alternatives may be considered as a basic concept of management accounting.

From the foregoing discussion, it is clear that the role of the accountant in the planning function is to foresee what information will be needed by all levels of water utility management in the planning process, and provide it. Usually it is also considered his duty to coordinate the preparation of the plans by sub-managers so that all employ the same assumptions and adhere to the same time schedule.

Control of Operations. Control describes that function of water utility management which has to do with guiding all parts of the water utility organization along planned paths. Therefore, a fifth principal concept is that the management accounting system should provide for the routine comparison of actual data with planned data and the prompt reporting of significant variances to individuals responsible for investigation of variances and for corrective action. Comparison of actual costs and operating statistics with planned costs and performance standards, by responsibility segment, enables water utility management to control costs and performance effectively and to improve future planning.

Control of Resources. If the operations, and changes in the operations, have been planned and controlled as outlined previously, it would appear that management has done its best to preserve and enhance the capability of the water utility to make a profit, to be self-sustaining, to furnish quality water service, and to attain any other goals set for it. Clearly, preservation of the capability of a water utility to achieve the goals set for it by its owners or their representatives is of more importance than merely safeguarding the resources used by the water utility. However, the resources must be safeguarded or there is considerable possibility that they will not remain available to the utility.

In order to safeguard the resources of the water utility, the management information system must provide for internal control in the broadest sense: accounting control, physical control, adequate and appropriate insurance coverage, and statistical controls. This is the sixth basic concept of management accounting for water utilities.

Internal and External Audit. Any management information system for a water utility is incomplete if it does not provide for continuing internal checks to make sure that the proper data is being correctly processed and reported to the proper managers of the water utility. Internal audits must also be made to insure that plans and policies of the owners and the managers of the water utility are being followed and that necessary changes and exceptions are brought to the attention of appropriate managers. Periodic independent, or external, audits are also a requirement of a good management accounting system for a water utility,

to make sure that the system itself is functioning as it is supposed to. Provision for internal and external audit is the seventh basic concept of management accounting.

Summary

A management accounting system for a water utility should provide utility management with sufficient timely information to facilitate planning and control. Plans (budgets) should be prepared for each responsibility segment of the water utility by those persons responsible for the operation of the segment, within the framework of plans and policies which have been set for that segment. The plans for each segment must be an expression of the action to be taken by the segment to reach concrete objectives. Each segmental plan must relate inputs of all resources (personnel, material, equipment, and money) to outputs of services, so that proposed plans for each segment of the water utility can be evaluated and coordinated by the general manager to insure the optimum allocation of resources available to the utility.

Further, effective control requires that actual performance be compared with budgeted or standard performance by responsibility segment, and that deviations from plans be investigated to determine necessary management control action. In addition, effective control over the activities of the water utility requires an adequate system of internal control over resources, and a provision for internal and external audits.

Application of the basic concepts of management accounting for water utilities is discussed in the remainder of Part Three (Planning and Controlling Operations) and Part Four (Planning and Controlling Assets, Liabilities, and Equities).

CHAPTER 9. PLANNING REVENUES

It is the responsibility of water utility management to insure that an adequate level of revenue is maintained and that revenue is collected equitably from all classes of customers using water service. The Water Utility Management Manual states that: "Each water utility, whether publicly or privately owned, should receive gross revenue sufficient to enable it to provide adequate service, to maintain the system, to pay taxes or make payments in lieu thereof when required, to earn a reasonable return, and to have the secure financial status necessary to obtain money at reasonable interest rates for system expansion. This gross revenue is obtained by establishing and charging rates for the water sold and the services furnished by the utility."[1]

Payments by customers for water service provide the principal continuing flow of cash into the utility. The maintenance of an adequate and continuing flow of cash into the utility requires effective planning and controlling of revenues by water utility management. In this chapter, management planning and controlling of revenues are discussed.

Sources of Revenue

The revenues of a water utility are divided into two broad categories: operating revenues and nonoperating revenues. Operating revenues are all revenues derived from the sale of water and from other activities closely allied to the sale of water. The nonoperating revenues category includes those revenues not derived from the utility's normal business of supplying water, such as rents from nonutility property, interest and dividends, and revenue for rendering supervision, management, engineering, and similar services to other organizations. Ordinarily, revenues from merchandising, jobbing and contract work also are classified as nonoperating (as shown in the system of accounts presented in the Appendix). Nonoperating revenues, together with the nonoperating ex-penses incurred in obtaining the revenues, normally are classified in the "Other Income" section of the income statement.

Operating revenues may be subdivided into two categories: Sales of Water, and Other Operating Revenues.

Sales of Water. Revenues derived from the sale of water represent the major source of operating revenue to the water utility. The types of sales of water are:

1. Unmetered Sales to General Customers
2. Metered Sales to General Customers
3. Private Fire Protection Service
4. Public Fire Protection Service
5. Other Sales to Public Authorities
6. Sales to Irrigation Customers
7. Sales for Resale
8. Interdepartmental Sales.

Sales to general customers ordinarily are subclassified as residential sales, commercial sales, and industrial sales. This subclassificiation is based upon the type of customer and the use made of the water supplied to the customer. Residential sales include all sales of water service to individuals for home or domestic uses. Commercial sales include sales to retail and wholesale businesses and sales of water for use by occupants of office buildings. Industrial sales include sales to manufacturing firms for use in manufacturing, as well as for use by their employees while employed.

Sales of water to general customers may be metered or unmetered. In the case of metered sales the charge to the customer is based on a rate schedule applied to the amount of water delivered through each meter. If meters are not used, the charge to the customer is based on a flat rate per period of time per fixture, foot of frontage, or other unit. Although the flat rate basis still is fairly common, meter-based rates are more widely used, and are generally considered to result in more equitable charges to consumers. In addition, when compared with unmetered service,

---

[1] American Water Works Association, Water Utility Management Manual, AWWA M5 (New York: American Water Works Association, 1959), p. 82.

metered service is said to result in more econom- ical use of a water plant by reducing water wast- age, thus tending to require comparatively less need for water system investments as the service area grows.[2]

The Private Fire Protection Service category includes revenues obtained for rendering fire protection service, and for the water delivered in connection therewith, to customers with specific facilities, located on private property, which are billed under distinct fire protection rate schedules. The Public Fire Protection Service category includes revenues obtained from munici- palities or property owners for fire protection service rendered to the general public. In the case of investor-owned water utilities, charges for public fire protection typically are levied against the municipality on the basis of the number of hydrants, miles of mains, or "inch-foot" calcula- tions (where "inch" refers to the diameter of mains and "foot" refers to the length of mains). In the case of municipally-owned water utilities, a charge for public fire protection may be levied against the municipality or directly against prop- erty owners on the basis of assessed valuation. The latter procedure is an equitable way of dis- tributing the cost of public fire protection among these benefiting from such service. The Other Sales to Public Authorities category includes rev- enues from municipalities or other governmental authorities for such purposes as supplying water to public buildings and parks, public swimming pools, and fountains. These other sales to public authorities are made under special contracts or agreements which call for the application of either metered or flat rate schedules.

In some localities sales to irrigation customers may compose a significant portion of the sales of water by a utility. The Sales to Irrigation Cus- tomers category includes revenues for water sup- plied for commercial irrigation purposes which are billed under either special metered or flat rate tariff schedules applicable solely to irrigation customers. The Sales for Resale category includes revenues from water supplied (including standby or breakdown service) to investor-owned water utilities or to public authorities for resale. Water supplied for resale is billed under special metered or flat rate tariff schedules. The Interdepart- mental Sales category includes amounts charged for water supplied to departments of the water utility under specified rate schedules.

There may, of course, be other special sales of water which, if significant in amount and billed under special rate schedules, should be classified separately. These special sales include revenues from water supplied for air conditioning, for refrigeration, for large industrial users or insti- tutions which consume a significant portion of the total water delivered by the utility and which are billed under special rate agreements, and for water furnished to builders, contractors, circuses, and other customers who use water for a limited time without permanent connections.

Other Operating Revenues. Although revenues derived from the sale of water represent the major source of operating revenues, other operating rev- enues may represent a significant amount. The sources of other operating revenues may be classified as follows:

1. Forfeited Discounts and Penalties. Includes the amount of discounts forfeited or additional charges to customers who do not pay their water bills within a specified time.

2. Miscellaneous Service Revenues. Includes items such as fees for changing or reconnecting service, and charges for maintenance of ap- pliances, piping, or other installations on cus- tomers' premises.

3. Rents from Water Property. Includes rents received from other organizations for use of prop- erty devoted to water operations.

4. Interdepartmental Rents. Includes rental charges made against other departments of the utility (electric, gas, etc).

5. Power Revenues. Includes revenues ema- nating from the sale of power. For example, self-produced power for pumping may be in excess of utility requirements; the excess may be sold to others.

6. Other Water Revenues. Includes revenues incidental to water operations not included in any of the foregoing accounts, such as income from the sale of material and supplies not ordinarily purchased for resale, commissions on sale or distribution of the water of other utilities, and sale of ice, trees, and similar items.

The Operating Revenue Accounts. State public service commissions require that separate ac- counts and subsidiary records be kept for each type of operating revenue. At a minimum, separate accounts and subsidiary records are generally required for each type of operating revenue dis- cussed in the preceding sections; these detailed operating revenue accounts are shown in the sys- tem of accounts presented in the Appendix. In

2 Emery Troxel, Economics of Public Utilities (New York: Rinehart and Company, Inc., 1947), p. 611.

Figure 9-1
THE NATIONAL WATER UTILITY
STATEMENT OF BUDGETED OPERATING REVENUES
For The Year Ending December 31, 19BY

Item	Orginal Budget 19CY	Actual[a] 19CY	Proposed Budget 19BY
Sales Of Water:			
Metered Sales:			
Residential	$3,783,000	$3,832,100	$4,017,000[b]
Commercial	1,127,000	1,193,400	1,392,000
Industrial	885,000	907,500	931,000
Public Authorities	43,900	42,120	59,200
Sales For Resale	126,200	137,500	145,300
Total Metered Sales	$5,965,100	$6,112,620	$6,544,500
Unmetered Sales:			
Sales to General Customers	$ 40,600	$ 38,800	$ 36,400
Private Fire Protection	69,200	72,100	77,900
Public Fire Protection	350,000	367,000	382,200
Other Public Authorities	5,300	5,300	5,400
Total Unmetered Sales	$ 465,100	$ 483,200	$ 501,900
Total Sales of Water	$6,430,200	$6,595,820	$7,046,400
Other Operating Revenues:			
Forefeited Discounts and Penalties	$ 57,000	$ 48,700	$ 53,000
Miscellaneous Service Revenues	45,000	41,500	48,000
Rents From Water Property	6,500	6,500	7,200
Other Water Revenues	4,600	4,900	5,000
Total Other Operating Revenues	$ 113,100	$ 101,600	$ 113,200
Total Operating Revenues	$6,543,300	$6,697,420	$7,159,600

[a] The figures in this column represent operating revenues for the first ten months of the current year plus estimated operating revenues for the remaining two months.
[b] See Fig. 9-2.

addition, operating revenue derived from other sources should, if significant in amount, also be classified in separate operating revenue accounts.

The careful maintenance of detailed operating revenue accounts (including the subclassification of revenue from general customers by residential, commercial, and industrial sales) is essential to water utility management and to regulatory authorities for determining and establishing rate schedules. Water utility management may utilize the information contained in the detailed operating revenue accounts to analyze trends in revenue and to aid in forecasting future water requirements. Trends and forecasts of water revenue requirements will, in turn, affect management decisions regarding the amount and type of capital expenditures to be undertaken by the utility, the securing of additional water rights and franchises, and other preparations for expansion.[3]

Planning Operating Revenues

Sound planning on the part of water utility management is a prerequisite to obtaining an adequate

level of revenue. Gross operating revenues must be sufficient to enable the water utility to provide adequate service and to assure the maintenance, development, and perpetuation of the system.

The operating budget is an important planning aid to water utility management. It allows management to develop plans for reaching the objective of realizing gross revenues sufficient to cover the cost of supplying the desired level of water service and to allow a fair and reasonable return. The cost of supplying the desired level of water service may be considered to be measured by the level of operating expenses. A fair and reasonable return, as measured by utility operating income, must be sufficient to pay interest (and dividends in the case of an investor-owned water utility) and to otherwise insure the secure financial position necessary to obtain money at reasonable interest rates for system expansion.

The first step in the development of the operating budget is to estimate the revenue component of the budget. Figure 9-1 shows a statement of estimated operating revenues, by class of customer, forecast for a budget period of one year.

[3] American Water Works Association, Water Utility Management Manual, AWWA M5 (New York: American Water Works Association, 1959), p. 100.

Estimates of operating revenues may, of course, be made for periods of less or more than one year. Operating revenues are a function of the demand for water service. In turn, the demand for water service in a given locality is a function of factors such as the population level, industrial concentration, weather conditions, customs of the people concerning the use of water for sanitary and other purposes, and economic conditions.

Operating revenues should be estimated for each class of customers (general customers, private fire protection service, sales for resale, and other significant classes) to which a separate rate schedule applies. Revenues obtained from general customers should be forecast by residential, commercial, and industrial customer components if the accuracy of the forecast can be materially improved by separately forecasting the revenue to be derived from each component. Forecasting by residential, commercial, and industrial customer components may improve the accuracy of the forecast when the historical water consumption pattern for each of these classes of general customers reflects a different trend in water usage, or when future trends may be expected to diverge.

In addition, if a water utility serves more than one community or district, each of which is subject to different rate schedules or which reflects different water usage characteristics, operating revenues should be estimated for each community or district served. To increase the accuracy of the forecast, large customers or customers having extraordinary demands for service may be requested to supply estimates of their probable demands for water during the budget period.

Since sales to residential customers typically produce the greatest portion of total operating revenues, it may be desirable to forecast residential sales by such components as single-family houses, multi-family houses, and apartment houses. The extent to which the revenue forecast is made by separate customer classes and by components of classes will, of course, depend upon the extent to which different customer classes and components of classes are subject to differing rate schedules, the extent to which different classes and their components reflect differing consumption characteristics, and the degree of accuracy desired in the operating revenue forecast.

The preparation of a statement of estimated operating revenues, such as that shown in Fig. 9-1, may be considered as a two-step process: (1) an estimate of the quantity of water required by each class of customer or an estimate of the amount of other quantities used as a basis for applying rate schedules; and (2) the application of rate schedules to the estimated quantity components to determine the estimated revenue obtainable from each class of customer.

Interrelation of Operating Budget and Capital Expenditures Budget. The forecast of demand for water service is the starting point of the entire budgetary process; that is, estimated customer demand for water service is the basis for quantification of the entire water utility operation plan. Obviously, the estimate of the quantity of water required by customers will affect the level of budgeted operating revenues (assuming, of course, that at least a portion of customers' water usage is metered).

The estimated amount of water required by customers will also affect the level of budgeted operating expenses. Many of the operating expense items of a water utility do not vary in amount in response to changes in operating activity by the utility. Accountants call such cost behavior "fixed." There are, however, other operating expenses which do vary in amount in response to change in operating activity. The accounting term for this behavior is "variable." Fuel expenses (for pumping) and chemical expense (for treatment), are examples of expenses which may vary in relation to the quantity of water demanded by customers. Meter reading, billing, and collecting expenses, are examples of expenses which vary with the number of customers served by the utility.

In addition to serving as a basis for budgeting operating revenues and some operating expenses, a forecast of future water consumption is needed by water utility management to aid in planning a capital expenditures program that will provide facilities sufficient to meet future demands for water. Total system capacity must be provided to meet the peak hourly demand placed on the system during the year by general customers, plus additional capacity to provide adequate public fire protection service even during times of peak demand of general customers. The impact of planned additional facilities on annual operating expenses and on revenue requirements also must be considered. In order to be an effective capital budgeting aid, the forecast of annual customer water requirements should be made for at least a five year period, and include forecasts of the peak demands for service. Inasmuch as the forecasts for the period beyond the first year are not used as a basis for the current operating budget, the forecasts need not be detailed by category of customers.

This chapter is concerned primarily with forecasting water requirements as a step in forecasting operating revenues for inclusion in the annual operating budget. The use of estimated future water requirements in preparing the operating expense budget is discussed in Chapter 11. The use of estimated future water requirements in preparing the capital expenditures budget is discussed in Chapter 16.

Forecasting Sales of Water to Metered Customers. Historical water consumption information accumulated from individual customer records may be used as a basis for estimating the amount of water to be sold to each particular class of metered customer, or component thereof, during the budget period. For example, the amount of water sold within each block of a block meter-rate schedule for each year of a series of years for each customer class or class component may be charted. A trend line can then be fitted to the historical data. The trend line can be extrapolated in order to estimate the amount of water to be sold within each block of the block meter-rate schedule applicable to the particular class of customer or class component for the budget period.

If, in addition to the block meter-rate schedule, a service charge or miminum charge is to be levied on customers, an estimate of the revenue to be obtained from service charges or minimum charges also must be made. The estimate of the revenue from service charges or minimum charges involves forecasting the number of customers who will be subject to the charges. This forecast can be made on the basis of historical information concerning the number of customers subject to the charges, in the same manner as the forecast of water consumption. If the service charge or minimum charge is based on the size of meter or other measure, the historical data must be assembled on that basis.

Figure 9-2 continues the example of revenue budgeting presented in Fig. 9-1. Figure 9-2 shows the computation of estimated quantities of water to be sold to residential customers who are subject to a three block meter-rate schedule. Amounts to be consumed by metered residential customers are estimated for each of the three blocks. In addition, Fig. 9-2 assumes that residential customers are subject to a service charge based on the size of meter, so the estimated number of meters of each size for residential customers is shown.

Forecasting Unmetered Sales. Charges for unmetered sales to a particular customer class are based on quantity components or measures other than the amount of water consumed. Budgeted revenue for a particular unmetered customer class, therefore, depends on (1) the estimated number of customers in the class, and (2) the estimated number of units (i.e. faucets, frontal footage, and hydrants) for each customer on which water charges are based. Customer records provide historical data about these factors and the historical data may be extrapolated as described previously.

Modification of Historical Trends. Historical data, such as per capita consumption records, must be examined to make sure that underlying

Figure 9-2
THE NATIONAL WATER UTILITY
ESTIMATED OPERATING REVENUE
METERED RESIDENTIAL SALES
For The Year Ending December 31, 19BY

Item	Estimated Quantity to be Sold (1000 gallons)	Block Rate (per 1000 gallons)	Estimated Revenue
Service Charge(a)			$ 796,600
Domestic Step	4,180,000	$0.68	2,842,400
Intermediate Step	840,000	0.45	378,000
Wholesale Step	0	0.24	0
Total Estimated Revenue, Metered Residential Customers (Carried to Fig. 9-1)			$4,017,000

(a) Service charge determined as follows:

Meter Size	Estimated # of meters	Annual Charge per Meter	Total Charge
5/8"	74385	10.00	$743,850
3/4"	2630	13.00	34,190
1"	480	20.00	9,600
1-1/2"	320	28.00	8,960
Total Service Charges			$796,600

conditions have not changed. Economic and social conditions in the service area of the utility may change rather abruptly, causing corresponding changes in the number of customers in a particular class, the quantity of water sold within each block of a block meter-rate schedule, the number of meters of various size, or other factors affecting demand and revenue. Thus, projections of historical trends must be adjusted in the light of changing conditions in the service area. Specifically, the estimated number of customers based on projections of historical trends should be adapted for the estimated effects of changes in population, changes in the number of building permits issued, and the number of new housing starts. Likewise, historical projections of the quantity of water sold within each block of a block meter-rate schedule should be adjusted for the estimated effects of changes in pricing policies, advertising and other promotional activities, and general and local socio-economic conditions.

Applying the Rate Schedules. After the quantity components are estimated they must be related to the appropriate rate schedule in order to determine the estimated revenue obtainable. For example, in the case of metered sales to a particular customer class or class component, the appropriate block meter-rate schedule is applied to the estimated water volume to be sold under the rate schedule in order to obtain a revenue estimate for that particular class or class component. Further, if a service charge or minimum charge is levied on metered customers, then the appropriate charge must be multiplied by the estimated number of customers (or number of meters, if the charge is based on meter size) to determine the total estimated revenue obtainable under the service charge or minimum charge. Figure 9-2 depicts the application of a three block meter-rate schedule and a service charge to the appropriate estimated quantity components in order to determine the estimated amount of revenue from metered sales to residential customers.

In the case of unmetered sales, the appropriate flat rate schedules are applied to the total estimated number of units (i.e., faucets, frontal footage, and hydrants) used by each customer class in order to determine the budgeted amount of revenue from unmetered customers.

After forecasting the amount of operating revenue (and determining water consumption for the

budget period), operating expenses are budgeted (as discussed in Chapters 11 and 12). If the existing rate structure is adequate and if costs are properly controlled, the completed operating budget will indicate a level of operating revenue allowing a fair and reasonable return. If the estimated operating revenue does not allow a reasonable return, and costs are considered to be under control, a rate study is required.

Planning the Rate Schedule[4]

The process of determining water rate schedules is a subject of controversy. At the present time there is no single set of rules established for determining a rate schedule for a water utility.

The particular rate-making procedure to be followed in establishing a rate schedule for a water utility depends on many factors, including differences in the form of ownership (investor-owned or municipally-owned), differences in regulatory control over water rates (control by a state public service commission or by a local authority), and differences in individual viewpoints and preferences concerning the appropriate procedure to be followed to meet local conditions and requirements. Nevertheless, there are some basic considerations involved in formulating a rate schedule, The purpose of this section is to discuss some of the basic considerations involved in, and to outline general procedures for, establishing a rate schedule for a water utility.

The preparation of the rate study is a joint effort between various expert groups, particularly accountants and engineers. The accounting records (property and expense records) supply the basic data for the rate study. The accountant also must develop pro forma statements of expense. The engineer generally is responsible for converting original cost records to rate base values which fall somewhere between original cost-less depreciation and replacement cost-new-less depreciation. Finally, the accountant and the engineer, working together, must allocate certain property values and expenses to permit the development of an equitable water rate schedule.

Revenue Requirements Under the Traditional Public Utility Approach. In the case of investor-owned water utilities and municipally-owned water utilities subject to rate regulation by state public

---

[4] The discussion in this section is largely dependent on three sources: American Water Works Association, Water Rates Manual, AWWA M1 (New York: American Water Works Association, 1960), American Water Works Association, Water Utility Management Manual, AWWA M5 (New York: American Water Works Association, 1959), pp. 82-92; and Paul J. Garfield and Wallace F. Lovejoy, Public Utility Economics (Englewood Cliffs, New Jersey: Prentice-Hall, Inc., 1964), pp. 220-233.

service commissions, revenue requirements generally are established by applying the traditional public utility approach: the determination of gross revenues sufficient to permit a given return on a defined rate base. The NCGA strongly recommends that municipally-owned utilities use the same approaches as those in private industry, including charging depreciation. Therefore, as mentioned in Chapter 6, the traditional public utility approach also is recommended for use by municipally-owned water utilities not subject to regulation by public service commissions, rather than the "cash needs" approach. The traditional public utility approach is consistent with the accrual basis of accounting and with depreciation accounting, whereas the "cash needs" approach is not.

Utilizing the public utility approach, operating revenues must be sufficient to cover operation and maintenance expense, depreciation, taxes, and must allow a return on the rate base. Figure 6-8 depicts a statement of estimated revenues, expenses, and income appropriate to summarize a rate study conducted in accordance with the traditional public utility approach.

There is, of course, some lapse between the date an application for new rates is prepared and submitted to the state public service commission for approval and the date the new rates become effective. Therefore, if rates are predicated on past or present costs, the revenues derived from the new rate schedule may become inadequate shortly after it goes into effect if operating expenses increase markedly. A realistic forecast of expenses may be based on past operation and maintenance expenses, taxes, depreciation, and amortization adjusted for known or anticipated changes and forecast for the applicable future period.

Further, frequent changes in rates are undesirable because of the cost incurred in conducting rate studies and the adverse effect on customer relations. Therefore, to reduce the frequency of rate changes and to insure adequate revenues, rate schedules should be predicated on the rate base and operating expenses that are forecast for the middle of a reasonably long period of time (such as 5 to 10 years) during which the rates are expected to be in effect. However, in the case of water utilities subject to public service commission regulation, the rate base and operating expense figures are essentially historical in nature and generally are developed for a "test year." The rate base and operating expense figures for the test year are typically those which existed during the twelve months prior to the rate study, adjusted for conditions which are expected to prevail in the future.

It should be mentioned that the NARUC procedure for accounting for property retirements assists in avoiding material changes in rate base value due to the retirements. At the time depreciable property is retired, the book cost of the property is (1) credited to the plant accounts, and (2) charged to the depreciation allowance account. In addition, the cost of removal is charged to the allowance account and the proceeds from salvage are credited to the allowance account. The retirement affects the net book value of utility plant only to the extent that the proceeds from salvage differ in amount from the cost of removal. The NARUC retirement procedure assists in stabilizing the rate base, thereby minimizing the need for frequent rate changes resulting from changes in the rate base due to property retirements.

The amount of the rate base and rate of return to be allowed on the defined rate base are established by the public service commission for those water utilities subject to its jurisdiction. The determination of rate base differs between states. Methods employed by public service commissions range from original cost-less depreciation to replacement cost-new-less depreciation or some combination thereof. In any event, a rate base and a rate of return must be fixed for a regulated water utility that will insure an income sufficient to attract the capital necessary to maintain and expand the facilities as required by customer demand.

Revenue Requirements Under the "Cash Needs" Approach. Municipally-owned water utilities may be required by law to use the "cash needs" approach to rate determination.

Depending on local policy and conditions there is a wide variation among municipally-owned water utilities as to the kinds of cash outlays which are to be covered by revenues. The rate study, in accordance with the cash needs approach, generally would determine the amount of operating revenue needed to cover operation and maintenance expense, debt service requirements, replacements, and normal extensions and improvements. In some instances operating revenues may also be required to cover other cash outlays such as appropriations for major improvements and contributions to other municipal funds. Figure 6-9 presents a statement which summarizes a rate study conducted in accordance with the "cash needs" approach.

The emphasis on cash needs in determining the revenue requirements for a municipally-owned water utility (not subject to commission regulation) is primarily a result of two factors: (1)

municipally-owned water utilities often are financed by bonds which must be serviced from cash generated by the utility; and (2) municipally-owned water utilities are ordinarily expected to recover the cost of service (measured in terms of annual cash outlays) through operations, but are not expected to earn a profit.

It should be noted that, in accordance with the "cash needs" approach, no explicit provision is made for depreciation expense; depreciation charges are non-cash expenditures and, as such, are properly excluded. However, the use of the "cash needs" approach does not imply that depreciation expense should be ignored in determining utility operating income; sound accounting requires that provisions be made for depreciation and other non-cash expenses.

The revenue requirements should be based on the average requirements for the period to which the new rate schedule will apply. Operation and maintenance expenses should be forecast as described in the preceding section. Forecast debt service requirements should include the interest and principal payments to be made on outstanding debt and on any borrowing expected to take place during the budget period.

The amount estimated for replacements should be sufficient to provide for the current renewals and replacements of water utility property which is no longer serviceable. The amount included in revenue requirements for current renewals and replacements should be at least equal to the amount charged to depreciation, so that over a period of time the utility's capital is not impaired. The requirement for normal extensions and improvements should provide for small main extensions, services, meters, hydrants, and other minor items. The amount of funds needed for major extensions and improvements often is not included in the estimate, since it is assumed that major improvements will be financed by issuing bonds. In addition, normal extensions and improvements

financed by contributions would not be considered.

Required contributions to other municipal funds, particularly if made in lieu of payment of taxes, must also be included in the computation of revenue requirements. And, if the policy of the utility is to avoid debt, operating revenue may be required to cover the cost of major extensions and improvements not otherwise financed from contributions.

Determining the Rate Schedule—General. The definition of rate base varies greatly from one public service commission to another, as does the allowable rate of return. Consequently, the rate schedules developed by two similar water utilities subject to regulation by two different public service commissions may vary greatly. In the case of municipally-owned water utilities not subject to the jurisdication of state public service commissions, rate schedules also may vary markedly depending on the capital structure of the utility, the requirements for payments of taxes (or payments in lieu of taxes), and policies regarding future financing methods.

Figure 9-3 summarizes the revenue requirements for a commission-regulated water utility determined in accordance with the utility approach. Figure 9-4 summarizes the revenue requirements for a non-regulated municipally-owned water utility determined in accordance with the "cash needs" approach. Ordinarily, the revenue requirements as determined by the two different approaches would differ, however, to facilitate comparison and discussion in this chapter, the revenue requirements in Figs. 9-3 and 9-4 are the same.

Most water utilities employ a meter-rate schedule of three to seven blocks which is applicable to all general customers (residential, commerical, and industrial). Under the block meter-rate schedule, charges per unit of water consumed by customers vary depending on the amount of water consumed within successive brackets. (An example of a block meter-rate

Figure 9-3
ESTIMATED REVENUE REQUIREMENTS
("Utility" Approach)

		Total
Estimated Operation and Maintenance Expenses		$1,036,000
Estimated Fixed Charges		
Depreciation..	$ 210,000	
Taxes	798,000	
Return (Utility Operating Income)(a)	1,008,000	
Total Estimated Fixed Charges		2,016,000
Total Estimated Revenue Needed to Cover Annual Costs		$3,052,000

(a) Return is computed at 6% on a rate base value of $16,800,000.

Figure 9-4
ESTIMATED REVENUE REQUIREMENTS
("Cash Needs" Approach)

		Total
Estimated Operation and Maintenance Expenses		$1,036,000
Estimated Fixed Charges		
Debt Service Requirements	$357,000	
Replacements	469,000	
Normal Extensions and Improvements	893,000	
Payments to General Fund in Lieu of Taxes	297,000	
Total Estimated Fixed Charges		2,016,000
Total Estimated Revenue Needed to Cover Annual Cash Needs		$3,052,000

schedule is shown in Fig. 6-10.) Separate rate schedules are provided for private fire protection, public fire protection, sales for resale, and other classes of use. In the following pages, the essential steps in the development of a three block meter-rate schedule for general customers and a special rate schedule for public fire protection are presented. The procedures may, of course, be altered to include more blocks or to provide for additional separate charges for other special uses.

Rates charged each class of customer should be reasonably related to the cost of rendering service to that class. The two primary methods for allocating costs to each customer class in an equitable manner and for determining rate schedules based on these cost allocations are the functional cost basis and the demand basis. These two methods are discussed in the succeeding paragraphs together with an illustrative application of each method. In the discussion the following terms are used as defined:

1. Costs. This term includes the total cost of operation and maintenance and fixed charges.

2. Fixed Charges (or Fixed Capital Costs). Under the traditional public utility approach to rate determination, fixed charges include the return on rate base, depreciation, and taxes. Under the "cash needs" approach, fixed charges include the annual debt service requirement, outlays for replacement, outlays for normal extensions and improvements, and taxes or payments in lieu of taxes.

The Functional Cost Basis. Under the functional cost basis of determining water rates, costs are classified as production costs (source of supply, pumping, treatment, and transmission), distribution costs, customers' costs (commercial, services, and meters), public fire protection costs, and costs of other special uses. The chart of accounts presented in the Appendix provides for the functional classification of operation and maintenance expense items. Many of these expenses are directly traceable to a given function. Some items, on the other hand, such as administrative and general expenses, must be allocated to functional cost categories on an equitable and clerically feasible basis. Figure 9-5 shows the allocation of operation and maintenance expenses. The total amount of operation and maintenance expenses allocated agrees with the "estimated operation and maintenance" figure in Figs 9-3 and 9-4. The basis for distribution of administrative and general expenses is indicated by the footnote in Fig. 9-5.

In addition to operating and maintenance expenses, fixed charges must also be classified within the functional cost categories. Inasmuch as fixed charges are related to rate base elements, the elements themselves must be classified by functional category. An example of the classification of rate base items is presented in Fig. 9-6; the bases used for allocation are explained in notes to the figure.

It is assumed in Fig. 9-6 that the total rate base value of $16,800,000 is equal to original cost-less depreciation. If a basis other than original cost is used (such as replacement cost-new-less depreciation), the figures depicted in Fig. 9-6 would, of course, be adjusted accordingly. A change in the rate base value from original cost-less depreciation, for example, not only would affect the values presented in Fig. 9-6, and the subsequent allocation of fixed charges, but also would affect the return on rate base as shown in Fig. 9-3. The fixed charges shown in Figs. 9-3 and 9-4 are classified in proportion to the allocation of rate base elements in Fig. 9-6. This allocation of fixed charges is shown in Fig. 9-7.

In the case of public fire protection service, the annual costs related to that portion of utility plant installed solely for public fire protection service have been determined (see Fig. 9-7). However,

Figure 9-5

ALLOCATION OF OPERATION AND MAINTENANCE EXPENSES

| | | Allocation to Functional Cost Categories | | | | |
Expense Item	Total	Production	Distribution	Commercial	Meters and Services	Public Fire Protection
Source of Supply						
Operation	$ 49,200	$ 49,200				
Maintenance	12,400	12,400				
Pumping						
Operation	456,400	456,400				
Maintenance	43,200	43,200				
Treatment						
Operation	40,800	40,800				
Maintenance	2,400	2,400				
Transmission	20,000	20,000				
Distribution						
Operation (Other than Meters, Hydrants & Connections)	56,000		$ 56,000			
Maintenance (Other than Meters, Hydrants & Connections)	45,200		45,200			
Meters	19,600				$19,600	
Services	24,400				24,400	
Hydrants	14,400					$14,400
Customer Accounts	180,800			$180,800		
Administrative and General(a)	71,200	14,240	21,360	21,360	7,120	7,120
Total	$1,036,000	$638,640	$122,560	$202,160	$51,120	$21,520

(a) Distributed to: Production, 20%; Distribution, 30%; Commercial, 30%; Meters and Services, 10%; and Public Fire Protection, 10%. Percentages used are for illustrative purposes only.

Figure 9-6
ALLOCATION OF RATE BASE ITEMS

Rate Base Item	Total	Cost Allocated to:			
		Production Facilities	Distribution Facilities	Customers' Facilities	Public Fire Protection Facilities
Intangible Plant[a]	$ 20,000	$ 4,000	$ 6,000	$ 8,000	$ 2,000
Source of Supply Plant					
Land and Land Rights	410,000	410,000			
Structures and Improvements	230,000	230,000			
Other	50,000	50,000			
Pumping Plant					
Land and Land Rights	90,000	90,000			
Structures and Improvements	780,000	780,000			
Power Production Equipment	88,000	88,000			
Steam Pumping Equipment	68,000	68,000			
Electric Pumping Equipment	440,000	440,000			
Water Treatment Plant					
Land and Land Rights	42,000	42,000			
Structures and Improvements	210,000	210,000			
Water Treatment Equipment	118,000	118,000			
Transmission Plant					
Land and Land Rights	40,000	40,000			
Structures and Improvements	150,000	150,000			
Transmission Mains	3,700,000	3,700,000			
Distribution Plant					
Distribution Reservoirs & Standpipes	380,000		380,000		
Distribution Mains	7,125,000		7,125,000		
Hydrants	629,000				629,000
Meters & Services	1,350,000			1,350,000	
General Plant[a]					
Land and Land Rights	40,000	8,000	12,000	16,000	4,000
Structures and Improvements	200,000	40,000	60,000	80,000	20,000
Office Furniture & Equipment	44,000	8,800	13,200	17,600	4,400
Transportation Equipment	90,000	18,000	27,000	36,000	9,000
Stores Equipment	4,000	800	1,200	1,600	400
Tools, Shop, and Garage Equipment	46,000	9,200	13,800	18,400	4,600
Laboratory Equipment and Other	6,000	1,200	1,800	2,400	600
Materials and Supplies[b]	200,000	60,000	80,000	50,000	10,000
Working Cash Requirement[a]	250,000	50,000	75,000	50,000	25,000
Total	$16,800,000	$6,616,000	$7,795,000	$1,680,000	$709,000

(a) Distributed to: Production, 20%; Distribution, 30%; Customers' Facilities, 40%; and Hydrants and Connections, 10%. Percentages used are for illustrative purposes only.
(b) Distributed according to the types of materials and supplies in inventory.

Figure 9-7
ALLOCATION OF ANNUAL COSTS TO FUNCTIONAL CATEGORIES

Functional Cost Category	Total	Fixed Charges[a]	Operation and Maintenance Expenses[b]
Production	$1,432,560	$ 793,920	$ 638,640
Distribution	1,057,960	935,400	122,560
Customers' Costs			
Commercial	$ 202,160		$ 202,160
Meters and Services	252,720	$ 201,600	51,120
Sub-Total	$ 454,880	201,600	253,280
Hydrants (Public Fire Protection)	106,600	85,080	21,520
Total	$3,052,000	$2,016,000	$1,036,000

[a] Fixed charges are distributed to functional categories in proportion to the distribution of rate base items to each of the function categories (see Fig. 9-6). The amount of fixed charges allocated to each category is equal to 12% of the rate base value distributed to that category.

[b] The distribution of operation and maintenance expense is in accordance with the distribution shown in Fig. 9-5.

since a production and distribution system of the water utility is fundamental to adequate public fire protection service as well as to meeting the water requirements of general customers, some portion of production and distribution costs (as shown in Fig. 9-7) is properly allocable to public fire protection.

There are a number of different approaches to the allocation of production and distribution costs to public fire protection. The AWWA Committee on Water Rates has taken the position that the prime function of a water supply system is to provide a commodity and that public fire protection service, although important, is a supplementary service. The charge for public fire protection service should not exceed the demonstrable additional costs involved in furnishing this service.[5] That is, the cost applicable to public fire protection service is considered the annual cost which would be incurred if a water utility which did not provide public fire protection service was adapted to provide such service. Additional costs include: (1) the cost related to plant installed solely for public fire protection purposes such as hydrants, connections, pumps, mains, and other facilities used only for public fire protection purposes (this cost is considered in Figs. 9-7 and 9-8); (2) the cost of water used for fire protection (shown in Fig. 9-8 as the production expense captioned "operation and maintenance"); and (3) costs related to the additional capacity needed for public fire protection service (shown as the fixed charges for

distribution and production in Fig. 9-8). The determination of incremental costs resulting from additional capacity for public fire protection requires careful analysis of each major production and distribution plant item. After estimating the differential investment in each major production and distribution plant item due to public fire protection, fixed charges may be allocated to fire protection service based on the differential investment.

Figure 9-8 depicts the allocation of costs to public fire protection based on the procedures discussed in the preceding paragraph.

After fixed charges and operation and maintenance expenses have been allocated to public fire protection, the cost of water service for other special uses, such as private fire protection, air conditioning, refrigeration, sprinkling, irrigation, and sales for resale, must be considered. Costs to be considered for each of these other special uses include direct costs (costs relating to items of utility plant used solely for special use and the cost of water furnished for the special use) and indirect costs (costs arising out of additional plant capacity required for a particular special use).[6]

After costs have been allocated to all special users, the next step is to establish rate schedules for general customers and special users. Figure 9-9 summarizes the information presented in Figs. 9-7 and 9-8. Based on the information in Fig. 9-9, rate schedules for normal and special uses may be determined under the functional cost basis as

[5] American Water Works Association, Water Rates Manual, AWWA M1 (New York: American Water Works Association, 1960), p. 14.

[6] For a further discussion of public fire protection service and other special uses, and techniques for determining the cost of these special uses, see: American Water Works Association, Water Rates Manual, AWWA M1 (New York: American Water Works Association, 1960), pp. 13-21.

Figure 9-8
ALLOCATION OF COSTS TO PUBLIC FIRE PROTECTION

Cost Item		Totals
Hydrants (see Fig. 9-7)		
Fixed Charges..	$ 85,080	
Operation and Maintenance Expenses..............................	21,520	
Total Cost—Hydrants..		$106,600
Distribution		
Fixed Charges—Distribution Reservoirs and Standpipes[a]	$ 22,800	
Fixed Charges—Distribution Mains[b]	139,200	
Total Cost—Distribution....................................		162,000
Production		
Operation and Maintenance Expenses[c]	$ 30,520	
Fixed Charges[d]	129,600	
Total Cost—Production......................................		$160,120
Total Cost—Public Fire Protection.................................		$428,720

[a] It is assumed that 1/2 of the capacity of distribution reservoirs and standpipes is devoted to public fire protection—a total investment of $190,000 (See Fig. 9-6). 12% of $190,000 results in annual fixed charges for distribution reservoirs and standpipes of $22,800.

[b] It is assumed that the differential investment for fire protection on 2,320,000 feet of distribution main is $0.50 per foot or $1,160,000. 12% of $1,160,000 results in annual fixed charges for distribution mains of $139,200.

[c] It is assumed that approximately 4.8% of the water produced is attributable to public fire protection. Therefore approximately 4.8% of total production operation and maintenance expense (see Fig. 9-7) or $30,520 is charged to fire protection.

[d] It is assumed that $1,080,000 or approximately 16% of production plant investment is attributable to public fire protection. 12% of $1,080,000 results in annual fixed charges for production of $129,600.

described in the following paragraphs.

A charge for public fire protection (total cost, from Fig. 9-9, $428,720) may be made in one of several ways. The charge levied on the municipality for public fire protection commonly is measured in terms of a hydrant charge (a fixed cash charge per hydrant per year), a charge related to the number of miles of water main providing fire protection service, or a combination of both. The public fire protection charge may also take the form of a lump sum charge against the municipality and may be based on "inch-foot" calculations. In the continuing example used in this section—assuming that a hydrant charge is levied and that the water utility serves an estimated 9,525 hydrants during the period for which the rate study applies—an annual per hydrant charge of ap-

proximately $45 would recover the total annual cost of $428,720 for public fire protection service.

Some water utilities charge fire protection costs to property owners based on the assessed valuation of the property of the owners. A less equitable procedure sometimes used is the basing of the charge to general customers on meter size or on water consumption. Bases of collecting charges for other special uses include size of service line (for private fire protection); tons of cooling capacity (for air conditioning); size of meter (for sprinkling); and special block meter-rate schedules (for irrigation and sale for resale).

The composition of the rate schedule for general customers can differ in numerous ways depending on the inclusion of a service charge or minimum charge and the number of blocks in the

Figure 9-9
SUMMARY OF FINAL ALLOCATION OF COSTS TO FUNCTIONAL CATEGORIES

Functional Cost Category	Total	Public Fire Protection	General Customers			
			Commercial	Meters and Services	Production	Distribution
Production	$1,432,560	$160,120			$1,272,440	
Distribution	1,057,960	162,000				$895,960
Customers' Cost	454,880		$202,160	$252,720		
Hydrants	106,600	106,600				
Total	$3,052,000	$428,720	$202,160	$252,720	$1,272,440	$895,960

block meter-rate schedule (in the example which follows, the rate schedule to normal users consists of a service charge and a block meter-rate schedule comprised of three blocks or steps).

Under the functional cost basis, the service charge—based on the size of meter—includes customers' costs (commercial, meters, and services). Production and distribution costs are collected through the block meter-rates. This approach to establishing a rate schedule is based on the premise that the fixed charges included in distribution and production costs should be collected on the basis of meter readings rather than on an arbitrary measure of the hypothetical demand of the water user (such as meter capacity). Under the demand basis, discussed in the next section, a portion of the fixed charges included in production and distribution costs are collected through a service charge as determined by the size of the meter; the functional cost basis avoids the problems involved in separating fixed charges into the portion collected through the service charge and the portion collected through block meter-rates.

To determine service charges, commercial expenses may be apportioned equally among all customers (unless there are known variations in commercial costs for different classes of customers). Annual costs related to meters and services may be distributed among customers on the basis of installation costs of meters and services. Based on the customer costs shown in Fig. 9-9, the

computation of service charges is presented in Fig. 9-10.

Many water utilities, however, do not levy a service charge, as such, on customers. A service charge may be thought by management to be unacceptable to the public; that is, the public may not understand being charged even though no water is delivered. In the place of the service charge, a minimum charge may be substituted. The minimum charge should be an amount sufficient to provide for the service charge and for the cost of the water allowed under the minimum charge. The minimum charge usually increases with the size of the meter since the service charge typically increases with the size of meter and the amount of water allowed under the minimum charge (and therefore the cost of the water furnished) usually increases with the size of meter.

The three blocks or steps in the continuing example of a meter-rate schedule are determined under the functional cost basis by establishing a wholesale rate, an intermediate rate, and a domestic rate. Based on the information shown in Fig. 9-9, the computation of the wholesale, intermediate, and domestic unit rates is presented in Fig. 9-11. In addition, Fig. 9-12 summarizes the expected operating revenue based on the proposed charges for water service. The proposed charges would generate estimated revenues of $3,094,668, an amount slightly greater than the required revenues of $3,052,000.

Figure 9-10
COMPUTATION OF SERVICE CHARGES—FUNCTIONAL COST BASIS

Meter Size (inches)	Number of Meters	Commercial Expense			Meters and Services			Total Annual Service Charge per Meter	Total Annual Service Charge All Meters
		Ratio	Charge per meter[a]	Ratio[b]	Equivalent Number of 5/8 inch meters	Charge per meter[c]			
5/8	47,172	1	$4.00	1	47,172	$ 4.00	$ 8.00	$377,376
3/4	1,818	1	4.00	1.5	2,727	6.00	10.00	18,180
1	1,544	1	4.00	2.25	3,474	9.00	13.00	20,072
1 1/2	332	1	4.00	4.0	1,328	16.00	20.00	6,640
2	402	1	4.00	6.0	2,412	24.00	28.00	11,256
3	192	1	4.00	10.0	1,920	40.00	44.00	8,448
4	132	1	4.00	20.0	2,640	80.00	84.00	11,088
6	20	1	4.00	35.0	700	140.00	144.00	2,880
8	2	1	4.00	50.0	100	200.00	204.00	408
	51,614				62,473			$456,348

(a) Commercial expense ($202,160) divided by total number of meters (51,614) is approximately equal to $4.00 per meter per year.

(b) These ratios are based on an estimation of installation costs of meters and services for each meter size, in relation to the cost of installation of meters and service for a 5/8 inch meter.

(c) Meters and services cost ($252,720) divided by total equivalent 5/8 inch meters (62,473) is approximately equal to $4.00 per equivalent 5/8 inch meter per year. To determine charge per meter size per year requires that $4.00 be multiplied by the appropriate ratio.

Figure 9-11
COMPUTATION OF BLOCK METER-RATES—FUNCTIONAL COST BASIS

Block	Quantity (1,000 gallons)	Cost to be Distributed	Incremental Rate Per 1,000 gallons	Unit Rate per 1,000 gallons
Wholesale Step	3,550,000	$1,272,440	$0.16(a)	$0.16
Intermediate Step.	1,560,000	447,980(b)	0.10(c)	0.26
Domestic Step	3,090,000	447,980(b)	0.14(d)	0.40
	8,200,000	$2,168,400		

(a) Total production costs ($1,272,440) divided by total water sales measured in 1,000 gallon increments (8,200,000) is equal to approximately $0.16 per 1,000 gallons.

(b) Distribution costs ($895,960) are allocated, 50 percent to the intermediate step and 50 percent to the domestic step (the 50% figure is used for illustrative purposes only).

(c) 1/2 of distribution costs ($447,980) divided by total water sales, except sales at the wholesale rate, measured by 1,000 gallon increments (4,650,000) is equal to approximately $0.10 per 1,000 gallons.

(d) 1/2 of distribution costs ($447,980) divided by sales at domestic rate measured in 1,000 gallon increments (3,090,000) is equal to approximately $0.14 per 1,000 gallons.

Figure 9-12
ESTIMATED OPERATING REVENUE—FUNCTIONAL COST BASIS

Item	Quantity (1,000 gallons)	Unit Rate (Per 1,000 gallons)	Estimated Revenue
Wholesale Step	3,550,000	$0.16	$ 568,000
Intermediate Step.	1,560,000	0.26	405,600
Domestic Step.	3,090,000	0.40	1,236,000
Service Charges			456,348
Public Fire Protection			428,720
Total Estimated Revenue.			$3,094,668

The wholesale unit rate is determined by dividing total production costs chargeable to general customers by total annual volume of water to be sold. The intermediate unit rate is established by adding to the wholesale rate an incremental charge, determined by dividing a portion of the distribution costs by the total volume of water to be sold, except sales at the wholesale rate. The domestic unit rate is established by adding an incremental charge to the intermediate rate. The domestic increment is determined by dividing the remaining portion of distribution costs not allocated to the intermediate step by the total water to be sold at the domestic rate.

The estimated volume of water to be sold at each rate may be determined by analyzing customers' bills. The analysis of bills permits the determination of the consumption characteristics of residential, commercial, and industrial customers. Based on these consumption characteristics for customer classes, the volume of water to be sold at wholesale, intermediate, and domestic rates may be determined. Depending on the consumption characteristics of customer classes, it

should be possible to establish limits on the amount of water which may be consumed by each customer at each rate, so that the water consumed by the majority of residential customers is billed at the domestic rate; the major portion of water consumed by commercial customers is billed at the intermediate rate; and the major portion of water consumed for industrial purposes is billed at the wholesale rate. Water utility management may, of course, find it desirable to establish more than three blocks in the block meter-rate schedule; this would require an allocation of production and distribution costs among the various blocks in a manner similar to the example given.

The Demand Basis. Under the demand theory of rate-setting, costs are classified or divided into three groups: customer costs, capacity (or demand) costs, and consumption (or commodity) costs. Customer costs include expenses resulting from the maintenance of services and meters, and expenses required for reading, billing, and collecting. That is, customer costs generally include those expenses which are proportional to the number of customers. Capacity costs include those expenses resulting from making plant capacity available and keeping it ready to serve. Consumption costs (primarily fuel, power, and chemicals) are those costs which are directly proportional to the actual amount of water produced by the utility.

Customer costs typically constitute a relatively small proportion of total costs. Generally, commodity costs also represent a small proportion of the total. The greatest proportion of expenses for a water utility are fixed and theoretically are to be classified as capacity costs. If the capacity costs are fully collected, either through a service or minimum charge or through a higher rate for the first block of the rate schedule applicable to general customers, the result to customers is a substantial charge that is primarily independent of the actual water consumed. The AWWA Committee on Water Rates suggests that the demand theory of rates should not be carried to extremes, that capacity costs should be limited to reasonable amounts, and that the consumption costs should assume the greatest portion of total costs. To encourage uniformity in the classification of costs under the demand basis and to promote a reasonable classification of costs into the three categories, the AWWA Committee on Water Rates suggests the following modified definitions:

1. Customer costs. These costs shall comprise all operation and maintenance and fixed charges arising out of service to customers, including meters and services, collection, and commercial expense, together with a suitable portion of general and administrative expense.

2. Capacity costs. These costs shall be limited to a portion only of the fixed charges of depreciation, taxes, and return. After suitable deductions for fire protection, customers' investment, and property devoted to special uses, the remaining fixed charges shall be divided between the capacity costs and the commodity costs of normal users.

3. Commodity costs. These costs shall include all operation and maintenance expenses, except those chargeable to customers and to fire protection or other special services, plus the balance of fixed charges not allocated to capacity or customer costs.[7]

Under the modified approach advanced by the AWWA Committee on Water Rates, customer costs and a portion of fixed charges (or capacity costs) relating to production and distribution would be collected from normal users through a service charge. Operation and maintenance expenses relating to production and distribution and the remaining portion of fixed charges relating to production and distribution would be collected from normal users through a block meter-rate schedule.

The major difference, therefore, between the functional cost basis and the demand basis is that under the demand basis, fixed charges (capacity costs) relating to production and distribution of water to normal users are collected through the service charge, while under the functional cost basis, all fixed charges related to production and distribution of water to normal users are considered as commodity costs and are collected through a block meter-rate schedule. However, under the modified approach advocated by the AWWA Committee on Water Rates, it is recommended that only a portion of fixed charges related to production and distribution of water to normal users be collected through a service charge, and the remaining portion be collected through a block meter-rate schedule. The Committee's recommendations, therefore, lessen the differences obtained under the functional cost basis and the demand basis.

A major problem arising under the modified demand basis concerns the determination of the amount of fixed charges (capacity costs), related to production and distribution of water to normal users, to be distributed as a service charge. The Committee recommends that the amount of fixed costs so distributed should be limited to fifty percent of the total, the balance being charged to commodity costs and collected through the block meter rate schedule. This recommendation is based on the following premise: "Excluding special uses, it is not uncommon to experience an average daytime delivery rate on the maximum day of approximately twice the average annual rate. Under such conditions, half of the capital costs would appear to be chargeable to the commodity and the other half to the demand."[8] Certainly, if the maximum rate for normal use were greater or less than twice the average rate, then the allocation of fixed charges between capacity costs and commodity costs should be modified accordingly.

The information developed in the preceding section on the functional cost basis can be utilized to demonstrate the application of the modified demand basis for rate determination. Figure 9-13, which summarizes cost data in a form convenient for computing water rates under the demand basis, is based on the information presented in Figs. 9-7

[7]Ibid., pp. 8-9.
[8]Ibid., p. 22.

Figure 9-13
DISTRIBUTION OF ANNUAL COSTS

Item	Total Cost	Customer Costs			Balance of Production and Distribution Costs	Balance of Production and Distribution Costs Divided Between(a)	
		Public Fire Protection	Commercial	Meters & Services		Service Charge	Meter-rate Schedule
Fixed Charges							
Production	$ 793,920	$129,600			$ 664,320	$332,160	$ 332,160
Distribution	935,400	162,000			773,400	386,700	386,700
Customers' Meters & Services . .	201,600			$201,600			
Hydrants	85,080	85,080					
Total Fixed Charges	$2,016,000	$376,680		$201,600	$1,437,720	$718,860	$ 718,860
Operation and Maintenance Expenses							
Production	$ 638,640	$ 30,520			$ 608,120		$ 608,120
Distribution	122,560				122,560		122,560
Customers							
Commercial	202,160		$202,160				
Meters and Services	51,120			$ 51,120			
Hydrants	21,520	$ 21,520					
Total Operation & Maintenance Expenses . .	$1,036,000	$ 52,040	$202,160	$ 51,120	$ 730,680		$ 730,680
Total Annual Costs	$3,052,000	$428,720	$202,160	$252,720	$2,168,400	$718,860	$1,449,540

(a) This distribution is premised on the allocation of fixed charges (capacity costs) equally between the service charge and the block meter-rate schedule.

Figure 9-14

COMPUTATION OF SERVICE CHARGES—DEMAND BASIS

Meter Size (inches)	Number of Meters	Commercial Expense		Production and Distribution Costs			Meters and Services			Total Annual Service Charge per Meter	Total Annual Charges All Meters
		Ratio	Charge per Meter(a)	Ratio(b)	Equivalent Number of 5/8 inch Meters	Charge per Meter(c)	Ratio(d)	Equivalent Number of 5/8 inch Meters	Charge per Meter(e)		
5/8	47,172	1	$4.00	1	47,172	$ 7.60	1	47,172	$ 4.00	$ 15.60	$ 735,883
3/4	1,818	1	4.00	2	3,636	15.20	1.5	2,727	6.00	25.20	45,814
1	1,544	1	4.00	4	6,176	30.40	2.25	3,474	9.00	43.40	67,010
1 1/2	332	1	4.00	10	3,320	76.00	4.0	1,328	16.00	96.00	31,872
2	402	1	4.00	25	10,050	190.00	6.0	2,412	24.00	218.00	87,636
3	192	1	4.00	45	8,640	342.00	10.0	1,920	40.00	386.00	74,112
4	132	1	4.00	90	11,880	684.00	20.0	2,640	80.00	768.00	101,376
6	20	1	4.00	170	3,400	1,292.00	35.0	700	140.00	1,436.00	28,720
8	2	1	4.00	300	600	2,280.00	50.0	100	200.00	2,484.00	4,968
	51,614				94,874			62,473			$1,177,391

(a) Commercial Expense ($202,160) divided by total number of meters (51,614) is approximately equal to $4.00 per meter per year.

(b) These ratios are based on rated capacity of each size of meter, in relation to the capacity of a 5/8 inch meter.

(c) Production and distribution costs ($718,860) divided by total number of equivalent 5/8 inch meters (94,874) is approximately equal to $7.60 per equivalent 5/8 inch meter per year. To determine charge per meter size per year requires that $7.60 be multiplied by the appropriate ratio.

(d) These ratios are based on an estimation of installation costs of meters and services for each meter size, in relation to the cost of installation of meters and services for a 5/8 inch meter.

(e) Meters and services cost ($252,720) divided by total equivalent 5/8 inch meters (62,473) is approximately equal to $4.00 per equivalent 5/8 inch meter per year. To determine charge per meter size per year requires that $4.00 be multiplied by the appropriate ratio.

Figure 9-15
COMPUTATION OF BLOCK METER-RATES—DEMAND BASIS

Block	Quantity (1,000 gallons)	Cost to be Distributed	Incremental Rate (Per 1,000 gallons)	Unit Rate (per 1,000 gallons)
Wholesale...................	3,550,000	$ 940,280	$0.115[a]	$0.115
Intermediate.................	1,560,000	254,630[b]	0.055[c]	0.17
Domestic....................	3,090,000	254,630[b]	0.08 [d]	0.25
	8,200,000	$1,449,540		

[a] Production costs allocated to meter rate schedule ($332,160 + $608,120) divided by total water sales measured in 1,000 gallon increments (8,200,000) is equal to approximately $0.115 per 1,000 gallons.

[b] Distribution costs ($386,700 + $122,560) are allocated, 50 percent to the intermediate step and 50 per cent to the domestic step.

[c] 1/2 of distribution costs ($254,630) divided by total water sales, except sales at the wholesale rate, measured in 1,000 gallon increments (4,650,000) is equal to approximately $0.055 per 1,000 gallons.

[d] 1/2 of distribution costs ($254,630) divided by sales at the domestic rate measured in 1,000 gallon increments (3,090,000) is equal to approximately $0.08 per 1,000 gallons.

Figure 9-16
ESTIMATED OPERATING REVENUES—DEMAND BASIS

Item	Quantity (1,000 gallons)	Unit Rate (per 1,000 gallons)	Estimated Revenue
Wholesale Step	3,550,000	$0.115	$ 408,250
Intermediate Step.	1,560,000	0.17	265,200
Domestic Step	3,090,000	0.25	772,500
Service Charge			1,177,391
Public Fire Protection			428,720
Total Estimated Revenue.			$3,052,061

and 9-8. The distribution of annual costs shown in Fig. 9-13 serves as the basis for the computation of service charges (shown in Fig. 9-14) and for the computation of block meter-rates (shown in Fig. 9-15). Finally, under the demand theory of rate setting an estimate of operating revenue based on the proposed charges for water service is presented in Fig. 9-16, where the proposed charges would generate estimated revenues of $3,052,061, an amount slightly greater than the revenue requirement of $3,052,000.

Some Additional Considerations. It should be noted that the block meter-rate schedules developed in the preceding discussion result in decreasing incremental charges to customers as consumption is increased; this is a normal characteristic of block meter-rate schedules for water utilities. There are two major reasons for decreasing unit water rates as consumption increases: (1) the saving involved in transporting water in large quantities for delivery to a single customer; and (2) the ratio of maximum use to average use is often smaller for the large water user than the small user and, therefore, the extra capacity costs are relatively less for large users.

It also should be noted that, at the present time, municipally-owned water utilities are subject to regulation by public service commissions in only six states. However, the usual exemption of municipally-owned water utilities from commission regulation does not necessarily hold when the utility renders service to customers located beyond the limits of the municipality.[9] Where commissions do regulate outside-of-city water charges, the water rates generally are required to be computed using the traditional public utility approach to rate determination. The AWWA Committee also recommends that the utility approach be used to establish rates to suburban areas served by a municipally-owned water utility,

[9]Paul J. Garfield and Wallace F. Lovejoy, Public Utility Economics (Englewood Cliffs, New Jersey: Prentice-Hall, Inc., 1964), p. 222.

whether subject to commission regulation or not.[10]

If the utility approach is used inside the city, as is required of investor-owned water utilities and by municipally-owned water utilities subject to commission regulation, differences between inside- and outside-city rates may be based on variations in the cost of serving the two groups of customers. If a municipally-owned water utility, using the "cash needs" approach to determine inside-city rates, were to follow the utility approach (using the procedures recommended by the AWWA Committee on Water Rates) to establish outside-city rates, the charges to the two groups of customers would most certainly differ.

Summary. In summary, it may be said that water rates must produce sufficient revenue to allow the water utility to operate, to meet financial obligations, and to attract investment capital. In addition, rates to each customer class should be based on the cost of supplying water service to that class. The specific rate schedules, for various classes of customers, which will permit the water utility to operate on a sound fiscal basis and which will not discriminate inequitably among customers, may be determined under the functional cost basis or the demand basis.

---

[10]American Water Works Association, Water Rates Manual, AWWA M1 (New York: American Water Works Association, 1960), p. 6.

CHAPTER 10. CONTROLLING AND ACCOUNTING FOR REVENUES

The general rule in accounting is that revenue is recognized at the time when possession, title, or use of a product or service is transferred to the customer. In following this rule, the accrual basis of accounting should be employed (see Chapter 3). Under accrual accounting the major item of revenue for a water utility—sales of water service—is recognized on the basis of customer billings. (If a utility is required to follow cash basis accounting, revenue is recognized when cash is received from customers.) Revenue from other sources should also be recognized, to the extent practicable, as it is earned during the accounting period.

Measuring Revenue

The use of meters for measuring the quantity of water delivered to customers results in a lag between the time that water is consumed and the time that meters are read. There is an additional interval between the time a meter is read and the time the bill is rendered to a customer. These lags result in some inaccuracies in assigning revenues to accounting periods. When remote reading systems become practicable their use will reduce the lag.

Presently, in an effort to decrease inaccuracies, some utilities estimate the amount of water delivered to customers but not represented by meter readings and determine the prospective billing based on monthly pumpage figures and customers' past consumption records. This method may be particularly useful if a water utility reads customers' meters every two months but prepares a monthly statement of revenue.

Even if all meters are read and all customers billed during the accounting period, revenues from the sale of water service based on meter readings and billings during the period will be understated by the amount due to the utility for water service rendered between the time meters are read and the end of the accounting period. For example, if meters are read regularly throughout the month, the deficiency is approximately equivalent to fifteen days' revenue. The deficiency may be largely offset by water service which was rendered to customers during the preceding accounting period but which is represented by meter readings and billings during the current accounting period. Variations in customer consumption from one accounting period to another, however, make reported revenue somewhat inaccurate, but the inaccuracy is seldom large enough to mislead users of water utility financial statements.

Comparing Budgeted and Actual Revenue

Actual revenues usually differ to some extent from budgeted revenues. Budgeted revenue estimates serve as useful standards only to the extent that they are valid and reasonable. Minor variations from budgeted revenue figures are to be expected. Significant variations in actual revenues from budgeted revenues should be investigated in order to determine necessary management action. In some instances variations arise from faulty budgeting procedures. In other instances managers or employees have erroneously failed to follow the operating plan. In still other instances, neither the planning nor the operations are at fault; the variations result from random causes.

As discussed in Chapter 6, revenue totals should be reported to management on a periodic basis, typically at monthly intervals. Revenue statements should be designed to display results both in total and in detail by geographical area and customer classes. During each year monthly statements should present both actual and budgeted data. Figure 10-1 shows a monthly statement in which actual operating revenues are compared with budgeted operating revenues and with actual operating revenues for the preceding year. The comparative figures are presented for the month and for the year to date. Figure 10-2 shows a monthly statement which analyzes in greater detail the revenue received from metered water service.

Variations in revenue from the budget standard due to unanticipated changes in volume of water used by customers may be largely beyond the control of management. The demand for water appears to be somewhat inelastic, and attempts to increase water usage (for example, through marketing activities) may be ineffective.

Figure 10-1
THE NATIONAL WATER UTILITY
STATEMENT OF REVENUE
For the Month Ending June 30, 19CY

	For the Month of June				Year to Date			
	Actual Last Year 19PY	Actual This Year 19CY	Budget 19CY	Over (Under) Budget	Actual Last Year 19PY	Actual This Year 19CY	Budget 19CY	Over (Under) Budget
Sales of Water:								
Metered Sales:								
Residential	$383,210	$421,200	$401,700	$19,500	$1,916,050	$2,122,450	$2,008,500	$113,950
Commercial	119,340	131,110	139,200	(8,090)	596,700	712,310	696,000	16,310
Industrial	90,750	98,200	93,100	5,100	453,780	489,750	465,500	24,250
Public Authorities	4,200	4,730	5,920	(1,190)	21,060	23,230	29,600	(6,370)
Sales for Resale	13,750	16,450	14,530	1,920	68,710	82,400	77,600	4,800
Total Metered Sales	$611,250	$671,690	$654,450	$17,240	$3,056,300	$3,430,140	$3,277,200	$152,940
Unmetered Sales:								
Sales to General Customers	$3,250	$2,470	$3,040	$(570)	$19,400	$15,800	$18,200	$(2,400)
Private Fire Protection	6,050	7,200	6,600	600	36,010	46,260	40,000	6,260
Public Fire Protection	30,600	33,400	31,800	1,600	183,500	200,310	191,100	9,210
Other Public Authorities	450	420	450	(30)	2,640	2,850	2,700	150
Total Unmetered Sales	$40,350	$43,490	$41,890	$1,600	$241,550	$265,220	$252,000	$13,220
Total Sales of Water	$651,600	$715,180	$696,340	$18,840	$3,297,850	$3,695,360	$3,529,200	$166,160
Other Operating Revenues:								
Forefeited Discounts and Penalties	$4,870	$5,170	$5,300	$(130)	$24,350	$25,650	$26,250	$(600)
Miscellaneous Service Revenues	4,150	4,650	4,800	(150)	20,730	23,110	24,000	(890)
Rents from Water Property	540	600	600	0	3,250	3,600	3,600	0
Other Water Revenues	490	540	500	40	2,470	2,430	2,500	(70)
Total Other Operating Revenues	$10,050	$10,960	$11,200	$(240)	$50,800	$54,790	$56,350	$(1,560)
Total Operating Revenues	$661,650	$726,140	$707,540	$18,600	$3,348,650	$3,750,150	$3,585,550	$164,600

Figure 10-2
NATIONAL WATER UTILITY
ANALYSIS OF METERED SALES(a)
For the Month of June, 19CY

Description	Billed Revenue	Estimated Billed Revenue Applicable to April and May(b)	Estimated Billed Revenue Applicable to June (1)-(2)(b)	Estimated Unbilled Revenue for June(b)	Total Estimated Revenue for June
Metered Sales to Residential Customers					
Single Family					
Billed Revenue—District 3 (includes misc. billings, Districts 1 and 2)	$361,810	$232,240	$129,570		
Estimated Unbilled Revenue—Districts 1 and 2				$207,230	$207,230
Total, Single Family	$361,810	$232,240	$129,570	$207,230	$366,800
Multi-Family (2-4)					
Billed Revenue—District 3 (includes misc. billings, Districts 1 and 2)	$ 46,850	$ 30,280	$ 16,570		
Estimated Unbilled Revenue—Districts 1 and 2				$ 34,040	$ 34,040
Total, Multi-Family	$ 46,850	$ 30,280	$ 16,570	$ 34,040	$ 50,610
Apartments					
Billed Revenue—District 3 (includes misc. billings, Districts 1 and 2)	$ 28,640	$ 18,380	$ 10,260		
Estimated Unbilled Revenue—Districts 1 and 2				$ 23,530	$ 23,530
Total Apartments	$ 28,640	$ 18,380	$ 10,260	$ 23,530	$ 33,790
Total Metered Sales to Residential Customers	$437,300	$280,900	$156,400	$264,800	$421,200
Metered Sales to Commercial Customers	131,110		131,110		131,110
Metered Sales to Industrial Customers	98,200		98,200		98,200
Metered Sales to Public Authorities	4,730		4,730		4,730
Metered Sales for Resale	16,450		16,450		16,450
Total Metered Sales	$687,790	$280,900	$406,890	$264,800	$671,690

(a) This analysis assumes that all meters, other than residential, are read each month and that all customers, other than residential, are billed each month. Residential meters are read, and customers billed, on a cycle basis. Under the cycle plan, one district (of three) is read and billed each month; the billed revenue is adjusted for the two previous months' estimate of revenues for that district. In addition, revenues are estimated for the two un—billed districts. Billing months are as follows:

District	Billing Months
1	Jan., Apr., July., Oct.
2	Feb., May, Aug., Nov.
3	Mar., June, Sept., Dec.

(b) Revenue estimates are based on customer consumption records for prior years and on monthly pumpage statistics.

The fact that water delivered for usage varies from anticipated levels is not necessarily an indication that the water used by customers has varied from anticipated levels. Variations in the level of water delivered for usage may be caused by such factors as leaks in the water delivery system, underregistration or overregistration of meters, and unauthorized usage of unmetered water. For revenue control purposes, water utility management is primarily interested in insuring that (1) user demands for water are met, (2) that the water which is produced is actually used by customers, and (3) that metered customers are billed for the correct amount of water that they use. User demands for water are met primarily by insuring that plant capacity is adequate to meet the water requirements of all customers and by remedying customer complaints concerning water service. Control over the latter two items is discussed in the following section.

Accounting for Water Output

Closely allied with the control of revenues is the concept of accounting for the water which is produced and delivered to the distribution system. This concept assists a water utility in increasing the effectiveness and efficiency of its operation.

Total delivery to the distribution system, measured, for example, by a master meter installed in the mains that supply the distribution system with treated water, less water used by customers (metered use and estimated flat rate use), is considered as unaccounted-for water. The determination of customer usage of water is facilitated when all users are metered. Even in a completely metered system some estimate of usage is necessary because all meters cannot be read simultaneously.

Residential, commercial, and industrial use is metered by the majority of water utilities. Public use, with the exception of fire protection, also may be metered. In order to account for treated water, all unmetered usage must be estimated. Estimates of water usage for fire fighting may be based on the number and size of hose streams, pressure, and the length of time water is used. Estimates of water used by street department water trucks, if not metered, may be based on the capacity of each truck and the number of tank loads used. Unmetered treated water used by the utility itself—for

example, to clean filter beds—must also be estimated. The ratio of total water used by customers to total water delivered to the distribution system provides one index to the efficiency of utility operation. A ratio of 85-90 percent, when the use of water is between 100 and 125 gallons per capita per day, is currently considered as good performance. If a utility has a higher per capita use the ratio should be higher.[1] Other factors which must be considered in determining whether or not the ratio of measured use to total water delivered to the system is satisfactory include:

1. Age of system and ground conditions. Water leakage is greater in an old system and it may cost more to locate and repair a leak than to permit it to exist. The more porous the ground the greater the losses through leakage.

2. Pressures and source of supply. The higher the pressure the greater the waste. Whether pressure is maintained by gravity or pumps affects the necessity of reducing unaccounted-for water. If pressure is maintained by gravity then there is little or no production cost, except water treatment. The need for a high ratio is not great because there is little or no pumping expense. If the water supply is ample then the need for water conservation is not as great and the ratio need not be as high as for a limited supply.

3. Quality of materials and workmanship. Higher quality should result in a higher ratio.

4. Use per capita and per mile of main. Higher than normal per capita use for residential, commercial, and industrial customers may indicate substantial leakage. In industrial and thickly populated apartment house areas, the consumption per mile of main can legitimately be high; in residential sections, the use per mile of main should be correspondingly low. In a residential community, leakage may be substantial and a low ratio permissible; for a water utility serving predominately commercial and industrial users, leakage should be less and the ratio high.

5. Amount of underregistration and unauthorized use. The amount of underregistration of meters depends on the meter maintenance program. Unauthorized use, most likely, may occur through unmetered fire lines.[2]

To attain, or to maintain, an acceptable percentage of accounted-for water (or revenue-producing water) in relation to the total treated

---

[1]Committee 4450D, "Revenue-Producing Versus Unaccounted-for Water," Journal American Water Works Association, Vol. 49, No. 12 (Dec. 1957), p. 1588.
[2]Ibid., pp. 1588-1591.

water delivered to the distribution system, programs of the nature suggested below may be conducted by a water utility.

1. An adequate program of meter testing and repair. Residential meters should be tested periodically and repaired or replaced as necessary. The period between testing should be based on experience in each system and on requirements of regulatory authorities.

2. An adequate leakage control program. The frequency of such programs should be determined by experience with program cost and effectiveness. Electronic equipment is available for use in leak detection.

3. Program for collecting operating statistics. Indexes of accounted-for water (or revenue-producing water) to delivered water, per capita consumption figures, and other statistics reflect conditions needing correction.

4. Unauthorized water usage control program. Methods for controlling unauthorized use include the use of detector-type meters in fire lines, comparisons of meters in service to the number of customer billings, and comparison of location of occupied buildings for which no meter reading is made to location of privately-owned wells or other sources of water.

5. Meter reader training and supervision program. Meter readers should be able to read meters accurately and efficiently. In order to attain good performance they must be adequately supervised. Control is further facilitated by rotation of routes among meter readers.

In summary, it may be said that with the increasing cost involved in expanding water utility plant capacity, it is imperative that existing plant capacity be utilized efficiently and effectively. The total accounted-for water (or revenue-producing water) in relation to the total water delivered to the distribution system is an effective measure of the efficiency and effectiveness of operations. By increasing the ratio of accounted-for water to water delivered, the need for expensive programs to increase plant capacity may be minimized, and increased net income should result from increasing the percentage of treated water which can be charged to users.

Controlling Revenues Through Customer Accounting

The term "customer accounting" is used broadly in this book to describe commercial relations with customers, particularly the organization and procedures used to establish and maintain accounts with customers. Customer accounting forms an important phase of a water utility's activities, in that the utility's revenues are derived primarily from charges for service rendered to customers. This phase of the operations of a water utility must be well planned and executed because of the importance of customers as a revenue source, and the expense of providing and maintaining accurate records of all transactions with customers. Providing and maintaining accurate records for each customer is extremely important because unless the records are accurate, the water utility will lose revenues as well as the goodwill of customers.

Customer accounting for a water utility is complicated by the fact that the number of customers served by the utility normally is quite large in relation to the dollar amount of billings. The service line of each customer must be physically connected to the utility's distribution system, each meter must be read periodically, periodic bills must be prepared and rendered to each customer, and a record of receivables for each customer must be maintained. It is apparent, therefore, that the functions of customer accounting include:

1. Opening and closing customer accounts and recording all essential information regarding each customer.

2. Determining at regular intervals the amount of water consumed by each customer as well as the extent of any other services rendered.

3. Billing each customer for water consumed or for other services rendered.

4. Receiving customers' payments and insuring that customers pay their bills.

5. Keeping a proper record of amounts due from each customer by providing for the prompt recording of collections and for the proper crediting of each customer with the amount paid.

6. Handling customer complaints and requests for information.

7. Providing water utility management with revenue and customer information for use in planning and control.

Organization for Customer Accounting. Customer accounting is of concern to those divisions of the water utility whose responsibilities are wholly or in part related to relations with customers. Organization for customer accounting varies substantially among water utilities. In many instances, the organizational structure of the water utility may provide for a single-purpose division, appropriately called the "commercial" or "customer services" division, which is responsible for most of the seven functions listed above. The relationship of the commercial division to other divisions of a water utility is shown in Figs. 6-1 and 6-2.

The commercial division of the utility organizations shown in Figs. 6-1 and 6-2 is responsible for opening and closing customer accounts, issuing orders to set or remove meters or to turn service off or on, reading meters, preparing and rendering bills to customers, receiving customers' complaints, and preparing revenue and customer reports for management. The meter operations shop (assumed to be located in the Operations Section of the Transmission and Distribution Division shown in Figs. 6-1 and 6-2) receives and executes orders from the commercial division to set or remove meters or to turn meters off or on.

Variations from the organizational structure set forth by Figs. 6-1 and 6-2 are to be expected. For example, in some water utilities meter reading may be performed by a meter division which is also assigned the tasks of setting and removing meters, turning meters off or on, and maintaining and testing meters. Further, in municipally-owned water utilities, the responsibilities for other customer accounting functions, such as meter reading, billing, and collecting may be assigned to departments of the municipal government which are external to the water utility organization.

Regulations Governing Water Service.[3] The relationship between the customer and the water utility is typically governed by a set of rules commonly known as "Regulations Governing Water Service." Usually, one section of these regulations specifies the obligation that the water utility has to its customers and a second section specifies the customer's obligations. Although the content and the extent of regulations governing water service varies among water utilities, the regulations customarily include information concerning:

1. Service Area. The regulation concerning the service area usually includes a statement that the utility is required to supply water service to all customers located in the service area, defined as the geographical area within which all water utility property has been dedicated to public service, in accordance with other rules and regulations governing water service. A water utility may also serve customers outside of the area dedicated to public service, although such service is not required.

2. Description of Service. The regulation that describes service provided by the water utility includes information concerning the utility's responsibilities for supplying a given quantity and quality of water, the classes of service provided, and the schedule of rates applicable to various classes of service.

3. Application for Service. The regulation governing application for service sets forth procedures for making application for service, including the stipulation of conditions which require special contracts before service can be rendered to the customer.

4. Establishment of Credit. The regulation governing the establishment of credit sets forth procedures required to obtain a satisfactory credit rating. If all or some applicants are required to make a report to establish credit, information is included concerning the circumstances requiring deposits, amount of the deposit required to establish or reestablish credit, applicability of deposits to unpaid accounts, interest on deposits, and refund of deposits.

5. Service Connections and Meters. The regulation governing service connections and meters includes information concerning ownership of service connections and meters and information concerning the extent of a customer's liability for the cost of installing service connections and meters, for changing the location of meters and services, for changing the size of meters, and for damages to, or loss of, service connections and meters.

6. Meter Readings and Billings. The regulation governing meter readings and billings includes information concerning the frequency of meter readings, the frequency of rendering bills, and due dates for the payment of bills.

7. Discontinuance of Water Service for Cause. The regulation governing discontinuance of service contains conditions which permit the utility to discontinue service, such as for nonpayment of bills, the use of unsafe appliances, fraud and abuse, service detrimental to others, and noncompliance with regulations. The regulation usually provides for the levying of charges for restoration of water service.

8. Other Aspects of Water Service. Other regulations may be included which are concerned with other aspects of water service, such as procedures for giving notice by the utility to the customer or by the customer to the utility regarding the discontinuance of service, remedies for settling disputed bills (including meter tests and adjustment

---

[3]This discussion largely depends upon: American Water Works Association, Water Utility Management Manual, AWWA M5 (New York: American Water Works Association, 1959), pp. 58-70.

of bills for meter error), fire protection service, temporary service, responsibility for damage to property of customer, and interruption in service to make necessary repairs or improvements to the water system.

It is apparent that the procedures employed to establish and maintain accounts with customers must be developed within the context of the regulations governing water service to customers.

Opening New Accounts. The first step in customer accounting is opening a customer's account. The prospective customer usually is required to file an application for service. Sometimes requests for service may be made by telephone or mail in which case an employee fills out the application form based on the information supplied by the applicant. The information required for opening a new account generally includes the date of application, name of the applicant, address of the applicant, location of premises to be served (if different from address of applicant), whether premises have previously been supplied with water by the utility, purpose for which service is to be used, size of service, date of service turn-on, the agreement of applicant to abide by all rules and regulations of the utility, and such other information as the utility may usually require.

In the case of real estate developers, large commercial customers, industrial customers, public authorities, or other large users of water service, who may require construction of extension facilities, special rate schedules, temporary service, connections with other water utilities, standby or fire service, or any other special arrangement, formal contracts are usually prepared to supplement, or replace, the ordinary agreement form.

After the application for service is made, the credit rating of the prospective customer is determined. (Some utilities, particularly municipally-owned utilities whose water charges are, under state laws, a lien against the property served, make no credit investigation of a property owner.) If the prospective customer has no credit rating, or an unsatisfactory one, the utility may require a deposit. (Municipally-owned utilities operating under a lien law may routinely require non-property owners to make a deposit before receiving service.) Utilities which charge flat rates seldom require a deposit since flat-rate charges are normally billed in advance. In most cases, however, the applicant must settle any unpaid water bills, or make arrangements for payment thereof, before water service can be obtained.

If a deposit is required from some or all applicants, a provision may be included in the regulations governing water service that the deposit shall be refunded after it has been held for a stipulated period of time during which all charges to the customer have been regularly paid. The deposit, less the amount of unpaid charges for service rendered by the utility, must, of course, be refunded (or applied to the final bill) upon termination of water service. In some cases, the payment of interest to customers on deposits may be required, particularly for the time beyond a stipulated period during which the customer has paid all bills. The utility must maintain appropriate deposit records for each customer including the name, address, and account number of the depositor, the date the deposit was received, the amount of the deposit, the date and amount of interest payments on deposits, and the date and amount of deposit refunds.

The feasibility of requiring a deposit should be given careful consideration. In the case of small users, the expense of maintaining deposit records and paying interest, where this is necessary, may more than offset the reduction of uncollectible accounts plus the earnings from cash deposits.

As soon as the prospective customer's credit position is found satisfactory, or upon receipt of a service deposit, the customer's application results in an order to establish service which is issued to the meter operations shop. The manner in which the order is executed by the meter operations shop will depend upon the status of the proposed connection. If the service connection is already established, a "turn-on order" (if a meter is presently installed on the customer's premises) or a "meter order" (if a meter needs to be installed at the customer's premises) would be prepared. Some utilities charge the customer for meter installation or the turn-on.

If customer premises have no service connection, an order for the installation of the service connection must be made. Procedures for installing service connections vary among utilities and depend upon the rules of the utility regarding such installations. Frequently the service connection from tap to curb line is installed and paid for by the utility, and the service connection from curb line to meter is installed by the customer's plumber and paid for by the customer. In other instances, the entire installation is performed by the utility and a charge for the cost of a portion of the installation is made to the customer. Procedures also are required for orders to relocate service connections and meters or to change the size of meters. After the order to install the service connection has been executed, a meter order normally is prepared and the procedure is identical to that described for a customer who has service connections at the time of application for service.

The execution of the turn-on order or meter order ordinarily includes reading the meter, turning on the water, and preparing a sketch showing the location of the meter. This information, together with the date on which service was established, is reported to the commercial division for use in preparing meter reading books and billings.

General customers residing within the area served by the water utility's existing distribution system generally can obtain service within a few hours or days after applying for it. For applicants located beyond the utility's distribution mains, delays in obtaining service may be experienced while the utility determines if it is feasible to supply water service and to establish the amount of the applicant's contribution, if any, to the cost of supplying service. Other circumstances, particularly those involving special use of water service, may also necessitate some delay in supplying service to customers.

Meter Reading and Billing Customers. Unless the water utility charges customers on a flat-rate basis, the quantity of water consumed by each customer, as determined by a meter, must be read and recorded by a meter reader at regular intervals.

A very small water utility may be able to have all meters read within a period of a few days and to prepare and mail bills to all customers monthly without placing an undue work burden on the utility clerical personnel. Ordinarily, however, meter reading and billing should be scheduled continuously throughout each month in order to provide level work loads. To implement a plan for continuous meter reading and billing, the area served by the water utility may be divided into meter reading zones. Routes within zones should be rotated among meter readers as an internal control measure.

Meter reading activity must be coordinated with the billing activity, if the work load of each section is to be even. In order to aid in attaining this objective, water utilities often use cycle billing. For example, if the service area is divided into six districts, three may be read during one month and the other three districts read during the succeeding month, with a reasonably constant number of routes being scheduled to be read each working day. At the end of each day the meter readings are sent to the billing department for processing. In this example each customer would receive a bill every two months. If desired, billings may be

made each month on the basis of estimated charges for months during which meters are not read.

There are various other ways to organize meter reading activities, limited only by the reading and billing frequency desired, the number of meter readers available to the utility, and the cost of such activities. The work schedule should be planned, of course, so that meter readings are conducted on a continuous and even basis throughout each month.

To assist the meter reader, and for billing and control purposes, a meter sheet is prepared for each customer. This sheet, which shows the name, address, and account number of the customer, the meter number, and previous meter readings, is initially prepared from the data recorded on the turn-on order or the meter order.

The meter sheets should at all times represent the actual situation with respect to all meters to be read within the service area. From the information contained on meter orders, and turn-on and turn-off orders, an up-to-date file may be maintained by district, zone, and route, in which a record of all meters set or removed is maintained (by meter number), and which shows a record of all meters in service (by meter number). Meter sheets, arranged by district, zone, and route, may then be checked periodically against the meter file to insure that all meters in service are being read. The meter sheets, which may be kept by the billing section, are ordinarily grouped by route number. The meter sheets for each route, in turn, may be arranged in the order in which the meter reader will visit customers' premises. Normally, a sufficient number of meter sheets will be included in a meter book to constitute a day's work for the meter reader.

If the utility utilizes electronic data processing, or punched card equipment, the customer's meter readings and periodic water consumption may be entered on a punched card by the meter reader, rather than on a meter sheet. There are a variety of ways in which this may be done. For example, the reading may be recorded as a series of marks in designated spots on the punched cards. These marks are made by use of a special pencil or pen, and are "sensed" by equipment which punches the reading into the card. In other instances, punched cards prescored to be punched out by the meter reader by use of a pencil point or a special tool may be used, or a punch (similiar to a conductor's punch) may be used by the meter reader to record meter readings on the punched cards. Other utilities prefer to have punched cards prepared in the office from meter sheets prepared by meter readers. Once the current meter reading data are available in machine processible form the machine can match the data with the prior reading for the same customer and prepare the bill automatically.

Unless curb meters are used throughout a route, it is safe to assume that a meter reader will be unable to read all meters on a given route on the day scheduled. Many different procedures are followed with respect to missed readings. One is for the meter reader to leave a self-addressed post card requesting the customer to read the meter, record readings on the card, and mail the card promptly. Other water utilities require the meter reader to return to the location the same day or the next day. Still other utilities have personnel whose duty it is to secure missed readings. Others simply send estimated bills to customers whose meters were not read. The latter is considered the most economical procedure and appears to provide adequate control from the revenue standpoint as well as the cost standpoint, as long as two or more consecutive estimated bills are not permitted.

Some water utilities require each meter reader to compute the quantity of water consumed at the time the meter is read so that he can note any abnormal consumption and make preliminary tests himself, recording his finding on the meter sheet. Whether the computation of consumption is made by the meter reader or in the office, proper control requires that meter readings be subjected to a reasonableness test. Abnormal consumption figures may result from erroneous meter readings, leaks, or defective meters.

Recent developments in water metering indicate many new possibilities concerning meter reading procedures. For example, portable meter reading equipment is available that can be used to record readings automatically either on punched cards or magnetic tape. Systems have also been designed that permit readings to be transferred automatically (by utilizing telephone lines) to a central facility for direct processing by computers. Automatic meter reading systems, although expensive to install at the present time, will no doubt become economically feasible in the future.

Customer Billing. Meter reading, billing, and customer record expenses may be reduced in total by extending the period covered by meter readings and billings. However, the saving in expense from an extended billing period would be at least partially offset by the cost of additional working capital required to carry unbilled water sales and by the increased loss from uncollectible accounts. In order to minimize these unfavorable effects, large users may be billed more frequently than average users.

Within the context of the particular meter reading and billing schedules employed by a water utility, there are a number of systems or combinations and variations of systems which may be used by the utility to prepare bills, to process collections, and to maintain records for each customer. It is appropriate for very small utilities to use manual procedures. Bookkeeping machines become appropriate as a utility outgrows manual procedures. As the volume of paper work increases, a utility finds it advantageous to convert to a computer system. Smaller utilities may share computer time with other businesses or municipal departments, while larger utilities find it efficient and economical to purchase or lease computers. Regardless of the data processing system employed, the basic considerations involved in developing customer accounting procedures (discussed below) are the same.

Individual customer records should be grouped according to the plan used by the utility to subdivide its service area for meter reading purposes—district, zone, and route in the example given in preceding pages. Bookkeeping controls should be maintained for each subdivision, and the individual account balances reconciled periodically with route control balances, route control balances reconciled with zone control balances, and zone control balances reconciled with district control balances, in order to facilitate discovery and correction of bookkeeping errors. Customer billing data, when summarized, become the source of entries to the Sales of Water revenue account and the current asset account, Customer Accounts Receivable.

All customer accounting systems should provide for the routine verification of each bill to see that consumption has been correctly computed, rates have been correctly applied (including proper application of the service charge or minimum charge, if used), unpaid balances have been correctly carried forward, and all miscellaneous charges have been correctly billed.

The information shown on a customer's water bill, in addition to the name and address of the customer, generally includes the period covered by the bill, present and previous meter readings, quantity of water used during the period, the amount due from the customer for consumption during the period, amounts past due from previous bills (if any), and the total amount due. If a discount is allowed for prompt payment or a penalty charge added for late payment, both the net and gross amounts due should be shown together with the last discount date or first penalty date. Service charges or minimum charges, if applicable, also should be shown. If the bill is subject to sales tax, the law in many jurisdictions requires that the amount of the tax must be indicated separately. For maintenance of good customer relations, information concerning the applicable rate schedule may also be shown so that the customer will be able to verify the accuracy of the charge for service, if he desires. In some municipalities, the water bill is used as a vehicle for charging customers for other services rendered by the municipality, such as sewerage service. In such instances information concerning charges for other municipal services would be included on the bill.

Customer Collections. Upon receipt of payment from customers, the utility must credit individual customer account balances and individual collections must be summarized so that the increase in Cash and decrease in the Customer Accounts Receivable control account can be recorded. In order to provide control over cash and receivables, the person receiving cash by mail or over the counter should have no access to either control accounts or the individual customer accounts. Persons receiving cash must provide for the input into the data processing system of information as to daily collections, properly classified as to customer, route, zone, and district.

When customers' bills are prepared, each customer's account balance is ordinarily increased by the net amount due. Therefore, when a customer does not make payments within the stipulated time period, and a discount is lost or a penalty assessed, the customer's account balance, as well as the route, zone, and district control accounts, must be increased by the amount of the penalty or lost discount. Individual customer accounts and control accounts must also be adjusted to reflect cash refunds for overpayments, bad debt write-offs, and similar items.

No matter how strict the credit and collection policies are, a small number of customer accounts may be expected to become uncollectible. In order to make sure that the credit and collection policies are being followed and that the percentage of uncollectible accounts is reasonable for that particular utility, listings of past-due customer account balances by age, should be prepared periodically. Accounts more than one month past due should be investigated to determine necessary action. Not all customer accounts that are in arrears involve the same degree of risk of nonpayment; therefore, the particular action required to force payment depends on each particular customer. For customers who have paid their bills regularly in the past, past-due accounts are not ordinarily a matter of concern. For customers who are new

or who have unsatisfactory records of payment, some action is required in order to obtain payment. Requests for payment of past-due accounts may be made by various means including post card reminders, telephone calls, and bill collectors.

Customer Inquiries. The handling of customer complaints and requests for information is ordinarily an important part of the work of the commercial or customer services division of a water utility. The nature of customer inquiries is quite varied, and includes complaints or requests for information concerning customer's bills, leaks, water pressure, taste and odor of water, and maintenance of service connections and meters. Customer inquiries should be routed directly to those utility personnel who are able to answer the inquiry to the satisfaction of the customer. If a customer's inquiry involves a problem that cannot be solved immediately, the inquiring customer should be kept informed of the action being taken, and the required action should be taken as promptly as feasible. After action is taken, the customer should be informed.

Information for Management. The commercial division, or other unit primarily concerned with customer accounting, is responsible for generating and supplying information to management for use in planning and controlling revenues. For example, the district control accounts and other summarizations of customer accounting data are the basis for entries necessary to record the monthly transactions concerning accounts receivable and revenues. The recording of these transactions, in a manner consistent with the prescribed system of accounts, is necessary for preparing monthly financial statements for management and other interested groups.

Customer accounting information also may be accumulated in a number of other ways (besides that required for recording transactions in a manner consistent with the system of accounts) for use in management planning and control of revenues. Monthly information can be accumulated and reported by classes of revenue, such as residential, commercial, industrial, private fire protection service, public fire protection service, and sales for resale. Further, revenue information can be analyzed by revenue classes within districts. Other information, such as the total number and type of new customers, the number and nature of customer inquiries, agings of accounts receivable, and bad debt write-offs may also be accumulated and reported, and historical trends in each of these areas presented, if meaningful.

pense, based on actuarial studies, is equal to the amount of the accrual made during the accounting period. A pension fund from which pension payments are made also may be established and maintained through contributions to the fund equal in amount to the periodic reserve accruals. If pension payments are made to retired water utility employees by an insurance company, employee pension expense is determined by the payments to be made by the water utility to the insurance company during the accounting period. In cases where accruals are not recorded in a pension reserve or where annuities are not purchased, employee pensions expense is determined by direct payments made by the water utility during the accounting period to, or on behalf of, retired employees.

Employee pensions expense for the budget period can be estimated by referring to the terms of the pension contract or agreement which indicate the basis for determining the expense. Where accruals are made to pension reserves (and contributions equal to the reserve accruals are made to a pension fund), the amount of the reserve accrual (and associated pension fund contribution) typically is determined by the number of water utility employees and the employees' salaries and wages. If an annuity is purchased from an insurance company, the periodic payments for the purchase also are based on the number of employees and the level of employees' salaries and wages. If no reserve accruals are recorded and no annuities are purchased, pension payments depend upon the number of retired employees and the level of the retired employees' salaries and wages earned during the time of their employment by the utility. While past experience may be useful in estimating employee pensions expense during the budget period, adjustment in historical data will be required for changes in contract terms based on new actuarial studies, for changes in the number of employees covered, and for changes in other factors influencing pensions expense.[4] When the pension contract terms are complex, the employment of the services of an actuary may be advisable.

Generally, retirement systems of municipally-owned water utilities fall into three main categories: (1) water utility employees may be covered by a plan for all municipal employees; (2) the water utility by itself, or as one of many departments of the municipality, may belong to a state-wide plan; or (3) the utility may have its own

retirement system. The amount of employee pension expense under any one of these plans depends upon the regulations and laws establishing the plan. Reference must be made to the particular regulations and laws in order to forecast pension expense.

Forecasting Other Employee Benefits Expense. Expenses associated with other employee benefit programs (e.g., accident, sickness, hospital, and death benefits) also can be estimated by referring to the appropriate contracts or agreements giving rise to the benefit plans and by using past experience regarding the cost of these plans. Historical data will require adjustment for changes in the terms of the contracts, changes in the number of employees covered, and changes in other factors affecting the cost of the employee benefit plans.

Forecasting Other Administrative and General Expenses. Rent expense associated with property used for administrative and general activities can be estimated by referring to existing and proposed lease agreements. Assessments to cover the expenses incurred by state public service commissions, and labor expense and materials and supplies expense incurred for the maintenance of general plant facilities, may be estimated by projecting historical trends. Adjustments of historical data will be required for extraordinary changes in factors influencing the level of these expenses.

Planning Centralized Activity Expenses

A water utility organization typically includes certain centralized activities which provide services to other segments of the organization. Examples of such activities are a central garage which provides transportation services and a central stores department which receives and issues materials and supplies. Since each centralized activity represents a responsibility center, costs associated with rendering centralized services should be budgeted for each centralized activity. Actual costs associated with rendering centralized services are accumulated in clearing accounts and allocated to particular operation and maintenance activities and to particular capital expenditure projects (allocation of centralized activity expenses is discussed later in this chapter). Depending on the size and the complexity of the utility organization, separate clearing accounts may be established for the expenses of

[4] For a comprehensive discussion of procedures for accounting for pension plan expenses, the reader is referred to Ernest L. Hicks, Accounting for the Cost of Pension Plans (Accounting Research Study No. 8; New York: American Institute of Certified Public Accountants, 1965).

transportation, power-operated equipment, stores, fuel stock, shops, and similiar activities.

In connection with stores and fuel stock expenses, the undistributed balances in the clearing accounts at the date of the balance sheet (i.e., the amount of stores and fuel stock expenses reasonably attributable to the inventory of materials and supplies and fuel stock on hand at the balance sheet date) are classified by the NARUC as current assets (see account 163, Stores Expense, and account 152, Fuel Stock Expenses, in the Appendix). In the case of expenses for transportation, power-operated equipment, and shops, any undistributed balances in the clearing accounts as of the balance sheet date are classified by the NARUC as deferred debits (see account 184, Clearing Accounts, in the Appendix).

To illustrate the budgeting process associated with centralized activity expenses, the remaining discussion in this section is devoted to forecasting two of the more common types of centralized activity expenses: transportation expenses and central stores expenses.

Forecasting Transportation Expenses. Transportation services are primarily used by operation and maintenance personnel in the transmission and distribution division, meter reading and bill collecting personnel, and supervisory personnel. The size of the central garage depends on the requirements of the entire water utility organization for transportation services.

Based on the anticipated needs of the water utility for transportation, the manpower, equipment, and materials and supplies requirements must be determined for the budget period. Wages and salaries of the garage supervisor, equipment operators, and equipment maintenance personnel may be budgeted in a manner analogous to the budgeting of other wages and salaries expense previously described in this chapter. Other expenses incurred (e.g., gas, oil, maintenance materials and supplies, depreciation of equipment and garage, and taxes on equipment) in operating and maintaining equipment may be estimated by using historical data regarding each individual piece of equipment modified in accord with anticipated changes in equipment.

Forecasting Central Stores Expenses. In the case of central stores, the major items of expense include wages and salaries, and materials and supplies.[5] Requirements for manpower to operate central stores and the level of materials and supplies needed to perform central stores activities depend on requirements of the water utility organization for the services rendered by central stores. Historical data may be used to budget wages and salaries expense, materials and supplies expense, and other items incurred in operating central stores. Adjustments in historical data may be required due to anticipated changes in factors affecting the expense items.

Summary of Planning Operation and Maintenance Expenses

Effective planning requires that alternative procedures for conducting operation and maintenance activities be evaluated. The combination of procedures which is expected to result in the most efficient use of resources should be the one selected. After determining procedures to be employed, operation and maintenance expenses should be budgeted for each organization responsibility segment, including those performing centralized service activities (such as central garages and central stores) as well as those directly involved with the operation and maintenance of water utility plant facilities, customer accounts activities, sales promotion and advertising activities, and administrative and general activities.

The end result of planning operation and maintenance activities, as described in the preceding sections of this chapter, is an annual budget of operation and maintenance expenses such as that shown in Fig. 11-2.

Controlling Operation and Maintenance Expenses

Effective control over operation and maintenance expenses is mandatory from the standpoint of avoiding frequent requests for changes in water utility rate schedules in response to increasing expenses. Unless operation and maintenance expenses are kept in strict control, frequent and costly rate studies may become necessary, and there is, of course, no assurance that rate increases will always be approved.

Comparing Budgeted and Actual Expenses. Effective management control of operation and maintenance expenses requires that actual results be compared with planned (budgeted) expenses on a routine basis. These comparisons should be made by developing a system of monthly comparative reports of actual and bud-

---

[5] Materials and supplies expense associated with central stores is to be distinguished from the cost of materials and supplies received and issued by central stores.

Figure 11-2
THE WILLING WATER UTILITY
STRUCTURE OF AN ANNUAL OPERATING BUDGET

Statement of Estimated Revenue and Expense
(see Fig. 6-3)

	Budget 19BY
Operating Revenues	$6,930,000
Operating Expenses:	
Operation Expense	$1,663,200
Maintenance Expense	346,500
Depreciation and Amortization Expense . . .	485,100
Taxes	2,564,100
Total Operating Expenses	$5,058,900
Utility Operating Income	$1,871,100

Budgeted Utility Operation and Maintenance Expenses

Cost Center	Budgeted Amount-19BY
Office of the General Manager	$ 36,400
Production Division	748,370
Transmission and Distribution Division	324,850
Commercial Division	268,960
General and Administrative Division	631,120
Total Budgeted Operation and Maintenance Expenses . .	$2,009,700

Transmission and Distribution Division
Budgeted Operating Expenses

Cost Center	Budgeted Amount-19BY
Office of the Division Manager	$ 23,200
Operations Section	116,485
Maintenance Section	185,165
Total	$324,850

Maintenance Section
Budgeted Operating Expenses

Cost Center	Budgeted Amount-19BY
Maintenance Supervision	$ 12,480
Maintenance of Mains and Storage Facilities . . .	61,120
Maintenance of Customer Services	70,365
Maintenance of Meters	41,200
Total	$185,165

Meter Maintenance Shop

Budgeted Operating Expenses	Budgeted Amount-19BY
Salaries and Wages:	
Foreman	$ 5,150
Meter Repairmen	13,435
Laborers	10,105
Total Salaries and Wages	$28,690
Materials and Supplies:	
Small Tools	$ 200
Maintenance Materials and Supplies	10,900
Other	710
Total Materials and Supplies	$11,810
Other Expenses:	
Maintenance of Meter Testing Equipment . . .	$ 210
Utility Services	360
Incidental Expenses	130
Total Other Expenses	700
Total Budgeted Operating Expenses	$41,200

geted operation and maintenance expenses for each responsibility segment of the water utility organization. Figure 11-1 presents an example of a monthly control report for a meter maintenance shop. Similar reports should be prepared for each segment of the utility.

Significant variances between budgeted and actual amounts should be investigated to determine needed corrective action. For example, an unfavorable variance between actual and budgeted chemical expenses might be explained by an unanticipated increase in the price of various kinds of chemicals, an unanticipated increase in the volume of water supplied to customers, or lower-than-expected quality of raw water being received for treatment.

In the case of significant unfavorable variances between actual and budgeted figures, the manager or supervisor in charge of the responsibility segment experiencing the variance should be required to indicate on the monthly report what corrective action, if any, is being taken to alleviate the problem. In no case should a manager or supervisor in charge of a responsibility segment of the water utility organization be held responsible for expenses over which he has no control. For example, expense variances due to the efficiency or inefficiency experienced by a centralized activity (such as a central garage or central stores) which provides services to other segments of the water utility should be attributed to the management of the centralized activity and should not be allocated to the serviced segments as a controllable variance.

The Use of Unit Cost Standards Based on Historical Data. For certain types of work performed by various segments of the water utility organization, unit cost standards can be developed for use in judging the efficiency of the work performed. Unit cost standards also provide the basis for distributing certain expenses, such as those incurred by central garages and central stores, among operation and maintenance activities and among construction projects.

The efficiency of operations is best measured by the relationships between cost incurred and the amount of work accomplished. Work is usually measured in terms of physical units, the cost per unit being determined by dividing total costs applicable to a number of units of work performed by the number of units. The procedure for developing unit cost standards is (1) to establish units of work for the activity, (2) to compile all the elements of cost entering into the performance of the work, and (3) to divide the total cost by the number of units in order to arrive at the cost per unit. Unit cost standards are usually developed from historical cost data for a particular period of time. Periods reflecting abnormal operating conditions should, of course, be eliminated from consideration.

One maintenance activity which leads itself

to the development of a unit cost standard is painting fire hydrants. The standard cost per hydrant can be used to evaluate the efficiency of current performance of this activity. Unit standards should also be developed for all other maintenance activities which involve a significant annual expense.

Unit cost standards also may be used to judge the performance of pumping and water treatment activities. For example, the current cost of chemicals used per million gallons pumped and the current cost of fuel and power used per million gallons of water pumped could be compared with standard unit costs. In addition, customer accounting costs over a period of time could be compared on a per customer basis. The cost of operating and maintaining transportation and other power operated equipment could be compared on a per mile driven or per hour operated basis.

It should be noted that unit cost standards require periodic updating. For example, changes in wage and salary levels and changes in the cost of materials and supplies associated with a particular activity affect the applicability of existing cost standards for that activity and will necessitate changes in the cost standards. Further, increases in productivity resulting from improved technology or improved management techniques also may affect the applicability of existing cost standards associated with particular activities and, therefore, require the determination of new cost standards.

Reconciling Expense Classifications for Planning and Control With Functional Expense Classifications

There are some expense classifications used for management planning and control purposes which are directly comparable with the functional classification of expenses shown in the Appendix; included among these expense classifications are chemicals expense (for water treatment), fuel or power expense (for pumping), and property insurance expense (considered as an administrative and general expense in the functional classification of expenses). The majority of expense classifications used for management planning and control purposes must, however, be reclassified and reaccumulated in order to determine expenses on a functional basis. For example, the maintenance expense accounts presented in the Appendix (account 676, Maintenance of Meters, for example) include wages and salaries expense, material and supplies expense, and other expense incurred in performing particular maintenance activities.

Wages and Salaries Expense. It is apparent, therefore, that records must be maintained for each responsibility segment regarding the amount of wages and salaries expense incurred with respect to specific activities and jobs performed by that responsibility segment. Generally, wages and salaries expense is allocated among various jobs and activities on the basis of time expended by employees with respect to particular activities or jobs. The time expended is recorded and maintained by the use of individual or group time sheets. Normally, not all wages and salaries paid to employees of a water utility will be classified as expense. If construction work is performed by the utility, the wages and salaries paid to employees engaged in construction activity should be capitalized.

Materials and Supplies Expense. As in the case of wages and salaries expense, records must be maintained for each responsibility segment regarding the amount of materials and supplies expense incurred with respect to specific activities and jobs performed by that particular responsibility segment. Generally, the cost of materials and supplies used is allocated among activities and jobs on the basis of information contained on stores requisition forms. As in the case of labor costs, a portion of the cost of materials and supplies used may require capitalization in the Construction Work in Progress accounts while the remaining portion is allocated to the various operation and maintenance expense accounts shown in the Appendix.

Centralized Activity Expenses. The expenses incurred in performing centralized service functions must also be allocated to particular activities and jobs, including stores expenses, fuel stock expenses, transportation expenses, power-operated equipment expenses, and shop expenses.

Stores expense represents the cost of handling materials and supplies. As materials and supplies are charged to activities and jobs, a proper proportion of the stores expense should be allocated to each activity and job. The amount to be charged is arrived at by applying a predetermined percentage to the cost of materials used. Estimated or actual total stores expenses are divided by the total estimated or actual cost of materials and supplies handled in order to determine the applicable percentage. As mentioned previously in this chapter, the balance in the Stores Expense account at the end of the accounting period should not exceed the amount of stores expenses reasonably attributable to the inventory of materials and supplies. This balance is classified as an asset on the balance sheet, as are balances in other centralized activity accounts. Fuel stock expenses are allocated to activities and jobs in an analogous manner.

Transportation expenses and power-operated equipment expenses must also be allocated to specific activities and jobs. The wages and salaries of equipment operators are allocated to activities and jobs on the basis of information contained on time sheets. The costs of operating and maintaining equipment (i.e., the cost of gas, oil, maintenance materials and supplies, maintenance labor, depreciation of equipment and garage, taxes on equipment, and general overhead) generally are allocated to activities and jobs on the basis of a rate established for each piece of equipment. That is, an individual equipment record sheet is maintained for each piece of equipment on which the costs of operating and maintaining that piece of equipment are gathered. Each activity or job is then charged for the cost of operating and maintaining the equipment on the basis of a rate per hour or mile operated.

Shop expenses include all the expenses connected with operating a central shop. Labor costs and shop overhead may be charged to activities and jobs on the basis of an hourly rate. The cost of materials and supplies may be charged on the basis of actual costs incurred for each activity or job.

Administrative and General expenses ordinarily are not allocated to other functional expense accounts. Administrative and general expenses which are directly traceable to construction activity should, however, be transferred to construction costs and capitalized in Construction Work in Progress accounts.

CHAPTER 12. PLANNING AND ACCOUNTING FOR DEPRECIATION AND AMORTIZATION EXPENSE

Although depreciation is of concern to most enterprises, it is of particular importance in the case of water utilities because of the relatively large investment in water utility plant required to produce a dollar of annual revenue. Amortization expense, similar in nature to depreciation expense, is also a significant item of expense for a typical water utility. This chapter deals with planning and accounting for depreciation expense and amortization expense as elements in the determination of rates, the budgeting of cash flow, and the determination of net income.

Depreciation Expense and Amortization Expense Defined

The NARUC defines depreciation as follows: "'Depreciation,' as applied to depreciable utility plant, means the loss in service value not restored by current maintenance, incurred in connection with the consumption or prospective retirement of utility plant in the course of service from causes which are known to be in current operation and against which the utility is not protected by insurance. Among the causes to be given consideration are wear and tear, decay, action of the elements, inadequacy, obsolescence, changes in the art, changes in demand and requirements of public authorities."[1]

For the purpose of clarifying the preceding definition as well as the discussion in this chapter, the following NARUC definitions are presented:

"Service value" means the difference between the original cost and the net salvage value of utility plant.

"Original cost," as applied to utility plant, means the cost of such property to the person first devoting it to public service.

"Net salvage value" means the salvage value of property retired less the cost of removal.

"Salvage value" means the amount received for property retired, less any expenses incurred in connection with the sale or in preparing the property for sale, or, if retained, the amount at which the material recoverable is chargeable to materials and supplies, or other appropriate account.

"Cost of removal" means the cost of demolishing, dismantling, tearing down, or otherwise removing utility plant, including the cost of transportation and handling incidental thereto.

"Property retired," as applied to utility plant, means property which has been removed, sold, abandoned, destroyed, or which for any cause has been withdrawn from service.

"Service life" means the time between the date utility plant is includable in utility plant in service, or utility plant leased to others, and the date of the retirement. If depreciation is accounted for on a production basis rather than on a time basis, then service life should be measured in terms of the appropriate unit of production.[2]

In view of the NARUC definition of "depreciation," and the definitions of associated terminology, the term "depreciation" is limited to the accounting for original cost. Depreciation accounting for water utilities involves procedures whereby the original cost-less net salvage value of tangible utility plant is distributed over the estimated useful life of the assets in an orderly and rational manner. In addition, the depreciation expense for a particular period of time is that portion of the original cost (less net salvage value) of water utility plant which is allocated to that particular period.

It should be made clear that depreciation, from the standpoint of accounting, is defined in terms of cost. The economic concept of depreciation, on the other hand, involves the process of valuation, that

---

[1] Committee on Accounts and Statistics, National Association of Regulatory Utility Commissioners, Uniform System of Accounts for Class A and B Water Utilities 1957 (Washington D.C.: National Association of Regulatory Utility Commissioners, 1958), p. 2.

[2] Ibid., pp. 2-3.

is, depreciation (appreciation) is measured in terms of the loss (gain) in value of property. The engineering concept of depreciation also differs from the accounting concept. Depreciation, from the engineer's viewpoint, is established by comparing the present physical condition of a depreciable asset against the physical condition of that asset when new.

Amortization Expense. The term "amortization" is defined by the NARUC as follows: "'Amortization' means the gradual extinguishment of an amount in an account by distributing such amount over a fixed period, over the life of the asset or liability to which it applies, or over the period during which it is anticipated the benefit will be realized."[3]

While the NARUC definition of amortization refers to both assets and liabilities (such as bond premium and other deferred credit accounts and liabilities), the discussion in this chapter is limited to the amortization of balances in particular accounts classified under the balance sheet heading "Assets and Other Debits."

It is apparent that the definition of "amortization" is closely associated with the concept of depreciation. However, as defined by the NARUC, the term "amortization" applies to both assets and liabilities, whereas the term "depreciation" applies only to assets. Depreciation expense is associated with distributing the cost of long-term tangible utility plant assets (excluding land), whereas amortization expense is associated with distributing the cost of intangible utility plant assets (limited-term franchises, patent rights, and licenses), limited-term interests in land, improvements on leased property (where the service lives of the improvements is terminable by action of the lease), utility plant acquisition adjustments, and extraordinary property losses (when included as a deferred debit).[4] "Amortization" is, of course, also associated with the distribution among accounting periods of bond premium, bond discount, and bond expense.

The Nature and Significance of Depreciation

Depreciation of utility plant assets is an economic fact which must be given explicit and systematic recognition by both investor-owned and municipally-owned water utilities as a cost of rendering water service. In order to plan appropriate procedures for distributing the cost of a depreciable asset over its estimated service life, it is helpful to understand the forces which tend to limit the service life of the asset.

Causes of Depreciation. Both physical factors and functional factors affect the usefulness of water utility plant assets. Physical deterioration of an asset is due either to wear and tear resulting from use of the asset, or to decay, rot, rust, and corrosion resulting from the action of time and the elements. Physical deterioration generally is capable of being observed, however; observation may be difficult, as in the case of water mains.

The physical lives of water utility plant assets are related not only to wear and tear from use, decay, and similar factors but also the extent to which maintenance is carried out with respect to the assets. That is, maintenance limits depreciation by reducing the effects of physical causes of depreciation. Obviously, failure to make even minor repairs on pumping equipment would quickly terminate the useful life of the equipment. A preventive maintenance policy will greatly prolong the physical life of many water utility plant assets; therefore, the estimated physical life of plant assets is, to a large extent, a function of the maintenance policy of the utility. Considerations in setting maintenance policy are discussed in Chapter 11.

Functional or non-physical causes of depreciation arise from factors external to the operation of the water utility plant. Functional depreciation exists when utility plant assets are no longer adapted to their use. Included among the functional causes of depreciation are obsolescence, inadequacy, and the actions of government authorities. Obsolescence indicates lack of economic usefulness due to new designs, inventions, and other improvements. Inadequacy occurs when facilities are no longer large enough to meet the demand for water service. Actions of government authorities, including regulatory commissions, may require that water utilities make changes in serviceable property so that the welfare (i.e. safety, convenience, or appearance) of the general public, water utility customers, or utility employees is improved. Property relocation due to urban renewal projects and highway construction projects is an example of this.

It is apparent from the above discussion that

---

[3] Ibid., p. 1.

[4] This classification of assets and deferred debits is consistent with NARUC recommendations. In addition, in the case of improvements on leased property where the service lives of the improvements are less than the term of the lease, the cost of improvements allocated to each accounting period is considered as depreciation expense.

there are a number of factors tending to limit the useful life of a plant asset. To the extent that these factors can be forecast with a reasonable degree of accuracy, they should be given consideration in determining the service lives of plant assets.

The Significance of Depreciation Expense to Interested Parties. Depreciation is of importance to a number of groups interested in the affairs of a water utility. The groups which are particularly interested in depreciation include public service commissions, management, customers, taxing authorities, and investors (bondholders and stockholders). Although the discussion in this section emphasizes the significance of depreciation expense, it is equally applicable to amortization expense.

Depreciation is of interest to public service comissions, management, and customers primarily because depreciation expense, as a cost of rendering water service, is an important factor in establishing the structure and level of rate schedules. The annual depreciation expense must be equitably apportioned among customer classes in order to develop a rate schedule based on the cost of supplying water service to each class (see discussion in Chapter 9 devoted to planning the rate schedule). In addition, depreciation is important for establishing rates because accumulated depreciation is an element to be deducted from the original cost (or reproduction cost new) in determining the rate base.

In the case of investor-owned water utilities, appraisals of security values by bondholders and stockholders depends upon the asset values and earnings information included in accounting reports, and upon the maintenance of the capital invested in the water utility. Depreciation accounting helps to determine appropriate balance sheet values for assets, helps to determine periodic earnings, and helps to maintain invested capital by allocating the cost of tangible plant assets over the service life of the assets. The credit standing of the water utility, as well as future earnings, may be jeopardized if present stockholders have profited too greatly from fictitious earnings resulting from inadequate recognition of depreciation expense.

In addition, depreciation expense is of interest to management as an element to be considered in the determination of net income and in the budgeting of cash flow. Depreciation charges are non-cash expenses and, as a result, these charges must be added back to net income to determine cash flow resulting from operations. It should be emphasized that depreciation charges are not a source of cash—the accounting recognition of depreciation expenses does not in itself produce additional funds. The recognition of depreciation expense by management does, however, influence cash flows because it is a factor in setting rates. In addition, management recognition of depreciation expense influences cash flow to the extent that such recognition prevents disbursements for dividends (in the case of investor-owned water utilities) or to the general fund (in the case of municipally-owned water utilities) which would otherwise be made from fictitious earnings resulting from inadequate depreciation charges. Further, depreciation expense, to the extent permitted by tax authorities, will influence cash flows by reducing the income tax liability of investor-owned water utilities. Since depreciation charges are allowable deductions in establishing an investor-owned water utility's liability for income taxes, procedures for calculating depreciation charges and the amount of such charges are of interest to tax authorities. The determination of depreciation charges for income tax purposes is discussed in a later section of this chapter.

Determining Depreciation Expense

Once the decision has been made to purchase or construct depreciable assets, management planning of annual depreciation charges is limited to the determination of the appropriate portion of the cost of the assets which should be allocated to each accounting period in the form of depreciation expense. The determination of periodic depreciation charges involves four steps: (1) estimating the service lives of the depreciable assets; (2) estimating the net salvage value of the assets; (3) selecting a depreciation formula to distribute the cost of assets over their estimated service lives; and (4) applying the selected depreciation formula to the depreciable property.

Each of these steps is discussed in the following sections of this chapter. It should be emphasized that depreciation rates and depreciation charges of investor-owned water utilities, and municipally-owned water utilities under the jurisdiction of state public service commissions, are subject to the approval of the commissions.

Estimating Service Life

The discussion of the factors causing depreciation of plant assets (in a preceding section of this chapter) points up one of the most difficult problems related to depreciation—estimating the service lives of depreciable assets. In estimating the service life of an asset, consideration must be given to a number of causes of depreciation acting simultaneously to terminate the useful life of the asset. Estimates of service life of a plant asset generally are based on the water utility's retirement experience for that type of asset (or the experience of other utilities) and information relating to probable future conditions.

Retirement experience and engineering studies are particularly useful for estimating the service life of an asset if the indication is that physical factors will terminate the life of the asset. In such cases, estimated service life may be expressed in terms of production units such as vehicle miles or machine hours operated. But it is by no means assured that the same causes which terminated the useful life of the same kind of asset in the past will produce similar results in the future. This is particularly true for assets which are exposed predominantly to functional causes of depreciation. Thus, the inability to know which factor, or combination of factors, will ultimately terminate the service life of a depreciable asset results in considerable uncertainty in estimating the useful life of the asset. As a result, the service lives of the majority of depreciable plant assets are expressed in terms of time rather than in terms of production units.

Use of Retirement Experience. Even though the retirement experience does not necessarily provide accurate estimates of future service lives of plant assets, detailed property records or other detailed plant mortality records are useful guides to the future. Past retirement experience can be analyzed by making actuarial studies and plant turnover studies. Actuarial studies require information concerning the retirement age of individual asset items, and retirement frequency curves can then be developed to estimate the average service life of an individual asset item. Whereas actuarial studies require detailed property records concerning individual asset items, plant turnover studies require less detailed information. Plant turnover studies provide estimates of average service life where historical information regarding the retirement age of individual asset items is unknown; that is, turnover studies determine the average service life of a group of individual asset items based on annual additions to, and retirements from, the group.

Use of Other Available Information. In some instances, the water utility may not have sufficient retirement experience or may lack sufficient records of asset retirements which can be used to estimate the service life of an asset or a group of assets. In such cases, retirement experience of other water utilities, information concerning service life provided by equipment manufacturers, or engineering studies may be available for use in making service life estimates.

Estimated service life based on retirement experience or other information described in the preceding paragraph must, of course, be adjusted in light of available information regarding probable future conditions affecting the service life of the depreciable asset. Future conditions may very well alter the relative effect of causes (both physical and functional) of depreciation which existed in the past. In brief, estimates of future service lives of assets are subjective and can reflect only the best informed judgment.

Estimating Net Salvage Value

Since the amount of a periodic depreciation charge is the function of the service value (original cost less the salvage value net of cost of removal) of the depreciable asset, it is necessary that the net salvage value also be estimated. As in the case of service life, net salvage value can only be estimated. Estimated net salvage value may be based on historical information and adjusted for probable future conditions affecting the salvage value and cost of removal.

Selecting a Depreciation Formula

There are a number of depreciation formulas that can be used to distribute the depreciable cost (or service value) of an asset over the estimated service life of an asset. The nature of each common method is discussed below.

Straight Line Method. The straight line method distributes the depreciable cost of an asset in equal amounts to each of the accounting periods during the estimated service life of the asset. Under this method, the depreciation rate per period is determined by dividing the depreciable cost (cost less salvage value), expressed as a percentage of original cost, by the estimated time units (either months or years) in the service life of the asset. Figure 12-1 presents a simplified example of the application of the straight line method; the example is in the form of an equipment ledger card (the use of equipment ledger cards is discussed in Chapter 15, "Accounting for the Cost of Utility Plant Assets"). The straight line allocation method is probably the predominant method used by water utilities for reporting to regulatory authorities and

Figure 12-1
APPLICATION OF STRAIGHT LINE METHOD

PLANT ASSET AND ACCUMULATED DEPRECIATION
SUBSIDIARY LEDGER CARD

ITEM Accounting Machine PRIMARY ACCOUNT CLASSIFICATION Office Furniture and Equipment

DESCRIPTION Excelsior, Model 140 FROM WHOM ACQUIRED Excelsior Company

SERIAL NUMBER R-1734 ESTIMATED SERVICE LIFE 10 years

WHERE LOCATED OR STORED Office COST $2,000.00

PERSON RESPONSIBLE FOR ASSET Office Manager SALVAGE VALUE $200.00 (10%)

DEPRECIATION RATE (YEAR) $180.00 (9%) (MONTH) $15.00 (0.75%)

Date	Description	Asset Account			Accumulated Depreciation			Net Book Value
		Dr.	Cr.	Bal.	Dr.	Cr.	Bal.	
July 1, 1964	Purchase of Asset	$2,000.00		$2,000.00				$2,000.00
Dec. 31, 1965	Annual Depreciation					$ 90.00	$ 90.00	1,910.00
Dec. 31, 1966	Annual Depreciation					180.00	270.00	1,730.00
Dec. 31, 1967	Annual Depreciation					180.00	450.00	1,550.00

Computations:

Original Cost $2,000 (100%)
Net Salvage Value 200 (10% of original cost)
Depreciable Cost (Service value) $1,800 (90% of original cost)

Annual Depreciation Rate = $\dfrac{90\%}{\text{Estimated Service Life}} = \dfrac{90\%}{10} = 9\%$ of Original Cost (or $180 per year)

Monthly Depreciation Rate = 9% ÷ 12 = 0.75% of original cost (or $15 per month)

Figure 12-2
APPLICATION OF A METHOD BASED ON USE

End of Year	Miles Operated	Depreciation Charge	Accumulated Depreciation	Net Book Value
1	16,000	$640	$ 640	$3,360
2	12,000	480	1,120	2,880
3	18,000	720	1,840	2,160
4	20,000	800	2,640	1,360
5	14,000	560	3,200	800

Computations:
Cost of Service Truck. $4,000
Net Salvage Value   800
Depreciable Cost (Service Value) $3,200
Service Life . . . .   80,000 miles
Depreciation Rate ($3200 ÷ 80,000 miles) . . . . $0.04 per mile

others (except the United States Internal Revenue Service), and for determining annual depreciation expense and accumulated provisions for depreciation for use in rate studies.

The straight line method is the only method in which time is considered to be the sole factor, other than asset cost and net salvage value, determining the depreciation charge. It is, of course, unlikely that the service value of an asset will expire uniformly throughout the service life of that asset; physical factors and functional factors which limit service life may cause more loss in service value of an asset in one period than in another. However, unless there is sufficient evidence that the rate of service value expiration differs substantially from one period to another (such as where service value expiration is due primarily to wear and tear from use), the assumption of uniform service life expiration is not unreasonable. In addition, the straight line method is the easiest depreciation method to apply and therefore the most acceptable from an administrative point of view. The use of the straight line method, as opposed to other depreciation methods, permits the recalculation of depreciation charges based on changing estimates of service lives or net salvage values with little difficulty.

Methods Based on Use. Depreciation is sometimes based on use, rather than time. For example, depreciation charges for transportation equipment may be related to vehicle miles driven, or depreciation charges for pumping equipment may be related to hours operated. Methods which allocate depreciable cost based on use are also commonly known as production allocation methods. Figure 12-2 presents an example of the application of depreciation based on use.

Depreciation based on use is appropriate when asset service life is actually a function of use.

However, for many types of assets, service life expiration results without regard to actual use of the assets.

Compound Interest Method. The compound interest method assumes that depreciation in any year will be the same in amount as the increase in the value of a sinking fund established for a period of time equivalent to the service life of the depreciable asset. Annual depreciation expense, therefore, is equal in amount to (1) an annuity that, at an assumed rate of interest compounded annually over the asset service life, will equal the depreciable cost plus (2) the annual interest on the compound amount of the accumulated annuities which are in the theoretical sinking fund during the year. The application of the compound interest method is shown in Fig. 12-3.

As indicated by Fig. 12-3, the compound interest method provides for increasing annual charges for depreciation. The compound interest method of computing depreciation results from a formula which has little or no relationship to the way in which the service life of an asset expires.

Sinking Fund Method. An alternative to the compound interest method is the sinking fund method. As in the case of the compound interest method, the sinking fund method also employs the concept of establishing a hypothetical sinking fund in which a regular periodic deposit is made, and compound interest earned at an assumed rate. Both the compound interest method and the sinking fund method are based on the same mathematical calculations, but the sinking fund method differs from the compound method as to the amount which is recognized as depreciation expense. Under the sinking fund method the annual depreciation expense would be equal in amount to the annuity (the amounts shown in column 3 of Fig. 12-3). The annual credit to the accumulated provision for depre-

Figure 12-3
APPLICATION OF COMPOUND INTEREST METHOD

Year	(1) Balance of Theoretical Sinking Fund Beginning of Each Year	(2) Interest Assumed Earned on Fund Each Year	(3) Annual Contribution Made to Theoretical Sinking Fund at End of Year	(4) Depreciation Expense (2) + (3)	(5) Accumulated Provision for Depreciation	(6) Net Book Value After Current Charge for Depreciation
1	$ 0	$ 0	$ 758.68	$ 758.68	$ 758.68	$9,741.32
2	758.68	45.52	758.68	804.20	1,562.88	8,937.12
3	1,562.88	93.77	758.68	852.45	2,415.33	8,084.67
4	2,415.33	144.92	758.68	903.60	3,318.93	7,181.07
5	3,318.93	199.14	758.68	957.82	4,276.75	6,223.25
6	4,276.75	256.61	758.68	1,015.29	5,292.04	5,207.96
7	5,292.04	317.52	758.68	1,076.20	6,368.24	4,131.76
8	6,368.24	382.09	758.68	1,140.77	7,509.01	2,990.99
9	7,509.01	450.54	758.68	1,209.22	8,718.23	1,781.77
10	8,718.23	523.09	758.68	1,281.77	10,000.00	500.00
		$1,413.80	$7,586.80	$10,000.00		

Assumptions and computations:

1. Total Cost of Asset $10,500.00

   Less: Estimated Net Salvage Value 500.00

   Depreciable Cost $10,000.00

2. Estimated Service Life . . . . 10 years

3. Theoretical sinking fund assumed to earn 6 percent.

4. Amount of an annuity of 1 at 6 percent for 10 years equals 13.180795 (arrived at using annuity tables which employ the formula $\dfrac{(1+i)^n - 1}{i}$ where n represents the number of years and i the rate of interest). $10,000.00 (depreciable cost) ÷ 13.180795 (amount of annuity of 1) equals $758.68, which is the amount that must be contributed annually to a sinking fund for a period of 10 years in order to accumulate an amount equal to $10,000.

ciation account would equal the amount of the annuity plus the annual interest earned by the hypothetical sinking fund (the amounts in column 4 of Fig. 12-3); and the difference between the annual amount charged to depreciation expense and the annual amount credited to the accumulated provision for depreciation account (which is the annual amount earned by the sinking fund) is charged to income (the amounts in column 2 of Fig. 12-3) as a nonoperating expense item.

The use of the sinking fund method has the same net effect on income as does the use of the compound interest method; however, under the sinking fund method, as opposed to the compound interest method, net operating income is greater by the amount of the annual interest earned by the sinking found which is charged to income as a nonoperating expense item. If the sinking fund method is required by a regulatory commission in a given jurisdiction, an undepreciated rate base is used for rate-making purposes to compensate for the fact that less depreciation expense is permitted to be included as an operating expense than under the compound interest method. Based on the necessary assumption that amounts equal to the balance found in the accumulated provision for depreciation account are reinvested in plant assets, Fig. 12-4 shows how the compound interest method and the sinking fund method are reconciled for rate-making purposes. The data used in Fig. 12-4 are based on those presented in Fig. 12-3.

As in the case of the compound interest method, the sinking fund method results in increasing annual accruals to the accumulated provision for depreciation account. This pattern of increasingly greater accruals usually bears little resemblance to asset service life expiration. In addition, the sinking fund method and the compound interest method both present more complex clerical problems than other methods described above.

It may be observed that under the sinking fund method (as well as the compound interest method), the lower the interest rate used to determine the annuity and the hypothetical sinking fund earnings, the closer will be the results of the method to those of the straight line method based on time.

Figure 12-4
RECONCILIATION OF COMPOUND INTEREST METHOD AND SINKING FUND METHOD FOR RATE-MAKING PURPOSES[a]

Compound Interest Method:
Revenue Requirement for Year 6:

Depreciation Expense for Year 6		$1,015.29
Return on Rate Base:		
Net book value of Original Asset at End of Year 5	$ 6,223.25	
Reinvestment in Plant Assets of an Amount Equal to 5 years' accruals to the Accumulated Provision for Depreciation Account	4,276.75	
Total Rate Base in Year 6	$10,500.00	
Rate of Return Allowed on Rate Base	×6%	
Return on Rate Base in Year 6 ($10,500 × .06)		$ 630.00
Revenue Requirement for Year 6		$1,645.29

Sinking Fund Method:
Revenue Requirement for Year 6:

Depreciation Expense for Year 6		$ 758.68
Return on Rate Base:		
Cost of Original Asset	$10,500.00	
Reinvestment in Plant Assets of an Amount Equal to 5 years' accruals to the Accumulated Provision for Depreciation Account	4,276.75	
Total Rate Base in Year 6	$14,776.75	
Rate of Return Allowed on Rate Base	×6%	
Return on Rate Base for Year 6 ($14,776.75 × .06)		$ 886.61
Revenue Requirement for Year 6		$1,645.29

[a] This example shows the calculation of revenue requirements (in the sixth year of the life of a depreciable asset costing $10,500) under two assumptions:

(1) The compound interest depreciation method is used and the depreciated cost of plant assets serves as the rate base.
(2) The sinking fund depreciation method is used and the undepreciated cost of plant assets serves as the rate base.

Operation and maintenance expenses, taxes, and the return on rate base resulting from other plant assets are ignored in determining revenue requirements; their inclusion would complicate the example and would not prohibit the reconciliation of the two depreciation methods.

The use of the sinking fund method (or the compound interest method) with an assumed interest rate of zero is the same as the straight line method based on time.

Sum of the Years' Digits Method. The sum of the years' digits (SYD) method may be used by investor-owned water utilities for income tax purposes. However, the SYD method is not presently acceptable to public service commissions as an appropriate method for determining the depreciation expense portion of the operating expenses of utilities. Under the SYD method, annual depreciation expense is determined by applying a constantly declining fraction to the depreciable cost (service value) of an asset. The applicable fraction to be applied in each year is determined thus: (1) the years of service life of the asset are numbered in reverse order (1 for the last year, 2 for the next-to-last year, until all years in the service life are assigned a number); (2) the sum of the numbers assigned is thus determined; and (3) the applicable fraction for each year has as its numerator the number assigned to the year in question and as its denominator the sum of the numbers assigned to all years. Figure 12-5 presents an example of the application of the SYD method.

Since the method weighs the early years of the service life of an asset with a greater amount of cost than the later years, there is a presumption that service value expires more rapidly in the early years than in the later years. Therefore, the method does recognize the fact that, in some cases, a plant asset makes a greater contribution to revenue when it is new than when it is old. Nevertheless, the method is arbitrary and, in most cases, will not match actual service value expiration.

Double Declining Balance Method. The double declining balance method (DDB) also can be used by investor-owned water utilities for income tax purposes. As in the case of the SYD method, the DDB method is not presently acceptable to public service commissions as an appropriate method for calculating the depreciation expense portion of operating expenses. Under the DDB method, annual depreciation expense is determined by multiplying the undepreciated balance of asset cost by a percentage which is twice the annual rate (computed without adjustment for net salvage value) used for the straight line method based on time. Figure 12-6 presents an example of the application of the DDB method. Like the SYD method, the DDB method seeks arbitrarily to weight the early years of the service life of an asset with a relatively greater amount of the depreciable cost of the asset.

Figure 12-5
APPLICATION OF THE SUM OF THE YEARS' DIGITS METHOD

(1) Year	(2) Annual Depreciation Rate	(3) Depreciable Cost	(4) Charge to Depreciation Expense (2) × (3)	(5) Annual Credit to Accumulated Provision for Depreciation	(6) Balance in Accumulated Provision for Depreciation Account	(7) Net Book Value After Annual Charge
0						$1,800.00
1	5/15	$1,500.00	$ 500.00	$ 500.00	$ 500.00	1,300.00
2	4/15	1,500.00	400.00	400.00	900.00	900.00
3	3/15	1,500.00	300.00	300.00	1,200.00	600.00
4	2/15	1,500.00	200.00	200.00	1,400.00	400.00
5	1/15	1,500.00	100.00	100.00	1,500.00	300.00
			$1,500.00	$1,500.00		

Computations:
Cost of Asset $1,800.00
Net Salvage Value 300.00
Depreciable Cost (Service Value) $1,500.00

Service Life . . . . 5 years
Sum of the Years' digits:
    Year 1 = 5
    Year 2 = 4
    Year 3 = 3
    Year 4 = 2
    Year 5 = 1
          15

Figure 12-6

APPLICATION OF DOUBLE DECLINING BALANCE METHOD

(1) Year	(2) Annual Depreciation Rate	(3) Undepreciated Cost Before Annual Charge	(4) Annual Charge to Depreciation Expense $(2) \times (3)$	(5) Annual Credit to Accumulated Provision for Depreciation	(6) Balance in Accumulated Provision for Depreciation Account	(7) Net Book Value After Annual Charge
0		$2,000.00				$2,000.00
1	.20	1,600.00	$400.00	$400.00	$ 400.00	1,600.00
2	.20	1,280.00	320.00	320.00	720.00	1,280.00
3	.20	1,024.00	256.00	256.00	976.00	1,024.00
4	.20	819.20	204.80	204.80	1,180.80	819.20
5	.20	655.36	163.84	163.84	1,344.64	655.36
6	.20	524.29	131.07	131.07	1,475.71	524.29
7	.20	419.43	104.86	104.86	1,580.57	419.43
8	.20	335.54	83.89	83.89	1,664.46	335.54
9	.20	268.43	67.11	67.11	1,731.57	268.43
10	.20		68.43(a)	68.43	1,800.00	200.00

Computations:

Cost of Asset $2,000.00

Net Salvage Value .... $ 200.00

Service Life .... 10 years

Annual Straight Line Rate(b) $= \dfrac{100\%}{\text{service life}} = \dfrac{100\%}{10} = 10\%$

Double Straight Line Rate $= 10\% \times 2 = 20\%$

(a) Note that depreciation expense in year 10 is not the product of columns 2 and 3. The amount charged to depreciation expense in year 10 is an amount sufficient to reduce cash value of the asset at the end of year 10 to an amount equal to estimated salvage value; in order to accomplish this, depreciation expense in year 10 is slightly higher than in year 9. To avoid the need for increasing depreciation expense in the last year, a formula is available for computing a fixed rate to apply each year to undepreciated asset cost; the computed rate, when applied annually to the undepreciated asset cost, will accumulate depreciation expense over the service life of the asset exactly equal to the depreciable cost of the asset. The fixed rate formula is: $r = 1 - \sqrt[n]{S/C}$ where $r =$ constant rate; $n =$ number of periods in the estimated service life; $S =$ net salvage value; and $C =$ cost of the asset. Applying the formula to our example results in the following fixed rate which is slightly greater than the straight line rate: $r = 1 - \sqrt[10]{\$200/\$2,000} = .2057$.

(b) Annual straight line rate must be computed without adjustment for estimated net salvage value. Compare with Fig. 12-1 where annual straight line rate is computed after consideration of net salvage value.

Methods of Applying Depreciation Formulas to Depreciable Property

There are a number of ways in which the depreciation formulas may be applied to the cost of depreciable assets. Depreciation expense and accumulated provision for depreciation may be accounted for by individual depreciable property items, by groups of property items, by functional groups of plant accounts, or by utility plant as a whole.

Accounting for Depreciation by Individual Property Items. Accounting for depreciation by individual property items requires that depreciation rates be fixed separately for each individual unit of property. Such a procedure is reasonable for large items of property such as pumps and vehicles. When an individual item is retired, the recorded cost of the item is credited to the primary plant account in which the cost of the item is included, and the accumulated provision for depreciation account is charged with the amount of accumulated depreciation related to that particular property item. Generally, a gain or loss from the disposal of the property item will result in, and is measured by, the difference between the net book value (original cost less accumulated depreciation) of the asset and the net salvage value. Accounting for depreciation by individual property items, while providing detailed information concerning accumulated depreciation related to each item, involves a great deal of work. Figure 12-1 presents an example of accounting for depreciation by individual property items.

Accounting for Depreciation by Groups of Property Items. Classes of property consisting of numerous small units, such as meters, having the same or similar service life expectancies, are generally accounted for by groups rather than individual units. In effect, each group is considered as one asset. Consequently, it is necessary to determine an average service life for each group. The aggregate cost of a group of property items having similar service life expectancies is represented by the balance in a primary plant account such as Services, Meters, or Hydrants. Based on the average service life and the cost of the group of similar property items, periodic depreciation expense is determined for the group by applying one of the depreciation formulas described in the preceding section. Typically, the straight line method based on time is employed in conjunction with the group method and a composite depreciation rate is determined for the group (or primary account). The amount of depreciation expense for any period is obtained by applying the composite depreciation rate to the balance in the primary account.

When an individual property item is retired, the cost thereof is credited to the primary plant account in which the cost of the item is recorded, and the accumulated provision for depreciation account is charged for the cost of the item less net salvage value. No gain or loss will result from the disposal of individual property items when they are accounted for on a group basis. This procedure for accounting for retirements of depreciable property is the one required by the NARUC systems of accounts. As discussed in Chapter 9, the NARUC procedure avoids fluctuations in the rate base which would otherwise occur when property is retired and not replaced.

The use of the group method is most logical when primary accounts are composed of the cost of individual property items having similar service life expectancies. However, the use of the group method can be extended to other primary accounts, such as Structures and Improvements, which are composed of the cost of a variety of property items which are not similar in nature and which do not have the same estimated life.

Accounting for Depreciation by Functional Groups of Accounts and by Utility Plant as a Whole. The use of the group method also can be extended to functional groups of primary plant accounts (source of supply, pumping, water treatment, transmission and distribution, and general plant), and even to the depreciable cost of utility

Figure 12-7
COMPUTATION OF A COMPOSITE DEPRECIATION RATE

Asset	Cost	Net Salvage Value	Depreciable Cost	Estimated Service Life	Annual Depreciation Expense
A	$100,000	$10,000	$ 90,000	30	$ 3,000
B	50,000	1,000	49,000	10	4,900
C	60,000	4,000	56,000	16	3,500
D	200,000	0	200,000	40	5,000
	$410,000		$395,000		$16,400

Composite Rate on Cost: $16,400 ÷ $410,000 = 4 per cent.

plant as a whole. The NARUC recommends that water utilities maintain subsidiary records showing the amount of accrued depreciation (as well as the book cost of property retired, the cost of removal, salvage, and other items such as recoveries from insurance) for each functional group of plant accounts. Retirements of depreciable property would be handled in the manner described in the preceding section concerning accounting for depreciation by groups of property items.

Using the straight line method, Fig. 12-7 presents the calculation of a composite rate for a group of assets. Each asset may be considered as an individual property item with the composite rate applicable to a primary plant account, or as a primary account with the composite rate applicable to a functional group of primary accounts, or as a functional group of accounts with the composite rate applicable to the cost of depreciable utility plant as a whole.

Reevaluating the Adequacy of Periodic Depreciation Charges

Since the service life of an asset or group of assets is based on estimates of future conditions, the service life chosen for use in the depreciation computation may prove to be inaccurate. Thus, service life estimates should be reviewed periodically to determine their reasonableness in the light of current knowledge and actual experience.

Remaining-Life Method. The use of the remaining-life method is helpful for maintaining and insuring adequate depreciation charges with respect to a depreciable asset or group of assets. The method is particularly useful in the case of long-lived assets and in cases in which it is difficult to determine with any degree of exactness the service lives of utility properties at the time of their purchase or construction.

The remaining-life method emphasizes estimated remaining service life as opposed to the estimate of total service life. Under this method an estimate of the remaining service life of an asset is made each year. The new estimate of service life is then applied against the undepreciated cost less estimated net salvage value of the asset to determine the depreciation expense for the year. The depreciation expense computed by the remaining-life method is compared with the depreciation expense computed in accord with the method currently in use in order to determine whether current charges are reasonable or if adjustments need to be made. The remaining-life method need not be employed on an annual basis for each asset

or asset-group. It should be used occasionally, however, so that the adequacy of depreciation charges is reviewed at reasonable intervals.

Engineering Studies. Periodic engineering studies are also useful in judging the adequacy of depreciation charges, particularly in cases where the causes of depreciation are predominantly physical in nature. Engineering studies may point up the need for changes in maintenance policies, which, in turn, may affect the adequacy of original estimates of service life.

Alternatives to Depreciation Accounting Based on Cost

A number of alternatives to depreciation accounting based on cost have been advocated for use by water utilities. Two examples are retirement reserve accounting, and depreciation accounting based on purchasing power of the dollar.

Retirement Reserve Accounting. Under retirement reserve accounting, the cost of utility plant assets is recorded in the utility plant accounts at the time the assets are purchased or constructed; then the cost of utility plant assets is charged to expense at the time the assets are retired. This method is based upon the contention that the annual retirements of an established water utility will tend to become uniform from year to year; therefore, based on the assumption that the cost of utilizing plant assets during each accounting period is the same, the cost less net salvage value of assets retired during an accounting period is considered as an expense of the period. The cost less net salvage value of these retired assets is charged to retirement expense, an operating expense item.

Under retirement reserve accounting, a retirement reserve account also is established to equalize any variations, among accounting periods, in the cost less net salvage value of assets retired in each period. Retirement expense can be increased for periods in which the cost less net salvage value of retirements is smaller than normal by increasing the credit balance in the retirement reserve account. Likewise, during periods when the cost less salvage value of retired assets is larger than normal, a portion of the cost less net salvage value of retired assets is charged to retirement expense, and the other portion (the amount in excess of normal) is charged to the retirement reserve account. The determination of an amount considered as normal for an accounting period usually is based on past experience. The balance in the retirement reserve account is not considered as a measure of loss in service value as is the balance in the accumulated provision for depreciation account under depreciation accounting. The sole purpose of the retirement reserve account is to equalize period charges to operating expense.

The retirement reserve method permits the amount considered as normal retirement expense to be manipulated, thereby affecting reported operating results for a given accounting period. Retirement reserve accounting is not considered by the accounting profession and by state public service commissions as an acceptable method of distributing the cost of depreciable assets among accounting periods. Since depreciation accounting provides a systematic and rational procedure for distributing the cost of depreciable assets among accounting periods, and is advocated by the accounting profession and required by state public service commissions, it is recommended that depreciation accounting be used by water utilities.

Depreciation Accounting Based on Purchasing Power of the Dollar. Another alternative to depreciation accounting as described in this chapter has been adopted in countries that have experienced severe inflation. In such countries periodic depreciation charges are based on the asset cost expressed in terms of the purchasing power of the original investment rather than historical cost. The practical justification for this view can be appreciated by water utility treasurers and controllers in the United States and Canada who have had to secure funds for plant improvement and expansion in the face of constantly rising price levels.

In theory, the primary purpose of depreciation accounting based on purchasing power changes is to permit a more meaningful calculation of actual water utility operating expenses and income, for the purpose of establishing realistic rate schedules and to permit the recovery of purchasing power originally invested in plant assets. Depreciation accounting based on purchasing power changes is not generally accepted for financial reporting purposes in the United States and Canada at present, nor is it accepted by tax authorities and regulatory authorities in these countries. Nevertheless, it is a concept which bears consideration by water utility management, regulatory authorities, and other interested groups, if the rate of inflation continues to increase.

Determining Amortization Expense

The determination of periodic amortization expense related to assets and deferred debits gen-

erally presents little problem. The service lives of the assets and deferred debits are established by law or contract (as in the case of limited-term franchises, patent rights, licenses, limited-term interest in land, and improvements on leased property where the service life of the improvements is terminable by action of the lessee) or are established by regulatory commissions (as in the case of utility plant acquisition adjustments and extraordinary property losses). The straight line method generally is employed to compute the amortization expense.

Utility Plant Acquisition Adjustments. The NARUC recommends that water utilities acquiring properties from another utility record such property at the original cost to the first utility devoting it to public service. If the purchase price differs from the original cost, the difference is recorded separately in an account called Utility Plant Acquisition Adjustments. As approved or directed by state public service commissions, the Utility Plant Acquisition Adjustments account balance may be amortized over a period of time with a corresponding charge to an amortization expense account.

Extraordinary Property Losses. The Extraordinary Property Losses account is provided by the NARUC to record extraordinary losses on property abandoned or otherwise retired from service which could not be reasonably anticipated (and therefore could not be avoided through greater accumulated provisions for depreciation or amortization) and which are not covered by insurance. The amounts to be included in this account are authorized or directed by state public service commissions. The period over which the extraordinary property loss is to be amortized or otherwise disposed of is also subject to the approval or direction of the regulatory commission.

Depreciation Expense for Income Tax Purposes

The United States Internal Revenue Code currently permits investor-owned water utilities to elect to use accelerated depreciation methods for tax purposes. These accelerated methods may be applied to the cost of water utility property purchased, or constructed, or reconditioned after 1953. The accelerated methods provide for the depreciation of property at a faster rate than under the straight line allocation method, resulting, for a particular item of property, in larger deductions for tax purposes during the early years of the service life of the property and smaller deductions during the later years. The accelerated depreciation methods permitted include the sum of the years' digits method (see Fig. 12-5 and related discussion) and the double declining balance method (see Fig. 12-6 and related discussion).

In addition, guideline lives are listed by the Internal Revenue Service for use in determining depreciation charges for various classes of property. These guideline lives may differ from the service lives used by the water utility for other than tax purposes. It is apparent that depreciation charges for tax purposes will differ from depreciation charges for other than tax purposes if (1) an accelerated depreciation method is used for tax purposes and straight line method is used for other purposes and, (2) the guidelines of useful lives employed for tax purposes differ from the estimated service lives of assets used for determining depreciation expense for other than tax purposes.

Effect of "Tax" Depreciation on Cash Flows. The use of accelerated depreciation methods for tax purposes has implications both from the standpoint of increasing cash flows and from the standpoint of rate determination. It is apparent that with respect to an individual property item, the use of accelerated depreciation for tax purposes, as opposed to the straight line method, will result in lower income taxes in the early years of the property life and higher taxes in later years. This will, of course, result in additional funds for working capital or plant investment during the early years of the life of the property. In later years, however, cash flows will decrease due to the smaller deduction for depreciation and the resulting increase in taxes. Therefore, accelerated depreciation results in a tax deferral as opposed to a tax saving. From the standpoint of the water utility as a whole, accelerated depreciation will result in a permanent tax saving only if the utility experiences a continual growth in plant investment sufficient to permit high depreciation charges on new plant investment to offset the lower depreciation charges on older plant investment.

Effect of "Tax" Depreciation on Rate-Making. For rate determination purposes, some state public service commissions consider accelerated depreciation methods as resulting in a tax deferral, while others consider the result as a tax saving. Considered as a tax deferral, the commission permits the utility to use accelerated depreciation methods for tax purposes, but requires the use of another method (generally straight line) to determine the appropriate depre-

ciation expense and tax expense for rate-making purposes. Therefore, if accelerated depreciation methods are employed for tax purposes, the actual income tax paid must be adjusted or "normalized" by recomputing income tax expense on the basis of the straight line depreciation. The amount of income tax computed by using the straight line method is charged to the Income Taxes account. The difference between the income tax computed by using the straight line method and the actual tax liability as determined by using accelerated depreciation methods is credited to a Reserve for Deferred Income Taxes account. The Reserve for Deferred Income Taxes is increased or decreased each year as necessitated by the difference between the normalized tax expense and the actual income tax liability.

Generally, the amount accumulated in the reserve for deferred income taxes is deducted from the cost of utility plant to determine the rate base (customers therefore are given free use of plant assets financed from interest-free funds arising from the use of accelerated depreciation methods). If the reserve for deferred income taxes is not deducted in determining the rate base, the water utility would retain the full benefit of accelerated depreciation methods for tax purposes.

If the state public service commission considers the results of accelerated depreciation for tax purposes as a permanent tax saving, water utilities using accelerated depreciation methods are not permitted to establish a reserve for deferred income taxes. For rate-making purposes, actual income taxes paid are considered as the income tax expense and included in the cost of service; however, depreciation expense for rate-making purposes is based on the straight-line method. This approach to the treatment of income taxes resulting from accelerated depreciation is known as the "flow-through" approach; that is, the benefits received from electing to use accelerated depreciation methods for tax purposes are allowed to flow through water customers as reduced rates resulting from the reduction in income taxes.

Obviously, there is little incentive to use accelerated depreciation methods for tax purposes where state public service commissions deny water utilities the benefits accruing from the use of the accelerated methods. This is true under the flow-through approach and under the normalization approach, if the reserve for deferred income taxes is deducted in determining the rate base.

CHAPTER 13. PLANNING FOR TAXES

Tax payments by water utilities comprise a substantial portion of the total cost of rendering water service. Planning and controlling tax expense is of greater concern to investor-owned water utilities than to municipally-owned water utilities since the latter are exempt from payment of federal income taxes and, in most cases, exempt from payment of state and municipal taxes.

However, in the case of a municipally-owned water utility, direct payments for taxes may not serve as the real measure of the tax burden placed on the utility. In measuring the extent of payments made by a municipally-owned water utility in support of government, the cost of free water service to other departments of the municipal government and the amount of cash transferred to the municipal general fund as a "payment in lieu of taxes," as well as direct tax payments, must be determined. Therefore, effective planning and control of the tax burden requires that both direct and indirect tax payments be given consideration.

Accounting for Taxes

Water utilities, particularly investor-owned utilities, are subject to a wide variety of taxes. At the federal level, the major types of taxes to which investor-owned water utilities are subject include income taxes, Federal Insurance Contributions Act (FICA) taxes, and Federal Unemployment Tax Act (FUTA) taxes. Municipally-owned water utilities also may be subject to payment of FICA taxes and FUTA taxes in those cases where states have adopted legislation permitting participation in the federal programs (see discussion in Chapter 5). At The state and municipal level, water utilities are subject to income taxes, property taxes, gross receipts or gross revenue taxes, unemployment insurance taxes, sales taxes on utility purchases, and a variety of other miscellaneous taxes. The nature of the major types of federal, state, and municipal taxes are described in Chapter 5.

The NARUC Account Classification. The NARUC account classification includes two control accounts for tax expense: Taxes Other Than Income Taxes, and Income Taxes (see accounts 408 and 409 in the Appendix). Each of these control accounts should be supported by subsidiary tax expense accounts, the number of which depends upon the number of federal, state, and local taxes for which the water utility is liable.

Tax payments made during a particular accounting period usually do not coincide with the tax expense for that period. Some payments, for example, are properly classified as prepaid taxes allocable to future periods while payment for other taxes properly classified as expenses of the current period are not made until a future period. The NARUC account classification provides for prepaid taxes (see account 165, Prepayments, in the Appendix), and for tax liabilities (see account 236, Taxes Accrued, in the Appendix).

Further, in the case of investor-owned water utilities, the recognition of accelerated depreciation techniques and the investment credit for income tax purposes may give rise to differences between the amount of the income tax payments made for a particular period and the amount considered as the income tax expense of the period. Differences between tax expense and tax liability resulting from the use of accelerated depreciation methods for income tax purposes are accounted for by establishing a reserve account for deferred income taxes (account 265, Miscellaneous Operating Reserves, shown in the Appendix may be used for this purpose).[1] Differences between tax expense and tax liability resulting from the recognition of the investment credit for income tax purposes are accounted for by establishing a deferred credit account for unamortized investment tax credit (account 253, Other Deferred Credits, shown in the Appendix may be used for this purpose).

The total amount of taxes applicable to a given accounting period is not always charged directly to expense, because a portion of the tax liability

---

[1] See the section entitled "Depreciation for Income Tax Purposes" in Chapter 12 for an explanation of the difference between tax liability and tax expense resulting from the use of accelerated depreciation methods for income tax purposes and for an explanation of the accounting treatment of this difference.

may be charged directly to various asset accounts. Any tax payments which are capitalized become expenses as the assets are depreciated and their costs charged as expenses of the appropriate accounting periods. Conditions which warrant the charging of tax payments to asset accounts include:

1. Taxes, including payroll taxes, specifically applicable to construction work, should be considered as a cost of construction and charged to the applicable plant account.

2. Special assessments for street and similar improvements should be included in the appropriate utility plant or nonutility plant account.

3. Gasoline and other sales taxes should be charged as far as practicable to the account which includes the cost of the materials on which the tax is levied.[2]

Not all tax expense incurred by the water utility is included in the two operating expense accounts, Taxes Other Than Income Taxes, and Income Taxes. For example:

1. Taxes applicable to nonutility property or investments should be charged to the account in which the income from the property or investments is included.

2. Taxes assumed by the utility on property leased from others for use in utility operations should be charged to the appropriate rent expense or clearing account.

3. Income taxes on income from utility plant leased to others should be charged to the Expense of Utility Plant Leased to Others account.

4. Where revenues less expense related to merchandising, jobbing, and contract work are considered as nonoperating income, taxes applicable to merchandising, jobbing, and contract work should be charged to the Costs and Expenses of Merchandising, Jobbing, and Contract Work account.

5. If a water utility agrees to pay income taxes on the interest income paid to others, the expense should be charged to the Other Interest Expense account.[3]

Only those taxes which are assessed directly against the water utility are accounted for as part of the utility's own tax expense. There are some taxes levied against customers and employees which the water utility collects and remits the amount collected to the appropriate tax authorities. Examples of taxes which are paid by the water utility but which are not classified as tax expense include: (1) sales taxes, which are levied against customers and which are collected from customers on the basis of separate charges designated on the bills for service;[4] (2) amounts withheld from employees' wages to be applied against the employees' federal and state income tax liability; and (3) amounts withheld from employees' wages as the employees' contribution for FICA taxes.

The Use of Estimates of Tax Expense. In some instances, the final determination of a tax liability cannot be made until after the end of the accounting period to which the tax expense is assignable. In such instances, the tax expense and tax liability must be estimated for financial statement purposes. Of course, if estimates are used for the purpose of making periodic charges to the tax expense accounts and periodic credits to the liability account, Taxes Accrued, adjustments will be required at a later date when the actual tax liability is known in order to account for any differences between estimated and actual taxes payable. In addition to the use of estimates of tax expense for the purpose of preparing periodic statements of income, tax expense estimates must be made to complete the operating expense budget.

Planning Tax Expense

The tax implications of each alternative course of action must be considered by the management of an investor-owned utility, as well as the other financial and nonfinancial factors discussed elsewhere in this book. It should be emphasized that not even the chairman of the board of directors should commit the water utility to any course of action until the tax implications of each practicable method of implementing the decision have been considered.

Decisions regarding expenditures for utility plant assets will affect the amount of property tax paid (by increasing the assessed valuation) and the amount of income tax incurred (by reason of the

---

[2] Committee on Accounts and Statistics, National Association of Regulatory Utility Commissioners, Uniform System of Accounts for Class A and B Water Utilities 1957 (Washington, D.C.: National Association of Regulatory Utility Commissioners, 1958), p. 87.

[3] Ibid., pp. 87-88.

[4] Sales taxes which are levied against customers are differentiated from gross receipts or gross revenue taxes which are levied on the water utility. The amount of the liability for gross receipts or gross revenue taxes is properly considered as part of the utility's own tax expense.

fact that depreciation is a deductible expense for income tax purposes and the fact that an investment tax credit may be recognized for income tax purposes). Further, the evaluation of the choice of leasing or purchasing property must give proper recognition to the tax advantages and disadvantages associated with each alternative (see the section entitled "Lease vs. Purchase" in Chapter 11). In addition, the evaluation of financing alternatives must give due recognition to the tax effects associated with each alternative. For example, interest payments on debt are tax deductible whereas dividend payments on stock (except for a percentage of dividends paid on preferred stock) are not tax deductible. For rate-making purposes, decisions regarding the level of rate schedules will also depend upon planned levels of taxes (since taxes are a cost of rendering water service). The planned level of taxes will, of course, depend upon other decisions regarding financing and capital expenditure activities.

It is apparent that management cannot make proper decisions regarding the activities of the water utility without a knowledge of the tax implications associated with alternative courses of action. Management may be kept aware of these tax implications through the use of a capable staff of tax experts whose duty it is to advise management concerning the tax effects associated with proposed alternatives.

For operating budget purposes, forecasting the liability and expense associated with any particular type of tax requires the application of the estimated tax rate to the estimated tax base to obtain the estimated tax liability and estimated tax expense. In the following sections, forecasting the major types of taxes incurred by water utilities is discussed.

Estimating Income Taxes

The estimation of federal income tax expense for the budget period requires that taxable income be forecast. The appropriate tax rates, expected to be in effect during the budget period, are then applied against estimated taxable income to determine the estimated federal income tax applicable to the budget period.

Taxable net income has no particular relationship to book net income as defined by the NARUC Uniform System of Accounts or net income which is shown in financial reports to stockholders, creditors, and regulatory commissions. Taxable net income is a legal concept which may be defined as gross income (revenue) not specifically exempt from taxation, less deductions (expenses) permitted by law. Revenue and expense items as described in the system of accounts shown in the Appendix usually do not coincide with revenue and expense items includible for income tax purposes.

Estimating Gross Income. The major sources of gross income as defined for income tax purposes include operating revenues, nonoperating revenues, and gains and losses from the sale or exchange of property and investments. Generally, operating revenues, as described in Chapter 9 of this book, are entirely includible in gross income for income tax purposes. The estimate of operating revenues for the tax period (which normally coincides with the annual budget or accounting period) may be determined by the procedures described in Chapter 9. Nonoperating revenues, as described in Chapter 9, are only partially includible in gross income for income tax purposes. Major nonoperating revenue items not included in gross income for income tax purposes are (1) interest earned on state and municipal obligations, and (2) eighty-five percent of dividends received from domestic corporations (the percentage exemption is somewhat less for dividends received on certain preferred stock of public utilities). Nonoperating revenues includible in gross income typically are small in relation to operating revenues. Historical data, adjusted for anticipated changes in revenue levels during the tax period, serve as a basis for estimating taxable nonoperating revenue.

As mentioned in the preceding paragraph, gains and losses from the sale or exchange of property and investments also is a factor in the determination of gross income for income tax purposes and therefore a factor influencing the determination of the utility's income tax liability. However, for general accounting purposes, gains and losses on the sale or exchange of property and investments is not a factor influencing income tax expense. Rather the tax effect of such gains and losses is netted against the gains and losses; these gains and losses net of related income taxes are closed directly to retained earnings or included in an extraordinary item classification on the income statement.

The correct income tax treatment of gains and losses from the disposition of assets, as well as the amount of gains and losses resulting from asset dispositions, may be difficult to determine. The advice of qualified tax consultants (certified public accounts, lawyers, or members of the tax staff of the utility) should be obtained before any decision is made regarding the sale or exchange of assets.

Estimating Deductions. Allowable expenses for income tax purposes as specified by the internal revenue code and regulations occasionally differ from expenses as determined for general accounting purposes. Items classified as operation and maintenance expenses, as described in Chapter 11, generally are allowable deductions for income tax purposes; major expenses such as wages and salaries, materials and supplies, chemicals, fuel, and rent incurred in the performance of operation and maintenance activities are allowable deductions from gross income. However, as described in Chapter 11, to the extent that property losses and injury and damages claims not covered by insurance are estimated, no permissible deduction from gross income is allowed (deductions are limited to those amounts representing actual losses during the tax year which are not covered by insurance). Further, for income tax purposes, a water utility may determine the expense for uncollectible accounts on the basis of a reasonable estimate or on the basis of accounts which actually become uncollectible during the tax year. Either alternative, once chosen, must be followed consistently from one tax year to the next.

In general, budgeted operation and maintenance expenses, as described in Chapter 11, serve as the basis for forecasting deductions from gross income for tax purposes. Expense estimates included in the operation and maintenance expense budget will require adjustment in those instances where the basis for estimating a particular expense item is inconsistent with the basis employed for income tax purposes.

The amount of depreciation expense included as a deduction from gross income for tax purposes may differ substantially from that computed for other than income tax purposes. Factors which may give rise to this difference include:

1. A depreciation method, such as straight-line, may be used for general accounting purposes, whereas an accelerated depreciation method, such as double declining balance or sum of the years' digits, may be used for income tax purposes (see Chapter 12).

2. Estimated service life of depreciable assets for general accounting purposes may differ from guideline lives used for tax purposes (see Chapter 12).

3. Depreciation of utility plant for general accounting purposes is based on original cost (cost of property to the person first devoting it to public service), whereas depreciation for tax purposes is based on cost to the taxpayer.

4. For general accounting purposes, interest during construction (the cost for the period of construction of funds used for construction purposes) may be capitalized and included among asset costs subject to depreciation. For income tax purposes, interest during construction is not an asset cost subject to depreciation (except to the extent of the cost of money borrowed specifically to finance construction).

It is apparent that two separate estimates of annual depreciation expense may be required—one estimate for general accounting purposes and one for tax purposes. If the water utility's income tax liability for any given year is based on a depreciation expense figure which differs from the depreciation expense figure employed for general accounting purposes, regulatory commissions may require that charges to income tax expense be based on depreciation charges employed for general accounting purposes. Such a requirement results in a difference between income tax expense and actual income tax payable for any given year. (See the discussion in Chapter 12 relating to the treatment of the difference between annual income tax expense and the annual income tax liability.)

For tax purposes, depreciation expense may be accounted for by individual property items, by groups of property items, or by total depreciable property as a single asset. Depreciation by individual property items requires that individual depreciation rates be established for each asset. Depreciation by asset groups requires that group rates be established and applied to the cost of each group of assets. Depreciation of property as a single asset requires that a composite rate be developed and applied to the total cost of utility property. (See the discussion in Chapter 12 regarding procedures for applying depreciation formulas to utility plant accounts.)

In general, taxes other than federal income taxes are deductible expenses for federal income tax purposes. A deduction from gross income also is allowed for charitable contributions to qualified organizations. Generally, estimates of contributions can be based on historical data adjusted for contemplated changes during the tax year. Further, interest paid or accrued by the water utility on indebtedness generally is permitted as a deductible expense for income tax purposes. Forecasting interest expense for the taxable year is discussed in Chapter 14.

Water utilities also are permitted a deduction for income tax purposes for a limited portion of dividends paid on a certain type of preferred stock. For general accounting purposes, dividends on preferred stock are treated as a distribution of earnings and not as an item of expense. The estimated deduction from gross income for dividends paid on preferred stock is based on the forecast preferred dividend payout during the tax year.

The preceding discussion concerning the components of gross income and the types of allowable deductions from gross income is intended only to suggest the nature of the problem of forecasting taxable income; it is not intended as a comprehensive study of all the considerations involved in estimating or determining taxable income. Federal tax laws and procedures for determining taxable income are extremely complicated and subject to frequent change; hence, the advice of certified public accountants or other qualified tax consultants or members of the tax department of the utility is required for effective and efficient planning and control of taxable income.

Estimating Tax Rates and Determining Tax Liability. The estimated income tax liability is a product of estimated tax rates and taxable income (gross income less allowable deductions) less any permissible tax credits. Federal income tax rates are set by the Congress of the United States and may vary from year to year. Normally, the best guide as to rates for the budget period is found in rates in effect at the time of budget preparation. However, when legislative bodies are contemplating revisions in income tax rates, the best available information concerning the revisions should be used in estimating income tax rates to be applied to estimated taxable income.

In the case of federal income taxes, a normal tax and a surtax are imposed on an investor-owned water utility's taxable income. The normal tax is a percentage of taxable income and the surtax is a percentage of the amount by which taxable income exceeds a surtax exemption. In addition, certain gains on the disposition of property and investments are subject to a separate capital gains tax.

The federal income tax as determined by the application of the normal tax rate, surtax rate, and capital gains rate is, in certain instances, reduced by tax credits. The primary tax credit available to investor-owned water utilities is the investment credit, which permits investor-owned water utilities to reduce federal income tax liability by a tax credit as a result of investments in certain types of property.

Typically, investor-owned water utilities, in accordance with public service commission requirements, do not consider the allowable investment credit in any tax year to be solely applicable to that year. Instead, the allowable investment credit is reflected in net income over the estimated service life of the property to which the credit applies and not in the year in which the property is placed in service. As a result of this particular treatment, the actual income tax liability in any year will be less than the recognized income tax expense, and the difference is accounted for by establishing a deferred credit account for the unamortized investment tax credit. The amount in the deferred credit account is then written off to income over the life of the property receiving the tax credit.

It is apparent that before capital expenditure decisions are made, managers of investor-owned water utilities should give consideration to the investment credit implications of the decision, since the investment credit will affect cash flows. Likewise, for the purpose of forecasting federal income tax expense, an estimate must be made of the amount of the investment credit associated with the budget period.

The above discussion of estimating income taxes has been primarily related to the federal level. However, in a number of cases, state and municipal income taxes are patterned after the federal income tax. In general, taxable income estimated for federal tax purposes can be used as a basis for income subject to state and municipal income taxes. The estimated state and municipal income taxes depend, of course, on the tax rates expected to be in effect for the budget period. Current state and municipal tax rates, adjusted for anticipated changes in the rates, serve as the basis for estimating rates applicable to the budget period.

Planning Property Taxes

Due to the large investment in plant facilities, property taxes generally comprise a large portion of the tax burden placed on water utilities. Both municipally-owned and investor-owned water utilities may be subject to payment of several different types of property tax. Frequently, too, a water utility pays property taxes to several different taxing bodies, i.e., states, counties, townships, school districts, and cities. The types of property taxes include general property taxes, real property taxes, personal property taxes, tangible property taxes, and intangible property taxes.

Property taxes are based upon the assessed valuation of property held as of a given date. (Property not held on that assessment date is not subject to property taxes.) The assessed value is then multiplied by the tax rate per unit of assessed value (such as per $1,000 of assessed value) to obtain the property tax liability.

Estimating Assessed Valuation. The bases for valuing property vary widely among the various taxing jurisdictions. Assessment of public utilities is frequently done by state agencies rather than by local assessors. In some instances the basis of value is cost-less depreciation; in other instances property valuation may be established by tax assessors who attempt to determine a "fair value" in terms of replacement cost new-less depreciation or in terms of cash or market value. In the case of a general property tax, assessed value also may be determined by the total market value of securities outstanding (stocks and bonds), by capitalizing average earnings (as measured by the results of prior years' earnings), or by a combination thereof. In the case of an intangible property tax, assessed value may be determined by the difference between the value of the utility as a going concern (as measured by capitalized earnings or by market value of outstanding securities), and the value of the physical property (determined by an inspection of individual property items, by cost-less depreciation of utility plant, or by some other measure).

Typically, all property of a water utility is not reassessed on an annual basis. Rather, property, once valued as a whole, is adjusted on an annual basis for the effect of additions to, and retirements of, individual property items. By law, general reassessment of all property must be made periodically in some states.

In estimating the valuation to be assigned to properties owned in order to arrive at estimated property tax liability, assessed value from the preceding year serves as a guideline. Utility management must, of course, adjust the prior year's assessed value for anticipated changes in properties owned during the budget period.

It is well to point out that utility management may take certain actions, or time those actions, to minimize property taxes. For example, management may plan to accomplish retirements of property items before the assessment date while delaying property acquisitions until after the assessment date. To the extent practicable, management may also save taxes by minimizing inventories of materials and supplies as of the assessment date.

Estimating Property Tax Rates. Property tax rates generally vary from year to year. Nevertheless, the best guide to the property tax rate for the budget year is the rate in effect during the current period. Except in years of general reassess-

ment, it is safe to assume that tax rates in the budget year will be somewhat higher than the rates for the current year. Occasionally the basis for property taxes or maximum rates are revised by state legislatures.

Accounting for Property Taxes. Property taxes have been charged against the revenues of various periods including (1) the year in which paid (the cash basis of accounting), (2) the fiscal year of the taxpayer during which the assessment date falls, and (3) the fiscal year of the governmental body levying the tax. The Committee on Accounting Procedure of the American Institute of Certified Public Accountants has taken the position that the most acceptable procedure is for the tax to be accrued over the fiscal period of the taxing authority even though the amount of the property tax has to be estimated for a considerable part of each period. However, the committee indicates that special circumstances may suggest the use of alternative accrual periods. They state that the important consideration is consistency from year to year and that the selection of any one of a number of periods over which property taxes are accrued is a matter of judgment.[5]

Planning Other Taxes

Other major taxes to which a water utility may be subject are the revenue tax, or gross receipts tax, and payroll taxes.

Estimating Revenue Taxes. The revenue tax is easy to administer in comparison with the property tax, and for that reason it is sometimes levied in lieu of the property tax. Revenue taxes may be levied on all operating revenue or on a particular class of operating revenue such as residential sales or commercial sales. Forecast operating revenues for the budget period, as described in Chapter 9 of this book, serve as the basis for determining estimated revenue or gross receipts taxes. In addition to the estimate of operating revenues subject to the tax, revenue tax rates must be estimated. Although rates may vary from year to year, revenue tax rates applicable to the current period serve as the basis for estimating tax rates during the budget period. Adjustments in current rates may be called for if there is evidence that revenue tax rates will be changed by the legislative body imposing the tax.

Payroll Taxes. The major types of payroll tax expenses are social security taxes and unemploy-

[5] American Institute of Certified Public Accountants, Accounting Research Bulletin No. 43 (New York: American Institute of Certified Public Accountants, 1961), pp. 83-84.

ment insurance taxes. Under the federal social security program, FICA taxes are levied upon both employee and employer. Only that portion of the tax levied upon the water utility is treated as a tax expense (see Chapter 5). The FICA tax expense is determined by the number of employees, the FICA tax rate, and the amount of each employee's wages or salary to which the rate is applied. At present (1969), the water utility must pay FICA taxes of 4.8 percent on the first $7,800 of each employee's wages or salary.

To forecast FICA tax expense applicable to the budget period the estimated payroll as forecast for the operation and maintenance expense budget (see Chapter 11), reduced by the amount of salaries and wages exceeding $7,800 per employee, serves as the base against which the FICA tax rate is applied. The product of the eligible payroll and the FICA tax rate results in the budget estimate for FICA tax expense.

Under the Federal Unemployment Tax Act (FUTA), a tax is levied on the employer based on each employee's income (see Chapter 5 for a describtion of the FUTA tax). Investor-owned water utilities having more than four employees are subject to the FUTA tax as described in Chapter 5. Municipally-owned water utilities are subject to the tax under conditions described in Chapter 5. In general, a tax of 3.1 percent is levied against the employer on the first $3,000 of each employee's salary or wages. The state government receives 2.7 percent of taxable wages, while the remaining 0.4 percent goes to the federal government. However, some state laws provide for a merit rating under which a reduction in the state contribution rate is allowed to employers who show a favorable and steady employment record.

To forecast FUTA tax expense applicable to the budget period the estimated payroll as forecast for the operation and maintenance expense budget (see Chapter 11), reduced by the amount of salaries and wages exceeding $3,000 per employee, serves as the base against which the FUTA tax rate is applied. The product of the taxable payroll and the estimated FUTA tax rate for the budget period (consistent with the anticipated merit rating for the utility) results in the budget estimate for FUTA tax expense.

Other Taxes. There are many other varieties of taxes such as franchise taxes based on a flat annual fee or other basis, to which a water utility may be subject. These taxes must also be forecast for inclusion in the annual operating budget. For minor taxes, historical data may be a sufficient guide in estimating for the budget period.

Controlling Tax Expense

The great number and variety of taxes levied on water utilities, as well as the importance of taxes as operating costs, requires that water utility management maintain effective control over the determination and incurrence of tax expense. The existence of a tax department within the utility organization is typical of large water utilities. The tax accountants and lawyers working within the tax department are responsible for the efficient planning and control of tax expense.

The tax department of the utility must insure that managers are aware of the tax implications of operating and capital budgeting decisions. In addition, the tax department is responsible for keeping abreast of current tax developments in order to insure that tax payments are minimized within the context of existing tax regulations and requirements. Further the tax department is responsible for meeting tax reporting and tax payment deadlines in order to avoid the incurrence of legal penalties associated with noncompliance. It is also important that appropriate tax records be maintained for use in justifying the amount of tax payments made, for disputing deficiency assessments, and in settling tax claims with tax authorities.

Periodic reports which compare actual taxes with budget estimates may prove helpful in discovering errors in tax computations. Further, such reports may indicate tax areas requiring additional or more efficient tax planning.

CHAPTER 14. PLANNING AND CONTROLLING THE COST OF MONEY

A large investment in plant assets is required in order for a water utility to render satisfactory water service to customers; the ratio of dollars of investment to dollars of revenue produced is extremely large for water utilities in comparison to most other types of business enterprises, including electric and gas utilities. As a result, obtaining money to finance the initial purchase or construction of a water utility plant, as well as to finance extensions and improvements, replacements, and relocation of plant assets is an important part of management planning and control activities.

There are a number of different financing sources available to the management of both municipally-owned and investor-owned water utilities. However, the use of the various alternative sources of financing is not available to the utility without cost; the cost of money is the price paid for the use of investible funds. It is the responsibility of water utility management to employ that combination of funds from various financing sources which, over the long run, minimizes the cost of the money to the utility. The use of a single source of funds cannot be utilized without bound; there are constraints, either of a legal or economical nature, which act to limit the use of each financing source.

In the sections of the chapter which follow, the nature of the sources of financing available to municipally-owned and investor-owned water utilities is described. In addition, the cost of using these sources and the constraints which limit their use are discussed.

Alternative Sources of Money

The major sources of money available to municipally-owned water utilities include long-term debt (general obligation bonds and revenue bonds), short-term debt, retained earnings, cash flows covered by depreciation charges, and contributions and advances in aid of construction. In the case of investor-owned water utilities, the major money sources available include long-term debt (mortgage bonds and debentures), short-term debt, preferred stock, common stock, retained earnings, cash flows covered by depreciation charges, and contributions and advances in aid of construction.

Long-Term Debt

The purposes for which water utilities may issue long-term securities (bonds in the case of municipally-owned water utilities, and bonds and stocks in the case of investor-owned water utilities) generally are limited. In the case of municipally-owned water utilities not regulated by state public service commissions, the purposes are customarily enumerated by statutes and ordinances under which bond issues are authorized. In the case of investor-owned water utilities and municipally-owned water utilities regulated by state public service commissions, statutes normally permit issuance of securities for the following purposes, subject to commission approval:

1. The acquisition of plant facilities
2. The construction of extensions and improvements to plant facilities
3. The replacement of plant facilities
4. In the case of investor-owned water utilities, the reorganization or readjustment of the capital structures of utilities in connection with a consolidation or merger
5. The repayment of temporary loans.

One very fundamental difference between municipally-owned and investor-owned utilities regarding debt obligations is that municipally-owned utilities often are faced with the legal requirement that they must retire their debt, and that the retirement must be provided for through cash generated during the period of time that the bonds are outstanding. With respect to investor-owned water utilities, corporate debt typically is issued with the intention of refunding such debt at maturity. In effect, investor-owned water utilities obtain debt capital and retain it as a permanent part of their capital structures, whereas municipally-owned water utilities obtain debt capital as needed, but retire it from cash resulting from income, thus replacing debt capital with retained earnings.

General Obligation Bonds. There are a number of types of long-term debt issued by water utilities. In the case of municipally-owned water utilities, long-term debt typically is represented by general obligation bonds and/or revenue bonds. General obligation bonds are bonds issued by the municipality which owns the water utility. These bonds are secured by the full faith and credit and the taxing power of the municipality. Authorization for the issuance of general obligation bonds to finance the capital expenditure activities of a water utility often must be gained through the approval of the electorate, or, in some instances, property owners, in a bond election. If general obligation bonds are issued by the municipality to finance the capital investment activities of the water utility, the utility should be required to service the bonds from its earnings. For all practical purposes, the bond issue is a liability of the water utility. Of course, a new water utility may rely upon the taxing power of the municipality to assist in the servicing of the bonds during the period of time necessary for the utility to become self-supporting. If general obligation bond financing is involved, the use of serial type bonds, which are designed to bring about a discharge of the total obligation by a series of installment retirements (a certain part of the total issue matures each year), has virtually displaced the use of the traditional term bond, the total face value of which matures on one date.

The use of general obligation bonds is limited by state laws. The legal debt limitation is usually expressed as a percentage of assessed valuation within the corporate limits of a municipality. General obligation bonds issued for water utility purposes may, in some instances, be considered a part of the municipal debt and be included in the total debt to determine the remaining borrowing capacity, if any. In such cases, all activities of the municipality are in competition for the remaining capacity; thus, the municipally-owned water utility may be forced to look to other means of obtaining long-term financing such as revenue bonds. Usually, general obligation water bonds are specifically excluded by charter or other provision from the debt limit, or if not, the limit is increased over what it would otherwise be. Consequently, general obligation water bonds are not in competition with the general obligation bonds, issued for other purposes, of the same governmental unit.

Revenue Bonds. Although general obligation bonds are utilized to finance the capital expenditure activities of a municipally-owned water utility, particularly in the early stages of the life of a utility, revenue bonds are becoming the dominant source of capital financing for municipally-owned water utilities. Water utility revenue bonds are bonds which pledge the revenues of the water utility to pay interest and repay principal when due. Revenue bonds are distinguished from general obligation bonds in that revenue bonds are serviced solely from a specific source of revenue. Water revenue bonds are issued by water districts, water authorities, and water departments. In the case of water districts and authorities, all the bonds are, in essence, revenue bonds regardless of the descriptive title employed, since the bonds are serviced from the revenues accruing to the districts and authorities. The authorization for issuing revenue bonds usually is found under existing statutes. Authorization to issue revenue bonds also may be included in the charter of the city, water district, or water authority. In many instances, revenue bonds can be issued without reference to the electorate. Where reference to the electorate is required, frequently a smaller percentage of favorable votes is required for revenue bonds than for general obligation bonds. As is true of general obligation bonds, the use of serial revenue bonds has virtually displaced term issues.

One disadvantage of revenue bonds is that generally they command a higher interest rate than do general obligation bonds. Another disadvantage of revenue bonds concerns the restrictions inherent in them because of such requirements as pledging of all gross revenues for debt service, the setting aside of reserves to cover periods of possible reduced income, replacement of worn-out facilities, and other covenants, which, in effect, give the bondholders a significant degree of control or, at least, influence over the issuer's future financial operations. Further, a broader market exists for general obligation bonds than for municipal revenue bonds.

Mortgage Bonds. In the case of investor-owned water utilities, long-term debt typically is represented by mortgage bonds and/or debentures. Mortgage bonds have specific utility plant and assets pledged as security for the debt. First mortgage bonds have the first lien upon the property named in the mortgage. Second mortgage bonds have a lien on the same property as named in the mortgage associated with first mortgage bonds, but the claims of the second mortgage bondholders can be satisfied only after claims of the first mortgage bondholders are satisfied. Invariably mortgage bonds for investor-owned water utilities mean first mortgage bonds. These first mortgage bonds are usually open-end bonds, which permit the water utility to issue additional first-mortgage bonds as additional bondable value arising from additional utility plant facilities come into existence, and as long as earnings coverage is adequate.

Debenture Bonds. In the case of debenture bonds issued by an investor-owned water utility, the general credit of the utility is the security for the bonds. The issuance of these bonds is not associated with any specific pledge of property. An investor-owned water utility must have a high credit standing if it is to issue debenture bonds advantageously.

The use of long-term debt financing by investor-owned water utilities is limited by sound water utility practice as defined by the marketplace. Customarily the use of long-term debt (bonds and long-term notes) does not exceed 70 percent of total capitalization. The remainder is composed of preferred stock and common stock equity.

The Cost of Long-Term Debt

The annual cost of long-term debt is the interest which is paid on the debt. The annual interest charge on presently outstanding debt is measured by the annual cash payments for interest (as determined by the interest rate stated on the face of the bonds) plus the annual amortization of debt discount less the annual amortization of any premium on debt. In addition, the annual amortization of the cost of issuing long-term debt serves to increase annual interest charges (see Figs. 14-2 through 14-6 and related text concerning methods of amortizing debt discount, debt premium, and issuing costs). The cost of future debt financing can be estimated by referring to the current interest rate (market rate of yield) on similar outstanding debt securities of the water utility and of comparable water utilities.

In the case of municipally-owned water utilities, revenue bonds may bear a slightly higher interest rate than general obligation bonds because the latter are secured by the full faith and credit and the taxing power of the municipality, whereas revenue bonds are secured by a specific revenue source. In the case of investor-owned water utilities, debenture bonds generally carry a higher rate than mortgage bonds of the same utility because of the fact that mortgage bonds receive a preferred claim on specific water utility property. Further, interest rates on bond issues of municipally-owned water utilities generally are lower than on bond issues of investor-owned water utilities because interest income earned by hold-

ers of municipal bonds is exempt from federal income taxation.

The Cost of Short-Term Debt

Many water utilities, particularly investor-owned organizations, issue short-term notes. In addition, water utilities usually maintain a line of short-term credit with one or more banks. Short-term debt is highly significant to water utility financing because the use of monies from short-term borrowing to meet relatively small and frequent financial needs enables a utility to avoid the sizable expenses associated with frequent offerings of long-term securities. The most economical use of debt by a water utility may be to accumulate short-term borrowings over an extended period of time and periodically refund the short-term debt with a reasonably large issue of long-term securities. Further, the use of short-term debt permits the utility to time long-term borrowings so as to obtain the most advantageous conditions for issuing new securities. If long-term interest rates are expected to fall in the future, short-term debt can be used to finance capital expenditure activities until interest rates are at a level favorable to long-term financing. The cost of short-term debt is analogous to that of long-term debt. The cost of short-term debt is measured by explicit interest payments on short-term credit such as in the case of interest payments on short-term bank loans.

The Cost of Preferred Stock

For a part of its equity, a typical investor-owned water utility will have a small block of preferred stock outstanding. Preferred stock has preference over common stock as to dividend payments (dividends of a stated amount must be paid on preferred stock before dividends can be paid on common) and usually has preference over common stock as to repayment of principal in the event of liquidation of the utility. The claims of preferred stockholders are, of course, subordinate to creditor claims. Generally, sound investor-owned water utility practice indicates that preferred stock not exceed 15 percent of total long-term capitalization and that the remainder be composed of up to 70 percent debt, with the balance common stock.

While the payment of preferred stock dividends is not considered as an expense of the water utility and does not affect the determination of net income, the use of monies obtained from the issuance of preferred stock nevertheless represents a cost to the investor-owned utility. The cost of preferred stock is determined in much the same way as is the cost of debt. The annual cost of preferred stock is the amount of dividends paid on the stock. The cost of future financing through preferred stock offerings can be estimated by referring to the current dividend rate on similar new issues of preferred stock of comparable water utilities, or by referring to the ratio of annual dividends per share to the market price of outstanding preferred stock of the water utility under consideration.

There are a number of benefits accruing to an investor-owned water utility from the use of preferred stock as an element in the capital structure of the utility. Since preferred stock typically carries no voting privileges, the ownership by common stockholders is not diluted. In addition, since the participation of preferred stockholders in the earnings of the utility normally is limited, the return on common equity is improved through the issuance of preferred stock (assuming, of course, that the additional earnings of the utility resulting from money invested by preferred stockholders is greater than the cost of preferred stock as determined by the contractual dividend rate). Further, the issuance of preferred stock improves the equity position of the utility, thereby providing a basis for the issuance of additional debt, which improves the return on common equity (again assuming that the additional earnings of the utility resulting from money invested by the holders of the debt instruments is greater than the cost of debt).

The Cost of Common Stock Capital and Retained Earnings[1]

Investor-Owned Utilities. The usual recommendation of financial experts is that common stock and retained earnings should comprise from 15 percent to 30 percent of the capital of an investor-owned water utility. It is generally agreed that there is an economic cost associated with the use of common stock capital even though such cost is not considered as an expense of the investor-owned water utility in determining net income. The determination of the cost of common stock capital is a very difficult and controversial subject. Since there is no contractual rate of pay-

ment for the use of common stock equity as there is in the case of monies obtained from borrowings or preferred stock issues, a concept frequently employed by theorists in corporate finance is that the cost of common stock capital is equal to the return required to attract common stockholders or to cause current stockholders to maintain their holdings.

Many corporate financial theorists maintain that the basis for common stock investment is similar to the basis for bond investment, the fundamental difference being that the monetary return on an investment in bonds can be forecast with more confidence than can the return on an investment in common stock. In the case of common stock, expected returns are comprised of an anticipated stream of dividend payments and anticipated appreciation in the market price of the stock. In theory, therefore, the expected return to common stock investors is the rate at which expected annual dividends and expected annual market price appreciation of the common stock is capitalized to determine the existing market price of the securities. However, since different investors have different views as to expected returns to be realized from common stock investment, it is difficult to determine the theoretical rate of return expected by common stockholders. Therefore, it is necessary that some practical measure be found to determine the cost of using common stock equity.

Assuming that investors are motivated to purchase the common stock of an investor-owned water utility by reason of future dividend income and by reason of expected appreciation in the market price of common stock, then current dividends on common stock may be taken as a measure of one portion of the return required on common equity, namely, future dividend income. Further, it is suggested by financial theorists that changes in the market price of common stock are due in part to changes in book value per share of common stock resulting from retention and reinvestment of earnings, as well as changes in the dividends payout ratio. Assuming a correlation between increases in book value per share and increases in market price per share of common stock, then current retention of earnings may be taken as a measure of the future price appreciation portion of the return required on common equity. As a result, current earnings (current

---

[1] For a further discussion of the cost of capital resources, and of the cost of common stock capital and retained earnings in particular, see: Harold Bierman Jr. and Seymour Smidt, The Capital Budgeting Decision (New York: The Macmillan Company, 1960), pp. 133-161; and Paul J. Garfield and Wallace F. Lovejoy, Public Utility Economics (Englewood Cliffs, New Jersey: Prentice-Hall, Inc., 1964), pp. 123-133.

dividends plus current earnings retained) in relation to the current market price of the water utility's common stock, serves as a measure of the return required on common stock. Therefore, the return on common stock of the water utility, measured by the earnings-price ratio of the stock, reflects the cost of common stock capital to the water utility. This rate of return must be maintained in order to satisfy the common stockholders.

The above described approach is by no means unchallenged. The dividend-price ratio has also been suggested as a measure of the cost of common stock capital. However, if it can be assumed that common stockholders prefer a stable dividend payout policy as opposed to irregular dividend payments, then a margin of current earnings over current dividend payments may be required to maintain stable divident payments; therefore, even if a stream of dividend payments is the prime consideration for investment in water utility common stock, the earnings-price ratio may serve as the best measure of the cost of common stock capital.

Indirectly, retained earnings of an investor-owned water utility also are contributed by common stockholders. It may be reasoned that retained earnings reflect the desire of stockholders to increase their investment in the water utility by permitting a portion of earnings to be reinvested in the company. It is frequently assumed that the cost of using retained earnings is the same as the cost of using common stock capital.

Municipally-Owned Utilities. The capital structure of municipally-owned water utilities also may reflect retained earnings. The use of retained earnings to finance the capital expenditure activities of a municipally-owned water utility results in a cost to water customers in the sense that charges for water service are higher than is necessary to cover current costs of providing the service by the amount used to finance capital expenditures from retained earnings. However, the cost of retained earnings to water customers is offset to the extent that future water rates should be lower than they would be if interest were being paid on funds borrowed to finance capital expenditures. In addition, the cost of retained earnings to customers is reduced to the extent that the utility which finances part of its expenditures from retained earnings generally can borrow at a lower interest rate than a utility which relies exclusively on long-term debt financing.

The Cost of Other Sources of Financing

Depreciation. Cash flows generated by the recognition of non-cash expenses, primarily depreciation charges, in setting rates, are an important internal source of financing to water utilities. (See the section in Chapter 12 entitled "The Significance of Depreciation Charges to Interested Parties" for a discussion of cash flows relating to depreciation charges.)

Cash retained in the utility for the purpose of preserving the original investment in plant facilities should not be recommitted indiscriminately for capital expenditures. Cash retained through recognition of depreciation charges should be regarded as available for alternate investments and should be committed on the most advantageous basis. For example, cash resulting from the recognition of depreciation charges could be used to retire outstanding debt, to finance capital expenditures, or for other purposes. The alternatives should be evaluated on the basis of "opportunity cost." The opportunity cost of using cash generated by the recognition of depreciation charges for a given purpose is the earnings foregone by not investing the cash in the next best alternative use. Cash retained through the recognition of depreciation charges should be employed for that purpose which minimizes opportunity cost.

Contributions and Customer Advances for Construction. The significance of contributions and customer advances for construction varies among water utilities and within the same utility at different times. Contributions or advances for construction are commonly required of customers desiring service which involves main extensions or other significant capital expenditures. Contributions in the form of grants from federal, state, or local governments may also be obtained for the purpose of financing capital expenditures. The use of contributions and customer advances generally is cost free to the utility in the sense that no interest is charged to the utility for the use of these financial resources. Planning and controlling contributions and customer advances for construction is discussed in Chapter 18.

A number of municipalities use special assessments to finance construction of some water utility facilities, particularly water mains and extensions. Special assessments to finance utility construction should be treated as contributions to the utility for construction. The use of cash resulting from special assessments is also cost free in the sense that no interest is charged to the use of these financial resources.

The Return on Rate Base and the Cost of Capital

It should be emphasized that there is a close relationship between the return allowed on the rate base of water utilities which are regulated by state public service commissions and the cost of capital to these utilities. The product of a reasonable rate of return and the allowable rate base must be sufficient to cover the cost of using capital resources.

The cost of using capital resources may be determined as shown in Fig. 14-1. In this illustration the hypothetical water utility has $33,000,000 of long-term debt outstanding, $4,500,000 of preferred stock, and the total common stock and retained earnings amount to $22,500,000. Applying the cost of each source, as defined in the illustration, the total annual cost of capital is $4,785,000 or approximately 8 percent of the total capitalization. This figure, of course, exceeds the total outlay for interest and dividends for reasons discussed at length in preceding sections of this chapter. The fact that cost of capital is greater than the cash outlays for interest and dividends emphasizes that the financial integrity of the utility can be maintained only if the allowable rate base and allowable rate of return are established at levels that enable their product to be at least equal to the cost of capital.

The weighted average cost of capital reflected in Fig. 14-1 reflects the historical cost of capital to the utility. Current interest rates on debt and current preferred stock dividend rates, as reflected in the capital market, may differ substantially from the historical rates presently being paid by the utility to its bondholders and preferred stockholders. Therefore, when outstanding bond issues are refunded, or when additional bonds and/or preferred stock are issued, the historical cost of capital will change. The return allowed a water utility should be sufficient to cover not only the historical cost of capital, but also anticipated changes in the cost of capital resulting from new security issues.

The above logic applies to municipally-owned water utilities regulated by state public service commissions, as well as to investor-owned utilities. The cost of capital is an important determinant of a reasonable return. For these municipally-owned water utilities, the cost of capital depends upon one type of capital resource, namely, long-term debt.

Planning the Cost of Money for the Budget Period

Water utility management is responsible for establishing plans for financing the activities of the utility. The financing plan for the budget period should be consistent with the goal of minimizing the cost of money over the long run.

Planning Sources of Financing for the Budget Period. Effective planning of the cost of money requires that various sources of capital be employed in the right combination so that money costs are minimized. The excessive use of a single source of capital tends to increase not only the future cost of the source but also the cost of other sources of financing. For example, under market conditions prevailing during the recent past, the cost of debt capital has been relatively cheap in comparison with equity capital, but only up to a point. The use of debt capital increases the risk and therefore the cost of future bond and stock issues. The margin of protection afforded bondholders decreases as additional debt is issued by the water utility. Provisions in bond indenture agreements which limit the issuance of additional debt reflect the desire of existing bondholders to protect their interests. Similarly, the margin of protection afforded preferred stockholders decreases as additional debt and preferred stock are issued and thereby higher yields are required by prospective preferred stockholders. In the case of common stock, increased use of debt and preferred stock tends to benefit common

Figure 14-1
COMPUTATION OF WEIGHTED AVERAGE COST OF CAPITAL

Source	Book Value	Applicable Rate	Cost of Capital
Long-Term Debt	$33,000,000	5.5%(a)	$1,815,000
Preferred Stock	4,500,000	6.0%(b)	270,000
Common Equity	22,500,000	12.0%(c)	2,700,000
Total	$60,000,000		$4,785,000

Weighted Average Cost of Capital $\dfrac{\$\,4,785,000}{\$60,000,000} = 7.975\%$.

(a) Cost of long-term debt is based on yield to maturity of outstanding debt.
(b) Cost of preferred stock is based on contractual dividend rate.
(c) Cost of common stock is based on earnings-price ratio of common stock.

stockholders as a result of leverage.[2] Obviously, heavy creditor financing when overall earnings are in excess of debt capital will greatly augment earnings on common stock. Nevertheless the position of common stockholders is jeopardized by the fact that the additional fixed obligation to pay interest charges on debt and dividends on preferred stock when combined with fluctuations in operating revenues and operating expenses may result in very little net income available to common stockholders. As a result, the return expected and required by common stockholders tends to increase as additional debt and preferred stock are issued.

In general, water utilities, with their large investment in long-lived plant facilities and relatively stable earnings, issue a large amount of debt capital. The reasonableness of the proportion of debt to total capital varies among individual water utilities and depends on each particular situation. As mentioned in a preceding section of this chapter, the use of long-term debt of up to 70 percent of total capitalization generally is considered reasonable for an investor-owned water utility. Practically, a margin for borrowing should be kept available to avoid the issuance of stock during a time of unfavorable market conditions. The retention of earnings in the utility serves to increase the common stock equity base and thereby generates an additional margin for borrowing.

In addition to financing capital expenditures, long-term debt (or stock) may be issued to pay off the principal amount of debt maturing during the budget period or to retire debt before maturity in order to obtain the benefit of favorable market conditions. Further, short-term borrowings also may be planned during the budget period in order to finance anticipated cash shortages and/or to delay the need for long-term debt borrowings until favorable market conditions prevail; short-term borrowings may also mature and need to be paid off during the budget period. Other sources of money which must be considered in developing the plan to finance the activities of the water utility during the budget period include internal sources (retained earnings and cash flows covered by depreciation), contributions, and customer advances for construction.

Forecasting Interest Expense. The financing plan developed for the budget period serves as the basis for forecasting the cost of money for the budget period. The financing plan should, in turn, reflect the desire of management to minimize the cost of money over the long run. Not all costs of money reflect actual cash outlays; some are opportunity costs, such as the cost of using cash retained through depreciation charges. In addition, not all money costs which are reflected, at least in part, by cash outlays are recognized as expenses for accounting purposes; for example, dividends paid on common stock. The only money costs which are recognized as expenses for accounting purposes are the costs (interest) associated with debt.

Outstanding debt at the beginning of the budget period adjusted for proposed debt issues and retirements during the budget period serves as the basis for forecasting interest expense. Major items of interest expense typically include interest on notes, interest associated with lines of credit established with banks, interest on customers' deposits, and interest on bonds.

The interest expense associated with notes outstanding during the budget period can be forecast by referring to the interest rate terms stated on the notes (in the case of notes outstanding at the beginning of the budget period) and/or by applying the current interest rate on notes to the amount of notes to be issued during the budget period. Interest expense associated with lines of credit at banks can be forecast by referring to the existing and/or anticipated interest payment terms accompanying the lines of credit. Historical trends regarding interest paid on customers' deposits, adjusted for anticipated changes in the rate of interest to be paid on the deposits, serve as a basis for forecasting the interest expense associated with customer deposits' held during the budget period.

Estimated interest expense on bonds is measured by the estimated amount of interest to be paid and accrued on bonds during the budget period plus the portion of unamortized bond discount and bond expense which is applicable to the budget period less the portion of unamortized bond premium which is applicable to the budget period. The amount of interest paid or accrued on bonds during the budget period can be forecast by referring to the interest rate stated on the bonds (in the case of bonds presently outstanding) and/or by applying the current market rate of interest on bonds to the amount of bonds to be issued during the budget period.

Debt discount on bonds arises when bonds are sold in the market at a price less than the face

---

[2] Financing with debt capital and preferred stock is frequently referred to as "trading on the equity" or as "applying leverage."

Figure 14-2
SCHEDULE OF AMORTIZATION OF BOND DISCOUNT AND EXPENSE FOR A TERM BOND ISSUE[a]
(Using Effective Yield Method)

(1) Interest Payment Period Number	(2) Nominal Interest Paid ($100,000 × 2.25%)	(3) Interest Charge (Amount in Col. 6 At End of Prior Period Multiplied by Effective Yield, 2.5%)	(4) Amortization of Bond Discount and Expense (3) minus (2)	(5) Unamortized Bond Discount and Expense	(6) Carrying Value at End of Period ($100,000 Less Unamortized Bond Discount and Expense)
				$3,897.29	$ 96,102.71
1	$ 2,250.00	$ 2,402.57	$ 152.57	3,744.72	96,255.28
2	2,250.00	2,406.38	156.38	3,588.34	96,411.66
3	2,250.00	2,410.29	160.29	3,428.05	96,571.95
4	2,250.00	2,414.30	164.30	3,263.75	96,736.25
5	2,250.00	2,418.41	168.41	3,095.34	96,904.66
6	2,250.00	2,422.62	172.62	2,922.72	97,077.28
7	2,250.00	2,426.93	176.93	2,745.79	97,254.21
8	2,250.00	2,431.36	181.36	2,564.43	97,435.57
9	2,250.00	2,435.89	185.89	2,378.54	97,621.46
10	2,250.00	2,440.54	190.54	2,188.00	97,812.00
11	2,250.00	2,445.30	195.30	1,922.70	98,007.30
12	2,250.00	2,450.18	200.18	1,792.52	98,207.48
13	2,250.00	2,455.19	205.19	1,587.33	98,412.67
14	2,250.00	2,460.32	210.32	1,377.01	98,622.99
15	2,250.00	2,465.57	215.57	1,161.44	98,838.56
16	2,250.00	2,470.96	220.96	940.48	99,059.52
17	2,250.00	2,476.49	226.49	713.99	99,286.01
18	2,250.00	2,482.15	232.15	481.84	99,518.16
19	2,250.00	2,487.95	237.95	243.89	99,756.11
20	2,250.00	2,493.89	243.89	- 0 -	100,000.00
	$45,000.00	$48,897.29	$3,897.29		

[a] Schedule relates to the sale of $100,000 face value (4-1/2 percent) 10 year bonds, interest payable semi-annually. Bonds were sold at a price of $96,102.71 (net of bond issue expense). Therefore, effective yield is 5 percent per year or 2-1/2 percent per interest payment period as determined from bond tables.

value of the bonds; as a result, the bonds yield a rate of return to the investor higher than the interest rate stated on the bonds. Bond debt expense refers to the cost of issuing bonds. Bond discount and expense are amortized over the life of bonds to which the discount and expense apply. The portion of unamortized bond discount and expense on outstanding bonds which is applicable to the budget period is determined by referring to bond discount and expense amortization schedules. A schedule should be maintained for each bond issue.

The most common methods used to schedule bond discount and expense are (1) the effective yield method, (2) the straight line method, and (3) the bonds outstanding method.

The effective yield method of amortizing bond discount and expense is based on the proposition that the interest charges relating to a bond issue should be at a uniform rate on the amount received for the bonds less any unamortized bond discount and expense. The uniform rate or effective rate usually is determined by the use of bond value tables.[3] The effective rate is multiplied by the face value of the bonds issued less unamortized bond discount and expense in order to determine the interest charge for the period. The nominal interest paid is then deducted from the interest charge in order to arrive at the amount of bond discount and expense to be amortized. Figure 14-2 depicts a bond discount and expense amortization schedule relating to a term bond, based on the effective yield method. The effective yield method can be applied to serial bonds as well as term bonds; bond value tables usually are employed to determine the effective rate on serial bonds.

The straight line method of amortizing bond discount and expense is much easier to apply than

[3] Two published bond value tables available are: Charles E. Sprague, Extended Bond Tables (New York: The Ronald Press, 1915); and Executive's Bond Value Tables (Boston: Financial Publishing Company, 1947).

Figure 14-3
SCHEDULE OF AMORTIZATION OF BOND DISCOUNT AND EXPENSE FOR A TERM BOND ISSUE
(Using Straight Line Method)

Face Value of 4-1/2 percent, 10 Year Bonds, Interest Payable Semi-Annually	$100,000.00
Sale Price of Bonds (net of Bond Issue Expense)	96,102.71
Bond Discount and Expense	$ 3,897.29
Semi-Annual Interest Payment ($100,000 × 2.25%)	$ 2,250.00
Semi-Annual Amortization of Bond Discount and Expense ($3,897.29 ÷ 20 periods)	194.86
Semi-Annual Interest Charge	$ 2,444.86

Figure 14-4
SCHEDULE OF AMORTIZATION OF BOND DISCOUNT AND EXPENSE FOR A SERIAL BOND ISSUE(a)
(Using Bonds Outstanding Method)

(1) Interest Payment Period Number	(2) Face Value of Bonds Outstanding During Period	(3) Ratio of Bonds Outstanding To Total	(4) Total Bond Discount and Expense	(5) Amortization of Bond Discount and Expense (3) × (4)	(6) Nominal Int. Paid (Face Value of Bonds Outstanding Multiplied by 2.5%)	(7) Int. Charge (5) + (6)
1	$ 100,000	10/110	$2,200	$ 200	$ 2,500	$ 2,700
2	100,000	10/110	2,200	200	2,500	2,700
3	90,000	9/110	2,200	180	2,250	2,430
4	90,000	9/110	2,200	180	2,250	2,430
5	80,000	8/110	2,200	160	2,000	2,160
6	80,000	8/110	2,200	160	2,000	2,160
7	70,000	7/110	2,200	140	1,750	1,890
8	70,000	7/110	2,200	140	1,750	1,890
9	60,000	6/110	2,200	120	1,500	1,620
10	60,000	6/110	2,200	120	1,500	1,620
11	50,000	5/110	2,200	100	1,250	1,350
12	50,000	5/110	2,200	100	1,250	1,350
13	40,000	4/110	2,200	80	1,000	1,080
14	40,000	4/110	2,200	80	1,000	1,080
15	30,000	3/110	2,200	60	750	810
16	30,000	3/110	2,200	60	750	810
17	20,000	2/110	2,200	40	500	540
18	20,000	2/110	2,200	40	500	540
19	10,000	1/110	2,200	20	250	270
20	10,000	1/110	2,200	20	250	270
	$1,100,000	110/110		$2,200	$27,500	$29,700

(a) Schedule relates to the sale of $100,000 face value (5 percent) serial bonds, interest payable semi-annually. $10,000 face value bonds mature each year until entire $100,000 issue is retired after 10 years. Bonds were sold at a price of $97,800 (net of bond issue expense) resulting in bond discount and expense of $2,200 to be amortized over 10 years.

the effective yield method. The bond discount and expense is simply written off in equal increments to each period of the life of the bond. Figure 14-3 depicts a bond discount and expense amortization schedule relating to a term bond based on the straight line method.

A modification of the straight line method, known as the bonds outstanding method, generally is used to amortize bond discount and expense related to serial bond issues. Under the bonds outstanding method, the amount of bonds that will be outstanding at the beginning of each period is determined and these amounts are totaled. Over all periods, a fraction is then determined, the numerator of which is the amount of bonds outstanding during that period and the denominator of which is the total amount outstanding for all periods. The fractions are then applied against total bond discount and expense to be amortized for each period. Figure 14-4 presents a bond discount and

Figure 14-5
SCHEDULE OF AMORTIZATION OF BOND PREMIUM FOR A TERM BOND ISSUE[a]
(Using Effective Yield Method)

(1) Interest Payment Period Number	(2) Nominal Interest Paid ($100,000 × 2.25%)	(3) Interest Expense (Amount in (6) At End of Prior Period Multiplied by Effective Yield, 2%)	(4) Amortization of Bond Premium[b] (2) minus (3)	(5) Unamortized Bond Premium	(6) Carrying Value at End of Period ($100,000 + Unamortized Bond Premium)
				$4,087.86	$104,087.86
1	$ 2,250.00	$ 2,081.76	$ 168.24	3,919.62	103,919.62
2	2,250.00	2,078.39	171.61	3,748.01	103,748.01
3	2,250.00	2,074.96	175.04	3,572.97	103,572.97
4	2,250.00	2,071.46	178.54	3,394.43	103,394.43
5	2,250.00	2,067.89	182.11	3,312.32	103,312.32
6	2,250.00	2,064.25	185.75	3,026.57	103,026.57
7	2,250.00	2,060.53	189.47	2,837.10	102,837.10
8	2,250.00	2,056.74	193.26	2,643.84	102,643.84
9	2,250.00	2,052.88	197.12	2,446.72	102,446.72
10	2,250.00	2,048.93	201.07	2,245.65	102,245.65
11	2,250.00	2,044.91	205.09	2,040.56	102,040.56
12	2,250.00	2,040.81	209.19	1,831.37	101,831.37
13	2,250.00	2,036.63	213.37	1,618.00	101,618.00
14	2,250.00	2,032.36	217.64	1,400.36	101,400.36
15	2,250.00	2,028.01	221.99	1,178.37	101,178.37
16	2,250.00	2,023.57	226.43	951.94	100,951.94
17	2,250.00	2,019.04	230.96	720.98	100,720.98
18	2,250.00	2,014.42	235.58	485.40	100,485.40
19	2,250.00	2,009.71	240.29	245.11	100,245.11
20	2,250.00	2,004.89	245.11	–0 –	100,000.00
	$45,000.00	$40,912.14	$4,807.86		

[a] Schedule relates to the sale of $100,000 face value (4-1/2 percent) 10 year bonds, interest payable semi-annually. Bonds were sold at a price of $104,087.86 (net of bond issue expense). Therefore, effective yield is 4 per-cent per year or 2 percent per interest payment period as determined from bond tables.

[b] Using the straight line method to amortize premium, amortization of bond premium for each of the 20 periods is $204.39 ($4,087.86 ÷ 20 periods) and interest charge for each of the 20 periods is $2,045.61 ($2,250.00-$204.39).

Figure 14-6
SCHEDULE OF AMORTIZATION OF BOND PREMIUM FOR A SERIAL BOND ISSUE[a]
(Using Effective Yield Method)

(1) Year	(2) Nominal Interest Paid (Face Value of Bonds Outstanding Multiplied by 4%)	(3) Interest Charge (Amount in (7) At End of Prior Year Multiplied by Effective Yield, 3%)	(4) Amortization of Bond Premium (2) minus (3)	(5) Unamortized Bond Premium	(6) Redemption ($20,000 Face Value Bonds each year)	(7) Carrying Value at End of Year ($100,000 + Amount in (5) minus (6))
				$2,800.00		$102,800.00
1	$ 4,000.00	$3,084.00	$ 916.00	1,884.00	$ 20,000	81,884.00
2	3,200.00	2,457.12	742.88	1,141.12	20,000	61,141.12
3	2,400.00	1,834.24	565.76	575.36	20,000	40,575.36
4	1,600.00	1,217.26	382.74	192.62	20,000	20,192.62
5	800.00	607.38	192.62	–0 –	20,000	– 0 –
	$12,000.00	$9,200.00	$2,800.00		$100,000	

[a] Schedule relates to the sale of $100,000 face value (4 percent) serial bonds. $20,000 face value bonds mature each year until entire $100,000 issue is retired after 5 years. Interest assumed to be paid annually. Bonds were sold at a price of $102,800.00 (net of bond issue expense). Therefore, effective yield is 3 percent per year, as determined from bond tables.

Figure 14-7
SCHEDULE OF AMORTIZATION OF BOND PREMIUM FOR A SERIAL BOND ISSUE[a]
(Using Bonds Outstanding Method)

(1) Interest Payment Period Number	(2) Face Value of Bonds Outstanding During Period	(3) Ratio of Bonds Outstanding To Total	(4) Total Bond Premium	(5) Amortization of Bond Premium (3) × (4)	(6) Nominal Interest Paid (Face Value of Bonds Outstanding Multiplied By 2.5%)	(7) Interest Charge (6) minus (5)
1	$ 100,000	10/110	$2,200	$ 200	$ 2,500	$ 2,300
2	100,000	10/110	2,200	200	2,500	2,300
3	90,000	9/110	2,200	180	2,250	2,070
4	90,000	9/110	2,200	180	2,250	2,070
5	80,000	8/110	2,200	160	2,000	1,840
6	80,000	8/110	2,200	160	2,000	1,840
7	70,000	7/110	2,200	140	1,750	1,610
8	70,000	7/110	2,200	140	1,750	1,610
9	60,000	6/110	2,200	120	1,500	1,380
10	60,000	6/110	2,200	120	1,500	1,380
11	50,000	5/110	2,200	100	1,250	1,150
12	50,000	5/110	2,200	100	1,250	1,150
13	40,000	4/110	2,200	80	1,000	920
14	40,000	4/110	2,200	80	1,000	920
15	30,000	3/110	2,200	60	750	690
16	30,000	3/110	2,200	60	750	690
17	20,000	2/110	2,200	40	500	460
18	20,000	2/110	2,200	40	500	460
19	10,000	1/110	2,200	20	250	230
20	10,000	1/110	2,200	20	250	230
	$1,100,000	110/110		$2,200	$27,500	$25,300

[a] Schedule relates to the sale of $100,000 face value (5 percent) serial bonds, interest payable semi-annually. $10,000 face value bonds mature each year until entire $100,000 issue is retired after 10 years. Bonds were sold at a price of $102,200 (net of bond issue expense) resulting in bond premium of $2,200 to be amortized over 10 years.

expense amortization schedule for serial bonds based on the bonds outstanding method.

Bond premium arises when bonds are sold in the market at a price greater than the face value of the bonds; as a result, the bonds yield a rate of return to the investor less than the interest rate stated on the bonds. The portion of unamortized bond premium on outstanding bonds which is applicable to the budget period is determined by referring to bond premium amortization schedules; a schedule should be maintained for each series of bonds issued at a premium. As in the case of bond discount and expense, the amortization schedule for bond premium on term issues can be determined by using either the effective yield method or the straight line method. Figure 14-5 depicts a bond premium amortization schedule for a term bond based on the effective yield method. Figure 14-6 presents a premium amortization schedule for a serial bond issue based on the effective yield method. Figure 14-7 depicts a premium amortization schedule for a serial bond issue based on the bonds outstanding method.

If interest is to be charged to construction, then such costs also must be estimated for the budget period. Interest charged to construction is based upon the net cost, during the period of construction, of borrowed funds used for construction purposes and a reasonable rate upon other funds when so used. The proposed capital expenditures budget serves as the basis for estimating interest charged to construction. Estimated interest to be charged to construction during the budget period reduces estimated interest expense otherwise charged as an expense applicable to the budget period.

PLANNING AND CONTROLLING
ASSETS, LIABILITIES, AND EQUITIES

CHAPTER 15. ACCOUNTING FOR THE COST OF UTILITY PLANT

Part Four of this book is concerned with planning and control of the major balance sheet items for a water utility. Accounting for the cost of utility plant is discussed in this chapter. Planning and controlling utility plant are discussed in chapter 16. Planning and controlling current assets and restricted assets are the subjects of Chapter 17. Planning and controlling liabilities and other credits are discussed in Chapter 18.

Water utility plant (or fixed assets) is of primary importance in the operation of the utility. Utility plant constitutes a very large percentage of the total assets of a water utility. It constitutes the principal source of the utility's earning power, and its valuation is of paramount importance in the determination of rate schedules. Because of the importance of water utility plant it is apparent that effective management planning and control of investment in plant assets is a prerequisite to successful operation of a water utility. This chapter is devoted to accounting as an aid to management in the performance of its task of planning and controlling investment in utility plant.

Accounts and Records for Water Utility Plant

Property of a water utility having an expected life of one year or more and employed for the primary purpose of rendering water service to customers (for example: mains, standpipes, pumps, etc.) is classifies as utility plant. In order to aid in understanding the problems involved in planning and controlling investment in utility plant it is worthwhile to review the account classification and nature of the cost elements includible in the utility plant accounts. Readers may wish to refer to the Appendix to note the relationship of utility plant accounts to other balance sheet accounts and to income accounts.

Control Accounts for Utility Plant. The classification of accounts shown in the Appendix provides for the segregation of the cost of utility plant into nine general categories, which serve as control or summary accounts. They are:

1. Utility Plant in Service Classified. This account includes the original cost of utility plant owned and used by the water utility in rendering water service. This account also includes the cost of additions to, and betterments of, property leased from others which is used to provide water service to customers. The cost of property included herein is subclassified in primary (detailed) accounts.

2. Utility Plant Purchased or Sold. This account is charged with the cost of utility plant acquired as an operating unit or system by purchase, merger, consolidation, liquidation, or otherwise, and is credited with the selling price of utility property transferred to others. The balance in this account is only temporary and is cleared by appropriate charges and credits to other accounts, including the other eight utility plant control accounts.

3. Utility Plant in Process of Reclassification. This account includes temporarily the cost of utility plant which has not yet been reclassified in a manner consistent with the NARUC classification of utility plant. This account is cleared as the cost of property included herein is appropriately reclassified into other utility plant control accounts and into the primary (detailed) accounts.

4. Utility Plant Leased to Others. This account includes the original cost of utility plant owned by the utility, but leased to others as operating units or systems. The cost of property included herein is subclassified into primary (detailed) accounts.

5. Property Held For Future Use. This account includes the original cost of property owned and held for future use in utility service under a definite plan for such use. The cost of property included herein is subclassified into primary (detailed) accounts.

6. Completed Construction Not Classified. This account includes the cost of utility plant which has been completed but which has not yet been subclassified into primary (detailed) accounts. The balance in this account is supported by work orders for construction which has been completed (work orders are discussed at a later point in this chapter and in Chapter 16).

7. Construction Work in Progress. This account includes the cost of utility plant in process

of construction but not yet completed. The balance in this account is supported by work orders.

8. Utility Plant Acquisition Adjustments. The difference between (1) the cost to the water utility of utility plant acquired as an operating unit or system by purchase, merger, consolidation, liquidation, or otherwise, and (2) the original cost of such property, estimated if not known, less the amount or amounts credited by the utility at the time of acquisition to accumulated provisions for depreciation and amortization and to contributions in aid of construction with respect to such property, is charged to this account.

9. Other Utility Plant Adjustments. This account includes the difference between the original cost, estimated if not known, and the amount at which property is recorded in other utility plant control accounts to the extent that such difference is not properly includible in the Utility Plant Acquisition Adjustments Account.[1]

In addition to the nine general categories used to classify the cost of utility plant, the classification of accounts provides seven control accounts for recording the accumulated depreciation and amortization of utility plant cost. These seven accounts are:

1. Accumulated Provision for Depreciation of Utility Plant in Service. This account is credited with amounts charged for depreciation of utility plant assets in service. At the time of retirement of depreciable utility plant in service, this account is charged with the cost less net salvage value of the property retired. The extent to which subsidiary accounts are maintained in support of the control account, Accumulated Provision for Depreciation of Utility Plant in Service, depends upon the extent to which charges are accounted for by individual property items, by primary accounts, by functional groups of primary accounts, or by treating, depreciable utility plant in service as a single asset.

2. Accumulated Provision for Depreciation of Utility Plant Leased to Others. This account is credited with amounts accrued for depreciation on utility plant leased to others. The preceding discussion, regarding retirement charges to, and the maintenance of subsidiary accounts in support of, the Accumulated Provision for Depreciation of Utility Plant in Service control account, also is applicable to this account.

3. Accumulated Provision for Depreciation of Property Held for Future Use. This account is credited with amounts charged for depreciation of property held for future use. Normally, this account includes the existing balance of accumulated provision for depreciation of property, when the property is transferred to the account, Property Held for Future Use. Except under special circumstances, current depreciation charges are not made with respect to property held for future use but only are made when property is placed in service (to the extent that a current depreciation charge is recognized on property held for future use, it is considered as a nonoperating expense). The preceding discussion regarding retirement charges to, and the maintenance of subsidiary accounts in support of, the Accumulated Provision for Depreciation of Utility Plant in Service control account also is applicable to this account.

4. Accumulated Provision for Amortization of Utility Plant in Service. This account is credited with amounts charged for amortization of limited-term utility plant in service. When any property to which this account applies is retired from service, the account is charged with the amount previously amortized with respect to such property. Subsidiary records should be maintained so as to show separately the balance applicable to each class of property which is being amortized.

5. Accumulated Provision for Amortization of Utility Plant Leased to Others. This account is credited with amounts charged for amortization of limited-term utility plant leased to others. The preceding discussion regarding retirement charges to, and the maintenance of subsidiary records in support of, the Accumulated Provision for Amortization of Utility Plant in Service control account also is applicable to this account.

6. Accumulated Provision for Amortization of Property Held for Future Use. This account is credited with amounts charged for amortization of limited-term property held for future use. Normally, this account includes the existing balance of accumulated provision for amortization of property, when the property is transferred to the account, Property Held for Future Use. Except under special circumstances, current amortization charges are not made with respect to property held for future use, but are made only when property is placed in service (to the extent that a current amortization charge is recognized on property held for future use, it is considered as a

---

[1] Based in large part on: Committee on Accounts and Statistics, National Association of Regulatory Utility Commissioners, Uniform System of Accounts for Class A and B Water Utilities, 1957 (Washington, D.C.: National Association of Regulatory Utility Commissioners, 1958), pp. 33-39.

nonoperating expense). The preceding discussion regarding retirement charges to, and the maintenance of subsidiary records in support of, the Accumulated Provision for Amortization of Utility Plant in Service control account also is applicable to this account.

7. Accumulated Provision for Amortization of Utility Plant Acquisition Adjustments. This account is credited or debited with amounts recognized for amortization of utility plant acquisition adjustments. Depending upon the directions of the public service commission, the periodic amortization is recognized either as an operating or as a nonoperating expense item.[2]

Primary Utility Plant Accounts. In addition to the proper identification, classification, and recording of the cost of utility plant and the associated depreciation and amortization accruals in the general ledger control accounts, proper accounting for utility plant assets requires that appropriate subsidiary utility plant assets accounts be maintained. As a practical matter, the Utility Plant in Service Classified control account is of primary importance. The other eight general or control accounts used to segregate the cost of utility plant assets are related to more or less temporary items or conditions and are normally of less consequence. Most of these eight accounts, while related to temporary items, may contain balances because the water utility is in the continuing process of constructing and replacing utility plant and may be buying or selling operating units.

In recognition of the importance of detailed information concerning investment in operating properties to efficient management and to sound regulation, the classification of accounts includes a listing of primary accounts in support of the following control accounts: Utility Plant in Service Classified, Utility Plant Leased to Others, and Property Held for Future Use.[3]

The primary utility plant accounts are comprised of both intangible and tangible plant accounts. The intangible plant accounts are classified in a single category while the tangible plant accounts are grouped by functional categories. As illustrated in the Appendix, the categories within which the primary or detailed plant accounts are grouped are:

1. Intangible Plant
2. Source of Supply Plant
3. Pumping Plant
4. Water Treatment Plant
5. Transmission and Distribution Plant
6. General Plant.

The intangible plant accounts require separate accounts for organization cost, franchises and consents, and miscellaneous intangible plant. Within each of the five functional groups of tangible plant accounts, the primary accounts are designed to afford classification of the costs of plant assets by general characteristics such as land and land rights, structures and improvements, and equipment.

Continuing Property Records and the Work Order System. A final requisite of proper accounting for utility plant assets is the maintenance of a continuing property record (CPR) system. Briefly, a CPR system involves the maintenance of a separate record for each unit of utility property. A "unit of property" (or "CPR unit") means an item of property which can be readily identified and accounted for by itself. A single record may, however, be used for a group of small items, such as meters. The property record card for each unit of utility property should contain such complete details on the unit as: (1) any information that will identify the unit of property (name of property item, brief description of the property item, and manufacturer's identification number); (2) location; (3) administrative custody; (4) from whom acquired; (5) when acquired; (6) where taxed; (7) information as to the cost of the asset, estimated service life, net salvage value, and any other factors which are useful for determining depreciation; (8) recorded depreciation (if depreciation is charged by individual property units); and (9) any data, such as account number, which will tie the record in with the proper primary utility plant account. (For examples of property record cards see Figs. 16-9 and 16-10.)

The CPR for each unit of property also must provide for recording changes in the cost of the property unit as a result of additions, replacements, and retirements. The recording of changes in the cost of a property unit as a result of additions, replacements, and retirements is based on

---

[2]Ibid., pp. 35-39.

[3]Normally, the control account, Utility Plant in Process of Reclassification, also would be supported by detailed accounts. However, the detailed accounts employed may differ from those presently recommended by the NARUC, since such a difference is one reason for categorizing the assets as Utility Plant in Process of Reclassification. The Utility Plant in Process of Reclassification account represents a clearing account until audit and analysis permits the asset costs to be reclassified in a manner consitent with the NARUC classification.

information contained in investment or construction work orders and retirement work orders. Completed work orders which have not been transferred to Utility Plant in Service provide supporting data for the Completed Construction Not Classified account, and incomplete work orders provide supporting data for the Construction Work in Progress account. The Completed Construction Not Classified account includes the total balances of work orders for utility plant that have been completed and placed in service but for which work orders have not been entered in the CPR's as of the balance sheet date, while the Construction Work in Progress account includes the total balances of work orders for utility plant in process of construction but not ready for service as of the balance sheet date. Most public service commissions require that water utilities under their jurisdiction maintain adequate work order systems to record all changes in water utility plant. Many public service commissions also prescribe the use of continuing property record systems for the larger water utilities under their jurisdiction. Further dicussion of work order systems and CPR systems is included in Chapter 16, "Planning and Controlling Investment in Water Utility Plant."

In summary, investment or construction work orders serve as a basis for accumulating charges to Construction Work in Progress. When the construction work is completed, the accumulated charges are transferred to Utility Plant in Service. The continuing property records support the balances in the primary or detailed utility plant accounts. The primary utility plant accounts, in turn, support the balances in utility plant control accounts, principally Utility Plant in Service Classified.

Retirement Units of Property

Proper accounting for the cost of plant assets requires that a distinction be made between expenditures which should be classified as maintenance expenses and expenditures which should be capitalized (charged to the utility plant accounts). In order to facilitate this distinction the concept of "retirement units" of property has been developed. "Retirement units" are defined by the NARUC as "those items of utility property which, when retired, with or without replacement, are accounted for by crediting the book cost thereof to the utility plant account in which recorded."[4]

In general any item of property that is readily separable, and separately useful, from a larger assembly of which it forms a part should be treated as a retirement unit. A retirement unit usually consists of items that on assembly perform a single function and are customarily installed or removed together. For example, a meter is a retirement unit. The cost of replacing any property item smaller than a retirement unit is accounted for, except for any substantial betterment involved, by charging such cost to maintenance expense.[5]

List of Retirement Units of Property. The NARUC and certain regulatory agencies provide lists which show the composition of retirement units of each kind of utility plant asset. Such lists furnish arbitrary but useful guides to the proper classification of expenditures. In the case of water utilities subject to the jurisdiction of a state public service commission, the commission customarily prescribes the list of retirement units to be used by the water utilities. The use of a prescribed list produces greater uniformity among utilities in accounting for replacements of property. If the list of retirement units is extensive and includes many small items, maintenance expense will be less than if the list includes only relatively large items. The cost of assets included in the utility plant accounts, and depreciation expense, vary directly with the size of units in the list. When a prescribed list of retirement units is furnished by a public service commission, the list may be expanded by any water utility within the jurisdiction of the commission, but the list cannot be condensed. A prescribed list includes retirement units for each of the structures and improvements accounts and for each of the

[4]Ibid., p. 3.

[5]The National Committee on Governmental Accounting, Governmental Accounting, Auditing, and Financial Reporting (Chicago: Municipal Finance Officers Association, 1968), p. 154, defines a "betterment" as follows: "An addition made to, or change made in, a fixed asset which is expected to prolong its life or to increase its efficiency over and above that arising from maintenance (q.v.) and the cost of which is therefore added to the book value of the asset."

The Committee on Accounts and Statistics, National Association of Regulatory Utility Commissioners, Uniform System of Accounts for Class A and B Water Utilities, 1957 (Washington, D.C.: National Association of Regulatory Utility Commissioners, 1958), p. 24, defines a "betterment" as making "the property affected more useful, more efficient, of greater durability, or of greater capacity."

equipment accounts making up the primary or detailed utility plant accounts.[6]

Minor Items of Property. Minor items of property include all parts or elements which make up a retirement unit of property. If a minor item of property is retired and not replaced, the accounting treatment of costs involved is the same as when a retirement unit of property is retired—namely, the cost of the minor item retired is credited to the utility plant account in which the cost is recorded, and the cost less net salvage value of this item is charged to accumulated provision for depreciation. When, however, the cost of a minor item of property will be accounted for by its inclusion in the cost of the retirement unit of property of which it is a part, no entry is made until the retirement unit itself is retired.

If minor items of property are replaced, the cost of replacement is charged as maintenance expense to the activity in which the item of property is used. As mentioned previously, if the replacement of a minor item of property constitutes a betterment, the replacement cost should be capitalized, the cost of the minor item retired should be credited to the appropriate plant account, and the cost less net salvage value of the replaced item charged to the accumulated depreciation account. However, even if the replacement of a minor item of property does constitute a betterment, the cost of the replacement normally should not be capitalized unless the replacement exceeds an established minimum (such as $100). If the replacement involves a cost of less than the established minimum, the expenditure is treated as maintenance expense.

Relationship Between Retirement Units and Continuing Property Records. As mentioned earlier in this chapter, a CPR system involves the maintenance of a separate record for each unit of utility property (CPR unit). Each CPR unit generally is composed of one or more retirement units. For a relatively large CPR unit, such as that representing structures (or major components thereof) and large items of equipment, the CPR unit may be composed of a number of retirement units. In the case of a smaller CPR unit, such as that representing a meter or hydrant, the CPR unit generally corresponds to a retirement unit.

Nature of Cost Elements Included in Utility Plant Accounts

Utility plant, whether purchased intact, constructed on a contractual basis by outsiders, or constructed by the utility itself, should be recorded at cost. "Cost" of assets acquired as an operating unit or system is defined by regulatory bodies as "the cost incurred by the person who first devoted the property to public service." All other items of utility plant are included in the accounts as the cost incurred by the water utility. The original cost of utility plant is determined by analysis of a water utility's records or those of previous owners. If original cost is not known, it must be estimated on the basis of available data concerning prevailing costs at the time utility plant was first constructed or first devoted to public service. If not subject to the jurisdiction of state public service commissions, municipally-owned water utilities may desire to record plant at cost to the utiility (the amount of cash, or cash equivalent, actually paid for the property) rather than cost to the "person who first devoted the property to public service."

There are many different elements of cost which make up the total cost of water utility plant. This section is concerned with these cost elements as they relate to the cost of the four general types of utility plant: intangible plant, land and land rights, structures and improvements, and equipment.

The Cost of Intangible Plant Assets. The most common items of intangible plant are organization cost, the cost of franchises and consents, and the cost of patent rights, licenses, and privileges necessary or valuable to the conduct of the water utility's operations. Organization expense represents the cost incidental to organizing the water utility enterprise to the time when revenues start to accrue. This cost includes the expense of securing governmental authorization to engage in the water utility business, the fees and expenses of incorporation, and other expenditures required to put the utility in a position of readiness to conduct operations.

Franchises and consents represent the expenditures incidental to securing from governmental agencies the right to use governmental property in the conduct of utility operations. These

---

[6]A list of retirement units is published by the NARUC. See: Committee on Accounts and Statistics, National Association of Regulatory Utility Commissioners, List of Retirement Units of Property for Water Utilities 1962 (Washington, D.C.: National Association of Regulatory Utility Commissioners, 1962).

rights may be for a stipulated period, or they may be in perpetuity. The expenditures which are recognized as assets represent advance payments for the right to use governmental property. When, in addition to these advance payments, annual payments must be made to preserve the rights, the annual payments are considered as operating expenses. If the advance payments are for a stipulated period of time, then the cost of limited-term franchises and consents should be amortized over those periods.

Miscellaneous intangible plant costs, such as the cost of patent rights, licenses, and privileges should be amortized over the life of the assets.

The Cost of Land and Land Rights. The accounts for land and land rights include the cost of land which is owned in fee by the water utility and the cost of all rights to the use of land. These rights include leaseholds, easements, water and water power rights, water diversion rights, submersion rights, rights of way, and other like interests in land. Although the rights to the use of land are really intangible plant assets, they typically are classified with land.

The cost of land owned in fee includes all the costs of acquisition and any expenditures necessary to place the land in a condition to serve the purpose intended by the utility. The costs of acquisition include the amount contracted to be paid to the vendor, liabilities assumed, legal expenses in connection with the perfection of title, and fees paid to brokers. Expenditures necessary to prepare the site for utility use include those associated with the demolition of buildings purchased with the land but not to be used, relocating of structures, surveying, clearing, draining, and grading the land, and other similar tasks. In addition, special assessments (benefit assessments) levied by public authorities for public improvements on the basis of benefits for new roads, bridges, sewers, curbing, pavement, and other public improvements are properly considered as a cost of land.

The cost of rights to the use of land which are to be recorded represent advance payments for rights. If no expenditure is incurred in their acquisition there is no cost to be recorded. If annual or other periodic payments must be made to preserve land rights, the periodic payments should be considered as operating expenses. If a land right is granted for a stipulated term, the cost of the right should be amortized over the period

during which the right may be exercised. Land rights which are in perpetuity need not be amortized unless there is an indication that the rights will become valueless with the passage of time.[7]

The Cost of Structures and Improvements. The primary accounts for structures and improvements include the cost of all buildings and facilities (including structures for impounding, collecting, and storing water) used to house, support, or safeguard property or persons, including all fixtures permanently attached to and made a part of buildings and facilities and which cannot be removed from the buildings and facilities without in some way impairing the buildings and facilities. Improvements include such items as fences, roadways, landscaping, bridges, and drainage systems. If structures and improvements are purchased intact or are constructed for the utility on a contractual basis by outsiders, the determination of the cost of structures and improvements so obtained is relatively easy. The purchase price or the contract price is the major determinant of cost to the water utility (except in the case where structures and improvements purchased intact must be recorded at original cost). If the purchase price relates to the acquisition of a number of utility plant assets, the amount of the lump sum payment must be allocated to each asset purchased in order to determine the cost of each asset. Typically, the lump sum payment is allocated to each asset on the basis of the ratio of the estimated fair market value (or appraised value) of the asset to the estimated fair market value (or appraised value) of all assets purchased.

If structures and improvements are constructed for the utility on a contractual basis by outsiders or if structures and improvements are constructed by the utility itself, there are certain costs incurred by the utility in connection with the construction work. These costs must be determined and charged to the appropriate utility plant accounts and records.

The NARUC System of Accounts recognizes 18 types of direct and indirect (overhead) construction costs which are to be included, where applicable, in the utility plant accounts. These 18 categories of costs are summarized as follows:

1. "Contract work" includes amounts paid for work performed and materials furnished by other persons and costs incurred in awarding contracts and inspecting work.

[7]For a detailed listing of cost items properly includible in the accounts for land and land rights, see: Committee on Accounts and Statistics, National Association of Regulatory Utility Commissioners, Uniform System of Accounts for Class A and B Water Utilities 1957 (Washington, D.C.: National Association of Regulatory Utility Commissioners, 1958), pp. 18-19.

2. "Labor" includes the pay and expenses (including payroll taxes) of utility employees engaged in construction work. Some labor costs are included as elements within other categories of construction costs.

3. "Materials and supplies" includes the cost of construction materials and supplies issued from stores.

4. "Transportation" includes the cost of transporting employees, materials and supplies, and construction equipment to and from points of construction.

5. "Special machine service" includes the costs incurred in operating construction equipment.

6. "Shop service" includes the proportion of costs incurred by utility shops assignable to construction work.

7. "Protection" includes the cost of protecting the utility's property from fire or other casualties and the cost of preventing damages to others or the property of others.

8. "Injuries and damages" includes expenditures or losses in connection with construction work due to injuries to persons and damages to the property of others.

9. "Privileges and permits" includes the costs incurred in securing temporary privileges, permits, or rights in connection with construction work.

10. "Rents" includes the cost of using the property of others during construction.

11. "Engineering and supervision" includes the portion of pay and expenses of engineers, surveyors, draftsmen, inspectors, and superintendents and their assistants applicable to construction work.

12. "General administration capitalized" includes the portion of the pay and expenses of the general officers and administrators and general expenses applicable to construction work.

13. "Engineering services" includes payments to outsiders for engineering services.

14. "Insurance" includes premiums paid or amounts provided for self-insurance for protection against loss and damages in connection with construction.

15. "Law expenditures" includes expenditures for court and legal services directly related to construction.

16. "Taxes" includes taxes on physical property (including land) and other taxes applicable to construction which are incurred during the construction period.

17. "Interest during construction" includes the net cost for the period of construction of borrowed funds used for construction purposes and a reasonable rate on other funds when so used.

18. "Earnings and expenses during construction" includes the revenues and expenses related to the operation of utility plant during the construction period.[8]

The distribution of construction costs, both direct and indirect, to particular construction projects and to particular plant assets and units of property involved in construction projects is discussed in more detail in a subsequent section.

The Cost of Equipment and Tools. "Equipment" is defined as all tangible utility plant except land and structures and improvements. If the utility constructs part of its own equipment, all the items of cost enumerated in connection with the construction of structures and improvements should be added to the cost of direct labor and materials in order to arrive at the cost of such equipment. If equipment is purchased, the cost includes, in addition to the purchase price, sales taxes, transportation expenses, and cost of installation.

Tools are distinguished from equipment by being defined as having a relatively small unit value ($50 each, for example). Small tools are particularly susceptible to pilferage, breakage, and loss. Although the unit value of each tool is small, which makes elaborate internal control procedures unreasonable, the total amount spent by the utility for tools is sizable enough to warrant some effort to discourage theft and encourage proper use. A common procedure is for utilities to maintain perpetual inventory records for tools in the storeroom (as described in Chapter 17 in relation to materials). Tools are issued on the basis of requisitions, which permits the cost of tools issued to be charged to the operating expense of the using department. Periodic physical inventories must be taken in order to bring to light errors in maintaining the perpetual inventory records and disappearance resulting from pilferage and circumvention of the requisition system.

---

[8]For a more detailed listing and explanation of cost items properly includible in the accounts for structures and improvements, see: Committee on Accounts and Statistics, National Association of Regulatory Utility Commissioners, Uniform System of Accounts for Class A and B Water Utilities 1957 (Washington, D.C.: National Association of Regulatory Utility Commissioners, 1958), pp. 10-14, 20-22.

Determining and Distributing Construction Costs

Direct Construction Costs. The cost of assets constructed by outside contractors ordinarily may be determined on the basis of payments to the contractors. If, as is often true, a single contract covers the construction and acquisition of a number of different kinds of assets, proper detail must be secured from the contractor to permit the determination and recording of costs by CPR units or retirement units.

If assets are constructed partially or completely by the utility's own personnel, labor and materials costs may be assigned to the project to which they relate on the basis of labor time records and materials requisitions. Other items of cost, as discussed below, are properly capitalizable but it is seldom clerically feasible to assign them directly to specific CPR units, or retirement units. Costs in the latter category are called "indirect" costs.

Indirect Construction Costs. Salaries and wages of utility employees whose time is not conveniently assignable to specific construction projects, labor-related costs commonly called "fringe benefits," transportations costs, the cost of special machine service, shop service costs, engineering and supervision costs, general and administrative costs, and the cost of taxes and interest during construction are examples of indirect construction costs. Some of these, particularly engineering and supervision costs, general and administrative costs, and the cost of taxes and interest during construction are incurred for the benefit of the utility in its entirety and are only partially assignable to the construction activity. Such costs must be allocated between construction work and operating expense.

Indirect construction costs should be charged to individual projects, plant assets, and property units on the basis of the amounts of such costs reasonably applicable thereto so that each project, plant asset, and property unit bears an equitable proportion of indirect costs. Therefore, valid bases must be found for allocating the several kinds of indirect costs between construction work and operating expense and for allocating indirect construction costs among construction projects, plant assets, and property units.

Two alternative methods are commonly used for determining the amount of indirect costs incurred by the utility in its entirety which should be allocated to construction work. One method is called the "incremental cost" method. Under this method, only the costs specifically incurred for construction—costs which would not be incurred by the utility if construction were not undertaken—are chargeable to construction. Under an alternative method, costs incurred by the utility are allocated to construction work in proportion to the construction activities performed by various divisions (such as the administration and general division) of the utility organization. This is called the "benefits-realized" method.[9]

Using the benefits-realized method, the indirect labor component of costs incurred by the utility in its entirety is allocated to construction work on the basis of studies to determine the proportion of time spent by personnel, such as administrators, supervisors, and engineers on construction work and on operations. Where expenditures made by the utility relate to things other than compensation for personal services, special studies are needed to determine that the expenditures have a beneficial relationship to construction and to determine a resonable basis for capitalizing a portion of the expenditures.

The use of the benefits-realized method has the effect of reducing expenses and increasing net income during periods of heavy construction activity. The use of the incremental cost method avoids the effect of showing greater net income merely because of increased construction activity.

Transportation and Special Machine Service Cost. The labor costs associated with transportation equipment operators and special machine equipment operators generally can be identified with construction projects, plant assets, and property units through the use of labor time sheets; therefore, such costs are direct construction costs. Other costs of operating equipment (gasoline, lubricants, depreciation of equipment and garage, taxes on equipment, and other garage overhead expenses) and the costs of maintaining equipment (maintenance labor, and maintenance materials and supplies) customarily are allocated to construction projects on the basis of a predetermined rate for each piece of equipment. The

---

[9] For an extended discussion of procedures for allocating indirect costs, see: Charles T. Horngren, Cost Accounting: A Managerial Emphasis (2nd ed.; Englewood Cliffs, N. J.: Prentice-Hall Inc., 1967), particularly pp. 68-97 and pp. 563-589; John J. W. Neuner and Samuel Frumer, Cost Accounting: Principles and Practice (7th ed.; Homewood, Illinois: Richard D. Irwin, Inc., 1967), particularly pp. 211-239; and Adolph Matz, Othel J. Curry, and George W. Frank, Cost Accounting (4th ed.; Cincinnati: South-Western Publishing Company, 1967), particularly pp. 123-148 and pp. 161-183.

rate is established for each piece of equipment on the basis of expected costs of its operation and maintenance. After the cost of operating and maintaining transportation equipment and special machine equipment is allocated to construction projects, it must be distributed among the plant assets and property units involved in the project. The cost must be allocated to plant accounts and property units on an equitable and clerically feasible basis.

Shop Service Cost. The cost of materials used or fabricated by a central shop may be charged to construction projects, plant assets, and property units on the basis of the cost of actual materials used plus an allowance for labor and overhead. The allowance is generally determined on the basis of a rate sufficient to absorb budgeted shop costs.

Engineering and Supervision Costs. A portion of engineering and supervision costs may be directly identified with construction projects, plant assets, or property units. However, if engineering and supervisory personnel are used jointly for construction and operating purposes, the associated costs must be appropriately allocated. Unless time sheets are kept by engineering and supervisory personnel, special studies will be required to determine the portion of costs allocable to construction work. After the portion of indirect costs of engineering and supervision is allocated to construction work, this portion must be distributed to individual projects, plant assets, and property units; this distribution must be made in an equitable and clerically feasible manner, such as in proportion to direct labor hours incurred with respect to the projects, plant assets, or property units.

Administrative and General Costs. A portion of administrative and general activities also generally is associated with construction work. Therefore, the portion of the pay of the general officers, administrators, and other general expenses applicable to construction work should be capitalized. The portions capitalized should, of course, have a provable relationship to construction work. As in the case of engineering and supervisory costs, the amount of administrative and general costs associated with construction

work typically is determined by special studies. The portion of administrative and general expenses must then be allocated to construction projects, plant assets, and property units in an equitable and clerically feasible manner.

Taxes During Construction. Payroll taxes should be included as part of the direct and indirect labor costs distributed to construction projects, plant assets, and property units. Sales taxes on construction materials and supplies should be included as part of the cost of materials and supplies distributed to construction projects, plant assets, and property units. The capitalization of property taxes generally is limited to substantial projects to which actual tax payments can be directly identified.

Interest During Construction. Interest paid, accrued, or imputed during the period of construction of a utility plant asset is included as a cost of the asset by the utility industry although it is not so treated by other businesses. The recognition of interest as a cost of construction is based on the theory that the use of money to finance construction activities involves an opportunity cost. The cost of using money to finance investment in plant assets during the period of construction is equal to the income foregone by being unable to invest the money in some immediately productive asset. Therefore, interest during construction is properly considered as a cost of constructing the productive asset. As soon as completed plant is placed in service, interest is treated as an expense to be matched against the revenues which presumably result from the use of the productive asset. The cost of the asset completed becomes, of course, a part of the rate base.

Interest during construction is measured by the net cost for the period of construction of borrowed funds used for construction purposes and a reasonable cost for other funds when so used. Since a number of different sources of money are available to finance construction projects (as discussed in Chapter 14), the weighted average cost of capital generally is the preferable measure of an appropriate interest rate to use to determine the cost of money during construction.

CHAPTER 16. PLANNING AND CONTROLLING INVESTMENT IN WATER UTILITY PLANT

Planning Investment in Utility Plant Assets

Within the framework of the major objectives and policies established for the water utility, management must plan and control the capital expenditure activities of the utility. Planning capital expenditure activities is one of the most important management considerations in the successful operation of water utilities and embraces the anticipation of the needs of customers for water service, the selection and design of the proper plant facilities to meet these needs, the timely purchase or construction of required additions to plant, the timely replacement and retirement of plant assets, and the development of financing programs to provide funds for plant investment.

Forecasting Demand. As discussed in Chapter 9, the forecast of demand for water service is the starting point for the entire budgeting process. In order to be an effective capital budgeting aid, the forecast of annual quantity requirements of customers for water service should be made for at least a five-year period. An extended period of time may be required for the construction and installation of additional utility plant; therefore, a long-range forecast of demand for water service is necessary in order to provide assurance that utility plant capacity will be adequate, but not substantially in excess of that required to meet anticipated peak demands for water service. In the case of investment in source of supply facilities, pumping facilities, water treatment facilities, and general plant facilities, a forecast of total demand for water service may be adequate for planning capital expenditure activities. However, in the case of transmission and distribution facilities, estimates of demand for water service by localities served, or to be served, are necessary. Only in this way can transmission and distribution system requirements be determined and capital expenditure plans for the system be developed.

Successful planning of capital expenditure activities often calls for a dovetailing of the projected service demands of customers with the proposed construction programs of federal, state, and municipal governments. For example, highway construction projects and urban renewal projects may force the relocation of existing facilities, or their abandonment and the construction of new ones. It is apparent that the impact of governmental programs on the water utility's capital expenditure activities must be anticipated.

In summary, a long term forecast of annual quantity requirements of customers for water service allows water utility management to anticipate requirements for plant facilities, to select and design facilities to meet the requirements, to time capital expenditure activities so as to provide plant capacity to meet demands for water service, and to make long-range plans for financing the capital expenditure activities.

Evaluating Alternative Investment Proposals. Consistent with the long term forecast of annual customer demand for water service, water utility management must determine the appropriate capital expenditures projects to be undertaken. There are, of course, certain investments which can be termed "imperative." The failure to meet imperative plant needs involving the replacement or extension of particular plant facilities would result in the inability of the utility to provide a minimum level of service to customers. There may, of course, be a number of alternative ways (mutually-exclusive investment alternatives) of meeting imperative plant investment needs. For example, it may be possible to increase needed capacity through either expanding water treatment facilities or expanding capacity to store treated water. In turn, additional storage capacity may be obtained through the use of additional distribution reservoirs or through the use of additional distribution standpipes. Alternative proposals for meeting imperative plant investment requirements should be evaluated in terms of expected costs in relation to expected benefits in order to determine the best alternative from the financial point of view.

In addition to imperative investments, other investments may be termed "optional." These investment proposals are desirable but not absolutely necessary during the forthcoming budget period. Optional plant investment proposals also should be evaluated in terms of earnings expectations. If expected earnings are insufficient (as determined by measures discussed later in this section), the project should not be undertaken unless regulatory authorities so require.

It is extremely difficult, if not impossible, to estimate the effect of certain investment proposals on earnings. For example, it is nearly impossible to predict the total effect on earnings of an investment in a locker room for employees or of investments which will increase the quality of water service. In such instances, it may be necessary to justify investment proposals primarily in terms of increased employee morale or better customer relations.

Four important factors are brought together in the evaluation of investment alternatives:

(1) The net amount of the investment
(2) The returns expected from the investment
(3) The expected rate of return on the investment, as determined by (1) and (2) above
(4) The lowest rate of return on the investment that will be acceptable to the utility.

It should be emphasized that although a water utility subject to the jurisdiction of a state public service commission is allowed a certain rate of return on rate base, the utility is not guaranteed such a return. Therefore, one way to make the allowed return is to screen investment alternatives so that only those proposals which indicate a sufficient expected rate of return are accepted. Regulatory agencies are concerned with the rate of return for an entire utility; therefore, it is possible for the utility to offset some projects or segments of their business which are in the public interest but which yield a lower rate of return with other projects which yield a higher-than-allowable rate of return.

The minimum acceptable rate of return for a capital expenditure project should be set at a level such that any return on investment greater than the required return will assist in maintaining or improving the financial integrity of the utility. The return on new investment must be equal to the return required to attract the financial resources of new investors and/or to cause present investors to maintain their holdings. Therefore, the mini-

mum acceptable return on new investment should be set at a level which is equal to or greater than the weighted average current cost of capital to the utility. (Chapter 14 is concerned with determining the cost of capital for the water utility.)

There are a number of different methods of measuring the rate of return on proposed investments. Two methods are average income on investment cost and yield on investment.[1] The first method requires that the cost, including both direct and indirect costs, of the proposed investment be estimated. In addition, the average annual income resulting from the proposed investment must be estimated. Estimated average income is the difference between the estimated change in average annual operating revenues resulting from the investment and the estimated change in average annual operating costs resulting from the investment. The percentage return on investment cost is then determined by dividing average annual income by the investment cost. In the case of an optional investment proposal, if the estimated percentage return on investment cost is greater than the minimum acceptable percentage return, the investment proposal is acceptable. If the estimated return is less than the required return, the investment proposal should be rejected; if it is mandatory, steps should be initiated to obtain increased revenue, if possible. Alternative proposals for meeting imperative investment requirements should also be evaluated in terms of rate of return, the best alternative generally being the one reflecting the highest estimated rate of return. If the best alternative proposal for meeting a particular imperative investment requirement reflects an estimated rate of return which is less than the minimum acceptable, then an attempt should be made to increase the estimated rate of return. In some instances the estimated rate of return can be increased by decreasing the net cost of the investment, which is reduced by obtaining greater donations or contributions in aid of construction from customers, subdividers, or governmental agencies. If imperative projects in general reflect an insufficient estimated rate of return, it may be necessary to increase returns by increasing water rates. An application of the "average income on investment cost" method is shown in Fig. 16-1.

Under the "yield on investment" method, the

---

[1]For an extended discussion of these two methods, as well as other methods of evaluating investment proposals, and of the advantages and disadvantages of using each method, see: Harold Bierman Jr., and Seymour Smidt, The Capital Budgeting Decision (2nd ed.; New York: The MacMillan Company, 1966); and Elly Vassilatou Thanopoulas, Financial Analysis Techniques for Equipment Replacement Decisions, NAA Research Monograph No. 1 (New York: National Association of Accountants, 1965).

Figure 16-1
ESTIMATING RATE OF RETURN ON INVESTMENT
(Using Average Income on Investment Cost Method)

Estimated Net Investment Cost of Construction Project:
  Direct Costs:
    Labor $20,000
    Material   30,000
    Contract Work   10,000
        Total Direct Costs $60,000
  Indirect Costs:
    Transportation and Special Machine Service .... $ 3,000
    Shop Service   1,500
    Engineering and Supervision   3,000
    Administrative and General   1,000
    Interest during Construction   5,500
    Other   1,000
        Total Indirect Costs   15,000
  Total Direct and Indirect Cost of Construction $75,000
  Less: Non-refundable Contributions in Aid of Construction ..   0
  Estimated Net Investment Cost of Construction Project $75,000

Estimated Average Income Available for Return:
  Increase in Revenue .... $ 0
  Decrease in Expenses:
    Operation Expenses .... $ 8,300
    Maintenance Expense   4,000
        Total Decrease in Expenses $12,300
  Increase in Expenses
    Depreciation Expense .... $ 1,500
    Taxes Other than Income Taxes   1,250
    Income Taxes   4,300
        Total Increase in Expenses   7,050
  Net Decrease in Expenses   5,250
  Estimated Average Income Available for Return .... $ 5,250

Estimated Rate of Return on Net Investment ($5250 ÷ $75,000) 7%

procedure is to find a rate of return that will make the present value of the cash proceeds expected from an investment proposal equal to the present value of the cash outlays required by the investment proposal. (This method is comparable to the method used in bond markets to determine yield on bonds.)[2] Through the use of present value tables, and by trial and error, the approximately correct rate of return can be determined.[3] This rate is referred to as the estimated yield of the investment. The "yield on investment" method considers only the incremental cash outlays and incremental cash proceeds associated with a particular investment proposal. Therefore, non-cash expenses, such as depreciation, associated with a particular investment do not directly affect the rate of return under this method. Depreciation expense associated with a proposed investment does indirectly influence the yield on investment of investor-owned utilities to the extent that additional depreciation charges increase cash proceeds by decreasing income taxes.

As in the case of the "average income on investment" method, for an optional investment proposal, if the estimated rate of return determined by using the "yield on investment" method is greater than the required percentage return, the investment proposal is accepted; otherwise, the proposal is rejected. In the case of an imperative investment proposal, an attempt should be made to insure that the estimated rate of return is sufficient. This may be accomplished through adequate contributions in aid of construction and/or by adequate water rates. An application of the "yield on investment" method is shown in Fig. 16-2.

[2]Other terms used to describe the "yield on investment" method include the investor's method, the marginal efficiency of capital method, the internal rate of return method, and the discounted cash flow method.

[3]Published annuity tables can be found in a number of sources including R. M. Mikesell and Leon E. Hay, Governmental Accounting (3rd ed.; Homewood, Illinois: Richard D. Irwin, Inc., 1961), pp. 710-717; and Harold Bierman Jr. and Seymour Smidt, The Capital Budgeting Decision (2nd ed.; New York: The MacMillan Company, 1966), pp. 369-403.

Figure 16-2
ESTIMATING RATE OF RETURN ON INVESTMENT
(Using Yield on Investment Method)

Estimated Net Cash Outlay for New Equipment:		
Cost of New Equipment		$130,000
Less: Cost of Repairs to Keep Old Equipment in Operation (Net of Income Tax Savings on Repairs Deduction)	$8,000	
Proceeds from Sale of Old Equipment (Net of Capital Gains tax on Sale of Old Equipment)	2,100	
Investment tax Credit (3% of $130,000)	3,900	14,000
Estimated Net Cash Outlay for New Equipment		$116,000
Estimated Annual Cash Proceeds From New Equipment:[a]		
Decrease in Cash Expenses:		
Operation and Maintenance Expenses.....................		$ 18,500
Increase in Cash Expenses:		
Taxes Other than Income Taxes	$1,800	
Income Taxes[b]	4,900	6,700
Estimated Annual Cash Proceeds From New Equipment		$ 11,800
Estimated Yield on Investment[c]		8%

[a] Service life of new equipment assumed to be 20 years. Depreciation is to be taken on a straight-line basis (net salvage value assumed to be negligible).

[b] Increase in income taxes computed as follows:

Increases in taxable income due to:		
Decrease in Operation and Maintenance Expense		$ 18,500
Decreases in taxable income due to:		
Increases in Taxes Other Than Income Taxes	$1,800	
Increase in Depreciation Expense ($130,000 ÷ 20 yrs.).................	6,500	8,300
Net Increase in Taxable Income		$ 10,200
Increase in Income Tax (48% × $10,200)		$ 4,900

[c] Assuming that annual cash proceeds from new equipment will occur each year for 20 years, the estimated yield on investment is computed as follows:

From published annuity tables it is determined that the present value of $1 received annually for 20 years (discounted at a rate of 8%) is approximately equal to $9.82. Dividing the net cash outlay for the new equipment ($116,000) by the present value of the 20 year annuity of $1 ($9.82) gives an answer of $11,812 which is approximately equal to the estimated annual cash proceeds from the new equipment. Therefore, the estimated yield on investment is approximately 8%.

The Capital Expenditures Budget. The capital expenditures budget is a plan for all changes to existing utility plant, both additions and retirements. In order to facilitate coordination of long range and short range plans the capital expenditures budget should be prepared for a period of at least five years. The process of developing the five-year capital expenditures budget should integrate all aspects of the planning function so that not only the facilities themselves are designed but also the financing implications and the impact the facilities would have on assignment of personnel and the use of material are foreseen. The effect of the capital expenditures budget on manpower and material requirements serves as the basis for planning the operating and construction activities to be performed by the utility. The capital expenditures budget also allows management to develop a financing program to meet the cash re-

quirements of the budget and allows management to time its trips to the money markets in order to minimize the cost of money. In addition, the capital expenditures budget serves as an instrument of management control over capital expenditures.

The five year budget should be revised annually. The current year is dropped, the plans for the next four years are reviewed and modified as necessary, and the plan is extended for an additional year, so that it remains a five year plan. Figure 16-3 presents an example of a five-year capital expenditures budget summary showing the estimated cost of additions and the credits to the utility plant accounts which reflect retirements. The budget depicted in Fig. 16-3 also shows estimated amounts expended as of the beginning of the budget period for unfinished capital investment projects.

Figure 16-3

THE WILLING WATER UTILITY

FIVE-YEAR CAPITAL EXPENDITURES BUDGET SUMMARY

19B1 to 19B5

Project Number	Brief Description of Projects	Estimated Expenditures or Retirements(a)	Expenditures or Retirements as of Dec. 31, 19CY	Expenditures or Retirements Required to Complete	Budgeted Expenditures or Retirements				
					19B1	19B2	19B3	19B4	19B5
	Source of Supply Plant								
307	Purchase of Reservoir Land—Expenditures	$ 41,000		$ 41,000	$ 41,000				
308	Extension of Roadway on Reservoir Land—Expenditures	20,000		20,000		$ 15,000	$ 5,000		
309	Replacement of Bridges and Culverts								
	Expenditures	37,000	$ 17,000	20,000	20,000				
	Retirements	(20,000)	(10,000)	(10,000)	(10,000)				
310–313	Construction of Wells—Expenditures(b)	200,000	20,000	180,000	40,000	40,000	40,000	40,000	20,000
	Total Expenditure—Source of Supply Plant	$ 298,000	$ 37,000	$ 261,000	$ 101,000	$ 55,000	$ 45,000	$ 40,000	$ 20,000
	Total Retirements—Source of Supply Plant	($ 20,000)	($ 10,000)	($ 10,000)	($ 10,000)				
	Pumping Plant								
314	New Booster Pumping Station (Structure & Parts)—Expenditures	$ 275,000	$ 10,000	$ 265,000	$ 85,000	$ 180,000			
315	Replacement of Pumps at Clear River Pumping Station								
	Expenditures	475,000		475,000		160,000	315,000		
	Retirements	(375,000)		(375,000)		(175,000)	(200,000)		
	Total Expenditures—Pumping Plant	$ 750,000	$ 10,000	$ 740,000	$ 85,000	$ 340,000	$ 315,000		
	Total Retirements—Pumping Plant	($ 375,000)		($ 375,000)		($ 175,000)	($ 200,000)		
	Water Treatment Plant(b)								
316–321	Total Expenditures—Water Treatment Plant	$ 540,000		$ 540,000				$ 270,000	$ 270,000
	Total Retirements—Water Treatment Plant	($ 290,000)		($ 290,000)				($ 200,000)	($ 90,000)
	Transmission and Distribution Plant								
322	New Distribution Tank—Expenditures	$ 75,000		$ 75,000			$ 75,000		
323	Landscaping Around Standpipes—Expenditures	10,000		10,000	10,000				
324–355	Extension and Replacement of Mains(b)								
	Expenditures	6,790,000	$ 190,000	6,600,000	1,130,000	$ 1,400,000	1,180,000	1,440,000	1,450,000
	Retirements	(340,000)	(40,000)	(300,000)	(60,000)	(40,000)	(70,000)	(70,000)	(60,000)
356	Services(c)								
	Expenditures	250,000		250,000	50,000	50,000	50,000	50,000	50,000
	Retirements	(10,000)		(10,000)	(2,000)	(2,000)	(2,000)	(2,000)	(2,000)
357	Meters(c)								
	Expenditures	525,000		525,000	100,000	100,000	100,000	110,000	115,000
	Retirements	(5,000)		(5,000)	(1,000)	(1,000)	(1,000)	(1,000)	(1,000)
358	Meter Installations(c)								
	Expenditures	105,000		105,000	20,000	20,000	20,000	20,000	25,000
	Retirements	(6,000)		(6,000)	(1,000)	(1,000)	(1,000)	(1,000)	(2,000)
359	Hydrants(c)								
	Expenditures	420,000	20,000	400,000	80,000	80,000	80,000	80,000	80,000
	Retirements	(35,000)	(5,000)	(30,000)	(6,000)	(6,000)	(6,000)	(6,000)	(6,000)
	Total Expenditures—Transmission and Distribution Plant	$ 8,175,000	$210,000	$ 7,965,000	$1,390,000	$1,650,000	$1,505,000	$1,700,000	$1,720,000
	Total Retirements—Transmission and Distribution Plant	($ 396,000)	($ 45,000)	($ 351,000)	($ 70,000)	($ 50,000)	($ 80,000)	($ 80,000)	($ 71,000)
	General Plant(b)								
360–384	Total Expenditures—General Plant	$ 1,050,000	$ 50,000	$ 1,000,000	$ 150,000	$ 200,000	$ 200,000	$ 250,000	$ 200,000
	Total Retirements—General Plant	($ 400,000)	($ 20,000)	($ 380,000)	($ 80,000)	($ 70,000)	($ 80,000)	($ 70,000)	($ 80,000)
	Total Expenditures—Water Utility Plant	$10,813,000	$307,000	$10,506,000	$1,726,000	$2,245,000	$2,065,000	$2,260,000	$2,210,000
	Total Retirements—Water Utility Plant	($ 1,481,000)	($ 75,000)	($ 1,406,000)	($ 160,000)	($ 295,000)	($ 360,000)	($ 350,000)	($ 241,000)

(a) Expenditure figures include the cost of removal less salvage value of assets being retired as well as the cost of new assets. Retirement figures indicate the book cost of assets being retired.

(b) In order to conserve space these categories have not been classified by individual projects.

(c) These categories of expenditures and retirements are considered as "blanket projects" as opposed to "major projects."

To be useful as a planning and control mechanism, a summary of budgeted capital expenditures, such as that shown in Fig. 16-3, should be based upon a carefully prepared and detailed analysis of individual projects. It is useful to classify capital expenditure projects as "major projects," and as "blanket projects." Major projects include proposed additions to and retirements of utility plant which involve relatively large outlays and are of a nonroutine nature. Examples of major projects include the construction or retirement of a water treatment plant, a pumping station, a standpipe, transmission mains, and other similar large additions or retirements of water utility plant. Each of these projects is of sufficient size to warrant individual attention and consideration by top management and policy making groups (the city council or board of directors).

Blanket projects include proposed additions to, and retirements of, utility plant which are routine in nature. Examples of blanket projects include the installation and retirement of customers' services, meters, and hydrants. The individual items included in blanket projects are so numerous, so similar in character, and so small in cost relative to major projects, that individual attention and consideration by management is unwarranted.

The summary of budgeted capital expenditures (Fig. 16-3) is supported by individual project budgets, for both major projects and blanket projects. Typically, each individual project budget includes a project number, a description of the project, the purpose and necessity of the project, scheduled starting and completion dates for the project, estimated cost of the project, estimated incremental operating revenues and expenses associated with the project, and estimated return on the investment. Individual project budgets would be prepared for uncompleted major projects (carryover projects from the current year) as well as for new projects. Figure 16-4 presents an example of an individual project budget.

Expenditure Authorization. The capital expenditures budget is an advance estimate of requirements for additions to, and retirements of, water utility plant; the expenditures are limited to those items approved by management and policy making groups and included in the budget as necessary to meet the demands of customers for water service. Customarily the construction budget has its origin in requests from division heads to the general manager of the utility for approval of specific pro-

jects, presented in the form of individual project budgets. It is the responsibility of the general manager and his staff to evaluate individual project requests and to consolidate those projects approved by the general manager. The consolidation of individual projects aids the general manager in coordinating the activities of the individual departments of the water utility so as to best meet the demands of customers for water service. The budget is then submitted to the policy making group (city council or board of directors) for final approval.

In the case of municipally-owned water utilities, the capital expenditures budget may become a legally binding document upon approval by the city council or other policy making group, although, as discussed in Chapter 6 of this book, the NCGA recommends that water utilities be allowed to budget in the same manner as investor-owned enterprises.[4] The approved capital expenditures budget serves as the authorization to issue commitment documents and to incur expenditures in the amount appropriated (approved) by the city council or other policy making group. In the case of investor-owned water utilities, the capital expenditures budget, while ordinarily requiring approval by the board of directors, is not a legally binding document. It is generally agreed that appropriations for capital expenditures should be stated in broad terms to provide reasonable latitude for water utility management consistent with the broad control needs of the policy making group.

In addition to the approval of the capital expenditure budget, specific management approval is customarily required in order to begin work on each individual project. A work order, when approved, serves as the authorization to commence a specific unit of work, places responsibility for the execution of the work, and serves as a review of a proposed expenditure at the time the request for authorization to make expenditures is received by management. In addition, the work order is the basis for accumulating costs, which are later transferred to appropriate plant accounts and continuing property records when the work is completed. A separate work order is sometimes issued for each primary plant account that will be affected by a particular capital expenditure project. Other utilities may desire to provide only one work order for each project even though the project affects the total in more than one primary plant account.

[4]National Committee on Governmental Accounting, Governmental Accounting, Auditing, and Financial Reporting (Chicago: Municipal Finance Officers Association, 1968), p. 51. Material from relevant pages of the NCGA text is quoted in Chapter 6 of this book.

Figure 16-4
INDIVIDUAL PROJECT BUDGET

THE WILLING WATER UTILITY CAPITAL EXPENDITURES PROJECT

PROJECT NO. _____333_____   CLASSIFICATION: Transmission and Distribution Mains

DESCRIPTION OF PROJECT:

Replacement of two miles of 8" main with 12" main

LOCATION OF PROJECT:

On Orchard Street, from Center Street to Broad Street

JUSTIFICATION FOR PROJECT:

12" main will replace badly deteriorated 8" main thereby reducing maintenance expenses and increasing reliability of service. Additional capacity resulting from replacement also will enable utility to meet service demands of new customers in adjacent areas.

ESTIMATED INCREMENTAL COST OF PROJECT:

Cost of Laying 12" Main:		
Direct Cost: Labor	$30,000	
Materials	32,000	$62,000
Indirect Cost: Transportation and Special Equipment	$ 3,000	
Engineering and Supervision	2,000	
Administrative and General	1,000	
Interest during Construction	1,600	7,600
Total Cost...		$69,600
Cost of Retiring 8" Main:		
Removal Cost	$ 500	
Less: Salvage Value......................................	100	400
Total Cost of Project		$70,000

ESTIMATED ANNUAL INCREMENTAL INCOME FROM PROJECT:

Increase in Operating Revenues	$ 2,000	
Decrease in Operating Expenses..........................	2,200	
Increase in Operating Income		$ 4,200
ESTIMATED RATE OF RETURN FROM PROJECT:[a] ($4,200 ÷ $70,000)		6.0%

ESTIMATED PERIOD OF CONSTRUCTION: FROM ____May 1, 19B1____   TO   August 31, 19B1

[a] It is assumed that rate of return is determined using the "average Income on Investment Cost" method. Other methods could be used as well.

In some instances, the individual project budgets which support the summary of budgeted capital expenditures serve as work orders. Frequently, however, there is a substantial time lag between the time a proposed capital expenditure project is tentatively approved and included in the capital expenditures budget and the time work is to begin on the project. Various factors may develop prior to the time project work is to begin, which affect management's plans and which make it undesirable to start or to complete a project previously approved. As a result, work orders permit management to review previously approved projects and to given final authorization to begin work or to cancel projects. In the case of project budgets which are blanket projects, each individual item of work, such as a customer service or meter installation, also may be supported by a work order.

Therefore, the work order system, together with the capital expenditure budget, serves as an instrument to assist management in planning and controlling capital expenditure activities. Separate work orders may be prepared for additions to and retirements of utility plant, or retirements may be included with additions on the same work order, provided that all items related to retirements are kept separate from those relating to additions. Figure 16-5 presents an example of an investment work order; the work order relates to the project described in Fig. 16-4. Figure 16-6 shows an example of a retirement work order which also is related to the project described in Fig. 16-4.

Planning the Conduct of Capital Expenditure Activities. Construction activities may be performed either by the utility itself or by outside

Figure 16-5
INVESTMENT WORK ORDER

THE WILLING WATER UTILITY
INVESTMENT WORK ORDER

INVESTMENT WORK ORDER NO. 786-CY   DATE   April 15, 19CY

BUDGET PROJECT NO. 333   ASSOCIATED RETIREMENT WORK ORDER (IF ANY)   593-CY

PURPOSE, LOCATION, AND DESCRIPTION OF PROJECT:

Installation of two miles of 12" main on Orchard Street, from Center Street to Broad Street. 12" main will replace badly deteriorated 8" main thereby reducing maintenance expenses and increasing reliability of service.
Additional capacity resulting from replacement also will enable utility to meet service demand of new customers
in adjacent area. Work to be conducted by utility's employees.

SUMMARY ESTIMATE OF COST:

Total Estimated Cost of Laying 12" Main (per reverse)[a] $69,600
Less: Contributions in Aid of Construction   – 0 –
Net Cost of Utility $69,600

SUBMITTED BY *Clarence Clearwater*, Head, Construction Section

APPROVALS:

ENGINEERING DEPARTMENT _____   DATE _____

CONTROLLER _____   DATE _____

GENERAL MANAGER _____   DATE _____

[a] Detailed estimates of cost, similar to those shown in Fig. 16-4, would be included on reverse side of form.

contractors. Specialized skills and services may be available within a large water utility organization which can be utilized for both operating and construction activities. The use of a utility's manpower resources to conduct construction activities may be more economical than construction by outside contractors if the special resources, such as engineering services, can be jointly applied to operating and capital expenditure activities. However, the performance of construction activities by the utility itself generally requires that special construction equipment be purchased, and that employees who are skilled in construction work be employed on a permanent basis. Construction equipment and manpower is expensive and, unless such resources can be utilized fully throughout the year (either for construction purposes or for operating purposes during periods of reduced construction activity), it may be uneconomical for the utility itself to construct plant assets. The use of outside contractors permits more flexibility, in that resources for carrying out construction activities are hired and paid for only when needed.

Therefore, the appropriate procedure for conducting capital expenditure activities depends on whether it is more economical for the utility or for an outside contractor to construct the asset. The best solution to the problem of choosing between self-construction and construction by outsiders may be to employ the utility's own equipment and manpower resources to complete relatively small and/or routine construction projects (replacement or extension of distribution mains, and service and meter installations, for example), and to contract with outsiders to complete relatively large and/or nonroutine construction projects.

Consistent with the level of construction activity indicated by the capital expenditures budget, a determination must be made as to whether particular construction projects included in the budget are to be completed by an outside contractor or by the utility itself. The manpower and equipment resources of the utility should be allocated to those

Figure 16-6
RETIREMENT WORK ORDER

THE WILLING WATER UTILITY
RETIREMENT WORK ORDER

RETIREMENT WORK ORDER NO. 593-CY   DATE   April 15, 19CY

BUDGET PROJECT NO. 333   ASSOCIATED INVESTMENT WORK ORDER (IF ANY)   286-CY

PURPOSE, LOCATION, AND DESCRIPTION OF PROJECT:

Removal and retirement of 8" main on Orchard Street, from Center Street to Broad Street. 8" main will be
replaced by 12" main. Work to be conducted by utility's employees.

COST SUMMARY:

Cost per books of assets being retired	$35,000
Estimated Cost of Removal	500
Estimated Salvage Value	(100)
Amount to be Debited to Accumulated Depreciation Account	$35,400

SUBMITTED BY *Clarence Clearwater* , Head, Construction Section

APPROVALS:

ENGINEERING DEPARTMENT _____ DATE _____

CONTROLLER _____ DATE _____

GENERAL MANAGER _____ DATE _____

projects for which they are best adapted. Projects should be matched with the capabilities and skills of the equipment and manpower resources available to the utility. The amount of equipment and manpower resources allocated to individual projects also must be sufficient to permit scheduled completion dates (or required completion deadlines) to be met. In some instances, the construction work necessitated by a particular project may be partly performed by outside contractors and partly performed by the utility itself.

Effective planning requires that, for those construction projects to be completed by outside contractors, the process of advertising and awarding bids (or by otherwise negotiating contracts) is initiated in time to permit that process to be completed prior to the scheduled date on which construction is to begin. Further, the process of purchasing construction materials and supplies, or the purchase of utility plant assets such as equipment, (either through competitive bidding or by negotiating contracts) should be initiated and completed in time to permit the delivery of the materials and supplies, or the delivery of the utility plant assets, as needed to meet scheduled completion dates.

With respect to costs in excess of a specified amount, municipally-owned water utilities are frequently bound by laws that require competitive bidding for construction contracts, contracts for the purchase of construction materials and supplies, and contracts for the purchase of items of utility plant. Normally, a contract will be awarded to the "lowest and best" bidder, but it should be kept in mind that the lowest bidder is not necessarily the best. The ability of the bidder to furnish goods and services promptly as needed, and the quality of goods and services furnished, as evidenced by past performance and current financial capability, are important factors in determining the best bid.

Controlling Investment in Utility Plant Assets

Due to the importance of the cost of water utility plant assets in determining the amount of periodic depreciation charges and as a measure of rate base, it is imperative that such cost be effectively controlled and accurately accounted for. Management control of capital expenditures is effected through the comparison of budgeted and actual costs. The actual costs of additions and retirements are accumulated through the use of a work order system. The use of the work order system and the transfer of costs from work orders to property records permits an accurate accounting for utility plant assets. Property records are also an important element of an internal control system.

Comparing Budgeted and Actual Expenditures. Actual capital expenditures usually differ to some extent from budgeted capital expenditures. Budgeted capital expenditure estimates serve as useful standards only to the extent that they are valid and reasonable. Minor variations from budgeted expenditures are to be expected. Significant variations in actual capital expenditures from budgeted capital expenditures should be investigated in order to determine necessary management action. In some instances, variations arise from faulty capital budgeting procedures. In other instances, managers or employees have failed to follow appropriate procedures for conducting capital expenditure activities. Variations between budgeted and actual capital expenditures may result from causes other than faulty budgeting procedures or faulty procedures used to conduct capital expenditure activities, such as unanticipated price changes for construction materials and supplies, and unanticipated price changes in labor wage rates.

If significant variances between budgeted and actual expenditures exist for individual projects, management should be informed of the variances and the reasons, so that proper control action can be taken for the remainder of the project and for subsequent projects.

As discussed in Chapter 6, the amount of capital expenditures and the status of capital expenditure projects should be reported to management on a periodic basis, typically at monthly or quarterly intervals. Capital expenditure control reports are usually composed of a listing of major projects and blanket projects. Figure 16-7 presents a monthly statement comparing actual and budgeted capital expenditures for projects completed during the month. Figure 16-8 presents a monthly statement of actual and budgeted capital expenditures for projects not yet completed. In instances in which total costs to complete a given project are expected to exceed budget authorization by a substantial amount, authorization to make additional expenditures should be required. In the case of those municipally-owned water utilities subject to

a legally binding capital expenditures budget, it may be necessary for utility management to obtain a supplemental appropriation in order to issue commitment documents and make expenditures beyond original authorizations.

The Work Order System. In addition to the capital expenditure budget, the work order system provides an accounting procedure to check the relationship between actual capital expenditures and the approved budget. The costs accumulated through the use of a work order system should be reported in sufficient detail so as to show the number and the cost of the various CPR (continuous property record) units involved in the capital expenditures project covered by the work order. A work order system operated in this manner permits management control of detailed capital expenditures for individual projects through comparison with authorizations.

In order to provide management with information concerning the costs associated with each project, or for each primary plant account and property unit involved in the project, a "work order record" is customarily maintained. In the case of an investment work order, direct and indirect labor costs, the cost of contract work, the cost of materials and supplies, transportation expense, and all other indirect (or overhead) costs are included on the work order record. Procedures for determining the direct and indirect construction costs and for associating such costs with individual projects, plant accounts, and property units are discussed in Chapter 15. In the case of a retirement work order, the cost of property retired, together with the cost of removal and salvage value, are included on the work order record. Therefore, by the use of work orders and work order records, the capital expenditures for, and retirements of, utility plant assets are identified, classified, and traced from the authorization stage, through the construction or retirement stage, to the continuing property records in support of the primary utility plant accounts. The cost of work in progress included on a work order record permits immediate reference to the corresponding work order estimate to determine the amount of variation between actual and budgeted expenditures for a particular project.

The Continuing Property Record System

It has been mentioned previously that additions to, and retirements of, water utility plant customarily are made under the authority of work orders (in the case of the construction or retirement of

Figure 16-7
THE WILLING WATER UTILITY
CAPITAL EXPENDITURE PROJECTS COMPLETED DURING OCTOBER, 19CY

Project Number	Description of Projects	Budgeted Expenditures	Actual Expenditures	Amount Over (Under) Budget
	Source of Supply Plant			
309	Replacement of Bridges & Culverts	$ 37,000	$ 34,300	($2,700)
310	Construction of Well	60,000	63,700	3,700
	Transmission & Distribution Plant			
323	Landscaping Around Standpipes	10,000	11,000	1,000
332	24" Main Extension—Cayuta Avenue	58,000	61,200	3,200
333	12" Main Replacement—Orchard Street	69,600	65,400	(4,200)
337	6" Main Extension—Elm Street	47,000	43,300	(3,700)
358	Meter Installations[a]	2,000	2,300	300
359	Hydrants*	7,000	7,400	400
	General Plant			
362	New Accounting Machine	2,000	2,000	– 0 –
364	Replacement of Service Trucks	18,000	17,900	(100)
	TOTALS	$387,000	$394,200	$7,200

[a] These projects constitute a number of minor projects included under blanket project numbers 358 and 359.

Figure 16-8
THE WILLING WATER UTILITY
STATUS OF UNCOMPLETED CAPITAL EXPENDITURE PROJECTS[a]
AS OF OCTOBER 31, 19CY

THE WILLING WATER UTILITY
STATUS OF UNCOMPLETED CAPITAL EXPENDITURE PROJECTS[a]
AS OF OCTOBER 31, 19CY

Project Number	Brief Description of Project	Originally Authorized	Amount		Not Expended or Committed	Status of Progress
			Committed	Expended		
	Source of Supply Plant					
307	Purchase of Reservoir Land	$ 41,000			$ 41,000	Not started
	Pumping Plant					
314	New Booster Pumping Station	275,000	$ 50,200	$ 12,000	212,800	25% completed
	Transmission and Distribution Plant					
327	20" Main Replacement—Clark Street	67,000	18,400	32,600	16,000	80% completed
328	12" Main Extension—Park Avenue	172,000	13,000	165,500	(6,500)	95% completed
334	24" Main Replacement—Waverly Street	104,000		21,400	82,600	20% completed
339	6" Main Replacement—Penna. Avenue	23,000	1,500	11,500	10,000	50% completed
340	8" Main Extension—Route 17	312,500	18,900		293,600	Not started
	General Plant					
366	Replacement of Special Service Equipment	22,000	12,500	4,200	5,300	75% completed
368	New Office Furniture	9,500		10,200	(700)	95% completed
369	Replacement of Office Equipment	4,500			4,500	Not started
	TOTALS	$1,165,500	$125,800	$316,300	$723,400	

a This list includes all capital expenditure projects scheduled to begin on or before December 31, 19CY which are not yet completed.

plant) or by purchase requisitions (in the case of the purchase of plant). In turn, charges and credits to the plant accounts and to the continuing property records in support of the plant accounts are based on cost information shown on the work order records (in the case of the construction or retirement of plant) or on invoices (in the case of the purchase of plant).

A continuing property record system is a rather elaborate and detailed system for matching property units (CPR units) with their costs. The CPR system supports the plant accounts with a perpetual inventory of the property represented by the plant accounts, and shows the portion of total plant cost associated with each individual unit of property or with each aggregate unit composed of similar, small items of property.

Uses of a CPR System. In general, public service commissions require that water utilities under their jurisdiction maintain CPR systems. A CPR system is a tool of regulation and a way to compile a complete record of the original cost of property owned by the water utility. However, the CPR system is a useful tool not only for regulatory commissions' purposes but also for management purposes as well. Some of its uses are:

1. A CPR system provides a record of plant costs for use in rate studies. Although the CPR system customarily shows the original cost of property units, the system facilitates the computation of other kinds of property values. The reproduction or replacement costs of plant assets can be determined by applying price indexes to the historical cost or original cost of property units.

2. A CPR system, as a record of the dates of property additions and retirements, provides historical information about the service lives of different property units. This facilitates service life studies to determine appropriate depreciation rates.

3. A CPR system provides cost data which may be useful to management in the preparation of capital expenditure budgets.

4. A CPR system assists in determining the cost of property retired.

5. A CPR system substantiates the costs included in the plant accounts. The cost of property as shown by the CPR system should be in balance with the cost of property shown by the plant accounts.

6. A CPR system is a useful tool for internal control of utility property. A physical inventory of utility property should agree with the inventory records generated by the CPR system.

Selecting Appropriate CPR Units. The construction of a CPR system begins with selection of the property units (CPR units) in terms of which physical inventory records are maintained and to which plant costs are allocated. In Chapter 15, the nature of a property unit (CPR unit) as an item of property which can readily be identified and accounted for by itself was discussed. The selection of property units also should be guided by reasonable limits of detailed property classification, since the cost of establishing and maintaining records increases with the degree of detail involved. The selection of appropriate property units should be guided by cost considerations as well as by anticipated usefulness of more detailed classification. It is desirable to establish and maintain property records in the degree of detail required to insure a reasonably close relationship between recorded cost and the actual cost of utility property in use.

In the case of land, each separate parcel of land constitutes a CPR unit. In the case of land rights, each land right having a useful life of more than one year constitutes a CPR unit. As mentioned in Chapter 15, a CPR unit of depreciable property generally is composed of one or more retirement units.

In the case of structures and improvements, and major items of equipment (such as those equipment items comprising source of supply plant, pumping plant, water treatment plant, transmission plant, and general plant), CPR units generally are relatively large in size. Each structure and improvement, or major item of equipment, sometimes is treated as a CPR unit; however, a particular structure, improvement, or major equipment item, may be composed of a number of retirement units. Of course, water utility management may desire to treat major components of structures and improvements, or major equipment items, as CPR units in order to provide better cost information concerning each component part. Distribution facilities are in large part composed of many small, similar, items of property, such as mains, services, meters, meter installations, and hydrants. Each item of property (for example, a given length of main, a service, a meter, a meter installation, or a hydrant) typically is chosen as a CPR unit. Each CPR unit is relatively small in size and generally corresponds to a retirement unit.[5]

It has been mentioned earlier that a major purpose or use of a CPR system is to permit tracing the cost of a particular property unit so that its cost can be eliminated from the plant accounts when that property unit is retired. However, a CPR system does not eliminate cost estimates in connection with the retirement of property items constituting less than a CPR unit or retirement unit. It would be impractical to establish and maintain cost records in detail sufficient to eliminate all cost estimates and to provide actual cost information for all property items retired.

Establishing CPR System. For relatively large CPR units (such as those representing land, land rights, structures and improvements, or major components thereof) it is advisable to provide a separate cost record for each unit. The type of information to be included on the cost record for each CPR unit is described in the section of Chapter 15 entitled "Accounts and Records for Water Utility Plant." An example of a property record card for a major item of equipment is presented in Fig. 16-9.

In the case of relatively small CPR units (such as those representing mains, services, meters, meter installations, and hydrants), a single cost record may be provided for groups of similar CPR units. For example, a single cost record may represent the aggregate cost of CPR units of the same size and the same year of installation. The average cost of similar units installed in each year can then be determined by dividing the aggregate cost by the number of CPR units represented by the aggregate cost. In the case of meters owned by the utility, it also is desirable to have a card showing the history of each meter, including its cost, date purchased, addresses at which used, and number of times repaired.

In the initial installation of a CPR system, an inventory of property must be made in accordance with the selected CPR units; this inventory can be prepared from existing utility records (such as maps and engineering reports) to the extent that such records exist. To the extent that records are unavailable or incomplete, a physical inventory of property units must be made.

After the inventory of property has been prepared, the cost of CPR units must be established.

Figure 16-9
PROPERTY RECORD CARD

THE WILLING WATER UTILITY
PROPERTY RECORD CARD

ITEM   Accounting Machine   PRIMARY ACCOUNT CLASSIFICATION   Office Furniture and Equipment

DESCRIPTION   Excelsior, Model 140   FROM WHOM ACQUIRED   Excelsior Company

SERIAL NUMBER   R-1734   ESTIMATED SERVICE LIFE   10 years

WHERE LOCATED OR STORED   Office   COST $2,000.00

PERSON RESPONSIBLE FOR ASSET   Office Manager   NET SALVAGE VALUE $200.00 (10%)

DEPRECIATION RATE (YEAR) $180.00 (9%)   (MONTH) $15.00 (0.75%)

| | | Asset Account | | | Accumulated Depreciation | | | Net Book Value |
Date	Description	Dr.	Cr.	Bal.	Dr.	Cr.	Bal.	
July 1, 1964	Purchase of Asset	$2,000.00		$2,000.00				$2,000.00
Dec. 31, 1965	Annual Depreciation					$ 90.00	$ 90.00	1,910.00
Dec. 31, 1966	Annual Depreciation					180.00	270.00	1,730.00
Dec. 31, 1967	Annual Depreciation					180.00	450.00	1,550.00

[5]The NARUC defines a retirement unit for a main as two or more standard lengths of main, including fittings, or one continuous run of 24 feet or more. Committee on Accounts and Statistics, National Association of Regulatory Utility Commissioners, List of Retirement Units of Property For Water Utilities 1962 (Washington, D.C.: National Association of Regulatory Utility Commissioners, 1962), p. 11.

Figure 16-10
EXAMPLE OF PROPERTY RECORD CARDS

PROPERTY RECORD SUMMARY CARD

ITEM __Pumphouse__ PRIMARY ACCOUNT CLASSIFICATION __321, Structures and Improvements__

LOCATION __Orchard Street__ ESTIMATED SERVICE LIFE __30 years (composite life)__

PERSON RESPONSIBLE FOR ASSET __Manager, Production Division__ NET SALVAGE VALUE __10% of Book Cost__

WHERE TAXED __Finewater City, Filter County__ SUMMARY CARD NO. __321-9__

CPR No.	Description of Structural Component	Cost
1	Floor	$15,500
2	Roof	18,300
3	Structure (Other than floor and roof)	33,800
4	Protective Fence	5,400
9	Plumbing System	4,200
10	Light and Power System	3,700
	TOTAL	$95,300

PROPERTY RECORD CARD

ITEM __Protective Fence for Pumphouse__ PRIMARY ACCOUNT CLASSIFICATION __321, Structures and Improvements__

PROPERTY RECORD CARD NO. __4__ ASSOCIATED SUMMARY CARD __321-9__

LOCATION __Orchard Street Pumphouse__ ESTIMATED SERVICE LIFE __25 years__

PERSON RESPONSIBLE FOR ASSET __Manager, Production Division__

WHERE TAXED __Finewater City, Filter County__ NET SALVAGE VALUE __5% of Book Cost__

Date of Installation	Description	Cost Debits	Cost Credits	Balance
Aug, 1957	Installation of five foot brick and wire fence around pumphouse (Investment work order 121-57)	$3,750		$3,750
May 1967	Removal of two foot wire topping on three-foot brick wall (Retirement work order 153-67)		$850	2,900
May 1967	Addition of four foot wire fence on top of three foot brick wall (Investment work order 174-67)	2,500		5,400

In the initial installation of a CPR system, direct and indirect costs (original cost in the case of commission-regulated water utilities) associated with inventoried CPR units should, if possible, be based on accounting entries and supporting documents such as work order authorizations and records, purchase requisitions and invoices, vouchers, and contracts. When accounting records are unavailable, or incomplete, costs of inventoried property units must be estimated by referring to labor wage rates, material costs, and other historical information relevant to the period when property units were constructed or purchased.

Maintaining the CPR System. After the CPR system has been installed, subsequent additions to and retirements of utility plant must be reflected in the property records in terms both of costs and quantities. To the extent possible, physical inventory tests also should be conducted periodically to establish the existence of property reflected by the CPR system.

The direct and indirect costs associated with additions to water utility plant are based on investment work order records and purchase invoices. These costs, which are transferred to property record cards, represent either the cost of individual property units (in the case of relatively large CPR units) or the aggregate cost of property units (in the case of relatively small, similar CPR units) installed during a given period of time.

The direct and indirect costs associated with retirement of water utility plant assets are based on retirement work order records. The cost of retirements credited to property record cards represents either the cost originally assigned to the individual property units being retired (in the case of relatively large CPR units) or the average cost of property units being retired (in the case of relatively small, similar, CPR units where the original cost is represented by the aggregate cost of similar units installed during a given period of time).

Figure 16-10 represents a simplified example of the continuing property record cards for a building, and they reflect the cost changes due to additions and retirements. If depreciation is accounted for by individual CPR units (such as might be the case for relatively large property items), rather than by treating each plant account, each functional group of accounts, or total depreciable property as a single account, accumulated depreciation charges should also be reflected by the property record cards. The property record depicted in Fig. 16-9 reflects accumulated depreciation on an individual item of equipment.

In summary, the elaborate procedures involved in a CPR system for allocating costs among property units permit the immediate determination of costs of property items being retired to the extent that the costs are recorded at the time of purchase or construction of property. In addition, the CPR system assists management in insuring that recorded costs correspond closely to the actual cost of property in service. This is important from the standpoint of establishing an appropriate rate base value to use in determining water rates. Further, the CPR system facilitates the placing of insurance by identifying the items of property that are insurable and by identifying the costs associated with insurable property items. The recorded cost of individual items of property frequently serves as the starting point for determining insurable value which, in turn, will determain the amount of premium payments required to obtain full (or adequate) insurance coverage. Finally, the CPR system functions as an important tool of internal control by serving as a perpetual inventory record of utility property.

CHAPTER 17. PLANNING AND CONTROLLING CURRENT ASSETS AND RESTRICTED ASSETS

As discussed in Chapter 15, utility plant comprises the greatest portion of the total assets of a water utility. Nevertheless, there also are other classes of assets which are of importance to a water utility. Among the more important classes of assets, other than plant, are current assets and restricted assets (or special funds). The NARUC defines "current and accrued assets" as follows: "Current and accrued assets are cash, those assets which are readily convertible into cash or are held for current use in operations or construction, current claims against other, payment of which is reasonably assured, and amounts accruing to the utility which are subject to current settlement, except such items for which accounts other than those designated as current and accrued assets are provided. There shall not be included in the group of accounts designated as current and accrued assets any item, the amount of collectibility of which is not reasonably assured, unless an adequate provision for possible loss has been made therefor."[1]

Current assets in relation to current liabilities (see Chapter 18) reflect the short term credit position of the utility. Asset items classified by the NARUC as current and accrued assets include cash, special deposits with fiscal agents, temporary cash investments, notes and accounts receivable, materials and supplies, and prepaid expenses.[2]

Restricted assets (or special funds) are comprised of cash and investments which have been segregated in special accounts and restricted for use for specific purposes such as bond debt service, replacement or construction of plant assets, and employees' pensions.[3] This chapter is concerned with planning and control of major kinds of current assets and restricted assets.

Planning and Controlling Liquid Assets

Current assets that are cash or near cash are called "liquid assets." Those assets customarily included in the liquid asset category include cash, temporary cash investments, and accounts receivable (primarily those from customers). In general, inventories of materials and supplies are not considered as liquid assets.

Nature of Cash. Cash includes demand deposits in banks, monies and checks (and other similar credit instruments that function as money) which are held by the utility for deposit, and petty cash (or working funds). Bank demand deposits generally comprise the greatest portion of cash. In order to be classified as cash, deposits with banks or other institutions must be available for use for general purposes. The deposits must be free and not restricted as to use either by contract or special trust agreement. The fact that water utility management may intend to use cash for the discharge of a particular obligation is not material so long as there is no legal compulsion to use the particular cash for that obligation. Therefore, special deposits with fiscal agents or others for the payment of interest, dividends (in the case of investor-owned water utilities), and for other special purposes are not considered as cash.

Sources of Cash. The sources of cash available to a water utility are many and varied. Most of the sources are described elsewhere in this book and are only briefly summarized here. The two major sources of cash for a water utility are cash received from the sale of water service to customers and cash received from investors in return for evidences of debt or ownership.

Other important sources of cash may include cash received from the rent of utility and nonutil-

---

[1]Committee on Accounts and Statistics, National Association of Regulatory Utility Commissioners, Uniform System of Accounts For Class A and B Water Utilities 1957 (Washington, D.C.: National Association of Regulatory Utility Commissioners, 1958), pp. 41-42.

[2]While special deposits with fiscal agents or others for the payment of interest, dividends, and for other special purposes are considered by the NARUC as current assets, the NCGA (National Committee on Governmental Accounting) considers such deposits as restricted assets.

[3]The NCGA recommends the use of the term "restricted assets" to describe cash and investments which have been segregated for use for specific purposes. The NARUC employs the use of the term "special funds".

ity plant assets leased to others, interest or dividends on securities owned, the sale of property and investments, customers' deposits, and advances and contributions for construction from customers, subdividers, and governmental authorities.

Uses of Cash. The disposition of cash can be considered to fall into four major categories: (1) payment of expenses (primarily operation and maintenance expenses and taxes) incurred in the conduct of utility and nonutility operations; (2) interest payments and repayment of principal amounts to creditors (and dividend payments to stockholders in the case of investor-owned water utilities); (3) capital expenditures; and (4) repayment of customers' meter deposits and advances for construction.

In general, the cash generated from the sale of water service and from the conduct of other miscellaneous utility and nonutility operations provides the source for payment of expenses incurred in the conduct of utility and nonutility operations and for payment of interest and, in the case of investor-owned water utilities, dividends. Of course, during periods when the generation of cash from operations is at a rate less than that required to discharge obligations, short term borrowings may be required to supplement cash resources. Short-term borrowings used to finance current operations are repaid during periods when the generation of cash from operations is at a rate greater than that required to finance current operations.

To the extent that retirement of long-term debt is not financed by new security issues, cash generated from the sale of water service is used to repay long-term debt obligations. For example, in the case of revenue bonds issued by a municipally-owned water utility, a portion of cash generated from operations typically is transferred periodically to asset accounts restricted for revenue bond debt service; these restricted funds are then used to pay interest and to repay debt principal. Debt service on general obligation bonds of municipally-owned water utilities also typically is payable from utility revenues. If operating revenues are insufficient, a general property tax levy may be required to meet debt service requirements.

Cash generated from the sale of water service (in excess of that required to pay operation and maintenance expenses, taxes, interest, and dividends, and to repay debt principal) can be used to finance current capital expenditures. In addition, a portion of cash generated from operations may be transferred to a restricted asset account (or depreciation fund) to be used to finance future replacement of plant assets. Cash received from investors, and advances and contributions in aid to construction, provide the other major sources for financing capital expenditures. In some instances, particularly in the case of municipally-owned water utilities, cash proceeds from a securities issue are segregated in a restricted asset account (or construction fund) to be used solely for capital expenditures.

In some jurisdictions, cash received as customers' deposits must be segregated in a restricted asset account. In such instances, the restricted assets serve as the source for repayment to customers of their deposits. If cash received from customers' deposits is not segregated, then cash generated from the sale of water service normally serves as the source for repayment of the deposits. In addition, repayment of advances from customers or others for construction typically is made from cash generated from the sale of water service.

If, during a given period of time, the cash accumulated by a water utility is in excess of needs for cash, the excess can be used to purchase investments, such as short-term government securities. This procedure permits the temporary use of idle cash to purchase earning assets with little risk of loss of principal when the investments are sold. Temporary investments are, of course, liquidated as required to meet obligations.

Cash Flow Statements. Information concerning the sources and uses of cash funds frequently is presented to water utility management in the form of cash flow statements. One form is depicted in Fig. 17-1. The preparation of the statement shown in Fig. 17-1 requires that cash receipts from operations and cash disbursements for operations be enumerated. This procedure is akin to the cash basis of accounting (as opposed to the accrual basis of accounting).

An alternate format for a cash statement is presented in Fig. 17-2. The preparation of the statement shown there is founded upon information contained in other statements, such as the income statement and balance sheet. The statement presented in Fig. 17-2 begins with the net income of the water utility (as determined under the accrual basis of accounting), together with necessary adjustments to reflect cash generated from operations. For example, depreciation and amortization expense must be added to net income since these expense items do not involve the disbursement of cash. In addition, other expense items (such as operation and maintenance expenses, taxes, and interest) as well as the pur-

Figure 17-1
THE WILLING WATER COMPANY
STATEMENT OF SOURCES AND USES OF CASH
For the Year Ended December 31, 19CY

Cash Balance, January 1, 19CY		$ 250,000
Cash Received From:		
Collection on Customer Accounts Receivable	$8,932,000	
Rent of Utility and Nonutility Property	37,000	
Interest and Dividends on Investments	14,000	
Net Cash Inflow—Advances and Contributions in Aid of Construction	125,000	
Net Cash Inflow—Customer Meter Deposits	10,000	
Sale of Property and Investments (Including Liquidation of Special Funds)	157,000	
Net Short-Term Borrowings	973,000	
Issuance of Long-Term Debt	2,947,000	
Other	15,000	
Total Cash Receipts During 19CY		$13,210,000
Total Cash Available During 19CY		$13,460,000
Cash Used For:		
Payments For Salaries and Wages	1,638,000	
Purchase of Materials and Supplies	2,947,000	
Purchase of Property and Investments	920,000	
Payments to Contractors For Construction	4,107,000	
Interest Payments	540,000	
Dividend Payments	1,312,000	
Tax Payments	1,283,000	
Repayment of Debt	300,000	
Other	142,000	
Total Cash Disbursement		$13,189,000
Cash Balance, December 31, 19CY		$ 271,000

Figure 17-2
THE CITY WATER DEPARTMENT
STATEMENT OF SOURCES AND USES OF CASH
For the Year Ended December 31, 19CY

Cash Balance, January 1, 19CY		$ 274,000
Cash was Provided By:		
Utility Operating Income Before Depreciation and Amortization Expense	$ 614,000	
Interest Income From Investments	23,000	
Sale of Utility Plant Assets	56,000	
Increase in Advances and Contributions in Aid of Construction	376,000	
Increase in Customer Meter Deposits	9,000	
Revenue Bond Issue	1,927,000	
Decrease in Non-Cash Current Assets	32,000	
Increase in Current Liabilities	78,000	
Other	14,000	
Total Cash Provided During 19CY		$3,129,000
Total Cash Available During 19CY		$3,403,000
Cash was Used For:		
Interest Charges	$ 306,000	
Retirement of Long-Term Debt	208,000	
Increase in Restricted Assets—Bond Debt Service	47,000	
Additions to Utility Plant	1,482,000	
Increase in Restricted Assets—Revenue Bond Proceeds	1,102,000	
Increase in Restricted Assets—Customer Meter Deposits	9,000	
Other	37,000	
Total Cash Used During 19CY		$3,191,000
Cash Balance, December 31, 19CY		$ 212,000

chase and construction of assets during the accounting period do not fully reflect cash disbursements; therefore, changes during the accounting period in the balances of current asset accounts other than cash, and in current liability accounts, must be considered in order to determine actual cash disbursements. For example, an increase in current liabilities generally indicates that cash disbursements are less than the amounts indicated by expenses and by the purchase and construction of assets during the period; therefore an increase in current liabilities can be considered as a source of cash. Similarly, an increase in current non-cash assets generally indicates a use of cash. For example, an increase in inventories of materials and supplies would be considered as a use of cash. Finally, revenues as shown in the income statement and the sale of plant assets and investments also will not fully reflect cash sources to the extent that there is a change in receivables during the accounting period. Therefore, an increase in receivables can be considered as a use of cash.[4]

Determining the Appropriate Amount of Cash. Perfect synchronization between cash realization from operations and the disbursement of cash in the discharge of obligations is impossible. Cash may be realized more rapidly than needed to discharge obligations, resulting in an excess of cash, or cash realization may not be adequate and borrowing may be required in order to discharge obligations. Cash held in checking accounts and cash on hand are nonearning assets. To the extent that cash balances are excessive, water utility management is withholding resources from possible profitable employment or is paying interest on borrowed money which is not needed by the utility to finance operations.

The amount of cash to be retained in bank accounts depends in part upon the amount to be held as minimum balances to compensate banks for services rendered, lines of credit or other credit agreements, and bank loans. In addition to minimum balances, cash in banks must be sufficient to permit the utility to conduct normal activities (both operating and capital expenditure activities). The amount held in banks for normal activities depends upon the seasonal requirements of the utility for cash needed for transactions. Finally, a utility may wish to maintain cash to meet contingencies. The amount of cash held as a safety factor to meet contingencies depends on the sub-

jective feelings of utility management toward risk. Contingencies should be interpreted as minor unforeseen requirements for cash. The amount of cash required to conduct normal utility activities and to meet contingencies, plus minimum balances required by banks, determines the appropriate amount of cash to be retained in bank accounts.

It should be noted that lines of credit or other credit agreements with banks may serve to reduce the appropriate amount of cash to be retained in bank accounts by reducing the amount of cash needed as a safety factor to meet contingencies. On the other hand, the use of lines of credit or other credit agreements will increase the appropriate amount of cash to be retained in bank accounts to the extent that additional compensating balances are required by banks under the terms of the credit arrangement. Lines of credit or other credit agreements are not for the purpose of meeting long-run cash needs; rather, they serve as a quick source of money to meet cash deficiencies which arise in the normal course of operations of the utility.[5]

Forecasting Cash Balances. While it is important that a water utility earn an adequate return, it is also important that the utility maintain an adequate cash position in order to discharge obligations as they mature. It is essential to sound financial planning and to the maintenance of an adequate cash position that forecasts of cash receipts and disbursements be made. Cash flow forecasts permit water utility management to anticipate future cash deficiencies and to augment cash balances by short-term borrowing or by issuing long-term securities. Likewise, cash flow forecasts permit management to formulate debt repayment plans and to plan the investment of excessive cash balances.

Forecasts of cash receipts and disbursements may be made for a year, a quarter, a month, or even for a week. For example, a one-year forecast of cash receipts and disbursements may be developed by months (or by quarters) and updated each month (or quarter) by dropping the elapsed month (or quarter) and adding the next month (or quarter). If the one-year cash flow forecast is made by quarters, the earliest quarter forecast should be made for each of the three months in that quarter. Figure 17-3 presents an example of a one-year forecast of cash receipts and disbursements by quarters, with the earliest quarter

[4] For an extended discussion of cash flow analysis, see: Perry Mason, Cash Flow Analysis and the Funds Statement, Accounting Research Study No. 2 (New York: American Institute of Certified Public Accountants, 1961).

[5] For a further discussion of the determination of the appropriate level of cash on hand, see: Harold Bierman Jr., Topics in Cost Accounting and Decisions (New York: McGraw-Hill Book Company, Inc., 1963), pp. 103-118.

Figure 17-3
THE CITY WATER DEPARTMENT
CASH FLOW FORECAST
For the Year 19BY

	1st Quarter—19BY			2nd Quarter —19BY	3rd Quarter —19BY	4th Quarter —19BY
	January	February	March			
Estimated Cash Balance, Beginning of Period	$250,000	$174,000	$ 69,000	$ 142,000	$ 96,000	$ 75,000
Estimated Cash Provided By:						
Sale of Water Service	$500,000	$500,000	$ 570,000	$1,630,000	$1,720,000	$1,790,000
Rent of Property	3,000	3,000	3,000	9,000	9,000	9,000
Interest on Investments	1,000	2,000	3,000	12,000	15,000	10,000
Sale of Plant Assets and Other Property	12,000	5,000	18,000	25,000	30,000	10,000
Advances and Contributions in Aid of Construction (net of repayment of Customer Advances)	10,000	12,000	14,000	50,000	60,000	60,000
Customer Meter Deposits (Net of repayments)	1,000	1,000	1,000	3,000	3,000	3,000
Use of Restricted Assets—Revenue Bond Proceeds				380,000	420,000	200,000
Short-Term Borrowings				300,000		
Issuance of Bonds			1,972,000			
Other	5,000	5,000	5,000	15,000	15,000	15,000
Estimated Total Cash Provided During Period	$532,000	$528,000	$2,586,000	$2,424,000	$2,272,000	$2,097,000
Estimated Total Cash Available During Period	$782,000	$702,000	$2,655,000	$2,566,000	$2,368,000	$2,172,000
Estimated Cash Disbursements:						
Salaries and Wages	$ 80,000	$ 80,000	$ 75,000	$ 250,000	$ 255,000	$ 235,000
Materials and Supplies	160,000	165,000	150,000	670,000	540,000	450,000
Payments to Outside Contractors for Construction	200,000	250,000	150,000	930,000	870,000	530,000
Purchase of Plant Assets and Other Property	75,000	60,000	65,000	225,000	210,000	100,000
Interest (Payments From Other Than Restricted Assets)	15,000	10,000	25,000	50,000	75,000	60,000
Taxes	8,000	10,000	20,000	75,000	32,000	98,000
Repayment of Short-Term Borrowings	15,000	5,000	10,000	20,000	60,000	310,000
Transfers to Restricted Assets—Bond Debt Service	40,000	40,000	35,000	200,000	195,000	190,000
Transfers to Restricted Assets—Customer Meter Deposits	1,000	1,000	3,000	3,000	3,000	3,000
Transfers to Restricted Assets—Proceeds from Sale of Bonds			1,972,000			
Other	14,000	12,000	10,000	47,000	53,000	32,000
Estimated Total Cash Disbursements During Period	$608,000	$633,000	$2,513,000	$2,470,000	$2,293,000	$2,008,000
Estimated Cash Balance End of Period	$174,000	$ 69,000	$ 142,000	$ 96,000	$ 75,000	$ 164,000

forecast by months. The forecast anticipates the need for short-term and long-term borrowing in order to meet cash deficiencies and to maintain a minimum cash balance. In general, the longer the period covered by the cash flow forecast and the more distant in time the period covered, the less reliable are the estimates; therefore, periodic revisions in cash flow estimates are required in order for the estimates to serve as useful financial planning guides.

The forecast of cash receipts and disbursements during the budget period is based in part on past experience and in part on anticipated changes in the activities of the water utility during the budget period. Forecast monthly or quarterly cash receipts from the sale of water service are based on the revenue budget, adjusted for differences between the revenue estimates as determined on the accrual basis and revenues as determined on the cash basis; this adjustment may be made by applying a ratio, based on past experience, of cash receipts to revenues. Forecasting other sources of cash, such as the rental of utility property, interest and dividends on securities owned, customers' deposits, and advances and contributions for construction, can be based on past experience adjusted for anticipated changes during the budget period. Cash receipts from the sale of utility property and investments generally are more difficult to estimate. To the extent possible, such estimates must be based on management's plans to dispose of property and investments and on prospective market prices for such property and investments.

Forecasts of monthly or quarterly cash disbursements for operations are based on the operating budget, adjusted for differences between expense estimates as determined on the accrual basis and expenses as determined on the cash basis. For example, cash disbursements for wages and salaries in any given month or quarter may vary depending upon the number of "paydays" falling within the period. Since monthly or quarterly labor expense included in the operating budget reflects expenses incurred (but not necessarily paid), an adjustment is necessary to place labor expense on a cash basis.

In addition, monthly or quarterly materials and supplies expense included in the operating budget ordinarily differs from cash outlays for operating materials and supplies. Particular material and supply items used usually are included in expenses at the average unit cost of the material and supply items on hand during the accounting period. Therefore, to the extent that materials and supplies are on hand at the beginning of the budget period, the cost of such items will influence the expense estimates included in the operating budget. On the other hand, cash disbursements for operating materials and supplies depend on actual outlays during the budget period, regardless of whether such materials and supplies are actually used during the period. Therefore, it may prove helpful in estimating cash outlays for operating materials and supplies to base such estimates on a separate materials and supplies budget (discussed later in this chapter) rather than the estimate of materials and supplies expense included in the operating budget. The materials and supplies budget is, of course, based on requirements for materials as reflected in the operating budget.

Cash outlays for taxes also differ from tax expense. Monthly or quarterly cash outlays for taxes depend upon the scheduled tax payment dates falling within each period. The operating budget reflects accrued taxes and is not affected by dates on which the taxes are actually paid.

Monthly or quarterly cash outlays for interest payments, repayment of debt principal, and dividend payments (in the case of investor-owned water utilities) must also be anticipated. Interest payment dates for short-term borrowings depend upon the terms of existing borrowing agreements. Dividends on capital stock typically are paid quarterly. Monthly or quarterly cash disbursements for repayment of debt principal depend upon existing repayment schedules as determined by debt agreements. Repayments of principal amounts of serial bond issues typically are made semiannually or annually. Cash disbursements for repayment of term bond issues must also be included in the cash budget if such issues mature during the budget period. Cash disbursements for repayment of debt principal (or for both the payment of interest and the repayment of debt principal) may, of course, be based on a schedule of payments to asset accounts (i.e., special funds) restricted for bond debt service.

Monthly or quarterly cash outlays for capital investment projects (both additions and retirements) are an important component of estimated monthly or quarterly cash disbursements. The capital expenditures budget, together with the construction work schedule and the schedule for purchasing plant assets during the budget period, serves as the basis for forecasting these disbursements. To the extent that the capital expenditures budget reflects accrued costs, as opposed to actual payments, the budget must be adjusted to a cash basis. In the case of contracts with outsiders, progress payment dates and final payment dates as provided by existing or proposed contracts determine when cash outlays will occur. In addition, monthly or quarterly outlays for the payroll of construction workers must be estimated. Further, the cost of construction materials and supplies as included in the capital expenditures budget may differ substantially from actual outlays for such items. (See the preceding discussion in this section concerning cash outlays for operating materials and supplies.) Therefore, it may prove helpful in estimating cash outlays for construction materials and supplies to base such estimates on a separate materials and supplies budget (discussed in a later section of this chapter).

To the extent that capital investment projects are paid for from assets (i.e., special funds) restricted for construction or replacement of utility plant, disbursements from general cash for capital investment are reduced. Therefore, total disbursements for capital investment, as shown in the cash budget, may be reduced by the amounts to be paid from restricted assets. As an alternative, the assets restricted for construction or replacement of utility plant, which are to be expended during the budget period, may be considered separately as a source of cash rather than subtracted from total cash disbursements for capital investments. By the same token, scheduled payments to restricted asset accounts during the budget period (for future expenditure for construction or replacement) must also be included among cash disbursements.

Past experience, adjusted for anticipated changes during the budget period, serves as the base for estimating repayments of customers' deposits and advances for construction. Estimated cash outflows resulting from repayment of customers' deposits and advances for construction may be offset against estimated cash inflows from customers' deposits and advances and contributions. Accordingly, estimated net cash inflow from customers' deposits and advances and contributions for construction should then be included as a source of cash.

After cash sources and uses (including interest and repayment of principal amounts on existing debt) are estimated for each month or quarter of the budget period, the resulting net cash balance for each month or quarter will indicate the need for, and timing of, additional financing through borrowings (and/or through the issuance of stock, in the case of investor-owned water utilities). The cash forecast must then be readjusted for the effect on monthly or quarterly cash flows of the additional required financing. The cash forecast included in Figure 17-3 includes anticipated borrowings during the budget period. The monthly or quarterly cash forecast, including the cash flows resulting from additional financing during the budget period, also permits management to plan for the temporary investment of excessive cash balances which are forecast as developing during the budget period.

Controlling Cash. Cash is perhaps the easiest asset to lose through theft and defalcation; therefore, rigid control over cash should be practiced. Proper internal control of cash requires that the persons handling cash should not be given the responsibility of accounting for cash (and vice versa). The work of every employee concerned with cash should be reviewed by other employees so that a continuous check and audit is made of all cash receipts and disbursements.

In the case of cash receipts, a requisite of an adequate system of internal control is the preparation of a receipt document at the time cash is received by the utility. The receipt document then passes through bookkeeping channels while the cash itself passes through cashier channels for deposit in bank accounts. Personnel responsible for receiving cash should not be given duties involving the keeping of accounting records. In addition, persons receiving cash should have no duties involving the preparation of customer bills.

Cashiers should be required to turn over to the head cashier each day the amount of cash collected through payments made in person by customers or received from other sources. The individual cashier reports summarizing cash receipts, together with the receipt stubs, should be reconciled by the head cashier with the amount of cash received from each cashier. Copies of the cashiers' reports, together with the receipt stubs, should be turned over to the bookkeeping personnel.

Remittances received by mail should be handled by employees under effective supervision, and each remittance should be accompanied by a bill. Remittances by mail should be turned over daily to the head cashier, while a report summarizing remittances by mail, together with bill stubs as verified by the head cashier, should be turned over to bookkeeping personnel. Each day's cash receipts should be deposited daily in a bank and a copy of the deposit slip should be reconciled with the daily cashiers' reports and the daily mail receipts report by an employee having no other connection with the accounting records or the handling of cash. Figure 17-4 presents a summary diagram of the flow of cash received by a water utility and of the accounting for cash receipts so as to obtain effective internal control over the receipts.

All cash disbursements, except for minor ex-

Figure 17-4
ACCOUNTING CONTROL OF CASH RECEIPTS

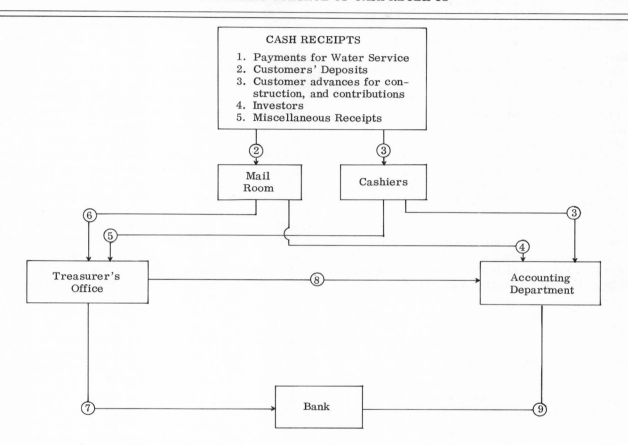

1. Payments from customers or other sources are made in person. Cashiers prepare a list of receipts showing customer account numbers or other sources of payment, and the amounts received.
2. Payments are received by mail. Mail clerks prepare a mail remittance list showing customer account numbers or other sources of payment, and the amounts received.
3. A copy of the list of receipts, together with receipt stubs, is routed to the Accounting Department where it is used as the basis for recording the receipt transactions as an increase in cash and a decrease in accounts receivable or an increase in liabilities or equities.
4. A copy of the mail remittance list, together with receipt stubs, is routed to the Accounting Department where it is used as the basis for recording the receipt transactions as an increase in cash and a decrease in accounts payable or an increase in liabilities or equities.
5. Cash received by cashiers, together with a list of the cash receipts is forwarded to the Treasurer's Office.
6. The mail remittances, along with a copy of the remittance list, are forwarded to the Treasurer's Office.
7. The Treasurer's Office deposits cash receipts intact in the bank on a daily basis.
8. A copy of the bank deposit slip is sent to the Accounting Department. It is compared with the list of receipts from cashiers and the mail remittance list to see that all cash receipts were deposited in the bank.
9. At month-end, the bank renders a bank statement showing the opening cash balance, the daily bank deposits, the checks drawn against the account (see Fig. 17-5), and the closing cash balance. The Accounting Department prepares a reconciliation of the bank balance of cash with the book balance of cash.

penditures made through the petty cash fund (or working fund), should be made by check. Invoices received should be properly vouchered after comparison with receiving reports or other documents to insure that value has been actually received by the utility. Cash disbursements should be authorized by the treasurer of the utility or his properly designated representative. In addition, all checks should be required to be signed by an authorized person who is responsible for examination of the voucher and other documents supporting the disbursement. Persons responsible fore the check signing function should be other than those responsible for the bookkeeping function.

Disbursements from the petty cash fund (or working fund) should be supported by sales receipts or other memoranda. At the time it is reimbursed the petty cash fund should be examined by someone other than the person in charge of the fund to verify that the amount of the reimbursement check (properly vouchered) corresponds with the amount by which the petty cash fund is depleted. Figure 17-5 presents a summary diagram of the flow of cash disbursed by a water utility and of the accounting for cash disburse-

ments so as to obtain effective control over the disbursements.

For proper control, it is also necessary that the bank balance per bank statement be reconciled monthly with the bank balance per the utility's books. This reconciliation should be performed by an employee having no other connection with the accounting records or the handling of cash. In addition to maintaining adequate internal control over cash in order to prevent theft and defalcation, it is also important that water utility management maintain close and continual control over cash balances in order to insure sufficient cash to meet maturing obligations. The general manager and/or treasurer customarily receives a daily cash report which summarizes cash receipts and disbursements and the cash balance; such a report is similar in nature to that shown in Fig. 17-1.

The daily cash report permits management to observe the present cash position of the utility and to compare the actual cash position with the position as forecast by the cash budget. If the actual cash position differs substantially from the forecast position, a revision of the cash forecast may be required. In addition, reports of actual cash position may indicate that financing plans

Figure 17-5
ACCOUNTING CONTROL OF CASH DISBURSEMENTS

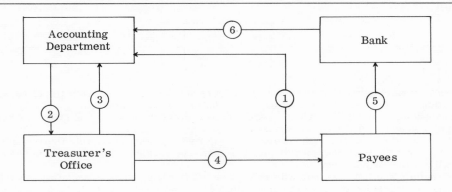

1. The Accounting Department receives invoices and bills from payees (vendors, contractors, employees, etc.) which are approved for payment. Included among the payees is "petty cash."
2. The Accounting Department prepares checks to be signed and forwards them, together with vouchers and supporting documents (invoices and bills approved for payment), to the Treasurer's Office.
3. The Treasurer examines the vouchers and supporting documents, and the checks to be signed. If satisfied that the disbursements are proper he signs the checks. The supporting documents are stamped "paid" and are returned to the Accounting Department where they are used as the basis for recording the disbursement transaction.
4. The signed checks are not returned to the Accounting Department, but are sent from the Treasurer's Office directly to the payees.
5. The payees present the checks to the bank for payment and the bank balance is reduced by the amount of the checks.
6. At month-end, the bank sends a bank statement, together with the cancelled checks, to the water utility. The Accounting Department or auditing department reconciles the bank balance with the book balance of cash.

should be altered, both from the standpoint of seeking additional sources of cash and from the standpoint of revamping planned borrowing and debt repayment schedules.

Planning and Controlling Other Liquid Assets. Temporary investments represent a short-term use of cash which is temporarily in excess of needs. Such excess amounts of cash might develop from sources such as seasonal or other periodic excesses of cash inflows from the sale of water service over cash outflows for operating expenses, or cash received through contributions or from investors (other than amounts transferred to restricted asset accounts) which is held temporarily pending more permanent investment in plant assets. In addition, cash may be accumulated from a number of sources in anticipation of future outlays for general utility purposes, such as payment of taxes, payment of interest (if not paid from restricted assets), and payment of dividends (in the case of investor-owned water utilities). Therefore, unless invested temporarily, pending future cash needs for ordinary utility purposes, or pending a more permanent investment decision, the cash would lie idle in a checking account rather than making a contribution to net income.

Temporary investments ordinarily consist of readily marketable securities. Municipally-owned water utilities usually are limited by statute or charter as to the types of securities in which cash can be invested, such as bank certificates of deposit, or federal, state, and municipal securities. Investor-owned water utilities may invest in certificates of deposit, stocks, bonds, or other debt instruments. In some instances, the board of directors may limit the type of securities which are eligible for investment. In all cases, the general manager or other members of top management should approve specific investments in temporary securities. An attempt should be made to invest in securities which will bring a reasonable return, but safety of principal should receive primary consideration. Certificates of deposit, governmental securities, and other debt instruments customarily offer a small risk of loss (or gain) of principal and offer a relatively safe investment; they provide interest income for whatever period they are held. Even among debt instruments there are variations in risk. For example, short term goverment securities are less risky than long term government securities in the sense that the price of short term securities may be expected to change less during the period of investment than would the price of long term securities. In addition to differences in risk due to differences in maturities, risk among debt instruments differs depending upon the issuing body. For example, investment in government securities generally is considered to involve less risk of loss (or gain) of principal for a given maturity than corporate debt instruments. Of course, the income from investment in high grade debt instruments may not be as great as it would if investment were made in securities such as stocks or low grade debt instruments.

General guidelines concerning the type of securities which can be purchased and the composition of the securities portfolio should be provided by the board of directors, city council, state legislature or other policy-making group. The guidelines should not, however, render management incapable of taking advantage of market conditions which permit the improvement of returns from temporary securities consistent with reasonable risk.

Within the limits set by law and by the board of directors, city council, or other policy-making group, it is reasonable for a water utility to invest in long-term securities or non-U.S. government securities and to bear the accompanying risk if management believes the differential in income, as compared with short term U.S. government securities, is such that the risk is outweighted by the expected return. Water utility management may also have a policy of buying securities which mature on a date close to the time when cash from the liquidation of securities is expected to be needed. However, utility management may desire to invest in securities which mature after the time cash is needed, but which can be readily converted into cash when needed.

From the standpoint of internal control, detailed inventory records regarding securities acquired should be maintained, and should include information regarding description, purchase price, maturity date, and income of the securities. Securities should be kept so that there will be no possibility of theft or mishandling. Only responsible officials should have access to them, and, whenever possible, securities should be registered. If they cannot be registered, they should be endorsed so as to prevent their negotiation without proper authorization.

Receivables. Receivables expected to be paid to the utility within a year are customarily classified as current assets. Included within the classification "receivables" are receivables from associated companies (in the case of investor-owned organizations), customer accounts receivable, receivables from officers and employees, and amounts due from other municipal departments (in the case of municipally-owned water utilities).

Typically, accounts receivable from customers comprise the major portion of receivables unless customers are billed in advance as is done in many flat rate territories.

Receivables, together with cash and temporary investments, represent purchasing power in suspense; as such, the utility is primarily interested in the market or cash value of the receivables. Therefore, the utility must provide for possible losses from uncollectible notes and accounts receivable. The appropriate amount to be included in the Accumulated Provision for Uncollectibles account will depend on the credit and collection policies of the utility (see Chapter 10), the existing economic conditions of the locality served by the utility, and the length of the meter reading and billing period used by the utility. The total investment in customer accounts receivable also depends upon the length of the meter reading and billing period; the longer the period the greater the investment in accounts receivable. The control of customer accounts receivable is discussed in other portions of this book, particularly in connection with controlling and accounting for revenues (Chapter 10) and in connection with the preceding discussion in this chapter dealing with the control of cash.

Planning and Controlling Materials and Supplies Inventory

The materials and supplies inventory of a water utility is comprised of many items including fuel stocks, chemicals for the treatment of water and other materials and supplies used in the operation of utility plant facilities, maintenance materials and supplies, construction materials and supplies, and materials and supplies held primarily for merchandising, jobbing, and contract work. In general, all material and supply items, regardless of their purpose, are considered as current assets. The NARUC classification of accounts (see the Appendix) provides a number of current asset accounts to be used to record the cost of materials and supplies. These accounts provide for the cost of supervision, labor, and other expenses incurred in purchasing, storing, handling, and distributing material and supply items as well as the invoice price of the items.

Particular material and supply items may be held in stock for a relatively short or relatively long period of time depending upon the nature of, and frequency of need for, the item. For example, fuel stocks and chemical stocks may be maintained in amounts sufficient for operating requirements for an extended period of time. The turnover of some operating material and supply items may be quite rapid because the items are continually used in operation and maintenance activities. The turnover of other operating items may be extremely slow because such items are held to meet emergency requirements.

The cost of materials and supplies purchased by the water utility are charged to the appropriate materials and supplies account and placed in stores until required for use by the utility. The cost of material and supply items is charged to expense accounts or investment work orders when the items are issued from stores for a specific purpose. Typically, the cost of material and supply items is charged to expense accounts or investment work orders and credited to inventory accounts on the basis of actual cost, average cost, first-in-first-out, or such other method of inventory accounting as conforms with accepted accounting standards consistently applied.[6]

Planning Investment in Materials and Supplies. Typically, investment in material and supply inventories for a water utility is substantial and requires careful planning. Such planning takes the form of a materials and supplies budget. The materials and supplies budget is a plan for the purchase of materials and supplies during the budget period. This budget is developed after considering the material and supply requirements of the operating budget and capital expenditures budget, the existing inventories of material and supply items, and the desired inventory level of material and supply items at the end of the budget period. Of course, the greater the construction work performed by the utility itself (as opposed to work by outside contractors) the greater will be the materials and supplies budget.

The materials and supplies budget should be prepared to show material and supply requirements in terms of dollars, as well as a detailed listing of material and supply items required for stock. In addition, a time schedule for the purchase of such items during the budget period should be prepared. The time schedule permits management to plan the purchase of material and supply items so as to avoid the cost of maintaining

---

[6] For an extended discussion of stores accounting, see: Adolph Matz, Othel J. Curry, and George W. Frank, Cost Accounting (4th ed.; Cincinnati: South-Western Publishing Company, 1967); Gordon Shillinglaw, Cost Accounting: Analysis and Control (Rev. ed.; Homewood, Illinois: Richard D. Irwin, Inc., 1967); and John J. W. Neuner and Samuel Frumer, Cost Accounting: Principles and Practice (7th ed.; Homewood, Illinois: Richard D. Irwin, Inc. 1967), particularly pp. 98-164.

higher-than-necessary levels of inventories of materials and supplies (resulting from premature purchases) while at the same time insuring that adequate levels of material and supply items are on hand to meet operating and construction requirements.

The materials and supplies budget in terms of dollars, together with the time schedule of purchases, facilitates the determination of cash disbursements resulting from the purchase of materials and supplies and provides information for the development of the cash budget (as discussed earlier in this chapter). The listing of material and supply items included in the budget, together with the proposed time schedule of purchases, permits stores personnel to plan their operations during the budget period.

The operation and maintenance budget and the capital expenditures budget are the foundation for the preparation of the materials and supplies budget. The operating and construction requirements for material and supply items are then adjusted for items already on hand and for planned reductions or increases in existing levels of inventory items during the budget period. Inventories of material and supply items should be maintained at levels which minimize cost. In the language of operations researchers, a proper inventory level for a particular item is one which minimizes the cost of carrying a given inventory level plus the cost of not carrying enough inventory. The cost of carrying inventory includes the risk of obsolesence, interest on investment, handling and storage cost, property taxes and property insurance, and clerical costs. The cost of not carrying enough inventory includes the costs incident upon an interruption of service supplied by the utility (loss of revenues, loss of customer goodwill, and extra cost of making emergency purchases). In determining the amount of purchases during the budget period, utility management should also consider the benefits of quantity discounts, transportation conditions, and possibilities of changes in market prices of material and supply items.

Stores Control. Because of the value of materials and supplies carried in inventory by a water utility, it is important that the utility establish a proper system for controlling and accounting for materials and supplies. Stores control involves not only the maintenance of inventory records but also the utilization of techniques to maximize profitability by balancing inventory investment against what is needed to sustain smooth operations. Each water utility should have a centralized stores system so that duplications and overstocking of materials and supplies is avoided and so that effective control over purchasing, receiving, storing, issuing, and transferring of materials and supplies is obtained. In some instances, due to the size of the utility, it may be desirable to maintain a number of storerooms close to facilities serviced in order to minimize travel and delivery cost; however, all inventories should remain subject to centralized planning and control.

Among the elements of an effective stores control and accounting system are proper procedures for the following:

1. Classification of materials and supplies
2. Purchasing
3. Receiving and inspecting
4. Handling and storing materials and supplies
5. Issuing items and transferring such items between jobs or storerooms
6. Conducting physical counts to verify recorded balances
7. Rendering reports on the status of inventories.

Classification of Materials and Supplies. Items carried in inventory must be properly classified and identified so that they can be accounted for and located when needed. A large water utility may, for example, have 20,000 separate items in its inventory;[7] therefore, proper classification and identification of inventory items is a requisite to efficient operation of the stores activity. As an example, pipe must be classified by type and diameter. In addition, a unit of issue must be chosen (feet of pipe, for example) and a stock number assigned to each item.

Purchasing Procedures. Although the size of the water utility will determine the complexity of its purchasing organization, the purchasing activity should be centralized. In some municipalities, a separate working capital fund handles purchasing, storing, and issuing. Centralized purchasing permits the realization of quantity discounts from combined purchases (as opposed to losing such discounts as a result of having each segment of the organization make its own purchases), the elimination of overstocking or duplications of materials and supplies inherent in a system of decentralized purchasing, and the utilization of

[7] American Water Works Association, Water Utility Management Manual, AWWA M5 (New York: American Water Works Association, 1959), pp. 103-107.

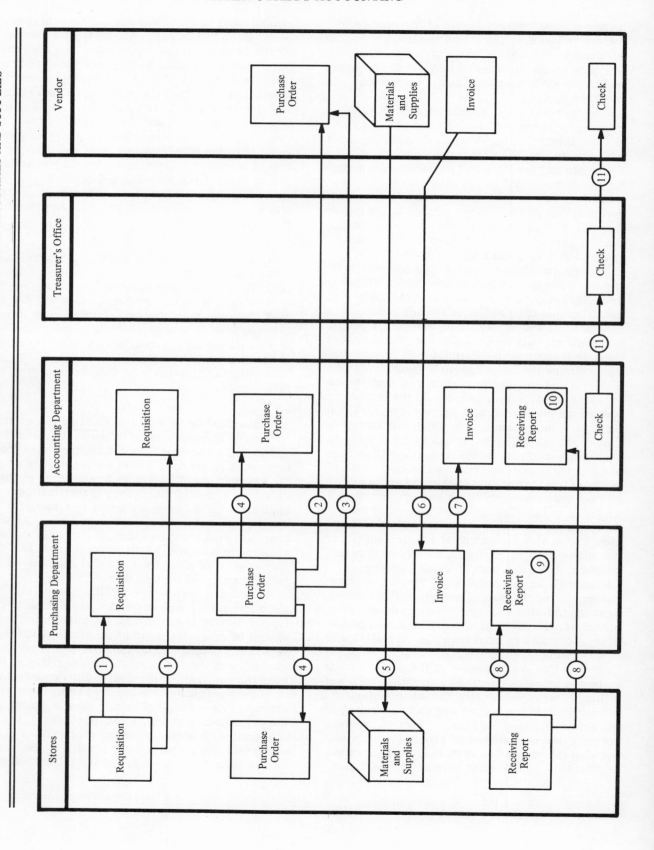

Figure 17-6

FLOW OF INFORMATION AND DOCUMENTS RELATED TO THE PURCHASING AND RECEIVING OF MATERIALS AND SUPPLIES

1. The purchase requisition is prepared by stores personnel indicating the item to be purchased and the quantity to be purchased (EOQ); copies are forwarded to the purchasing department and accounting department.

2. A purchase order is prepared by the purchasing department indicating the desired items to be purchased, the quantities to be purchased, and the desired time and place of delivery; typically, the order is placed with a supplier on the basis of competitive bidding.

3. Receipt of purchase order is acknowledged by vendor.

4. A copy of acknowledged purchase order is forwarded to the accounting department for the purpose discussed in item 10 below. A copy of the purchase order also is sent to stores as notification of the status of the order and expected delivery date.

5. Materials and supplies shipped by vendor and received by stores.

6. Invoice (showing description and quantity of items shipped, date shipped, carrier, prices for which the utility is being billed, and payment terms) is forwarded from vendor to purchasing department.

7. Copy of invoice forwarded from purchasing department to accounting department.

8. Upon receipt of the purchased goods from suppliers, stores personnel count, weigh, or otherwise measure the quantity of goods received; the quality of the goods also is determined. A receiving report is prepared by stores personnel indicating the quantity, conditions, and description of all items received. Copies of the receiving report are forwarded to the purchasing department and to the accounting department.

9. The purchasing department compares the receiving report with the sales invoice and purchase order to determine any discrepancies which require settlement with vendors.

10. The accounting department also compares the receiving report with the purchase order and the sales invoice. If the three documents agree (if the utility is being billed for the quantities actually received and at the agreed prices) then the invoice can be approved for payment. The accounting department then records the acquisition of the materials and supplies and the related liability to the supplier.

11. A check, properly vouchered and supported by the sales invoice and other documents, is prepared by the accounting department and forwarded for signature to the treasurer's office. The signed check is then mailed to the vendor (see Fig. 17–5).

personnel who are skilled or specially trained in purchasing activities.

Two major decisions are required in placing a purchase order for a particular item—when to place an order, and the size of the order. When to place an order will depend on the lead time (the time interval between placing an order and receiving delivery) and the rate of use of an item. For example, if the lead time is twenty days and the average rate of use of an item is four units per day, then a purchase request should be initiated when the inventory level for the item reaches eighty units. Normally, however, a safety factor would be included to allow for fluctuations in usage of an item. This would increase the order point for the item.

The size of the order depends upon factors such as the quantity of an item used per unit of time, the incremental cost of placing an order, the cost of carrying one unit of an item in stock per unit of time, the cost of being out of stock one unit, and quantity discounts. The optimum size of order or economic order quantity (EOQ) is that quantity which minimizes the costs enumerated above. A number of mathematical techniques and formulas have been developed to determine the EOQ for an item of inventory.[8] It is apparent that a decrease in the order point and/or a decrease in the order size will decrease the carrying cost of inventory and increase the cost of being out of stock. An increase in the order point and/or an increase in the order size will increase the carrying cost of inventory and decrease the cost of being out of stock.

When the level of a particular material of supply item approaches the order point, a purchase requisition should be prepared by stores personnel and forwarded to the purchasing department. The ordering procedure will depend upon the amount to be ordered and the requirements of law. As in the case of contracts with outsiders for construction, municipally-owned water utilities typically are required by law to obtain competitive bids for purchases in excess of a stated amount. Even if not required by law, it may be desirable for a utility to request formal bids before placing an order. In any event, the purchasing activity should obtain information regarding prices, payment terms, reliability of vendors with respect to meeting delivery dates, and quality of products, before selecting vendors.

In addition to selecting vendors, the purchasing department also is responsible for obtaining proper authorization to make purchases. The approved materials and supplies budget may serve as authorization. If the budget is a legally binding document for municipally-owned water utilities, the purchasing department must insure that limits on committing funds are not exceeded. In cases where budgeted amounts are inadequate, additional authorization to commit funds must be obtained.

Procedures for Receiving Materials and Supplies. When materials are received in the storeroom, they should be inspected, counted, and recorded by the storekeeper. A copy of the purchase order should be on hand so that the storekeeper can verify that the goods received are in compliance with the specifications. A receiving report should then be prepared by the storekeeper for comparison with the vendor's invoice and with the purchase order, to ascertain that the prices, quantities, and terms are in agreement. Any irregularities between amounts ordered, amounts received, or amounts billed for by vendors should be resolved before payments are made to vendors. Figure 17-6 presents a diagram which summarizes the flow of information and documents related to the purchasing and receiving of materials and supplies. This diagram also reflects the segregation of duties necessary for effective internal control.

Handling and Storing Materials and Supplies. Several considerations should be kept in mind in connection with the storing of material and supply inventories. Materials and supplies should be stored in a safe place. This means not only that the inventories should be protected from loss due to weather, fire, theft, and other hazards, but also be protected from unauthorized use by employees of the water utility. Materials and supplies should be removed from storerooms only with proper authorization, and only those persons responsible for material and supply inventories should have access to the storerooms.

All materials and supplies should be stored so that they can be issued, moved, and inventoried easily. Items should be readily identified by descriptive tags and stock numbers to ease the task of issuing and inventorying materials and supplies.

Issuing Materials and Supplies. Materials and supplies should be issued from the storeroom only upon receipt of a properly approved material requisition. The requisition serves two basic

---

[8] For an extended discussion of the optimum order point and the EOQ and the associated mathematimatical formulas, see: Harold Bierman Jr., Charles P. Bonini, Lawrence E. Fouraker, and Robert K. Jaedicke, Quantitative Analysis for Business Decisions (Rev. ed.; Homewood, Illinois: Richard D. Irwin, Inc., 1965) pp. 128-156; and Charles T. Horngren, Cost Accounting-A Managerial Emphasis (2nd ed.; Englewood Cliffs, N. J.: Prentice-Hall, Inc., 1967) pp. 531-555.

purposes: the charging of the cost of the material to the appropriate construction order or expense account, and the recording of the transaction as it affects the detailed stores records. The requisition should include information concerning the quantity and description of each item ordered, delivery instructions, the job or account to which the material is to be charged, and the proper approval or authorization for issuance of the materials and supplies. On the requisition the storekeeper should record the quantity of each item furnished, enter the proper code numbers for the items, and forward a copy of the requisition to the stores accounting section.

Of importance equal to the material requisition is the material credit, or return, which accompanies the return of material and supplies from a job or account to the storeroom. The same information should be shown on the material return as on the material requisition, and the processing should follow the same procedure.

The third type of document to record stores transactions is the material transfer, which is used to record the transfer of materials and supplies from one job to another or, in those instances where a number of storerooms are maintained, from one storeroom to another. Material transfer documents should carry the same information as the material requisitions and returns, showing both the job, account, or storeroom from which the material is taken, and the one to which it is transferred.

If all the transactions discussed in the preceding paragraphs regarding the receipt, issuance, return, and transfer of materials and supplies are properly recorded on stock records, it is possible to know at any given time exactly how many units of each category of materials and supplies are in the storeroom, and the cost of each category. Such a system of records is known as a "perpetual inventory."

The mechanics of posting the information will vary depending upon the frequency of transactions and the number of categories of materials and supplies. If the transactions are few and the number of categories small, the transactions may be manually posted to ledger cards. If the number of transactions is large, bookkeeping machines or electronic data processing equipment may be used. In all instances, however, the basic procedure for maintaining stock records is the same.

Figure 17-7 presents an example of a stock ledger card for a material or supply item. It is assumed in this example that material and supply items are charged to accounts or jobs on the basis of the average cost per unit of inventory; this

method simply involves the computation of a new average cost after each acquisition.

Physical Inventories. For several reasons it is necessary to supplement the maintenance of the perpetual inventory records with an actual physical count of the materials and supplies on hand. A physical count will verify the inventory records and will substantiate the figures which appear in the utility's financial reports. It is also necessary to take the physical inventory regularly in order to adjust the records because of any errors which may have occurred in the preparation or recording of the material documents. All materials and supplies in stores should be physically inventoried at least once a year. The physical inventory can be conducted by counting all stores items at the end of a fiscal period, at a time of minimum activity, or when minimum quantities of stores items are on hand. Further, the physical count can be made on a piecemeal basis by inventorying only certain items at one time, since separate records are available for each category of materials and supplies. The responsibility for the physical inventories should be vested in a different individual, or department, from the one responsible for the maintenance of the storerooms and inventory records. This segregation of responsibility helps to insure that inventory shortages are discovered and not covered up (by falsifying inventory counts) by those persons responsible for the maintenance of stocks.

Any significant differences between the inventory records and the physical count should be investigated to determine whether they are due to shrinkage, breakage, counting errors, recording errors, or theft. After this is completed, and the proper steps taken to correct the situation, the inventory records should be adjusted to the figures disclosed by the physical count.

Material and Supply Status Reports. To facilitate the operation of the stores control system, and to obtain benefits from the system, periodic reports showing the status of materials and supplies should be prepared for management. These reports should be prepared weekly, monthly, or as otherwise needed. Reports on materials and supplies should show, for the period covered by the reports, information regarding the activity of each major type of material and supply item. For each type of material and supply item, activity information includes the balance at the beginning of the period, quantities of the item received and issued during the period, the balance at the end of the period, and amounts of the item on order but not yet received.

In addition, it is desirable to indicate in the

Figure 17-7
STOCK LEDGER CARD

WILLING WATER UTILITY				LOCATION Storeroom #3, Bin #47-C		STOCK LEDGER CARD
DESCRIPTION OF ITEM Materials "A," size #3					STOCK NUMBER SO-413	
MAXIMUM STOCK 260 units			REORDER QUANTITY 200 units		REORDER POINT 60 units	ACCOUNT NUMBER 154

RECEIPTS

Date	Req. No.	Qty.	Unit Cost	Amount
19CY				
Jan. 2	Bal. For.	100	$0.50	$ 50.00
Jan. 28	165	200	0.522	104.40
Apr. 12	312	200	0.5305	106.10

ISSUES

Date	Req. No.	Qty.	Unit Cost	Amount
19CY				
Jan. 12	320	80	$0.50	$40.00
Mar. 2	413	100	0.52	52.00
Mar. 29	512	70	0.52	36.40
Apr. 10	594	40	0.52	20.80

BALANCE

Date	Qty.	Unit Cost	Amount
19CY			
Jan. 2	100	$0.50	$ 50.00
Jan. 12	20	0.50	10.00
Jan. 28	220	0.52	114.40
Mar. 2	120	0.52	62.40
Mar. 29	50	0.52	26.00
Apr. 10	10	0.52	5.20
Apr. 12	210	0.53	111.30

status report the order point and maximum inventory level for each type of material and supply. The maximum inventory level typically should be equal to the order point quantity plus the economic order quantity (as discussed earlier in this chapter). For example, if the order point is 200 units of an item and the EOQ is 800 units, then the maximum inventory level should be set at 1000 units for that item. Normally, the maximum inventory level for a particular item will not be reached, since units comprising the order point will be issued during the time interval between placing an order and receiving delivery.

If, for a particular item, the inventory on hand is less than the order point and no action has been taken to reorder, an explanation should be sought to explain the lack of reordering. Likewise, if units of a particular item on hand plus amounts ordered but not yet received are in excess of the maximum inventory level, an explanation of the excess should be sought by the management. In summary, status reports on materials and supplies permit management and personnel of the purchasing department to observe the status of inventory levels and to initiate corrective action where necessary to increase or reduce inventory levels of particular items of materials and supplies.

Planning and Controlling Restricted Assets

As discussed earlier in this chapter, restricted assets are comprised of money and investments which have been segregated and are to be used for specific purposes such as debt service, replacement or construction of plant assets, and employees' pensions. The restriction of assets may be voluntary or in compliance with the provisions of a contract. A balance in a restricted asset account is established through the transfer of cash from the general cash account of the water utility to the restricted asset account or through the direct transfer of cash to the restricted asset account at the time the cash is originally received by the utility (proceeds from the sale of bonds, for example). When the money in restricted asset accounts is to be held for extended periods of time, it is commonly invested in interest-bearing securities administered by the utility or by a trustee. These securities should not, of course, be classified as temporary investments (since temporary investments are current assets, the proceeds from

which, upon liquidation, are available for general utility purposes).

A distinction can be made between restricted assets which are classified as current assets and restricted assets which are classified as non-current assets. Special deposits are made with fiscal agents or others for the purpose of meeting liabilities (interest payments and repayment of debt principal, for example, and dividend payments in the case of investor-owned water utilities) maturing within a relatively short period of time. These deposits represent a segregation of cash for a specific purpose and are appropriately considered as restricted assets. The NARUC classification of accounts considers special deposits as current assets (see the Appendix). Other restricted assets, entitled "Special Funds" by the NARUC, are classified as non-current assets. On the other hand, in the case of municipally-owned water utilities, the NCGA recommends that special deposits with fiscal agents be included among the restricted asset accounts as non-current assets.[9]

Assets Restricted for Bond Debt Service. In the case of term bonds issued by water utilities, the bond indenture frequently calls for the accumulation of restricted assets (commonly called a "sinking fund") during the life of the bonds to provide for the redemption of the bonds at maturity. The restricted assets may be administered by a trustee to whom the utility periodically transfers cash generated from operations for investment by the trustee, or may be administered by the utility itself. If the restricted assets are administered by a trustee, the income from investments, less trustee's fees, is retained by the trustee for reinvestment, and the amount is reported periodically to the water utility for inclusion in net income.

The amount of the periodic contribution to asset accounts restricted for the retirement of term bonds may be calculated by compound interest methods. Procedures for determining periodic contributions are similar to those discussed in Chapter 12 in connection with the compound interest method and sinking fund method of determining depreciation charges. Figure 17-8 presents an example of a schedule of periodic contributions to a restricted asset account (or sinking fund) to provide for the retirement of a term bond issue, assuming that the restricted cash can be invested to earn a net return of 4 per cent per year. Referring to Fig. 17-8, at the end of the twentieth year the restricted assets represented by securities

---

[9]See: National Committee on Governmental Accounting; Governmental Accounting, Auditing, and Financial Reporting (Chicago: Municipal Finance Officers Association, 1968), p. 55.

Figure 17-8
ACCUMULATION OF RESTRICTED ASSETS (SINKING FUND) TO
PROVIDE FOR THE RETIREMENT OF 20 YEAR TERM BOND ISSUE

Year	(1) Restricted Asset Account Balance Beginning of Year	(2) Income Earned on Restricted Assets Each Year	(3) Annual Contribution At End of Each Year [a]	(4) Restricted Asset Account Balance End of Year (1) + (2) + (3)
1	$ 0	$ 0	$ 3,358.18	$ 3,358.18
2	3,358.18	134.33	3,358.18	6,850.69
3	6,850.69	274.03	3,358.18	10,482.90
4	10,482.90	419.32	3,358.18	14,260.40
5	14,260.40	570.42	3,358.18	18,189.00
6	18,189.00	727.56	3,358.18	22,274.74
7	22,274.74	890.99	3,358.18	26,523.91
8	26,523.91	1,060.96	3,358.18	30,943.05
9	30,943.05	1,237.72	3,358.18	35,538.95
10	35,538.95	1,421.56	3,358.18	40,318.69
11	40,318.69	1,612.75	3,358.18	45,289.62
12	45,289.62	1,811.58	3,358.18	50,459.38
13	50,459.38	2,018.38	3,358.18	55,835.94
14	55,835.94	2,233.44	3,358.18	61,427.56
15	61,427.56	2,457.10	3,358.18	67,242.84
16	67,242.84	2,689.71	3,358.18	73,290.73
17	73,290.73	2,931.63	3,358.18	79,580.54
18	79,580.54	3,183.22	3,358.18	86,121.94
19	86,121.94	3,444.88	3,358.18	92,925.00
20	92,925.00	3,717.00	3,358.00 [b]	100,000.00
Totals		$32,836.22	$67,163.78	

[a] Amount of an annuity of 1 at 4 percent for 20 years equals 29.778 (arrived at using annuity tables which employ the formula $\frac{(1 + i)^n - 1}{i}$ where n represents the number of years and i the rate of interest). $100,000 (amount of bonds to be retired) ÷ 29.778 (amount of an annuity of 1) equals $3,358.18, which is the amount that must be contributed annually to the restricted asset account (sinking fund) for a period of 20 years in order to accumulate an amount equal to $100,000.

[b] An adjustment of $0.18, due to rounding errors, required to bring restricted assets to $100,000.

are converted into cash which is used to pay off the bondholders. Any deficiency must be made up from other sources, while any excess in the restricted asset account over $100,000 would be handled as prescribed by law or at the discretion of management. Of course, if average return actually realized for several years is substantially different from original estimates upon which periodic contributions are calculated, it would be advisable to recompute periodic contributions.

Sometimes the trustee or other administrator of restricted cash has the power to buy the utility's own bonds as restricted assets. In such cases, two alternative treatments are possible: the bonds are cancelled, or the bonds are held "alive" as restricted assets. If the bonds are cancelled, the carrying value of the bonds is eliminated from the books. However, due to the dependence on interest income accumulation to make up part of the cash necessary to redeem

bonds at maturity, the use of restricted cash to purchase and cancel a portion of the bond issue before maturity may impair the ability of the restricted cash to redeem the remaining bonds at maturity; therefore, contributions to the restricted asset account may be increased to cover the loss of interest income accruing to the restricted asset account. There is, of course, no net loss to the utility because of the offsetting saving of interest expense on the cancelled bonds.

If the bonds are held "alive" among restricted assets, they are accounted for in the same manner as any other investment and the utility pays the regular interest to the trustee or other administrator. However, this investment does create a balance sheet and income statement problem since the repurchased bonds are shown both as assets and liabilities, and interest expense and interest income earned by restricted assets are overstated. This situation should be disclosed in a note to the financial statements.

In the case of serial bonds (or in the case of term bonds which are callable and are to be regularly redeemed), restricted asset accounts also may be employed. Indenture agreements associated with serial bonds (or callable term bonds which are to be regularly redeemed) issued by investor-owned water utilities may provide for periodic contributions to restricted asset accounts sufficient to meet the periodic payments for serial bonds as they mature or to meet the periodic payments for term bonds to be called. In the case of callable bonds, the indenture agreement typically provides that the utility may deliver either cash or redeemed bonds to the trustee. If cash is delivered, the cash must be used by the trustee to redeem the bonds which are callable. It is apparent that the balance in a restricted asset account associated with serial bonds or term bonds which are to be regularly retired will be relatively small at any given time.

In the case of revenue bonds issued by municipally-owned water utilities, the bond indenture typically provides for several restricted asset accounts to be created to protect the bondholders against late or inadequate payment of interest and repayment of debt principal as the serial bonds mature. Three typical restricted asset accounts associated with a revenue bond issue are Assets Restricted for Debt Service, Assets Restricted for Reserve Use, and Assets Restricted for Contingencies. These three accounts, together with amounts transferred from the three accounts to fiscal agents for the purpose of making periodic interest and principal payments, are known as the "Asset Group of Accounts Restricted for Bond Debt Service."

With respect to the "Assets Restricted for Bond Debt Service" account (usually called an "Interest and Sinking Fund"), a typical provision is that there be contributed to this account a monthly amount equal to one-sixth of the next maturing semi-annual interest payment plus one-twelfth of the next annual repayment of debt principal. Amounts are then transferred from this account to fiscal agents as required to make debt service payments.

The purpose of the "Assets Restricted for Reserve Use" account is to provide for the payment of matured bonds and interest in the event of a deficiency in the "Assets Restricted for Debt Service" account. The balance in this account is usually accumulated over the first sixty months following the issuance of a series of revenue bonds. The amount to be accumulated is specified (an amount equal to the average or maximum annual debt service, for example) by the bond indenture. Under normal circumstances, the cash accumulated in this account is invested in interest-bearing securities and will not be used until the final retirement of the bond issue.

The purpose of the "Assets Restricted for Contingencies" account is to provide cash for meeting unforeseen operating expenditures of an emergency nature or for replacement of plant assets. The balance to be accumulated in this accounts over a prescribed number of months following a bond issue is specified in the bond indenture. Figure 17-9 presents an example of a statement which summarizes the annual changes which take place in an asset group of accounts restricted for revenue bond debt service.

As in the case of temporary investments, municipally-owned water utilities generally are limited by statute or charter as to the types of securities in which cash restricted for debt service can be invested, such as certificates of deposit, and federal, state, and municipal securities. Investor-owned water utilities are subject to no such legal restrictions regarding the investment of restricted cash. However, the trustee administering the restricted assets must exercise reasonable care in investing restricted cash. In some instances, the board of directors may specify the types of securities which can be purchased. Within the limits set by law, or directives of policy-making groups, an attempt should be made to invest restricted cash in securities which will bring the greatest return consistent with the maintenance of a reasonably low degree of risk against loss of principal. In general, securities should be selected so that they mature as required to meet disbursements which must be made from restricted assets. In this way, realization of loss of principal due to the sale of securities before maturity is eliminated.

Particularly in the case of municipally-owned water utilities, there may be several restricted asset accounts or group of restricted asset accounts for each bond issue outstanding. For the purposes of investment, it may be desirable for the utility to pool cash belonging to the various accounts, in which case earnings on investments must be prorated among each of the accounts on the basis of the amount of cash contributed by each.

Assets Restricted for Capital Expenditures. In the case of municipally-owned water utilities, the proceeds of both general obligation bonds and revenue bonds issued for or by the water utility usually are segregated in a restricted asset account. This segregation is made to insure that the

Figure 17-9

THE MUNICIPAL WATER UTILITY

STATEMENT OF CHANGES IN THE GROUP OF ASSETS RESTRICTED FOR REVENUE BOND DEBT SERVICE

For the Year Ended December 31, 19CY

	Cash With Fiscal Agents	Assets Restricted For Debt Service	Assets Restricted for Reserve Use	Assets Restricted for Contingencies	Total Restricted Assets
Total Balance, Cash and Investments, January 1, 19CY	$240,000	$ 6,000	$168,000	$22,500	$436,500
Cash Balance, January 1, 19CY	$240,000	6,000	8,000	2,500	256,500
Cash Receipts					
Transfers from General Cash (see Fig. 17-2)		230,000	50,000	6,000	286,000
Income from Restricted Investments			5,600	700	6,300
Inter-Group Transfer of Cash Restricted For Revenue Bond Debt Service	226,500				226,500
Total Cash Available	$466,500	$236,000	$ 63,600	$ 9,200	$775,300
Cash Disbursements					
Principal Payments	$108,000				$108,000
Interest Payments	216,000				216,000
Fiscal Agents' Fees	500				500
Purchase of Investments			$ 59,000	$ 9,000	68,000
Inter-Group Transfer of Cash Restricted For Revenue Bond Debt Service		$226,500			226,500
Total Disbursements	$324,500	$226,500	$ 59,000	$ 9,000	$619,000
Cash Balance, December 31, 19CY	$142,000	$ 9,500	$ 4,600	$ 200	$156,300
Investment Balance, January 31, 19CY			$160,000	$20,000	$180,000
Additions			59,000	9,000	68,000
Deductions					
Investment Balance, December 31, 19CY			$219,000	$29,000	$248,000
Total Balance, Cash and Investments, December 31, 19CY	$142,000	$ 9,500	$223,600	$29,200	$404,300

cash proceeds are spent only on authorized capital expenditure projects and are not commingled with general utility cash. Cash is disbursed from the restricted asset account as required to meet liabilities incurred with respect to authorized capital expenditure projects. Eventually, the balance in the restricted asset account is depleted to zero or to an amount near zero, as all authorized expenditures from the bond proceeds are completed. If the proceeds exceed the total of all authorized expenditures, the balance is returned to general utility cash or is disposed of in accordance with the terms of the bond indenture or other applicable statutory provisions. The restricted cash should be invested in interest-bearing securities until needed to meet authorized expenditures. Generally, investments should be made in highly marketable securities which can be liquidated as needed without loss of principal.

Investor-owned water utilities may also desire to segregate proceeds from security issues in restricted asset accounts. In addition, water utilities may desire to restrict a portion of cash generated from operations in order to provide for future replacement of plant assets. Typically, the cash so restricted is invested in securities until needed for replacement of plant assets.

Assets Restricted for Other Purposes. In the case of municipally-owned water utilities, proceeds from customers' deposits typically are placed in a restricted asset account. The restricted proceeds may be invested in authorized securities with the income from such investments being used to pay required interest to customers on their deposits or to increase general utility cash. Disbursements are made from the restricted asset account as required to reimburse customers for their deposits. Investor-owned water utilities ordinarily do not place proceeds from customers' deposits in a restricted asset account; rather, the proceeds are placed in general utility cash, and repayment of deposits is made from general cash.

Assets (cash and investments) may be restricted for many other purposes. Included among other types of restricted assets are those established for the redemption of preferred stock (in the case of investor-owned water utilities) as a result of contractual agreement or management policy; those established for self-insurance; and those established for employees' pensions. While assets restricted for employees' pensions (i.e., pension funds) may be established, many utilities enter into contracts with insurance companies to provide for employees' pensions. This procedure eliminates any beneficial interest in amounts of cash paid to the insurance companies and no restricted asset account is called for. Similarly, amounts deposited with a trustee under the terms of an irrevocable trust agreement for pensions are not included in a restricted asset account. In the event that the pension plan is revocable by the utility, regardless of whether the fund is internally managed or trusteed, amounts contributed under such a plan should be included in a restricted asset account. Disbursements for pensions likewise are made from restricted assets.

Some municipally-owned water utilities maintain their own retirement systems and establish a separate fund (as used in the governmental accounting sense) to account for the transactions associated with the retirement systems. Payments made by the utility to the Retirement Fund are classified as pensions expense to the utility and no related restricted asset accounts are required to be maintained within the Water Utility Fund.

Related Appropriations or Liabilities. The restricted asset accounts discussed in this section are often associated with appropriations of retained earnings or with liabilities to be paid from restricted assets. See Chapter 18 for discussions.

CHAPTER 18. PLANNING AND CONTROLLING LIABILITIES AND OTHER CREDITS

The "Liabilities and Other Credits" side of the balance sheet presents the sources from which the utility's assets are financed. These sources reflect both external financing (liabilities, contributions, and, in the case of investor-owned organizations, amounts paid in by stockholders) and internal financing (through the retention of earnings). This chapter is devoted to a discussion of six major categories of liabilities and other credits, which are: (1) current and accrued liabilities, (2) long-term liabilities, (3) capital paid in by stockholders (applicable in investor-owned water utilities), (4) retained earnings, (5) operating reserves, and (6) customer advances for construction and contributions.

Current and Accrued Liabilities

As in the case of assets, the cost standard should be employed to record liabilities. In general, current liabilities represent liabilities which are definite in amount and which are due either as of the date of the balance sheet, within a year from the date of the balance sheet, or upon demand by creditors. Accrued liabilities represent those liabilities which are not yet payable but which will mature within one year and which are being provided for or accumulated over the period to date of maturity. The NARUC, however, makes some exceptions to these definitions as indicated by the following description of current and accrued liabilities: "Current and accrued liabilities are those obligations which have either matured or which become due within one year from the date thereof; except, however, bonds, receivers' certificates and similar obligations which shall be classified as long-term debt until date of maturity; accrued taxes, such as income taxes, which shall be classified as accrued liabilities even though payable more than one year from date; compensation awards, which shall be classified as accrued

liabilities regardless of date due; and minor amounts payable in installments which may be classified as current liabilities. If a liability is due more than one year from date of issuance or assumption by the utility, it shall be credited to a long-term debt account appropriate to the transaction, except, however, the current liabilities previously mentioned."[1]

It should be noted from the above definition that the NARUC recommends that bonds payable be classified as current liabilities only if the bonds have matured and have not yet been retired. On the other hand, the NCGA recommends that debt obligations be classified as current liabilities if matured or if due within a year from the date of the balance sheet, the latter view being consistent with generally accepted accounting principles.

Sources of Current and Accrued Liabilities. The NARUC classification of accounts provides a number of current and accrued liability accounts under which are recorded various types of liabilities (see the Appendix). Among the more important types of current and accrued liabilities of a water utility are accounts payable to vendors resulting from the purchase of materials and supplies, notes payable to banks or other institutions or persons resulting from short-term borrowings, payables to associated companies (in the case of investor-owned water utilities), amounts due to other municipal funds (in the case of municipally-owned water utilities), customers' deposits, accrued taxes, accrued interest, construction contracts payable, wages and salaries payable, dividends payable (in the case of investor-owned water utilities), matured long-term debt, and, under NCGA recommendations, long-term debt maturing within the year.

Disposition of Current and Accrued Liabilities. Obligations classified as current and accrued liabilities generally are discharged by payments from cash or, particularly for municipally-owned water utilities, by payments from restricted as-

---

[1] Committee on Accounts and Statistics, National Association of Regulatory Utility Commissioners, Uniform System of Accounts for Class A and B Water Utilities 1957 (Washington, D.C.: National Association of Regulatory Utility Commissioners, 1958), pp. 57-8.

sets. Due to the fact that municipally-owned water utilities frequently discharge current obligations through payments from restricted assets, the NCGA recommends that current and accrued liabilities be subdivided into two groups entitled Current and Accrued Liabilities (Payable from Current and Accrued Assets), and Current and Accrued Liabilities (Payable from Restricted Assets). This subdivision of current and accrued liabilities permits the reader of financial statements to associate restricted assets with the liabilities against which the restricted assets will be applied. The earmarking of current and accrued liabilities, together with appropriations of retained earnings, to offset or balance the amounts in restricted asset accounts is discussed at greater length in a later section of this chapter.

Statement of Sources and Uses of Working Capital. Current and accrued assets, less current and accrued liabilities, are often called "working capital," and sometimes, "net working capital." As in the case of statements of sources and uses of cash (cash flow statements) described in Chapter 17, statements concerning working capital are frequently prepared for water utilities to explain the sources and uses of working capital over a given period of time. Figure 18-1 presents a statement of sources and uses of working capital for an investor-owned water utility; the statement is supported by a detailed schedule of changes in working capital depicted in Fig. 18-2. Figure 18-3 presents a similar statement for a municipally-owned water utility; this statement also is supported by a detailed schedule of changes in working capital as shown in Fig. 18-4.[2]

It is apparent from Figs. 18-1 and 18-3 that the sources and use of working capital are similar to those for cash. The major exceptions are that a

Figure 18-1
THE PURE WATER COMPANY
STATEMENT OF SOURCES AND USES OF WORKING CAPITAL
For the Year Ended December 31, 19CY

SOURCES OF WORKING CAPITAL

Operations:			
Net Income		$ 340,000	
Add: Expenses not Using Working Capital:			
Depreciation and Amortization Expense		541,000	
Bond Discount and Expense Accumulated		800	$ 881,800
Less: Income not Providing Working Capital:			
Interest Income from Bond Sinking Fund			3,000
Total Working Capital Provided From Operations			$ 878,800
Sale of Plant Assets			56,000
Sale of $100 Par Value Common Stock (1500 shares @ $130 per share)			195,000
Sale of $2,000,000 Face Value First Mortgage Bonds			2,050,000
Advances and Contributions in Aid of Construction			142,000
Other			14,000
Total Sources of Working Capital			$3,335,800

USES OF WORKING CAPITAL

Additions to Utility Plant			
Mains	$2,242,000		
Other	857,000	$3,099,000	
Reacquisition of Securities			
Preferred Stock	$ 24,000		
Bonds	102,000	126,000	
Addition to Bond Sinking Fund		50,000	
Cash Dividends Paid			
Preferred	$ 30,000		
Common	220,000	250,000	
Other		41,000	
Total Uses of Working Capital			3,566,000
Decrease in Working Capital (see Schedule—Fig. 18-2)			$ 230,200

[2] Accountants and financial analysts who are not concerned with governmental entities often use the term "funds" to mean working capital, accordingly, a "Statement of Sources and Use of Working Capital" may be called a "Statement of Sources and Use of Funds." The term "working capital" is used in this book because it is more descriptive and less confusing than the term "funds."

Figure 18-2
THE PURE WATER COMPANY
SCHEDULE OF CHANGES IN WORKING CAPITAL
For the Year Ended December 31, 19CY

Increases in Working Capital Due to:		
Customer Accounts Receivable (net) increase	$ 39,600	
Materials and Supplies increase	116,000	
Prepaid Expenses increase	4,200	
Accounts Payable decrease	41,000	
Accrued Interest Expense decrease	7,000	
Total Increases in Working Capital		$207,800
Decreases in Working Capital Due to:		
Cash decrease	$ 52,000	
Temporary Investments decrease	115,000	
Special Deposits decrease	15,000	
Interest and Dividends Receivable decrease	5,000	
Notes Payable increase	200,000	
Income Tax Liability increase	41,000	
Customer Deposits increase	10,000	
Total Decreases in Working Capital		438,000
Net Decrease in Working Capital		$230,200

Figure 18-3
THE MUNICIPAL WATER UTILITY
STATEMENT OF SOURCES AND USES OF WORKING CAPITAL
For the Year Ended December 31, 19CY

SOURCES OF WORKING CAPITAL

Operations:			
Net Income		$ 357,000	
Add: Expenses not Using Working Capital:			
Depreciation and Amortization Expense		380,000	$ 737,000
Less: Increase not providing Working Capital			
Bond Premium Amortized			1,000
Total Working Capital Provided from Operations			$ 736,000
Sale of Plant Assets			167,000
Sale of $2,000,000 Face Value Serial Revenue Bonds			2,050,000
Advances and Contributions in Aid of Construction			675,000
Other			23,000
Total Sources of Working Capital			$3,651,000

USES OF WORKING CAPITAL

Additions to Utility Plant			
Mains	$1,743,000		
Other	632,000	$2,375,000	
Retirement of Serial Revenue Bonds		400,000	
Increase in Restricted Assets—Revenue Bond Debt Service		32,200	
Increase in Restricted Assets—Revenue Bond Proceeds		692,800	
Transfers to General Fund		43,000	
Other		11,000	
Total Uses of Working Capital			$3,554,000
Increase in Working Capital (see Schedule—Fig. 18-4)			$ 97,000

Figure 18-4
THE MUNICIPAL WATER UTILITY
SCHEDULE OF CHANGES IN WORKING CAPITAL[a]
For the Year Ended December 31, 19CY

Increases in Working Capital Due to:
Cash increase	$190,000	
Customer Accounts Receivable (net) increase	148,000	
Interest Receivable increase	7,000	
Accrued Taxes Payable decrease	4,000	
Interest Payable on General Obligation Bonds decrease	6,000	
Total Increases in Working Capital		$355,000

Decreases in Working Capital Due to:
Accounts Payable increase	$ 32,000	
Accrued Wages Payable increase	17,000	
Construction Contracts Payable increase	137,000	
General Obligation Bonds (due within 1 year) increase	20,000	
Prepaid Expenses decrease	2,000	
Notes Receivable decrease	50,000	
Total Decreases in Working Capital		258,000
Net Decrease in Working Capital		$ 97,000

[a] Only those current liabilities which are payable from current assets are included as factors in the determination of working capital. Therefore, changes in the account balances of liabilities payable from restricted assets are not included in a schedule of changes in working capital. Current liabilities payable from restricted assets frequently include a portion of construction contracts payable, accrued interest payable, and bonds payable within one year. In this illustration it is assumed that any revenue bonds due within one year and accrued interest on revenue bonds are payable from restricted assets.

transaction which increases cash through an increase in a current liability does not affect working capital, and a transaction which decreases cash through a decrease in a current liability does not affect working capital. Further, the conversion of a non-cash current asset into cash, or the conversion of cash into a non-cash current asset, while affecting cash, does not affect working capital.

To determine the amount of working capital provided by operations, the dollar amount of items which were recorded as expenses but which did not require the use of working capital must be added back to net income, just as expenses not using cash must be added to net income to determine cash provided by operations (see Fig. 17-2). As in the case of cash, transactions which affect only non-current assets (and other debits), and/or non-current liabilities (and other credits) do not result in a source or use of working capital. However, an increase in current assets through an increase in a non-current liability (or other credit) or through a decrease in a non-current asset (or other debit) is a source of working capital, while a decrease in current assets through a decrease in a non-current liability (or other credit) or

through an increase in a non-current asset (or other debit) is a use of working capital. Similarly, a decrease in a current liability through an increase in a non-current liability (or other debit) is a source of working capital while an increase in a current liability through an increase in a non-current asset (or other debit) is a use of working capital.[3]

Planning Current and Accrued Liabilities. Management planning of current and accrued liabilities begins with the budget process. Past experience, adjusted for changes reflected by the operating budget, capital expenditures budget, and materials and supplies budget, provides a forecast of probable levels of current and accrued liabilities during the budget period. The forecast level of current and accrued liabilities are residual amounts, resulting from the forecast level of activity of the water utility and from the terms of payments associated with the purchases of goods and services necessary to the fulfillment of plans.

To the extent not dictated by legal requirements or existing contractual agreements, payment terms associated with the discharge of current obligations should be arranged to help insure prompt payment of maturing liabilities.

[3] For an extended discussion of working capital statements, see: Perry Mason, Cash Flow Analysis and the Funds Statement, Accounting Research Study No. 2 (New York, New York: American Institute of Certified Public Accountants, 1961).

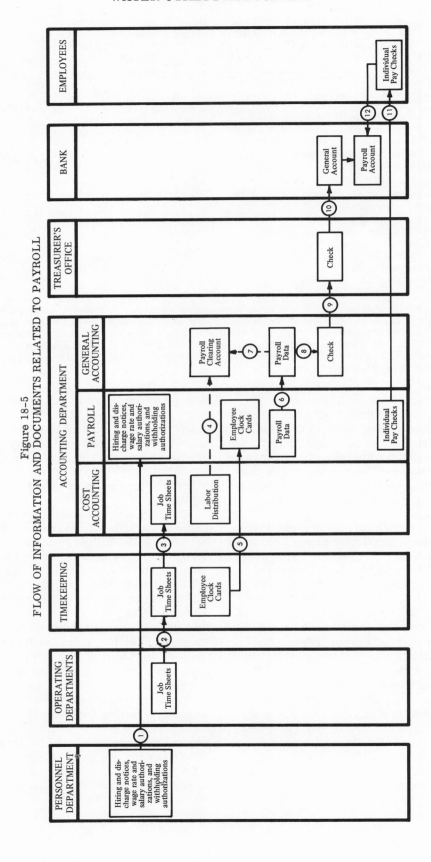

Figure 18-5

FLOW OF INFORMATION AND DOCUMENTS RELATED TO PAYROLL

1. Notices of employee hirings and discharges, wage rate and salary authorizations for each employee, and withholding authorizations (income tax, pension contributions, etc.) for each employee are prepared by the personnel department and forwarded to the payroll section.

2. Individual and/or group time sheets concerning employees' time devoted to each operating activity and each capital expenditure project are prepared by utility personnel (either by individual employees or by supervisors of groups of employees); these time sheets are forwarded to the timekeeping section where total time spent by each employee on various jobs is compared and reconciled with the time registered on the employee's clock card.

3. Job time sheets are forwarded to the cost accounting section where they are used as the basis for distributing labor costs to individual operating activities (expense accounts) and to individual investment and retirement work orders.

4. Labor distribution data are forwarded to the general accounting section thereby enabling the payroll clearing account (which is charged with total payroll costs) to be credited (cleared) by a labor distribution entry.

5. Employee clock cards are forwarded to the payroll section as basis for preparing payroll information and individual employee pay checks.

6. Payroll information, including amounts due employees, and amounts to be withheld from employees' pay for income tax, social security, and other purposes, is forwarded to the general accounting section.

7. The payroll clearing account is charged for total payroll cost and the payroll liability accounts (accrued wages and salaries payable, income tax withheld, F.I.C.A. withheld, etc.) are credited.

8. A single payroll check, properly vouchered, in the amount of the net payroll is prepared by the general accounting section.

9. The master payroll check is forwarded to the treasurer's office for signature (see procedure described in Fig. 17–5 concerning control of cash disbursements).

10. The master payroll check is forwarded to the bank, where it is drawn on the utility's general checking account and is deposited to a special payroll account (in the same or another bank).

11. Individual pay checks are distributed to employees; occasional distributions should be made by auditors to positively identify pay checks with employees.

12. Individual employee pay checks are charged against the special payroll bank account.

For example, to the extent possible, payments to contractors and trade creditors, and dividend payments to stockholders (in the case of investor-owned water utilities), should be scheduled during periods when cash generated from operations or other sources is expected to be substantial rather than during periods when the cash balance of the utility is otherwise expected to be small. Of course, scheduled payments to tax authorities or creditors as determined by law or existing contractual agreements generally cannot be altered, without difficulty, to meet the needs of the utility. These scheduled payment dates must be met in order to avoid the cost of legal penalties. Further, payments to other persons, such as employees (wage and salary payments), and customers (for repayment of meter deposits and advances in aid of construction), must be met when due to avoid the costs associated with the impairment of employee and customer relations. In addition, payment terms with trade creditors, once established, must be met in order to avoid the costs associated with a poor credit rating and the cost of purchase discounts lost. For example, the failure to take advantage of the purchase discount terms of "2/10, n/30" is equivalent to paying interest at an annual effective rate of 36 percent, which even the largest water utility cannot afford.

It is apparent that in addition to the level of current and accrued liabilities forecast for the budget period, current and accrued assets must be planned so as to provide an adequate working capital position for the utility throughout the budget period. A negative working capital position during a particular period may, of course, be considered adequate as long as cash is generated from operations or otherwise provided to meet the discharge of current obligations as they mature or become due. The cash flow forecast (see Fig. 17-3 and related discussion in Chapter 17) serves as the plan for obtaining cash resources to meet these maturing obligations.

Controlling Current and Accrued Liabilities. Satisfactory management control of current and accrued liabilities requires that all proposed commitments associated with the incurrence of a liability be reviewed before they are approved and become actual liabilities. Proposed commitments should not exceed the limits established by the operating budget, capital expenditure budget, or the materials and supplies budget, unless additional authorization to commit funds is obtained through the approval of top management or policy making groups. Procedures associated with the purchase of materials and supplies are discussed in Chapter 17. In the case of the purchase of man-

power services, procedures also must be adopted to insure proper control over commitments associated with the payment of wages and salaries. Typically, control over the hiring and firing of employees is centralized in a personnel department, which is responsible for insuring that manpower requirements, as reflected by the operating budget and capital expenditure budget, are met. The selection of new employees, the discharge of employees, the transfer of employees between positions in the utility organization, and the setting of wage rates and salary levels should be subject to review and approval by top management. This review and approval helps insure that proposed commitments associated with wages and salaries are properly considered before they become actual liabilities and that manpower requirements are being adequately and efficiently met.

Satisfactory management control of current and accrued liabilities also requires that all obligations be properly recorded, that proper procedures for cash disbursement be followed, and that all due dates for the payment of obligations be met. A sound routine for the recording of liabilities is basic to a sound disbursements procedure. Procedures related to the recording and discharge of obligations arising from the purchase of materials and supplies have been described previously. (See Fig. 17-6 and the related discussion in Chapter 17.) Procedures similar to those required for the recording and discharge of obligations arising from the purchase of materials and supplies are also required with respect to the purchase of labor services. Figure 18-5 presents a diagram which summarizes the flow of information and documents related to the payroll; it also reflects the segregation of duties necessary for effective internal control.

Detailed records pertaining to other current obligations such as those related to bank borrowings, taxes, customer meter deposits, interest, construction contracts, dividends, and matured or maturing long-term debt also must be maintained. These detailed or supporting records permit the identification of current obligations of the water utility with specific individuals or other entities; obviously, such identification is necessary to the proper discharge of obligations through payments to the proper individuals or other entities and in the correct amounts. All disbursements associated with current obligations should be vouchered and properly authorized and approved for payment. (See Fig. 17-5, which presents a summary diagram of the flow of cash disbursed by a water utility and the accounting for cash disbursements so as to obtain effective internal control over the disbursements.)

To insure that all due dates for the payment of obligations are met, schedules of due dates for the payment of taxes, interest, and other contractual obligations should be maintained. This will permit the scheduling of disbursements and will help insure that legal penalties and other costs associated with late payment are avoided. In the case of accounts payable, files of vendors' invoices should be maintained by purchase discount dates to facilitate payment within the discount period.

Long-Term Liabilities and Capital Paid in by Stockholders

As indicated at the beginning of this chapter, in the NARUC definition of current and accrued liabilities, all liabilities not qualifying for inclusion as current and accrued liabilities are classified as long-term liabilities. Generally, long-term liabilities of a water utility take the form of bonds or long-term notes, with bonds typically comprising the major portion of long-term debt. In addition to long-term debt, the other major source of long-term financing through investors is by the sale of capital stock; the sale of stock applies, of course, only to investor-owned water utilities.

The various types of bonds and stocks, and planning and controlling the issuance of long-term securities, have been described in Chapter 14, "Planning and Controlling the Cost of Money". This section is devoted to a brief discussion of the accounting control of bond and stock issues.

Accounting control of bond and stock issues does not require the same continuous vigilance which is necessary for proper control of assets and current liabilities. Transaction activity related to long-term liabilities and capital stock is less frequent than in the case of assets and current liabilities. This does not imply that planning for the issuance of long-term securities is a minor management consideration. On the contrary, it is extremely important that management give careful consideration and exercise sound judgment with respect to security issues so as to minimize the cost of capital over the long run. (See Chapter 14.) However, after securities have been issued, the accounting control procedures associated with the securities are quite routine.

Bond Records. At the time bonds are sold, entries should be made in the proper accounts to show the receipt of the proceeds and to indicate

the liability. Separate accounts should be provided for the face value of each bond issue, any premium or discount associated with the issue, and the bond issue costs. In addition, supporting documents containing general information regarding the bond issue, the amount of interest due each interest payment date, and the amount of principal due at each maturity date should be established. Further, an amortization schedule for bond discount and issue expense (or bond premium and issue expense) should be prepared. (See Chapter 14). In the case of registered bonds, where the utility acts as its own registrar, appropriate records must be maintained by the utility with respect to individual bondholders.

Other forms of debt, such as long-term notes, long-term advances from associated companies (in the case of investor-owned water utilities), and long-term advances from municipalities (in the case of municipally-owned water utilities) must also be properly recorded in the accounts. Supporting records concerning names and addresses of persons to whom payment of interest and repayment of principal are to be made, the amount of principal due at each maturity date, and the amount of interest due each interest payment date also should be established and maintained with respect to these other forms of debt.

Capital Stock Records. At the time capital stock is sold by a water utility, entries associated with the stock issue must be made to the appropriate capital stock accounts (see the Appendix). In addition to the maintenance of the capital stock accounts, supporting records are needed as described below:

1. Subscription Register. In this book are recorded the names and addresses of each subscriber, the number of shares subscribed for, and the amount.

2. Subscription Ledger. In this ledger are kept the accounts for each subscriber, showing the amount subscribed for, the amount paid in, and the amount receivable. When full payment on the stock is received and the stock is issued, the accounts are closed.

3. Capital Stock Certificate Book. This book contains the stock certificates to be issued to the subscriber when full payment is received. They are attached to stubs on which full information as to ownership of the stock, the date issued, and the amount paid is recorded.

4. Capital Stock Ledger. A separate account is provided in this record for each stockholder, showing the number of shares issued to him as well as their total stated or par value. The ac-

counts are closed when stock is retired or transferred to another owner.

5. Stock Transfer Register. In this book are recorded transfers of stock, the register only being needed if the utility itself makes records of transfers. If a transferring agent is employed, the utility will not need to keep this record.

Reacquisition of Securities. It may prove advantageous for a water utility to discharge a portion of its bond obligations prior to maturity. For example, if the water utility has an excessive cash balance which will not be depleted in the near future to finance operations or capital investments, the excess cash may be used to retire bond obligations before maturity, thereby reducing future interest expense. In addition, a water utility may desire to reacquire bonds before maturity and to replace the retired bonds with a new bond issue. This process is called "refunding." The purpose of refunding bonds before maturity is to obtain the benefits of favorable market conditions, namely lower interest rates. Bonds should not be refunded unless the incremental cash savings resulting from the lower interest payments (over the remaining life of the old bond issue, had the issue remained outstanding until maturity) exceed the incremental cash outlays associated with the refunding (the difference between the amount paid to retire the old issue and the net proceeds from the new issue). The reacquisition of bonds before maturity may be accomplished either by purchasing the bonds in the open market or, where the issuer has reserved the right, by calling the bonds as of an interest payment date.

When bonds are reacquired before maturity and retired or cancelled, the face value of the retired bonds, together with any unamortized bond premium or discount and unamortized bond issue expense, is removed from the accounts and supporting records. If the bonds are kept "alive" and not retired or cancelled, an amount equal to the face value of the bonds is charged to the Reacquired Bonds account and shown on the balance sheet as a deduction from the face value of bonds outstanding. The NARUC recommends that any gain or loss (the difference between face value, adjusted for unamortized premium, discount, or issue expense, and the amount paid upon reacquisition) associated with the reacquisition of bonds be credited or debited, as appropriate, directly to retained earnings. Of course, when bonds are retired at maturity, the face value of the bonds must also be removed from the accounts and supporting records.

In the case of an investor-owned water utility, capital stock may also be reacquired by the utility. If the reacquired stock is kept "alive," the amount paid to reacquire the stock is charged to the Reacquired Capital Stock account. When reacquired stock which is kept "alive" is reissued, the amount paid to reacquire the stock is credited to the Reacquired Capital Stock account and the difference between the amount paid to reacquire the stock and the proceeds from reissue is charged either to retained earnings or credited to the Gain on Resale or Cancellation of Reacquired Capital Stock account, as appropriate.

If the reacquired stock is retired or cancelled, the paid-in capital associated with the reacquired stock is removed from the capital stock accounts and supporting records. The difference between the amount paid in by stockholders and the amount paid to reacquire and retire the stock is charged either to retained earnings or credited to the Gain on Resale or Cancellation of Reacquired Capital Stock account, as appropriate.

Operating Reserves and Retained Earnings

The term "reserve" frequently is used to describe two different types of accounts found in the "Liabilities and Other Credits" section of the balance sheet. One type of account, called "operating reserves" generally represents provisions which have been made for contingent or estimated liabilities or losses; the accruals to these accounts customarily offset charges to operating expense. The other type of account represents an appropriation or restriction of retained earnings; appropriations of retained earnings arise directly from charges to the Unappropriated Retained Earnings account. In the case of either type of account, a portion of retained earnings has, in effect, been set aside to reflect the fact that assets equal in amount to the balances in the two types of accounts are available only for specific purposes. The discussion in this section is devoted to a further description of the nature and purpose of operating reserves and appropriated and unappropriated retained earnings.

Operating Reserves. The NARUC classification of accounts includes a number of accounts which are categorized as "Operating Reserves" (see the Appendix). Customarily, the accruals to the operating reserve accounts are a result of credits which correspond to charges made to operating expense. For example, to the extent that coverage by insurance companies is incomplete, a reasonable allowance for self-insurance against property loss may be charged to operating expense by debiting the property insurance expense account, and making a corresponding credit to the Property Insurance Reserve account. When a property loss actually occurs which is not covered by self-insurance, the amount of the loss is charged to the Property Insurance Reserve account.

Similarly, to the extent that insurance against injury and damage claims of employees and outside parties is not complete, a reasonable allowance for expected loss due to claims may be charged to operating expense by debiting the injuries and damages expense account, and making a corresponding credit to the Injuries and Damages Reserve account. When a loss due to claims not covered by insurance actually occurs, the amount of the loss is charged to the Injuries and Damages Reserve account.

A Pensions and Benefits Reserve account also is included in the NARUC classification of accounts. This account is used only in conjunction with employee pension and benefit plans in which pension and benefit payments are made from cash or restricted assets (special funds). If employee pension or benefit plan funds are not included among the assets of the utility but are held by outside trustees, or if the utility has entered into contracts with insurance companies to provide for employees' pensions, the use of the Pensions and Benefits Reserve account is not required.

The amounts credited to the Pensions and Benefits Reserve account are equal to the charges made by the water utility to the employees pensions and benefits expense account, plus amounts contributed by employees for pensions and benefits. At the time pension and benefit payments are made to employees, cash (or restricted assets) is decreased and the Pensions and Benefits Reserve account is charged for the amount of the payments.

In the case of investor-owned water utilities, differences between tax expense and tax liability resulting from the use of accelerated depreciation methods for income tax purposes are accounted for by establishing a reserve for deferred income taxes. The use of an operating reserve account for deferred income taxes is discussed in the section entitled "Depreciation for Income Tax Purposes" in Chapter 12.

Retained Earnings—General. The retained earnings of a water utility can be characterized as that portion of the ownership interest in the utility's assets which is not represented by paid-in or contributed capital. Retained earnings represent the ownership interest in the net increment in assets resulting from water utility operations. The retained earnings balance is affected by:

1. Income or loss from the normal and incidental operating activities of the water utility
2. Extraordinary gains and losses of the utility
3. Corrections of errors of prior periods concerning (1) and (2) above
4. Recapitalizations (in the case of investor-owned water utilities)
5. Distributions of retained earnings through asset transfers to other municipal funds (in the case of municipally-owned water utilities) or through the payment of dividends to stockholders (in the case of investor-owned water utilities).

The existence of retained earnings is one obvious requisite for the distribution of retained earnings through the transfer of assets to other municipal funds or through the payment of dividends to shareholders. In addition, in order to distribute retained earnings the utility must have cash, or assets in a form readily convertible into cash, which can be distributed. However, even if retained earnings exist together with assets in a form which can be distributed, the utility may be unable to distribute retained earnings because such earnings have been appropriated or restricted and are unavailable for distribution to the municipality or to shareholders.

Appropriated Retained Earnings. Whereas operating reserve accounts customarily arise as a result of charges to operating expense (thereby indirectly decreasing retained earnings), appropriations of retained earnings are created by direct charges to unappropriated retained earnings.[4] The general theory underlying the restriction or appropriation of retained earnings is as follows: If transfers to the general fund or other municipal funds (in the case of municipally-owned water utilities) or dividend payments (in the case of investor-owned water utilities) are restricted by an appropriation of retained earnings, assets which might otherwise be paid out in the form of transfers to municipal funds or in the form of dividends will be retained by the utility. Therefore, the utility will be in a better position to discharge its obligations than it would have been if the assets had been distributed to the municipality or to the shareholders.

[4] Appropriations of retained earnings also are commonly referred to as "reserves." However, to avoid confusion in terminology between "retained earnings reserves" and "operating reserves," the term "retained earnings appropriations" is used in this book in place of "retained earnings reserves."

The appropriation of retained earnings may be required by law or contract, or may be an expression of utility policy. In some states, for example, the law requires that retained earnings of an investor-owned water utility be restricted in an amount equal to the legal capital (par or stated value, or amounts paid in on no par stock) associated with reacquired capital stock (treasury stock). This requirement, in effect, substitutes retained earnings for legal capital of the reacquired stock. Bond indentures typically require that an annual appropriation of retained earnings be made so that the sum of the appropriations will, over the life of the bonds, equal the bond indebtedness at the time the bonds mature. In addition, creditors supplying relatively short-term funds may require that no distribution of retained earnings be made during the time the short-term debt is outstanding; this implies a restriction of the entire retained earnings balance. Restrictions of retained earnings as an expression of utility policy include appropriations for plant expansion or replacement, and appropriations to provide working capital.

The appropriation of retained earnings for specific purposes does not, of course, insure that assets of the utility will be available in a form that can be used by the utility for the specific purposes giving rise to the appropriations. To insure the availability of assets for use for a specific purpose, assets (cash and investments) must be segregated or restricted for specific purposes (see Chapter 17).

As mentioned earlier in this chapter, in the case of municipally-owned water utilities, retained earnings typically are restricted in amounts which, together with the amount of current and accrued liabilities earmarked to be paid from restricted assets, are sufficient to balance or offset the restricted assets. In some instances, no appropriated retained earnings are necessary to offset a particular restricted asset account because current and accrued liabilities to be paid from restricted assets are equal to the balance in the restricted asset account. Such is the case for assets restricted for repayment of customer meter deposits. In other instances, such as for restricted asset accounts associated with a bond issue, current and accrued liabilities to be paid from restricted liabilities may be less than the balance in the restricted asset account; therefore an appropriation of retained earnings is required to offset the restricted asset account. Figure 18-6 presents a portion of a balance sheet for a municipally-owned water utility which shows a number of restricted asset accounts together with the current and accrued liabilities (payable from restricted assets) and appropriations of retained earnings required to offset the balances in each of the restricted asset accounts.

Statement of Changes in Retained Earnings. A statement of changes in retained earnings customarily is prepared at the end of each accounting period. This statement presents an analysis of the changes in both appropriated and unappropriated retained earnings balances which have taken place during the accounting period and reconciles the beginning and ending retained earnings balance. Figure 18-7 presents a retained earnings statement for a municipally-owned water utility; Fig. 18-8 presents a similar statement for an investor-owned water utility.

Customer Advances for Construction and Contributions

Customer advances for construction and contributions arise from a number of sources. Municipally-owned water utilities may be established by capital contributions from the governmental unit of which the utility is a part and/or from persons and organizations outside the governmental unit. The amount of cash or value of services and property so contributed should be credited to an appropriately labelled contributions equity account (see accounts 272-275 in the Appendix). To the extent that the establishment of municipally-owned water utilities is financed by the issuance of bonds or by advances from the municipality, the amounts so obtained should, of course, be included in the appropriate liability accounts. The establishment of investor-owned water utilities usually is financed by bond and stock issues.

Once a water utility is established, a portion of the financing of plant expansion frequently is provided by advances and/or contributions from customers, subdividers or developers, and governmental agencies. Contributions from governmental units may also be provided for plant replacement, particularly in instances where utility plant assets must be relocated due to highway construction and urban renewal projects.

The NARUC classification of accounts provides deferred credit account 252, Customer Advances for Construction, to which are credited amounts advanced by or in behalf of customers for construction and which are to be refunded either wholly or in part. Upon completion of the project, if a person is refunded the entire amount to which he is entitled according to the agreement or rule under which the advance was made, any amounts

Figure 18-6
THE MUNICIPAL WATER UTILITY
STATEMENT OF RESTRICTED ASSETS,
CURRENT LIABILITIES (PAYABLE FROM RESTRICTED ASSETS), AND APPROPRIATED RETAINED EARNINGS
As of December 31, 19CY

Restricted Assets:

Group of Assets Restricted for Revenue Bond Debt Service:

Debt Service Account:
  Cash with Fiscal Agents $142,000
  Reserve Use Account 9,500
  Cash .... $ 4,600
  Investments (Certificates of Deposit) 219,000 223,600
  Contingencies Account
  Cash .... $ 200
  Investments (Certificates of Deposit) 29,000 29,200
  Total .... $ 404,300

Proceeds—Revenue Bond Issue:
  Cash .... $ 92,800
  Investments (Certificates of Deposit) 600,000 692,800

Proceeds—Customers' Deposits:
  Cash .... $ 400
  Investments (Certificates of Deposit) 127,600 128,000

Total Restricted Assets $1,225,100

Current Liabilities (Payable from Restricted Assets):

Payable from Revenue Bond Proceeds:
  Construction Contracts Payable $230,000
  Accounts Payable (Purchase of Equipment, Construction Materials and Supplies) .... 52,800 .... $282,800

Payable from Assets Restricted for Revenue Bond Debt Service:
  Due to Fiscal Agent .... $ 250
  Accrued Revenue Bond Interest Payable 33,750
  Revenue Bonds Payable 108,000 142,000
Customers' Deposits 128,000
  Total Current Liabilities (Payable from Restricted Assets) .... $ 552,800

Appropriations of Retained Earnings:
  For Revenue Bond Debt Service .... $ 9,500
  For Revenue Bond Reserve Use 223,600
  For Revenue Bond Contingencies 29,200
  For Additions to Utility Plant 410,000
  Total Appropriations of Retained Earnings .... $ 672,300

Total Current Liabilities (Payable from Restricted Assets) and Appropriated Retained Earnings $1,225,100

Figure 18-7
THE MUNICIPAL WATER UTILITY
STATEMENT OF CHANGES IN RETAINED EARNINGS
For the Year Ended December 31, 19CY

Unappropriated Retained Earnings:

Balance, January 1, 19CY			$469,000
Add: Net Income for 19CY		$357,000	
Correction of Prior Years' Excessive Depreciation Charges		23,000	380,000
Total			$849,000
Less: Transfers to General Fund			$ 43,000
Increase in Retained Earnings Appropriations:(a)			
Retained Earnings Appropriated for Revenue Bond Debt Service	$ 3,500		
Retained Earnings Appropriated for Revenue Bond Reserve Use	55,600		
Retained Earnings Appropriated for Revenue Bond Contingencies	6,700		
Retained Earnings Appropriated for Additions to Utility Plant	410,000	475,800	
Total Transfers and Current Appropriations			518,800
Unappropriated Retained Earnings, December 31, 19CY			$ 330,000

Appropriated Retained Earnings:

	Balance Jan. 1, 19CY	Current Appropriations	Balance Dec. 31, 19CY
For Revenue Bond Debt Service	$ 6,000	$ 3,500	$ 9,500
For Revenue Bond Reserve Use	168,000	55,600	223,600
For Revenue Bond Contingencies	22,500	6,700	29,200
For Additions to Utility Plant	- 0 -	410,000	410,000
Totals	$196,500	$475,800	672,300

Total Retained Earnings, Appropriated and Unappropriated, December 31, 19CY ... $1,002,500

(a) Reductions in retained earnings appropriations, if any, would be added to Unappropriated Retained Earnings.

Figure 18-8
THE PURE WATER COMPANY
STATEMENT OF CHANGES IN RETAINED EARNINGS
For the Year Ended December 31, 19CY

Unappropriated Retained Earnings:

Balance, January 1, 19CY			$1,630,000
Add: Net Income for 19CY		$340,000	
Reduction of Retained Earnings Appropriation for Plant Expansion		50,000	390,000
Total			$2,020,000
Less: Dividends Declared			
Preferred Stock	$ 30,000		
Common Stock	220,000	250,000	
Increase in Retained Earnings Appropriations:			
on Account of Reacquisition of Preferred Stock	$ 24,000		
per Bond Indenture	50,000		
for General Contingencies	20,000	94,000	
Total Dividends and Current Appropriations			344,000
Unappropriated Retained Earnings			$1,676,000

Appropriated Retained Earnings:

	Balance Jan. 1, 19CY	Current Appropriations	Balance Dec. 31, 19CY
On Account of Reacquisition of Preferred Stock	$ - 0 -	$ 24,000	$ 24,000
For Plant Expansion	300,000	(50,000)	250,000
Per Bond Indenture	200,000	50,000	250,000
For General Contingencies	100,000	20,000	120,000
Totals	$600,000	$ 44,000	

Total Retained Earnings, Appropriated and Unappropriated, December 31, 19CY		644,000
		$2,320,000

originally advanced but no longer refundable because of the expiration of the agreement normally are transferred to an appropriately labelled contributions account. As indicated in the Appendix, the NARUC classification of accounts provides account 271, Contributions in Aid of Construction, for investor-owned water utilities to use for this purpose. Consistent with NCGA recommendations, the accounts, Contributions from Municipality (account 272), Contributions from Customers (account 273), Contributions from Subdividers (account 274), and Other Contributions (account 275), as shown in the Appendix, may be used by municipally-owned water utilities to record transfers from the Customer Advances for Construction account. Amounts given by or in behalf of customers for construction, in the nature of contributions or donations of cash, services, or property, which are not subject to any agreement calling for repayment of any amounts either wholly or in part, are credited directly to an appropriately labelled contributions account at the time the contributions or donations are made.

Extension Policies. A large portion of advances or contributions made by or in behalf of customers for construction frequently arises in connection with the extension of distribution facilities to provide water service to new customers. The reasons for requiring customer advances or contributions for this purpose are to protect existing customers served by the system by insuring that the existing customers do not bear, in a discriminating manner, the specific costs of extending service to new customers; and to insure that an adequate return will be realized on the incremental plant investment required to service prospective customers.

The cost of providing service to new customers varies depending upon the distance such customers are located from existing distribution mains and upon requirements for any special construction required to provide the quality and quantity of water service required by the customers. In addition, with rising construction costs, the construction expenditures required to add new customers frequently exceed the expenditures which were made with respect to existing customers. As a result, customer advances or contributions may be required in order to equalize investment per customer in relation to revenue per customer. Further, customer advances or contributions must be sufficient to permit the water utility to earn an adequate return on its investment in the new facilities. To this end, customer advances and contributions may be considered as a sharing of the cost of plant construction. In lieu of requiring

advances or contributions, some utilities recover the cost of construction by means of special rate agreements. (Municipally-owned water utilities frequently charge rates for water service rendered to customers located beyond city limits which are higher than rates to inside-of-city customers in order to compensate for the added cost of serving outside-of-city customers.)

The types of main extension policies employed by water utilities vary widely. In the case of water utilities subject to public service commission jurisdiction, extension policies generally are a result of commission rule or are subject to the approval of the commission. Customarily, amounts paid by or on behalf of customers for construction are in the form of advances, with a provision for refunds against the advances. Refund provisions typically reflect a desire to return that portion of the advance which is in excess of the contribution necessary to permit the utility to make an adequate return on the incremental plant investment which is financed by the utility itself. It is, of course, extremely difficult to devise extension policies which result in the water utility retaining only that portion of the advance, as a contribution, which is necessary for the realization of an adequate return on investment and which avoids all discrimination among customers.

In some cases, an advance of the entire estimated construction cost is required by the utility. In other instances, the excess of estimated construction cost above a fixed limit is required to be advanced. The fixed limit typically is based on the construction costs associated with a minimum size and length of main. Advances made by customers, groups of customers, and subdividers or developers typically are not interest-bearing. Frequently, different policies regarding the portion of cost to be advanced are applicable to customers and to subdividers.

Methods of making refunds of customer advances for main extensions also vary widely among utilities. Any excess of the advance over actual construction cost is refunded in a lump sum. Additional refunds frequently are based on established schedules which permit refunds according to the number of customers using the extension or the amount of revenue derived from customers using the extension.

It is, of course, imperative that detailed records be maintained concerning advances and contributions from customers, subdividers, and other persons. Such records include information concerning the names and addresses of those providing advances and contributions, the amounts advanced or contributed by each, and the terms of the extension agreements. These detailed records serve not only as supporting documents for the Customer Advances for Construction account and for the contributions accounts but also as evidence supporting refunds of advances or portions of advances. When a person is refunded the entire amount to which he is entitled, as evidenced by the detailed records, any remaining balance of advances is transferred to the appropriate contributions account.

Frequently, the customer is charged for the cost of the service line, either from the meter to the curb or from the meter to the distribution main; the cost of the meter, in some instances, also is paid by the customer. Amounts paid by customers with respect to service and meter installations should be considered as contributions for construction.

Customer advances and contributions with respect to main extensions, service and meter installations, and other plant construction should not be considered as a reduction of the cost of plant construction (unless a utility is required to do so by a public service commission). The construction should be recorded in the plant accounts at its full cost, with the advances or contributions for construction included on the liability side of the balance sheet.

Appendix
A SUGGESTED SYSTEM OF ACCOUNTS
FOR CLASS A AND B WATER UTILITIES

A SUGGESTED SYSTEM OF ACCOUNTS FOR CLASS A AND B WATER UTILITIES[1]

The following system of accounts is based on the recommendations of the National Association of Regulatory Utility Commissioners (NARUC) for Class A and B water utilities and the recommendations of the National Committee on Governmental Accounting (NCGA). The letter "M" to the left of an account designates the account as applicable only to municipally-owned water utilities. The letter "I" designates the account as applicable only to investor-owned water utilities. All other accounts are applicable to both ownership forms.

I. BALANCE SHEET ACCOUNTS
 A. Assets and Other Debits
   1. Utility Plant
    (a) Utility Plant
       101 Utility Plant in Service Classified
       102 Utility Plant Purchased or Sold
       103 Utility Plant in Process of Reclassification
       104 Utility Plant Leased to Others
       105 Property Held for Future Use
       106 Completed Construction not Classified
       107 Construction Work in Progress
    (b) Accumulated Provision for Depreciation and Amortization of Utility Plant
       111 Accumulated Provision for Depreciation of Utility Plant in Service
       112 Accumulated Provision for Depreciation of Utility Plant Leased to Others
       113 Accumulated Provision for Depreciation of Property Held for Furture Use
       114 Accumulated Provision for Amortization of Utility Plant in Service
       115 Accumulated Provision for Amortization of Utility Plant Leased to Others
       116 Accumulated Provision for Amortization of Property Held for Future Use
    (c) Utility Plant Adjustments
       117 Utility Plant Acquisition Adjustments
       118 Accumulated Provision for Amortization of Utility Plant Acquisition Adjustments
       119 Other Utility Plant Adjustments
   2. Other Property and Investments
    (a) Other Property
       121 Nonutility Property
       122 Accumulated Provision for Depreciation and Amortization of Nonutility Property
    (b) Investments
     M 123 Long-Term Advances to Other Municipal Funds
     or I 123 Investment in Associated Companies
       124 Other Investments
    (c) Restricted Assets (or Special Funds)
     M 125 Cash and Investments Restricted for Bond Debt Service
     or I 125 Sinking Fund
     M 126 Cash and Investments Restricted for Replacement
     or I 126 Depreciation Fund
     M 127 Cash and Investments Restricted for Construction
     or I 127 Construction Fund
       128 Cash and Investments Derived from Customers' Meter Deposits

---

[1] For a definition of each account and instructions as to the types of transactions to be recorded in the separate accounts, see: Committee on Accounts and Statistics, National Association of Regulatory Utility Commissioners, Uniform System of Accounts For Class A and B Water Utilities 1957 (Washington, D.C.: National Association of Regulatory Utility Commissioners, 1958).

M 129 Other Restricted Assets
or I 129 Other Special Funds
3. Current and Accrued Assets
  (a) Cash, Special Deposits, and Temporary Investments
    131 Cash
  I 132 Interest Special Deposits[2]
  I 133 Dividend Special Deposits
  I 134 Other Special Deposits[2]
    135 Working Funds (Petty Cash Fund)
    136 Temporary Cash Investments
  (b) Receivables
    141 Notes Receivable
    142 Customer Accounts Receivable
    143 Other Accounts Receivable
    144 Accumulated Provision for Uncollectible Accounts
  I 145 Notes Receivable from Associated Companies
  I 146 Accounts Receivable from Associated Companies
  M 147 Due from Municipal General Fund
  M 148 Due from Other Municipal Funds
  (c) Materials and Supplies
    151 Fuel Stock
    152 Fuel Stock Expenses
    154 Plant Materials and Operating Supplies
    155 Merchandise
    156 Other Materials and Supplies
    163 Stores Expense
  (d) Other Current and Accrued Assets
    165 Prepayments
    171 Interest and Dividends Receivable
    172 Rents Receivable
    173 Accrued Utility Revenues
    174 Miscellaneous Current and Accrued Assets
4. Deferred Debits.
    181 Unamortized Debt Discount and Expense
    182 Extraordinary Property Losses
    183 Preliminary Survey and Investigation Charges
    184 Clearing Accounts
    185 Temporary Facilities

    186 Miscellaneous Deferred Debits
B. Liabilities and Other Credits
  1. Proprietary Capital
    (a) Common Capital Stock
    I 201 Common Stock Issued
    I 202 Common Stock Subscribed
    I 203 Common Stock Liability for Conversion
    (b) Preferred Capital Stock
    I 204 Preferred Stock Issued
    I 205 Preferred Stock Subscribed
    I 206 Preferred Stock Liability for Conversion
    (c) Other Stockholder Contributed Capital
    I 207 Premium on Capital Stock
    I 208 Donations Received from Stockholders
    I 209 Reduction in Par or Stated Value of Capital Stock
    I 210 Gain on Resale or Cancellation of Reacquired Capital Stock
    I 211 Miscellaneous Paid-in Capital
    I 212 Installments Received on Capital Stock
    I 213 Discount on Capital Stock
    I 214 Capital Stock Expense
    (d) Retained Earnings (or Earned Surplus)
    215 Appropriated Retained Earnings
    216 Unappropriated Retained Earnings
    (e) Treasury Stock
    I 217 Reacquired Capital Stock
  2. Long-Term Debt
    (a) Bonds
  M 221 Revenue Bonds Payable
or I 221 Bonds Payable
    222 Reacquired Bonds—Dr.
    (b) Other
  M 223 Advance from Municipality-General Obligation Bonds
or I 223 Advances from Associated Companies
    224 Other Long-Term Debt
  3. Current and Accrued Liabilities[3]
    231 Notes Payable
    232 Accounts Payable

---

[2] Accounts 132 and 134 include deposits with fiscal agents or others for the payment of interest or other special purposes. In the case of municipally-owned water utilities, such deposits should be included in the appropriate restricted asset accounts, 125-129. For example, deposits with fiscal agents for the payment of interest would be included in "Cash and Investments Restricted for Bond Debt Service."

[3] Municipally-owned water utilities may desire to subdivide Current and Accrued Liabilities into two groups entitled (1) Current and Accrued Liabilities (Payable from Current Assets) and (2) Current and Accrued Liabilities (Payable from Restricted Assets). This division allows one to more easily associate assets restricted for particular purposes with any corresponding liabilities.

I 233 Notes Payable to Associated Companies
I 234 Accounts Payable to Associated Companies
M 233 Due to Municipal General Fund
M 234 Due to Other Municipal Funds
235 Customer Deposits
236 Taxes Accrued
237 Interest Accrued
I 238 Dividends Declared
239 Matured Long-Term Debt
240 Matured Interest
241 Tax Collections Payable
242 Miscellaneous Current and Accrued Liabilities

4. Deferred Credits
251 Unamortized Premium on Debt
252 Customer Advances for Construction
253 Other Deferred Credits

5. Operating Reserves
261 Property Insurance Reserve
262 Injuries and Damages Reserve
263 Pensions and Benefits Reserve
265 Miscellaneous Operating Reserves

6. Contributions
I 271 Contributions in Aid of Construction
M 272 Contributions from Municipality
M 273 Contributions from Customers
M 274 Contributions from Subdividers
M 275 Other Contributions

II. Income Accounts
A. Utility Operating Income
400 Operating Revenues
401 Operation Expense
402 Maintenance Expense
403 Depreciation Expense
404 Amortization of Limited-Term Utility Plant
405 Amortization of Other Utility Plant
406 Amortization of Utility Plant Acquisition Adjustments
407 Amortization of Property Losses
408 Taxes Other Than Income Taxes
409 Income Taxes
412 Revenues from Utility Plant Leased to Others
413 Expenses of Utility Plant Leased to Others

B. Other Income
415 Revenues from Merchandising, Jobbing, and Contract Work
416 Costs and Expenses of Merchandising, Jobbing and Contract Work
417 Income from Nonutility Operations
418 Nonoperating Rental Income
419 Interest and Dividend Income
421 Miscellaneous Nonoperating Income

C. Miscellaneous Income Deductions
425 Miscellaneous Amortization
426 Other Income Deductions

D. Interest Charges
427 Interest on Long-Term Debt
428 Amortization of Debt Discount and Expense
429 Amortization of Premium on Debt-Cr.
430 Interest on Debt to Associated Companies or Municipality
431 Other Interest Expense
432 Interest Charged to Construction-Cr.

E. Retained Earnings (or Earned Surplus)
216 Unappropriated Retained Earnings (at beginning of period)
433 Balance Transferred from Income
434 Miscellaneous Credits to Retained Earnings
435 Miscellaneous Debits to Retained Earnings
436 Appropriations of Retained Earnings
Net Additions to Retained Earnings
I 437 Dividends Declared-Preferred Stock
I 438 Dividends Declared-Common Stock
M 439 Transfer to Municipal General Fund
216 Unappropriated Retained Earnings (at end of period)

The preceding groups of accounts are known as the principal, summary, or control accounts and they make up the three principal statements: The balance sheet, the income statement, and the statement of changes in retained earnings. Some of the principal accounts are supported by detailed (or subsidiary) accounts and records. Each of these principal accounts are listed below, together with the detailed accounts and records supporting it.

III. DETAILED BALANCE SHEET ACCOUNTS AND RECORDS

A. Utility Plant in Service Classified (101)
   1. Intangible Plant
        301 Organization
        302 Franchise and Consents
        303 Miscellaneous Intangible Plant
   2. Source of Supply Plant
        310 Land and Land Rights
        311 Structures and Improvements
        312 Collecting and Impounding Reservoirs
        313 Lake, River, and Other Intakes
        314 Wells and Springs
        315 Infiltration Galleries and Tunnels
        316 Supply Mains
        317 Other Water Source Plant
   3. Pumping Plant
        320 Land and Land Rights
        321 Structures and Improvements
        322 Boiler Plant Equipment
        323 Other Power Production Equipment
        324 Steam Pumping Equipment
        325 Electric Pumping Equipment
        326 Diesel Pumping Equipment
        327 Hydraulic Pumping Equipment
        328 Other Pumping Equipment
   4. Water Treatment Plant
        330 Land and Land Rights
        331 Structures and Improvements
        332 Water Treatment Equipment
   5. Transmission and Distribution Plant
        340 Land and Land Rights
        341 Structures and Improvements
        342 Distribution Reservoirs and Standpipes
        343 Transmission and Distribution Mains
        344 Fire Mains
        345 Services
        346 Meters
        347 Meter Installations
        348 Hydrants
        349 Other Transmission and Distribution Plant
   6. General Plant
        389 Land and Land Rights
        390 Structures and Improvements
        391 Office Furniture and Equipment
        392 Transportation Equipment
        393 Stores Equipment
        394 Tools, Shop and Garage Equipment
        395 Laboratory Equipment
        396 Power Operated Equipment
        397 Communication Equipment
        398 Miscellaneous Equipment
        399 Other Tangible Property

The above detailed utility plant accounts could apply to most of the other principal accounts listed under Utility Plant, but usually pertain to Utility Plant in Service Classified. For this reason they are shown as supporting the latter group.

B. Completed Construction Not Classified (106) and Construction Work in Progress (107)
    The principal accounts 106 and 107 should be supported by individual work orders. The principal accounts include the total of the balances of work orders for Completed Construction Not Classified or Construction Work in Progress.

C. Accumulated Provision for Depreciation and Amortization of Utility Plant (111-116)
    Subsidiary accounts should be maintained for sub-classifications of property in support of the principal accounts 111-116.

D. Receivables (141-148)
    The principal accounts 141-148 are supported by subsidiary accounts where necessary. For example, Customer Accounts Receivable (142) may be supported by district or route summaries, each of which controls the individual customer accounts.

E. Materials and Supplies (151-162)
    The principal accounts are supported by detailed inventory records, where necessary.

F. Stores Expense (163) and Clearing Accounts (184)
    Stores Expense and Clearing Accounts should be kept in sufficient detail to allow for the proper accumulation and redistribution of costs among the jobs and activities benefited.

G. Payables and Customer Deposits (231-235)
    Principal accounts 231-235 are supported by records of individual accounts payable.

IV. DETAILED INCOME ACCOUNTS
A. Operating Revenues (400)
   1. Sales of Water
        460 Unmetered Sales to General Customers
        461 Metered Sales to General Customers

462 Private Fire Protection
Service
463 Public Fire Protection Service
464 Other Sales to Public Authorities
465 Sales to Irrigation Customers
466 Sales for Resale
467 Interdepartmental Sales

2. Other Operating Revenues
470 Forfeited Discounts and
Penalties
471 Miscellaneous Service Revenues
472 Rents from Water Property
473 Interdepartmental Rents
474 Other Water Revenues

B. Operation and Maintenance Expense (401 and 402)

1. Source of Supply Expenses
(a) Operation
600 Operation Supervision and
Engineering
601 Operation Labor and Expenses
602 Purchased Water
603 Miscellaneous Expenses
604 Rents
(b) Maintenance
610 Maintenance Supervision and
Labor
611 Maintenance of Structures and
Improvements
612 Maintenance of Collecting and
Impounding Reservoirs
613 Maintenance of Lake, River, and
Other Intakes
614 Maintenance of Wells and
Springs
615 Maintenance of Infiltration Gal-
leries and Tunnels
616 Maintenance of Supply Mains
617 Maintenance of Miscellaneous
Water Source Plant

2. Pumping Expenses
(a) Operation
620 Operation Supervision and
Engineering
621 Fuel for Power Production
622 Power Production Labor and
Expenses
623 Fuel or Power Purchased for
Pumping
624 Pumping Labor and Expenses
625 Expenses Transferred—Cr.
626 Miscellaneous Expenses
627 Rents
(b) Maintenance
630 Maintenance Supervision and
Engineering

631 Maintenance of Structures and
Improvements
632 Maintenance of Power Production Equipment
633 Maintenance of Pumping
Equipment

3. Water Treatment Expenses
(a) Operation
640 Operation Supervision and
Engineering
641 Chemicals
642 Operation Labor and Expenses
643 Miscellaneous Expenses
644 Rents
(b) Maintenance
650 Maintenance Supervision and
Engineering
651 Maintenance of Structures and
Improvements
652 Maintenance of Water Treatment
Equipment

4. Transmission and Distribution Expenses
(a) Operation
660 Operation Supervision and
Engineering
661 Storage Facilities Expenses
662 Transmission and Distribution
Lines Expense
663 Meter Expenses
664 Customer Installations Expenses
665 Miscellaneous Expenses
666 Rents
(b) Maintenance
670 Maintenance Supervision and
Engineering
671 Maintenance of Structures and
Improvements
672 Maintenance of Distribution Reservoirs and Standpipes
673 Maintenance of Transmission
and Distribution Mains
674 Maintenance of Fire Mains
675 Maintenance of Services
676 Maintenance of Meters
677 Maintenance of Hydrants
678 Maintenance of Miscellaneous
Plant

5. Customer Accounts Expenses
(a) Operation
901 Supervision
902 Meter Reading Expenses
903 Customer Records and Collection Expenses
904 Uncollectible Accounts
905 Miscellaneous Customer Accounts Expenses

6. Sales Expenses
   (a) Operation
      910 Sales Expenses
      914 Revenues from Merchandising, Jobbing and Contract Work
      915 Costs and Expenses of Merchandising, Jobbing and Contract Work

7. Administrative and General Expenses
   (a) Operation
      920 Administrative and General Salaries
      921 Office Supplies and Other Expenses
      922 Administrative Expenses Transferred—Cr.
      923 Outside Services Employed
      924 Property Insurance
      925 Injuries and Damages
      926 Employee Pensions and Benefits
      927 Franchise Requirements
      928 Regulatory Commission Expenses
      929 Duplicate Charges—Cr.
      930 Miscellaneous General Expenses
      931 Rents
   (b) Maintenance
      932 Maintenance of General Plant

The subsidiary accounts and records outlined above are an indication of the more important detailed information which must be maintained by a water utility. For a particular water utility, detailed accounts and records will be required to support other principal accounts. In Addition, some of the subsidiary accounts may, in turn, control accounts subsidiary to them. Any account which controls other accounts may be referred to as controlling account, even though it is itself subsidiary to some other controlling account.

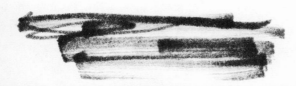